What Experts Are Saying About *Backing U!*

"*Backing U!* will start your career search with passion, then guide you step by step with rigorous screening tools Vaughan Evans developed during his extensive business experience. You'll end up with a career option that not only inspires you but gives you every chance of success. This is a terrific, original addition to career guidance books."
—**Barbara Sher**, author of *Wishcraft: How to Get What You Really Want* and *I Could Do Anything If I Only Knew What It Was*

"Uncertain that you're in the right job or career? *Backing U!* is a fresh, lively, in-depth guide on how to assess your work situation and shift to work you'll feel passionate about. What makes it stand out from so many other career books is its business perspective. It guides the reader through original tools and realistic case studies on the route to achieving career happiness and success."—**Julie Jansen**, author of *I Don't Know What I Want, But I Know It's Not This*

"If you are wondering whether you are in the right job or business, Vaughan Evans's *Backing U!* will re-ignite your passion. Rich, detailed examples bring his innovative ideas to life. As you apply his time-tested business tools to your career, you'll gain insight, clarity, and the motivation to succeed!"—**Carol L. McClelland**, author of *Your Dream Career for Dummies*

"This is a thorough work on achieving career success, full of innovative tools and charts, which I love! Readers will appreciate how they clarify the issues that are key to career development."—**Daniel Porot**, author of *The PIE Method for Career Success* and summer workshop co-leader with **Richard N. Bolles,** author of *What Color Is Your Parachute?*

BACKING

U!

A Business-Oriented Guide to BACKING YOUR PASSION and Achieving Career Success

VAUGHAN EVANS

Published by Business & Careers Press
PO Box 59814
2 Mortlake High Street
London SW14 8UR
www.businessandcareerspress.com

Printed and bound in the United States of America

First printing 2009

ISBN 978-0-9561391-0-8

ATTENTION CORPORATIONS, UNIVERSITIES, COLLEGES, AND PROFESSION-AL ORGANIZATIONS: Quantity discounts are available on bulk purchases of this book for educational, professional, or gift purposes, or as premiums for increasing magazine subscriptions or renewals. Special books or book excerpts can also be created to fit specific needs. For information, please contact the publisher.

To Gwyneth, ten years on,
wyt ti gwerth y byd i gyd i fi, wyt, wyt,
Ivor, Evan, Frances, and Mon,
who backed me.
And to Carys, Natasha, and Stefan…
I'm backing U!

Table of Contents

Preface: On Recessionary Times

This book is primarily addressed to people who are uncertain whether they are in the right job or business. It can help them improve their prospects where they are, or switch to a job or business where their passion lies.

But the techniques apply as effectively to those who are without a job.

I started writing this book in fall 2005. The global economy had in the previous couple of years pulled through the recessionary aftermath of the dot-com boom and hard times seemed behind us. By the time I had finished the first draft in fall 2007, prospects remained reasonable. Some astute observers were apprehensive over the potential ripple effects of the subprime lending collapse. But few anticipated the financial meltdown of fall 2008 and the subsequent steep recessionary spiral.

Have you been laid off in this recession?

If so, you should still follow the approach of this book as set out. But with a twist. You'll need to use the past tense to start with. When you *were* employed, or running your own business, how backable were you? *Were subsequent events predictable or just bad luck?* Were they the result of market demand decline, affecting the many, or your relative lack of competitiveness, affecting just you? Part I helps answer those questions.

If you were backable then, and your current circumstances merely unfortunate, what should you be doing now to make yourself *more* backable for the upturn? Part II can help here.

Carpe diem!
(Seize the day!)—*Horace*

Suppose, however, that you find you weren't backable in your former job. Your peers may have fared all right through this recession. This may be the moment to start afresh, to launch into a new career. You may even have a decent severance check in hand, poised for investment in your future. This is your chance to back your passion. Part III is for you.

You won't be the first. Many have faced such a cloud before and found a silver lining. An architect friend was made redundant during the great construction recession of 1989–1992. She retrained as an osteopath and hasn't looked back since. She turned anxiety at job loss into an opportunity to reshape her life. You could do likewise.

Carpe diem! And good luck!

Introduction

One-half of U.S. employees are dissatisfied with their jobs, up from two-fifths 10 years ago. Likewise, on the other side of the pond, one-half of U.K. employees feel they are "stuck in the wrong job."

Are you one of them?

But are you really in the wrong job or business? Or is it just a case of the grass being greener on the other side of the fence? Are you dissatisfied or unfulfilled for little or no reason? How can you tell?

If you are seriously dissatisfied, it's going to affect your attitude. And that may show up in your performance. *Are you at risk of losing out to others who are more satisfied with what they do?*

How do you change to a career where you can be truly satisfied and inspired? To a career in which you can excel?

If you're among the half of employees who *are* satisfied with their jobs, would you like to move to an even better job? Within your company or organization? Or to a new one? How can you improve your chances of success? Would you like to do what you're doing now—but as a self-employed businessperson?

Backing U! helps you answer these questions. It asks you to imagine on the one hand that you had some spare cash and were looking to invest it somewhere. You're going to be very careful indeed where you invest that cash. You're only going to invest in a business that has promising prospects, one that looks like it's going to grow profits.

Imagine, on the other hand, that you ("U") need some cash. This could be for further education or training. Or if you're self-employed, it could be for new equipment or taking on an employee. Alternatively, you may need the cash for personal reasons, for example, to move to a bigger or better house. Whatever the reason, U need a backer.

Would *you* back *U* in your current job or business? Are your income prospects that reliable, that promising, over the next few years? Would you be more backable if you worked elsewhere? Perhaps in work to which you felt passionately committed?

Backing U! is a step-by-step guide and personal toolkit on how to assess your prospects in your current job or business, and how to improve

Note: The employee satisfaction surveys above were conducted by The Conference Board, February 2007 (for the US), and Cranfield School of Management, March 2005 (for the UK.)

those prospects. Or how to switch to a career where your passion lies and where you can excel.

There are many excellent books you can read that address some of these issues, and many will be referred to in this book. But the approach of this book is distinctive. *It treats each of you as a business, whether you're employed or self-employed.*

If you're an employee, you have your own distinct set of customers, competitors, and capabilities. Just as for the self-employed. You work with your own set of market demand and competitive forces, your own set of personal strengths and weaknesses. You face your own set of challenges and risks. You have your own set of opportunities out there waiting to be grabbed hold of by you. Just as for the self-employed.

Backing U! uses tools developed by the author over years of experience in assessing small businesses and adapts them to assessing you as an individual—tools such as the Suns & Clouds, Going for Goal, Strategic Bubble Bath and *Hwyl* Star charts. The tools work whether you are a manual worker or a salesperson, a local Government official or an actress, a paramedic or an investment banker. They help you to decide if you should back yourself in your current job or business. Or switch to another.

Backing U! is divided into three parts:
➤ *Would You Back U?*—Are you in the right job or business?
➤ *Becoming More Backable*—If yes, how can you improve your chances of success?
➤ *Backing the* "Hwyl" *(or passion)*—If no, how can you switch to a field that inspires you?

Part I assesses how sound your prospects are and how backable you are in your current job or business. If you're self-employed, what are the chances of your business being hit by market downturn? Or tougher competition? How could you make your business more competitive?

If you're an employee, what are the chances of your company—or your job within your company—being affected by market downturn? Are there too many people with your skills? Do you have what it takes to compete? Is your attitude right? As the management pyramid narrows, will it be you who moves up? Or will you be one of the many cast aside?

In summary, are you in the right business or job to meet your earnings and lifestyle expectations? In short, *would you back U?*

If you conclude from Part I that your prospects are indeed sufficiently promising in your current work, Part II shows you how to do better. How you can improve your chances of succeeding in your current work. Be promoted, or shift to a more attractive role within your organization. How to set your sights, build on your strengths, work on your weaknesses. Voluntarily outsource yourself, perhaps, and set up your own company. In short, how to *become more backable.*

Part I may conclude, however, that it's time to look elsewhere. But where to start? Many excellent books will show you how to identify your "transferable strengths" and then look for where they can best be applied. Fine, if that works for you. But this book introduces a new, complementary approach that may work well for many.

Part III starts from where you want to be, where you will be inspired. It then shows you how to work out whether these jobs or businesses are as attractive as they seem, and how well placed you would be if you were in that field. Some of your dream jobs or businesses may lose their shine; others will be unattainable. But some will be promising and worthy of pursuit. This book shows you how to zero in on the most backable opportunities and how to improve your chances of getting in there—and succeeding once in. How you should *back the passion* in you, the Celtic *hwyl*—the spirit, the passion, the fervor—that can lift you to extremes of success.

Before we launch into the meat of Part I, let's pause to meet our main cast of characters. All four are fictional, but aspects of their situation may of course have been influenced by people I have known over the years. We'll peek into their lives and their work challenges throughout this book, whenever we need to show how some analysis, which may at first sight seem rather theoretical, makes sound sense when applied to realistic case studies. Here they are:

Elizabeth at ConsultCo

Elizabeth is employed as a personal assistant at ConsultCo, a Chicago-based management consulting company. She's in her early forties and married with one teenage son. She looks after one director and six other consultants. She helps organize their diaries, sorts out their travel plans and handles many of their other administrative duties. She types most letters for the director and helps all of them from time to time with producing reports and presentations.

These days, though, her consultants are supposed to be able to produce their own reports, whether in Word or PowerPoint. She has recently been helping her senior manager with market research on some of his assignments. She has really enjoyed this work—digging around for market information and calling up some of the client's customers and suppliers to find out what's happening in the market. She'd like to do more of it.

Leila at Helping Hands

Leila is a self-employed aromatherapist in her mid-thirties and lives in Notting Hill, an arty, lively, and cosmopolitan area of West London, England. She was a flight attendant in her early career, before marrying in her mid-twenties. She had two children close together, but unfortunately her marriage split up soon after. Leila has long been fascinated by alternative health therapies and she decided to

retrain as an aromatherapist. She kicked off her business from home, marketing her services initially to her fellow stay-at-home moms. Despite horrors of toys and candy wrappers left lying around the living-cum-therapy room, let alone muffled shrieks from the back room when working during weekends or school holidays, she has enjoyed the job. Her business has done well and she is now poised for expansion.

Carwyn the Carpenter

Carwyn is a self-employed carpenter of Irish-Welsh heritage and has lived in Boston, Massachusetts, his entire life. He's in his early fifties and has held many jobs over the years, both self-employed and as an employee. He has long been married, with three grown-up, healthy children. His full-time jobs have included working for two construction companies and as a member of the buildings maintenance team at Harvard University. He's currently self-employed, and for the last couple of years has been working almost exclusively for a specialist contractor in loft conversions called Boston Heights.

Randy at Homes 4U

Randy is an African-American in his late twenties and works at a real estate company called Homes4U in Atlanta, Georgia. He's single but is seldom seen without a date on his arm. He's an exceptional Realtor. He seems naturally attuned to the sensitivities of both buyers and sellers, a pivotal skill during final negotiations. His deal conversion rates eclipse all other colleagues. He's also a keen amateur basketball player and has long been tempted at the idea of turning pro. His father runs an air-conditioning maintenance and repair business, and his uncle is a plumber. Randy enjoys helping them both out now and again.

Two of these exemplars, Elizabeth and Randy, are employees. Leila and Carwyn are self-employed. All of them are in need of backing. During the course of this book, we'll find that each of the four will receive backing conditional upon either developing their career where they are now or switching to another career, as follows:

> ➤ One employee will stay put but with some retraining.
> ➤ The other employee will shift to self-employment where the passion lies.
> ➤ One of the self-employed will stay put and grow the business.
> ➤ The other self-employed person will seek employment and greater security.

These case studies won't cover every situation pertinent to every reader, but there should be aspects of at least one of their situations which are relevant and illuminating to most readers.

Take Care!

The case studies developed for this book are for illustrative purposes only. Readers interested in pursuing one of the careers illustrated, such as massage therapy, market research, carpentry, real estate, or plumbing, should conduct their own due dilligence on the market following the tools laid out in Part I.

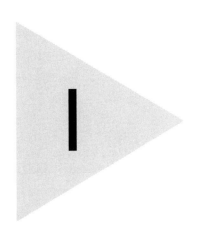

Would You Back U?

Introduction

In the Introduction to this book, we broached the concept of you as an investor considering backing U as a business. In short, would you back U?

What should you look for when considering whether to back a business? What would a serious pro investor look for, someone who does just this day in, day out. Let's meet one. He's called Chuck Cash.

Sure, Chuck will consider backing U. But Chuck will also be looking at investing in a host of other business opportunities, including the cast of characters we met in the introduction to this book—Leila, Elizabeth, Carwyn, and Randy. He's going to invest his money where he sees the highest return for the lowest risk. Period.

Don't be fooled by Chuck's name. Like other investors, Chuck is highly selective where he invests his money. He doesn't chuck cash any old where. Before he signs a check, he does some serious digging around. If Chuck backed entrepreneurs just because he liked the idea, the sector, the location, or the product; because he liked the people; or worst of all, in his business, because he sympathizes with them, that may make him a great guy, but he won't stay in business for long. If before investing, however, Chuck undertakes a rigorous, systematic series of checks—called "due diligence" in business-speak—then the odds of him losing his money become much smaller. And the prospect of him getting a good return on his investment becomes much higher.

In Part I we examine how Chuck would go about doing some systematic checking on you and your job or business. Chuck is looking for answers to one basic question, and one supplementary. The basic question is: *Are you likely to achieve your plans in your current job or business over the next few years?* And the supplementary: *Do the opportunities to beat your plan outweigh the risks of you not making your plan?*

The first thing Chuck and his team need to do is to figure out what exactly your "business" is and what plans you have for the future. Then he's going to set about checking how risky those plans are. He's going to look for risks and opportunities in four main areas:

1. *Demand risk*—How risky is future market demand for your type of service?

2. *Competition risk*—How risky is it that competition will get tougher?

3. U risk—How risky are *you* as a provider of services in your current job or business?

4. Your plan risk—How risky are your plans?

Your Backer's Risk Jigsaw

Each of these areas of risk and opportunity goes toward making up a *Risk Jigsaw,* as shown in the diagram. Chuck's challenge will be to piece together the four pieces of the jigsaw, assess the overall balance of risks and opportunities, and conclude on whether or not to back you.

The nine chapters of Part I of this book are therefore arranged primarily around how to piece together Chuck's Risk Jigsaw:

1. What's your "business"?—Preparation for the risk analysis to follow
2. Where's market demand going?—Demand risk
3. What about the competition?—Competition risk
4. What do customers need?—Preparation for Chapter 6
5. What do you need to do to succeed?—More preparation for Chapter 6
6. How do you measure up?—U! risk
7. Will you make your plans?—Your plan risk
8. How risky?—The Risk Jigsaw completed
9. Would you back U?—Assembling the storyline

First, Chuck needs to understand the nature of your job or business...

> **If You're Self-Employed**
>   **What are your services?**
>   **Who are your customers?**
>   **Which business chunks really count?**
>   **And in the future?**
> **If You're an Employee**
>   **You as a "business"**
>   **Suppose you were outsourced**
>   **Management outsourced?**
> **What Are Your Plans in Your Current Work?**

What services do you offer and to whom? Or perhaps, although less often in today's world, what products do you make and for whom? Which service or product to which customer group counts for most in your business?

Your backer needs to know this information because he doesn't like wasting his precious time. He wants to focus his effort on researching and analyzing those parts of your business that are most important. There is little point in him spending hour after hour checking out a service you offer to a customer group that only contributes to 1 percent of your sales. He wants to put in the work on the 80 percent.

This first step is relatively straightforward for the self-employed. But if you're an employee, you're going to need a little more imagination. We'll start with the self-employed, but employees will need to read this section too.

If You're Self-Employed

What are your services?

A self-employed person is a businessperson. Whether you see yourself as that, no matter—the taxman certainly does. Whether you're a hairdresser or a potter, a car mechanic or basketball coach, a travel agent or insurance broker, a domestic worker or nonexecutive director, a TV presenter or a stonemason, you need customers. Revenues from those

5

customers need to more than cover your costs. You live off the profit. You're a business.

As a business, what services or products do you offer? To what groups of customers? It's unlikely that you offer just the one service to just the one group of customers. But it is possible, for example:

> The aromatherapist, Leila, launched her business offering with just the one service, aromatherapy, to one customer group, her fellow stay-at-home moms

> A surveyor specializing only in home-buyers' surveys

> A consultant in management information systems (MIS) specializing in the retail sector and serving only small- to medium-sized shops

Most self-employed people tend to offer a number of services to a number of customer groups. The services are typically related, but each one is distinct. You can usually tell if a service is distinct when the competition you face is different from one service to another. Some competitors may also offer all of your services; others may specialize in just one or two of them. Others still may offer only one of them as a spin-off to a largely unrelated business.

Let's have a look at how Leila's business developed. Her aromatherapy offering soon became popular, buoyed by word-of-mouth among stay-at-home moms and spreading from school to school. She was not only good at what she did, but she was likeable, chatty, and uplifting. Customers felt better in both body and spirit when they left her house. She learned from her customers that they had experienced and benefited from other forms of massage. Leila undertook further training at night school and soon started to offer shiatsu and reiki, in addition to aromatherapy.

She now had three service offerings to one customer group. She found that no one else in her area offered all three, although some offered one or two of these services. This gave her an angle, she thought, to market her services to a broader market.

Who are your customers?

Most self-employed people tend to offer more than one service, and they also tend to serve more than one customer group. Customer groups can be defined as sets of customers with distinct characteristics and typically reachable through distinct marketing routes.

For example, the surveyor we referred to above could perhaps branch out from serving home buyers to commercial property buyers, a distinct customer group and one which would require a different marketing strategy. Or the MIS consultant could diversify his customer base into a related sector, say retail banking.

Leila believed that her offering of three services should be of benefit to a wider range of clientele, not just to stay-at-home moms. She relaunched herself as Healing Hands, broadened her pitch, and started marketing directly to stressed-out business people. This involved extending her hours of work into early evening and Saturday mornings to catch businesspeople when home from work. She soon developed a new, thriving customer group, and she now offers three sets of services to two customer groups, a total of six service/customer group offerings.

Which business chunks really count?

Most self-employed businesspeople likewise have a number of service/customer group offerings. In business-speak, these chunks of business are called, rather unattractively, "product/market segments." We'll call them "business chunks."

If you offer two services to one customer group, you have two business chunks. If you stick with the same two services but develop a new customer group, you'll have four chunks. Leila offers three services to two customer groups, so she has six chunks.

How many services do you offer? To how many customer groups? Multiply the two numbers together and that's how many business chunks you serve.

Your number of services provided
x Your number of customer groups served
= Your number of business chunks

The main aim of this chapter is to help you to identify which of these chunks is most crucial to your business. We do this in two stages:

1. Look at your current business and see which chunks count most toward your overall profit today (or more simply, sales, if all chunks have a similar cost profile).
2. Think about which chunks are going to make the greatest contribution to your business in three- to five-years' time. These may or may not be the same chunks as today.

Returning to Leila: She has now been in business for four years. Her launch into new services was only modestly successful with her stay-at-home mom market, but once she broadened her customer base to include businesspeople she found that the reiki service started to do well too. She now turns over around £20,000 a year, or roughly U.S. $40,000, to which the six business chunks contribute revenues as shown in Figure 1.1.

Looking at this table, it's clear where her main business comes from. The chunks that make the greatest contribution to her business are:

➢ Aromatherapy to stay-at-home moms, her original business ($20,000, or half of revenues)
➢ Reiki to businesspeople, a new service to a new customer group ($11,000, or over a quarter of revenues)

The importance of these two chunks can be further emphasized in a pie diagram (see Figure 1.2). Together they contribute to more than three-

Figure 1.1 **Leila's Revenues From Healing Hands Last Year**
(Thousands of U.S. Dollars)

Service	Customer Groups		
	Stay-at-Home Moms	Business-people	Total
Aromatherapy	20	2	22
Shiatsu	3	2	5
Reiki	2	11	13
Total	**25**	**15**	**40**

Figure 1.2 **Leila's Revenues From Healing Hands Last Year**
(Thousands of U.S. Dollars)

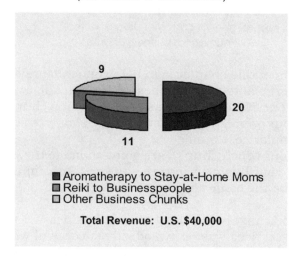

■ Aromatherapy to Stay-at-Home Moms
■ Reiki to Businesspeople
□ Other Business Chunks

Total Revenue: U.S. $40,000

quarters of her business. She offers three services to two customer groups, but her business is really centered around just two out of the six business chunks. The other four don't count for much for the time being. This is an important feature of Leila's business, one she should be conscious of, for example, when drawing up marketing plans.

It's important too for a potential backer, in this case Chuck Cash. He won't need to do much research, if any, on less prominent business chunks—for example, shiatsu to businesspeople. It's likely to be only the two chunks highlighted on which Chuck will need to spend time and money.

Which business chunks contribute to the bulk of your business or job?

And in the future?

There's one more preparatory step you need to make for your backer. Things change. Your most important business chunks of today may not be the same as those of tomorrow. Will market forces favor some at the expense of others? Do you have plans to invest in a particular chunk or develop into a new chunk?

Chuck asks Leila about her future plans. If the two highlighted chunks are her most important now, are they likely to stay that way? What about in three years', five years' time?

> We know what we are, but know not what we may be.
> —William Shakespeare, Hamlet

It so happens that Leila has big plans. Compared to when she set out, she has already extended her average working hours from three hours per day to five hours, and she now feels ready to do a full eight hours per day. She has at last found reliable childcare with a reputable daycare center as a comforting fall-back option.

She has also been speaking to a fellow mom, Ying, a Thai whose son has recently transferred to Leila's kids' school. Many years back, Ying trained in traditional Thai massage, and on her recent visit back to her homeland undertook further short training in reflexology, currently a booming business in Thailand. Ying is eager to work with Leila under the marketing umbrella of Healing Hands, with Leila taking a reasonable cut of Ying's sales.

Working out of Leila's front room will no longer be feasible. Dedicated space needs to be found. One day, they were discussing this with another mom who's married to a barber. He works out of premises just off Main Street and is willing for them to take the back room, currently used for

Figure 1.3 Leila's Forecast Revenues From Healing Hands in Three Years' Time
(Thousands of U.S. Dollars)

Service	Customer Groups		
	Stay-at-Home Moms	Business-people	Total
Aromatherapy	30	3	33
Shiatsu	5	3	8
Reiki	3	16	19
Reflexology	15	25	40
Total	53	47	100

storage. It would be big enough for both Leila and Ying. The barber will let them have the room rent-free, as long as they thoroughly redecorate, upgrade the plumbing, and install heating—all on their own account.

Leila and Ying don't have a sophisticated business plan. All they know is that they are going to need around $9,000 for heating, plumbing, decorating, furnishing, and advertising. Following a couple of planning sessions with Chuck, however, they came up with their vision of what the business should achieve over the next few years.

Their forecast of likely revenues from each of their business chunks—now eight of them—in three years' time is shown in Figure 1.3.

Leila and Ying are convinced that reflexology is going to take off in the area, appealing to both businesspeople and stay-at-home moms. This means that the chunks contributing most to the business of Healing Hands in the future will be the following four:

> ➢ Aromatherapy to moms, as for today
> ➢ Reiki to businesspeople, also as for today
> ➢ Reflexology to businesspeople, a new chunk
> ➢ Reflexology to moms, another new chunk

This means that Chuck needs to do serious checking—not just on two business chunks, based on today's business, but on four.

In fact, it is a little more complicated than that. If a backer is going to lend money to Leila, he'll be more interested in researching the business chunks that count most today, namely the first two chunks. Bankers are less interested in expectations of future growth, the so-called "upside." They're more concerned with the "downside," what can go wrong to the basic business of today. If, however, the backer (like Chuck) is going to buy some shares in Leila's business, he'll want to investigate all four chunks. Upside is very important to an equity investor.

Another added complication may be the relative profitability of each chunk. If all the reflexology is to be done by Ying, then Chuck may find that other chunks give more profit to Leila than the reflexology chunks, where Leila only takes a cut on Ying's work. But we'll keep this example simple for the time being.

We've now identified which chunks count for most in a self-employed person's business. These are the chunks around which the research and analysis of Part I will be concentrated. But what if you're not currently self-employed, but you work as an employee in a company or other organization, large or small?

If You're an Employee

Just a reminder: This step-by-step guide and toolkit works just as well for an employee as it does for a self-employed businessperson. But first you have to *think of yourself as self-employed*—as a business.

Let's take an example from the world of sport. There are many professional sports people who seem to run themselves as a business as effectively as they run around on the pitch, course or court. Think of David Beckham, Tiger Woods, and Maria Sharapova. A Briton, an American, and a Russian, they all excel in their chosen sports, but they are just as proficient in marketing themselves as a global brand.

Yet one of them is effectively an employee. David Beckham is contracted to Los Angeles Galaxy, as he was previously to Real Madrid Club de Fútbol. His obligations to those who contract him are little different than those of an employee to an employer. Yet his individual marketing power is as valuable as his playing skills. When Real Madrid bought him from Manchester United for $50 million in 2003, the club is reported to have recouped that investment within a year or two from replica shirt sales alone.

Beckham is an individual, effectively an employee, but runs himself as a business. His earning power depends partly on his continued sporting success—as for Woods and Sharapova—but also on a carefully crafted strategy of self development and brand promotion.

This book doesn't suggest that we should all seek to endorse a soft drink, a line of clothing, or a perfume, but it does suggest that it can be useful to regard yourself as a business. An employee, just like a self-employed person, needs to establish a sound position in an attractive market and engage in the kind of self-development and promotion appropriate to his or her marketplace.

You as a "business"

Think of your whole earnings package, including wage or salary, vacation, sickness benefits, medical insurance, pension contribution, and so forth, as *revenues* for your business. What services are you providing to your company or organization to merit those revenues? Which people or groups of people in your organization find your services so useful they are prepared to pay those revenues for them?

That's it then. You are a "business"! You provide services and you have "customers." All you have to do is carve up the main tasks you undertake in your job into distinct services. And allocate the people who use your services into customer groups. Then work out which business chunks are most important to your business. Your business is not that much different from a self-employed person's, like Leila's.

Although it may not always be quite as simple as that, it usually is—as you'll see from the following example.

Elizabeth, the PA we met in this book's introduction, laughed when she was first asked to think of herself as a business. "Who in their right mind would pay for my services?" she quipped. But her colleagues do pay. She thought it through and found she could categorize her work as providing three distinct services to two sets of colleagues. Her three types of service are administration ("admin"), typing, and research. As for her customers, she works directly for seven consultants, but she can readily divide them into two customer groups, namely senior staff (a director and a senior manager) and other staff (a manager and four junior consultants). Three services for two sets of colleagues (or "customer groups") makes six business chunks. Just as for Leila.

Elizabeth works 40 hours a week, and she has figured out that during the course of a year her time is divided very roughly as in Figure 1.4.

Figure 1.4 **Elizabeth's Workload at ConsultCo This Year**
(Average Hours/Week)

Service	"Customer Groups"		
	Senior Staff	Other Staff	Total
Admin	10	**15**	25
Typing	5	0	5
Research	10	0	10
Total	**25**	**15**	**40**

If we assume her time is equally valuable to the company for each of these services, then the business chunks that count most toward Elizabeth's "business" are:

➢ Admin support to the less senior staff (the largest chunk)
➢ Admin support to the senior staff
➢ Research for the senior staff

Before we conclude that these three chunks are those an investor needs to check out before backing Elizabeth, we first need to think of Elizabeth's future prospects in the job and whether she thinks she'll be providing these same services in five years' time.

Like Leila, Elizabeth has challenging plans for the future. She would like to develop her career within the company. She has been a PA for 15 years, and she doesn't want to be one forever. She used to like the job much more in the old days, when she did everything, including all the typing, for just one or two consultants. But times have changed. She now has to look after seven consultants, and very often it's the most junior who give her the hardest time.

Figure 1.5 Elizabeth's Target Workload at ConsultCo in Three Years' Time
(Average Hours/Week)

Service	"Customer Groups"		
	Senior Staff	Other Staff	Total
Admin	5	5	10
Typing	0	0	0
Research	25	5	30
Total	30	10	40

Meanwhile, she has really taken to the research work she has been doing recently. She finds it more stimulating, her colleagues say that she's pretty good at it, and she would like to do more of it. She would even like to do it full-time if there were enough work to go around. Ideally, in three years' time, she would like to find herself still working in the same company, but with a different emphasis on the kind of work she'd be doing. Her target for which chunks might contribute most to her future "business" is shown in Figure 1.5.

Chuck won't spend any time assessing her prospects in typing support, whether to senior or other staff. It's clear that Elizabeth is set on redefining her career, preferably within the company and possibly outside the company. Chuck will need to look at the demand for research services in the company over the next few years, as well as in the Chicago market as a whole, what alternatives the company will have to supply that demand, and how well placed Elizabeth will be to succeed as a market researcher.

I wonder if I've been changed in the night? Let me think: was I the same when I got up this morning? I almost think I can remember feeling a little different. But if I'm not the same, the next question is 'Who in the world am I?' Ah, that's the great puzzle!"—Lewis Carroll, Alice in Wonderland

Suppose you were outsourced

Some readers who are employees may find it difficult to imagine themselves as a "business." If that's so, it may help if you try to imagine what would happen if your job were "outsourced."

In its simplest form, outsourcing is when one, two, or a whole bunch of jobs are replaced by bought-in services from individuals or a company who specialize in providing just that service. This became popular during the 1990s. Organizations gain through these noncore services being done by companies with more focus, dedication, and scale-related cost-efficiency.

Sometimes the outsourcing service providers are located in areas with lower costs, and companies benefit from their cheaper labor and/or cheaper space. Many telemarketing companies, set up to relieve utility and other companies of their huge telemarketing departments, chose to locate in middle America rather than the more expensive East or West Coast. Likewise, in Britain, many chose Wales or Scotland. Where outsourcing becomes rather more controversial is when North American or Western European manufacturing operations get relocated to the Far East or Eastern Europe, or service operations to countries with both lower costs and language proficiency, such as India. This is called "offshoring" and can be of benefit to both the outsourcing and outsourcer countries in the long-term. But it can also cause disruption and distress to families and communities in the short-term.

Many—even most—jobs can be outsourced, and many have been in recent years, from customer service, IT, and maintenance workers to book-keepers and surveyors. Television network companies have outsourced much of their program making to specialist production boutiques. The British government has even outsourced some prison services.

Suppose your job were outsourced. You're no longer an employee in your present company, but you're still doing the same job. You're not on the payroll, so you have no salary. Nor do you have any vacation, pension, or other benefits paid by the company. You have revenues. Your services are the same as you are providing today. Your "customers" are those same colleagues who today use your services. Each customer pays you directly for the services you provide. Scary, perhaps, but that's your "business."

Does this help in assessing Elizabeth's "business"? Not obviously, since we've already been able to break down which chunks contribute most to her "business." But it can be useful as a check. If Elizabeth left the company, would she be replaced? Or would her services be carved up and supplied by external suppliers?

Certainly Elizabeth's market research services could be supplied by specialist market research houses, but the senior staff would then lose the advantages of immediate response and in-house intellectual capital. Again, her typing services could be bought in from external suppliers, although this might lead to problems of availability and meeting deadlines. Finally, her admin services are so widespread, so many, and so irregular that they would be difficult to buy in externally, even with a "temp" coming in two or three days a week. In conclusion, if Elizabeth left, ConsultCo would probably need to replace her.

Consideration of outsourcing can also be useful in assessing how valuable each chunk of a job, or "business," is to a company. If each of Elizabeth's services had to be ordered separately and paid for directly by her "customers," then the findings may be quite revealing. We might find, for example, that the senior staff would be happy to pay cash for Elizabeth's research work, but that the more junior staff would rather do their admin work themselves than pay for it out of their own pockets. This gives us clues on job security, which may be useful in later chapters.

Management outsourced?

Imagining your job as being outsourced can help managers and supervisors to identify which chunks contribute most in their "business." It is difficult to outsource management, since management is often defined as the core competence of any organization. It can be what distinguishes one group of people—one "company" of people—from another. But other roles in a manager's work may be outsourceable.

Let's return to Elizabeth's company, ConsultCo. The senior manager she does research for has three distinct roles in his job. He is by profession a management consultant, advising companies on how to improve some aspect of their performance. He also has to be a salesman, helping to win client mandates, often in the face of ferocious competition from other consulting groups. The more senior he gets, the more his selling skills will be appreciated by ConsultCo over his consulting skills. Finally, he's a manager—recruiting, training, guiding, and managing more junior consultants and support staff.

His consulting and selling chunks could conceivably be outsourced. His consulting tasks on each assignment could perhaps be bought in from an external consultant, one preferably as experienced and competent as he. He understands no one is irreplaceable. The selling tasks could also perhaps be undertaken by an external consultant on a sale commission basis. But his managerial role cannot be outsourced. His whole group, with him as manager, could be outsourced, but not he alone. Otherwise his juniors would remain in the company unmanaged, not a recipe for success.

What Are Your Plans in Your Current Work?

We've already taken a quick look at where you want to be in your current job or business in three- to five-years' time. We had to do that to be able to derive the most important business chunks.

Now is the time, however, to put some flesh on the bones. If yours was a business employing one, ten, a hundred, or a thousand people, this is when I would ask (or help!) you to draw up a business plan. Since this book is about you as an individual, a well-crafted business plan is not essential. But assuming you stay in your current job, or business, where do you see yourself in three- to five-years' time? And how are you going to get there?

Leila is self-employed, and she has plans to expand into new services (and a new location). Elizabeth is an employee and has plans to switch to a more gratifying role within the company.

What are your plans? You may have quite clear plans, like Leila and Elizabeth, and are reading this book as a "sanity check." *Backing U!* will help you address how realistic these plans are, whether you would back U in these plans, and how you can make yourself more backable in your plans.

Many—probably most—readers will be uncertain of what their plans are and that is why they are reading this book. If that's you—and you currently have no concrete plans to develop your positioning in your company, or to reshape your business—then let's assume for now that *things stay more or less as they are now.* Sure, as an employee, you may hope to receive some additional responsibility, a promotion, a pay rise (hopefully above inflation). Sure, as a self-employed person, you may hope to win some new customers and grow the business somewhat. But if you have no specific plans, let's for the time being assume that your "plan" for your job or business in five years' time is a steady, unspectacular improvement on what it is today.

The advantage of this assumption is its clarity. Because after you've worked through the tools in Part I of this book, you'll have a much firmer idea of whether staying as you are today is a practical scenario. Is it realistic that you would thrive in the same job or business in three or five years' time?

If you're a frustrated employee now, if you're dissatisfied, will you lose out to colleagues—present or yet to be hired—who are less frustrated and more satisfied? How would you compete with colleagues who actually love their work? Would you back U in your current work?

Part I's analysis may produce some stark results.

Where's Market Demand Going?

2

- ▷ **Is Market Demand Going to Grow?**
- ▷ **Remember the Chunks**
- ▷ **Look Beyond Your Catchment Area**
- ▷ **Weave Your Web of Information**
- ▷ **Use the Four-Stage Process for Demand Checking**
- ▷ **Some Examples for the Self-Employed**
- ▷ **Employees Need to Check Demand at Two Levels**
- ▷ **Some Examples for Employees**
- ▷ **Market Demand Risks and Opportunities**

This chapter is about demand for the type of services you provide. You are not alone. There are others out there who do what you do. This chapter asks you to think about how market demand for *all* these people, including you, has changed in the last few years and how it is likely to change in the future. Will demand for *you all* grow? We need to know this before we can address the crucial question in the next chapter: Is there any chance there may be too many of you competing for the same jobs or business in the future?

Again, if you're an employee, it will help if you think of yourself as a business. You need to think about what will happen to demand for your kind of service over the next few years. That's demand for your services not just within your current company but *overall demand for your type of service across all companies and organizations.*

Any market is made up of demand and supply. Whether the market is for things or people—apples or actors, MP3 players or musicians, trucks or truckers—the fundamentals of economics apply. When demand and supply are in balance, that's good news for all concerned. When demand outstrips supply, that's good for the suppliers—though usually only for a while, until more supplies and/or suppliers arrive.

When demand falls and supply exceeds demand, that's bad news for suppliers. In the labor market, these suppliers include you. You're a supplier of labor.

We're going to apply those fundamentals to the market for *your* services. We'll look at market supply in the next chapter, but first we'll examine market demand. We'll forecast what's going to happen to market demand over the next few years. Your backer will also want to know what the risks are of things turning out worse than that. And, on the other hand, what the opportunities are of things turning out better.

Is Market Demand Going to Grow?

This is the big question. Is demand for providers of your kind of services, in each of your main business chunks, going to grow over the next few years? Is it going to be bigger in a few years' time, or smaller? Or more or less the same?

It's not the only question, of course. Equally important, as we'll see in the next few chapters, is the nature of the competition you're going to face and how you are placed to compete.

It's better to be in a market with the wind behind you than in your face.—*Unattributed, but a common quote in the business world*

But it's all a question of odds. You have a better chance of prospering in a market that's growing than one that's shrinking.

Remember the Chunks

We need to remind ourselves that we are probably not looking at just the one market. Most of us work in a number of business chunks, some of which are more important than others, as we found out in Chapter 1. If so, we need to look at market demand prospects in *each* of the important chunks.

In the case of the aromatherapist Leila, she and her backer, Chuck Cash, will look at how demand from stay-at-home moms for aromatherapy and reflexology services is likely to change over the next few years. Likewise they'll need to examine future demand by businesspeople for reflexology and reiki services. But they won't waste time checking out, for example, demand by moms for shiatsu.

For Elizabeth, she and Chuck will look at likely future demand from her senior and junior staff in ConsultCo for admin and research services. But they won't need to look in detail at demand for typing, unless they think there's a chance that the trend toward executives doing their own typing will reverse.

Look Beyond Your Catchment Area

Most self-employed people address a local or regional market. Car mechanics in Berkeley, California, for example, mainly address the local demand for car repair in Berkeley itself, not even the other side of the Bay Bridge in San Francisco. San Franciscan residents tend to use their own neighborhood car mechanics. Most Berkeley car mechanics wouldn't advertise in the Yellow Pages of San Francisco, let alone in those of, say, Los Angeles, unless they were highly specialized in, for example, the complete rebuilding of 1950s Chevrolets.

There are comparatively few self-employed occupations where the market addressed is a national one. Examples include professional speaking, writing, acting, management consulting, and highly specialized areas of medicine or law.

Leila's market is mainly local. When she started off, her market was literally down the road, fellow stay-at-home moms at her child's primary school in Notting Hill. But with her growth into new services and new customer groups, she has since extended her catchment area to include the whole of Notting Hill, as well as neighboring villages such as Bayswater and Holland Park. Still a local market, but a broader definition of local.

Even if your market is local, it's always useful to start by looking at what's happening across the region or across the country. There are two reasons for this:

> Trends taking place on a wider scale tend to be similar to those taking place in your direct catchment area.

> It's usually easier to find information and data on what's happening in any market on a regional or national level.

Once you've identified what's happening at a broader level, it's quite easy to then gauge to what extent this is reproduced at your local level. We'll see how below, but first a word on sources of information.

Weave Your Web of Information

I've been advising clients on market trends for 35 years. In the old days, you used to have to call up trade associations; write to companies active in the market asking for their annual reports; visit reference libraries to wade through reams of trade magazines, journals, and so forth. Or you might have to purchase an expensive market research report, often only of tangential relevance to the market you were researching.

Now it's a breeze. All you have to do is switch on your laptop, click onto your Internet connection, pop into Google or Yahoo, and type in the name of your market alongside such words as "market," "growth," "forecasts," "trends."

You'll find that Google comes up with hundreds—maybe thousands—of websites to visit. Most of them will be irrelevant. One, two, or more will be spot on. You'll begrudge having to waste time trawling through dozens of useless sites, but hang on! Think of the hours and hours of effort you're saving compared to the old days. You just need a bit of patience and perseverance and systematically wade through the referred sites. Open up a Word file, and whenever you come across an article on a website that seems useful, copy it and drop it into your document.

You're weaving your own web of information on your market.

You may find that your search directs you to reports produced by specialist market research companies. These should be used as a last resort. Some can be quite good, reflecting the direct access they may have had to market participants and observers, but too many turn out bland. And expensive. Better to do your own digging around on the Web.

There are some good news websites where you can search directly without having to subscribe. The National Public Radio website, www.npr.org, offers fully searchable archived broadcasts, as does www.pbs.org. Also try the major newspaper websites. Both *The New York Times* (www.nytimes.com) and the *Washington Post* (www.washington post.com) offer free searchable archives for a limited period (one and two weeks, respectively). That should be time enough for you to research what you need for your own market, although while you're there you may choose to do a couple more searches on new markets you're interested in (see Part III of this book) before your allotted time runs out. *The LA Times* (www.latimes.com) offers free abstracts on searches through its archives, but you need to pay for the full article. For more detailed company and financial information, *The Wall Street Journal* website (www.online.wsj.com) will cost you US$59 per year.

In Britain, the BBC's website (www.bbc.co.uk) is a hugely informative, internationally focused resource and doesn't cost a penny. Similarly international in outlook, the website of *The Economist* (www.economist.com) offers free search on articles less than a year old, but a subscription is needed for older articles. The websites of the main broadsheet national and regional newspapers are also good sources, such as *The Guardian* (www.guardianunlimited.co.uk), which is free and requires no registration. There are also *The Times* (www.timesonline.co.uk), *The Daily Telegraph* (www.telegraph.co.uk), *The Independent* (www.independent.co.uk), *The Western Mail* (www.icwales.icnetwork.co.uk), *The Scotsman* (www.scotsman.com), and *The Irish Times* (www.ireland.com), some of which require registration. *The Financial Times* website (www.ft.com) offers a wealth of financial, company, and market information, but to search through back copy requires you to subscribe at £75 (roughly US$150) per year.

You can find similarly useful websites from the main national television, radio, newspaper, and magazine companies in most countries.

You can also find out much about the companies working in your market. Many will have their own websites into which you can tap. Smaller companies tend to use their websites just as product or service showcases, but some may provide snippets of information on where the market is heading, such as a press release summarizing a recent speech by the CEO at a trade conference. Publicly quoted companies will attach their annual reports and Form 10-Ks, in which you'll be able to find the company's views on market trends.

Another good source of market info on the Web is online trade magazines. Typically they will have at least some sections open to the public without subscription, which can often be expensive. If you work in the automotive industry, for example, you could look up www.automotive

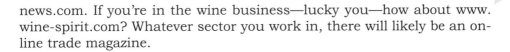

news.com. If you're in the wine business—lucky you—how about www.wine-spirit.com? Whatever sector you work in, there will likely be an online trade magazine.

Use the Four-Stage Process for Demand Checking

There is a four-step process you need to follow in any assessment of market demand trends. Get this process right and all falls logically into place. Get it out of step and you may end up with a misleading answer. You need to apply these steps for each of the main business chunks. The four steps are:

1. *Assess past growth*—Check how market demand has grown in the past.
2. *Assess past drivers of growth*—Identify what has been driving that growth in the past.
3. *Assess changes in drivers*—Assess whether there will be any change in influence of these and other drivers in the future.
4. *Forecast future growth*—Forecast market demand growth, based on the influence of future drivers.

Let's look at each of these briefly, then at some examples.

1. Assess past growth. This is where it would be good to get some facts and figures. It's surprising how the most straightforward of searches can reveal recent growth rates in the markets you're looking for.

Be careful not to fall into the trap of relying on one recent number. Just because demand for a service jumped by, say, 8 percent last year doesn't mean that trend growth in that market has been 8 percent each year. The latest year may have been an aberration. The previous year might have seen a dip in the market, followed by the 8 percent recovery.

You should try to get an average annual growth rate over a number of recent years, preferably the last three or four. As long as there haven't been serious annual ups and downs (if so, see the box on page 22), you can usually get a usable approximation of average annual growth by calculating the overall percentage change in, say, the last four years and then annualizing it. The annualizing should, strictly speaking, be on a compound basis (see box again), but you're not going to get a rap on the knuckles from your backer (that's you!) if you just divide the overall percentage change by the number of years to get a simple average. Then you can express your result as a range, preferably narrow, as in, say, 5 to 7 percent per year.

Most markets served by the self-employed, however, are so small—called "niches" in business-speak—that there is little or no data to be found on them. No matter. Useful information can still be uncovered. All you need to find out is whether the market has been growing fast, growing slowly, holding flat, declining slowly, or declining fast. We can define grow-

A Moving Average Approach to Deriving Trend Growth Rates

(WARNING! ONLY FOR THE MATHEMATICALLY INCLINED!)

There is one major complication in deriving trend growth rates, and that is when annual changes have been irregular, showing no consistent trend. One way to deal with this is to translate your data into three-year moving averages. This smooths out fluctuations and a trend growth rate can be readily derived. An example may help.

Here's a set of market data (in US$ millions, say) for the 2000s:

Year	2000	2001	2002	2003	2004	2005	2006	2007
Market demand	1476	1223	1150	1201	1387	1452	1582	1555
Change	n/a	-17%	-6%	4%	15%	5%	9%	-2%

If we were to ignore all that happened in the middle years, and just consider growth between the start point of 2000 and the end point of 2007, that would give us an overall increase of 5 percent, or growth in the range of 0.5 to 1 percent/year.

But 2000 was the peak of a boom, so using that as the base year has under-estimated growth in the 2000s. Likewise, if we'd used the trough year 2002 as the base, that would have overestimated growth in the 2000s. We therefore translate the above data into three-year moving averages—namely the sum of this year's number plus the previous year's number plus the following year's number, divided by 3—as follows:

Year	2000	2001	2002	2003	2004	2005	2006	2007
Market demand	n/a	1283	1191	1246	1347	1474	1530	n/a
Change	n/a	n/a	-7%	5%	8%	9%	4%	n/a

This has the effect of smoothing the annual fluctuations and we begin to get a clearer picture of what has been happening. Taking 2001 as the start point and 2006 as the end point now gives an overall increase of 19 percent, or 3 to 4 percent/year. This seems to be more reflective of trend growth in the 2000s in this market.

ing slowly as moving along at the same pace as the economy as a whole (Gross Domestic Product in economics-speak), which is roughly 2 to 2.5 percent each year in the United States, Britain, and other large Western economies. That's in "real" terms—in other words, in terms of tangible, wealth-creating growth. On top of that sits inflation, typically around the same 2 to 2.5 percent each year these days, although it has been much higher in the past. Slow growth in terms of "money of the day," or in "nominal" terms, can therefore be defined as roughly 5 percent each year.

2. *Assess past drivers of growth.* Once you have uncovered some information on recent market demand growth, you now need to find out what has been influencing that trend. Typical factors that influence demand in many markets are:

- Per capita income growth
- Population growth in general
- Population growth specific to a market (for example, of pensioners or baby boomers, or general population growth in a particular area)
- Some aspect of government policy
- Changing awareness, perhaps from high levels of promotion by competing providers
- Business structural shifts (such as toward outsourcing)
- Price change
- Fashion—even a craze
- Weather—seasonal variations, but maybe even the longer-term effects of climate change

Not all of these drivers will be relevant for your business chunks. You need to pick those that are the most important. There may also be factors that are purely specific to your market. Fashion, fads in particular, can have a huge effect on some markets.

Sometimes the element of fashion can be rooted in sound economic sense. For example, in the micro-economy of Boston, the demand for carpentry and other building trades has been boosted by the demand for loft conversions. Owners of older townhouses and commercial premises realized they could create sought-after living space from their often spacious lofts. This realization later spread to the Boston suburbs, where homeowners began to appreciate the benefits of creating a living or working space bathed in natural light at the top of the house. This demand has kept Carwyn, our imaginary Bostonian carpenter, very busy for the last few years, subcontracting his services to specialist loft contractor Boston Heights.

3. *Assess changes in drivers.* Now you need to assess how each of these drivers is going to develop over the next few years. Are things going to carry on more or less as before for a particular driver? Or may things going to change significantly for that driver?

Will, for instance, immigration continue to drive local population growth? Is the government likely to hike up a local tax? Could this market become less fashionable?

The most important driver is, of course, the economic cycle. If it seems the economy is poised for a nosedive, that could have a serious impact on demand in your business chunk over the next year or two. You need to think carefully about the timing of the economic cycle when approaching your backer.

4. *Forecast future growth.* This is the fun bit. You've assembled all the information on past trends and drivers. Now you can weave it all together, sprinkle it with a large dose of judgment, and you have a forecast of market demand—not without risk, not without uncertainty, but a systematically derived forecast nevertheless.

Let's take a simple example. You're offering a relatively new service to the elderly. Step 1: You find that the market has been growing at 5 to 10 percent per year over the last few years. Step 2: You identify the main drivers as (a) per capita income growth, (b) growth in the elderly population, and (c) growing awareness of the service by elderly people. Step 3:

Change is inevitable—except from a vending machine.— Robert C. Gallagher

You believe income growth will continue as before, the elderly population will grow even faster in the future, and awareness can only get more widespread. Step 4: You conclude that growth in your market will accelerate and could reach over 10 percent per year over the next few years.

Personally, I find that a simple chart helps in coming to the final judgment, especially when things are not as straightforward as in this example—see Figure 2.1. The chart shows clearly whether demand is set to grow faster or slower, and what drivers are causing that. It concludes that this service seems to have the wind behind. I wonder what it is...!

Figure 2.1 **Market Demand Prospects for a New Service to the Elderly**

Demand Drivers for a New Service to the Elderly	Impact on Demand Growth			Comments
	Recent Past	Now	Next Few Years	
Growth in incomes	+	+	+	▪ Economic forecasts in newspapers seem fine
Growth in elderly population	+	+	++	▪ Proportion of U.S. population aged 65+ forecast to grow from 13% to 18.5% by 2025 (U.S. Census Bureau)
Increased awareness of service	++	++	+++	▪ Newspaper coverage, national and local, greater all the time
Overall Impact	+	+	++	
Market Growth Rate	*5 to 10%/yr*	*5 to 10%*	*Over 10%/yr*	

Key to Impact		O	None
+++	Very strong positive	-	Some negative
++	Strong positive	- -	Strong negative
+	Some positive	- - -	Very strong negative

Some Examples for the Self-Employed

Leila at Healing Hands

While we are looking at promising market demand forecasts, let's see what Chuck may have dug up on future demand for services such as Leila's Healing Hands. Figure 2.2 shows his conclusions for two of her main business chunks.

Chuck has been unable to come up with any numbers from his research. But this doesn't faze him, as this is often the case. He's found that demand prospects for Leila's original business of aromatherapy to stay-at-home moms should be steady and there's good growth potential from businesspeople for Ying's new reflexology offering. Of the other two business chunks, not shown in the chart, he's found that reflexology to moms also has good growth prospects, while demand by businesspeople for reiki may slow down and be replaced by demand for reflexology.

Overall, Chuck sees demand prospects for massage service providers such as Healing Hands as most promising. It's difficult to be sure which branches of massage will prosper and which will stall, but as long as a broad service is offered, there seems to be plenty of demand to be shared between the different types of massage.

Finally, Chuck has found that there is no reason why the demand trends he has researched for Britain as a whole should be less promising in the area of West London where Healing Hands is based. Indeed, given that the Notting Hill area has a standard of living much higher than the national average, he feels confident that demand growth in Leila's catchment area will be at least as high as he has found for the country overall.

Figure 2.2 Market Demand Prospects for Massage Therapy Services in London

Demand Drivers for Aromatherapy to Stay-at-Home Moms	Impact on Demand Growth			Comments
	Recent Past	Now	Next Few Years	
Growth in London incomes	+	+	+	▪ Economic forecasts in local papers seem fine
Need for relaxation	++	++	++	▪ Stay-at-home moms ever conscious of stress
Increased awareness	++	+	O	▪ Most moms now know about it
Overall Impact	++	+	+	
Market Growth Rate	*Rapid*	*Bit Slower*	*Steady*	

Demand Drivers for Reflexology to Businesspeople	Impact on Demand Growth			Comments
	Recent Past	Now	Next Few Years	
Growth in London incomes	+	+	+	▪ Economic forecasts in local papers seem fine
Need for stress relief	+	+	++	▪ Business life gets ever more stressful
Increased awareness	O	+	+++	▪ Should take off with availability
Lack of time	- -	- -	-	▪ Likely to remain a market dampener, although reflexology can take just a half-hour
Overall Impact	+	+	++	
Market Growth Rate	*Slow*	*Picking Up*	*Fast*	

Carwyn the Carpenter

For another example for the self-employed, let's return to Carwyn, the Boston carpenter. For the last few years, he has been working almost exclusively for a loft conversion contractor, Boston Heights. He's a highly experienced and competent carpenter, however, and he feels he could readily switch back to other areas of carpentry should he need to. Chuck, on his return to the United States from visiting Leila in London and other prospective investees, decides to assess market demand prospects for the whole of carpentry in the Boston area—see Figure 2.3.

Chuck finds that the loft conversion boom has had a large impact on the demand for carpentry in Boston over the last few years. Once that boom starts to abate, however, the impact on demand for carpentry in Boston could be as large again, but in the opposite direction. It may leave the market completely flat.

This could raise concerns for Carwyn's employability over the next few years. Chuck will need to do further research on the supply of carpenters in Boston (Chapter 3) and on how well placed Carwyn will be to compete for work (Chapter 6) given that his legs aren't quite as sprightly as they used to be.

Figure 2.3 Market Demand Prospects for Carpentry in Boston

Demand Drivers for Carpentry in Boston	Impact on Demand Growth			Comments
	Recent Past	Now	Next Few Years	
Growth in incomes	+	+	+	• Economic forecasts in newspapers seem fine
Commercial development	+	+	+	• Commercial forecasts likewise
Commercial maintenance	O	O	O	• Little growth, but good jobs to be had
Housebuilding (excl lofts)	+	+	+	• Steady growth
Loft conversions	+++	O	- -	• Boom to slacken off as more homes done
Residential odd jobs	O	O	O	• Growth offset by popularity of DIY
Overall Impact	**++**	**+**	**O**	
Market Growth Rate	***Strong***	***Slow***	***Flat***	

Employees Need to Check Market Demand at Two Levels

So far we've looked only at market demand prospects for self-employed people. If you're an employee, the approach is similar but a little more complicated. You need to look at market demand prospects at two levels:

➤ At the level of the economy (local, regional, or national, as for the self-employed, depending on your willingness—or ability—to relocate): Where's overall market demand for your type of service heading?

➤ At the level of your company: Where's demand for your type of service heading *within your company*?

You should look at both these levels because your backer needs to know how employable you would be if things go wrong in your current company or organization and you need to leave. This could be for a whole variety of reasons. It could involve personality conflict. Your boss may move on and you don't get on with the new one. Maybe an ingratiating colleague is promoted undeservingly above you. It might be that you can't tolerate working in the same room as a colleague. Companies are no more than gatherings of people. People fall out. You may be forced to leave your company even though you do your job extremely well and everyone knows it.

But there's another reason. If there's a chance that your company gets into trouble—performing badly relative to the competition—then that could have a major impact on the *demand by your company for your type of services*. If your company is forced to restructure, then you and your colleagues may face a redundancy program. If the worst happens, and your company closes down, then you and your fellow service providers will find yourselves on the labor market all at the same time. Not a good place to be.

Suppose you were a production line foreman at the grand old British motorcycle manufacturer, BSA, in the early 1960s. Originally a gunsmith, the Birmingham Small Arms Company ventured into bicycles in the late nineteenth century and motorcycles in the 1900s. After its acquisition of Triumph in the 1950s, it was the largest motorcycle company in the world. By the time the Japanese motorcycle company, Honda, commenced operations in Britain in the 1960s, BSA virtually owned the British motorcycle market and was highly profitable. This wasn't surprising, since it had been spending precious little on research and development for years. Within a year or two, BSA was hemorrhaging cash. It never recovered.

Japanese motorbikes were technologically streets ahead of BSA—not in performance perhaps, but in reliability, fuel efficiency, and style. They were also much cheaper. Competition had for years been so fierce between the half-dozen Japanese motorcycle producers in Japan itself that taking on foreign producers in their domestic markets was a cakewalk. Within 10 years or so, the British motorcycle industry virtually disappeared. Much the same happened in the United States, with producers like Harley-Davidson surviving only through refocusing their strategy to become a distinctive, cult, high-performance, high-price, niche producer.

If you, a foreman at BSA, were looking for backing in the early 1960s, you'd have thought it would be straightforward: Yours was a respected blue-collar job in a venerable, prestigious, highly profitable company. But if your prospective backer had done her job properly and rigorously analyzed the prospects for your employer over the next three to five years, she may have unearthed some advance warnings of the impending catastrophe for the British motorcycle industry. She may have suggested that you started looking elsewhere before you were forced to do so—along with hundreds of fellow employees.

If, however, your company is performing well, and from what you can tell, better than most of the competition, then that's good news. Demand in your company for your type of service is likely to be higher than overall market demand (whether nationally, regionally, or locally, however you choose to define your market) for your type of services.

Your backer will also need to look at both these levels when considering the competition (Chapter 3) and how well placed you are to compete (Chapter 6). As with market demand in this chapter, the approach will be similar to that used for the self-employed.

For assessing market demand prospects for employees, again we use the four-stage checking process—both at the level of the economy and at the level of the company. Let's go straight into an example.

Some Examples for Employees

Elizabeth at ConsultCo

Elizabeth has told the truth to her prospective backer—yes, it's Chuck Cash again. Although she excels at doing admin work and typing for her consulting colleagues, she has set her sights on specializing more on the market research opportunities in her job. She understands that this may be higher risk, but she believes she will find the work more fulfilling.

Chuck will assess what Elizabeth's prospects are for doing this within ConsultCo. He'll also need to assess her prospects should anything go wrong for Elizabeth at ConsultCo, or should anything go wrong for ConsultCo itself, and Elizabeth finds herself on the open job market.

First he needs to find out how flexible she is in terms of location.

Would she be prepared to move out of town for the right job? No way, it turns out. Elizabeth has no desire to move from Chicago. She was born there, her elderly parents live there, her son is happy in school there, and Elizabeth's husband, a self-employed martial arts coach, has taken years to build up a healthy clientele there. Elizabeth is staying put in Chicago, come what may.

Chuck needs to assess demand prospects for market research services in Chicago as a whole and in ConsultCo specifically—see Figure 2.4.

Chuck's findings on market demand for Elizabeth's most important future business chunk, market research services, are favorable. There are two main types of employers providing these services (this example is simplified)— market research companies and management consulting companies doing their own market research on assignments for their clients. Chuck finds that both sets of employer are set to grow their businesses over the next few years, with consulting groups set to recover strongly from their recession in the wake of the dot com crash.

Chuck finds that demand for market research services at Elizabeth's employer, ConsultCo, is also set to grow faster than in the rest of Chicago. This is because ConsultCo is a consulting group that specializes in strategy consulting, rather than operations or IT consulting, and to help a client develop a sound strategy typically requires much primary market research.

Figure 2.4 **Market Demand Prospects for Market Research Services in Chicago and at ConsultCo, Inc.**

Demand Drivers for Market Research in Chicago	Impact on Demand Growth			Comments
	Recent Past	Now	Next Few Years	
National economic growth	O	+	+	• Economic forecasts seem promising
Business demand for research	+	+	+	• Internet has not dampened demand
Local company performance	+	+	+	• Chicago research companies doing well
Business need for consulting	-	O	+	• Order books at last recovering
Local company performance	O	O	O	• Chicago consulting companies doing okay
Overall Impact	**O**	**O/+**	**+**	
Market Growth Rate	*Flat*	*Better*	*Steady*	

Demand Drivers for Market Research at ConsultCo, Inc	Impact on Demand Growth			Comments
	Recent Past	Now	Next Few Years	
ConsultCo performance	-	+	++	• Tough action taken, so ConsultCo now set to outperform rival consulting groups
Need for market research	+	+	+	• ConsultCo's focus on strategy, rather than operations consulting, is research-intensive
Overall Impact	**O**	**+**	**++**	
Market Growth Rate	*Flat*	*Picking Up*	*Fast*	

Randy at Homes4U

Chuck doesn't always find such promising market demand prospects for his employee clients. In the case of Randy, our young Realtor at Homes4U in Atlanta, Chuck didn't bother to break down his "business" into chunks. Randy only has one service offering— selling houses, a service he carries out exceptionally well. Chuck could have broken down his customer groups into type of property, or maximum purchase price, but there was no point. The residential property market in Atlanta had been booming on the back of greatly inflated prices, and it was poised for a heavy correction. Realtors had ridden the boom, taking more commissions from more transactions, as well as higher commissions per transaction because of the booming prices. Now that virtuous circle was poised to turn vicious. And it was going to affect each customer group, as vendors were likely to hold on to their properties until the market picked up again—see Figure 2.5.

At the second level of demand, that of the company, prospects looked little better for Homes4U than they did for the Atlanta real estate business as a whole. Homes4U was one of the best-rated realty companies in Atlanta, but all real estate businesses were on the verge of toppling into the vortex of market collapse. Market demand prospects for Randy didn't look promising, concluded Chuck.

Figure 2.5 Market Demand Prospects for Realtor Services in Atlanta and at Homes4U, Inc.

Demand Drivers for Realtor Services in Atlanta	Impact on Demand Growth			Comments
	Recent Past	Now	Next Few Years	
Atlanta economic growth	+	+	+	• Economic forecasts in local papers seem fine
New homes built	++	+	O	• Boom over but some developments planned
House prices	+++	O	- -	• Extraordinary house inflation over last few years unsustainable, poised for a tumble
Overall Impact	++	O	- -	
Market Growth Rate	*Over 20%/yr*	*Flat*	*Down, Down!*	

Demand Drivers for Realtor Services at Homes4U, Inc	Impact on Demand Growth			Comments
	Recent Past	Now	Next Few Years	
Homes4U performance	+++	O/+	- -	• Homes4U is good but so are many others, and all will be hit in impending market crash
Overall Impact	+++	O/+	- -	
Market Growth Rate	*26%/yr*	*3%*	*Down, Down!*	

Market Demand Risks and Opportunities

Whether you're self-employed or an employee, you've now come to a reasonable forecast of what's likely to happen to market demand for your type of services over the next few years. But your backer needs to know a little more than that. You've assessed what's *most likely* to happen. But what are the risks of something happening to market demand that could make things worse than that? What could happen to make things much worse? How likely are these risks to happen?

On the other hand, what could make things better than you have forecast? What could make things much better? How likely are these opportunities to happen?

Your backer's going to be very interested in these risks and opportunities. She's going to use your market demand forecasts to help her assess whether you're going to make your plan in Chapter 7. But then she's going to look at all the risks and opportunities around that plan in Chapter 8. And market demand issues will be the first set to be factored in.

In these matters the only certainty is that nothing is certain.—Pliny the Elder

It may help if you draw up a table, setting out each main risk or opportunity in the left-hand column and assessing in the next two columns first the likelihood of it happening and then the impact on your forecast if it should happen. This will help you to assess how important are each of the issues that you identify, as follows:

➢ If likelihood is medium (or high) and impact is high, then that is a big issue.

> ➢ If likelihood is high and impact is medium (or high), then that too is a big issue.

Any other issues that you don't include in the table can be assumed to be either unlikely to happen or not to have much impact if they do happen. An example of such a table can be found in Appendix A, Figure A.2.

This table on market demand risks and opportunities, together with similar tables you'll draw up on those concerning competition (Chapter 3), your capabilities (Chapter 6), and your plan (Chapter 7) will form the inputs for completing your Risk Jigsaw in Chapter 8.

Leila at Healing Hands

Let's see what market demand risks register on Chuck's radar when he looks at the four prospective clients we've discussed earlier in this chapter. We'll start with Leila's marketplace, as in Figure 2.6.

There's little in this chart to register on Chuck's radar. There are a couple of risks that would seriously affect the massage therapy trade if they happened, but they are rather unlikely to happen. Likewise with the opportunities that Leila and he have identified. This makes Chuck feel more comfortable around his forecasts.

Figure 2.6 **Market Demand Risks and Opportunities for Massage Therapy Services in London**

Market Demand Risks	Likelihood	Impact	Comments
London economic recession	Low	High	• High proportion of London economy is in financial services, so vulnerable to stock market crash, perhaps triggered by 2007-08 sub-prime mortgage credit crunch
Customers switch to new de-stress solutions, like meditation	Low	Med	• Perhaps but likely to be gradual and partial
Massage therapy gets bad name	Low	High	• Massage and sauna parlors long associated with vice trade, but seldom a problem for businesses clearly positioned as clinical therapy
Market Demand Opportunities	**Likelihood**	**Impact**	**Comments**
Businessmen lose reluctance to be seen to be needing to unwind	Low	High	• Culture of macho men not needing lunch, let alone massage therapy, difficult to break
Celebrity backing for reflexology	Med/ High	Low/ Med	• Celebrity endorsement can help build awareness, though could work in reverse with the wrong celebrity

Carwyn the Carpenter

Chuck sees no big risks or opportunities around his forecast of market demand for Boston carpentry. He believes it's inevitable that things are going to flatten out. There is the outside chance that Boston may bid for—and win—the 2016 Olympic Games. If that were to happen, demand for carpentry would soar, but chances at present seem low—so this opportunity doesn't really register for Chuck.

Elizabeth at ConsultCo

For the first of our employee exemplars, Elizabeth, Chuck also finds few market issues to get him concerned or excited beyond what he has already forecast. He still has an uneasy feeling that the phenomenal growth of information available on the Internet should in some way dent demand for market research services, but it hasn't happened so far because of strict copyright control. This is likely to remain the case, so he concludes that the Internet threat remains of low probability, therefore of little importance, despite potentially large impact.

Randy at Homes4U

In Randy's marketplace, however, Chuck comes across a risk that does register—the risk of demand decline overshooting. In a cyclical market, when prices have risen beyond where they should be on a long-term trend line, they often plummet to well below the trend line during a market correction. They seem to aim for the trend line, then overshoot. Look at the dollar exchange rate against major currencies over time. Often it can seem over- or undervalued by much more or for much longer than would seem economically rational.

So too (let's suppose again, for the sake of a useful example) with the number of Atlanta house transactions. Sure, there has been a supply shortage of houses in Atlanta in the last few years. Houses were being snapped up within a day or two of being put on sale, and this led to extraordinary house price inflation, way beyond what was expected. Now that supply has caught up, the number of house transactions should in theory return to its long-term trend line. But homeowners the world over are notoriously reluctant to lower prices on their "castles." Buyers will hold back and the number of house transactions could well overshoot and fall to well below the trend line.

If this were to happen, Chuck thinks, there could be carnage in the Atlanta real estate marketplace. Lower prices, competitive commission rates, and the number of transactions not 10 percent down but conceivably 25 to 50 percent down are all possible. Employment prospects for Realtors under this scenario would be grim.

Chuck therefore rates the risk of overshooting in Chuck's marketplace as medium likelihood, high impact. This is an important and worrying risk. All is not necessarily lost for Randy, though. When Chuck comes to assessing Randy's capabilities as a Realtor in relation to his colleagues and competitors, the findings may be less bleak. Even if the real estate job market were to shrink by a third, or even a half, somebody would still need to help buy and sell houses in Atlanta, so why shouldn't it be Randy? We'll return to Chuck's views on this in Chapter 8.

In this chapter, you've forecast where demand is likely to be headed in the market for your services. And you've assessed the risks and opportunities around these forecasts. In the next chapter you're going to look at the supply of services in your market and whether competition among you and your fellow service providers is tough and likely to get tougher.

What About the Competition? 3

- Is Competition Going to Get Tougher?
- Again, Remember the Chunks
- Who's the Competition?
- Who's the Competition for Employees?
- May the Five Forces Be With You!
- Some Examples for the Self-Employed
- Some Examples for Employees
- Market Balance and Pricing
- Competition and Pricing Risks and Opportunities

This chapter is in some ways unfortunate. Life would be simpler if you were the only person who could provide your service, who could do your job. If your customers (or colleagues if you're an employee) had no choice but to come to you, you could shape your job to suit your own needs and charge the customer what you wanted, within reason.

Life isn't like that. First, if a job's worth doing, there will be more than one of you wanting to do it. Second, none of us is irreplaceable. Don't kid yourself. There's always someone who can do any job just as well as you. A screenwriter may have a certain actress in mind when he creates a screen role, but there's no guarantee she'll be available or willing to take the part. And when the second or fourth choice wins the Oscar for Best Actress, who then remembers the actress for whom the role was initially created?

> Competition's a bitch—but that's what gives us puppies.
> —*Unattributed, heard in the world of finance*

There's always competition. There are others out there, often many others, who are either doing, or may be thinking of doing, what you are doing. This chapter asks you to think about what's happening, and what's likely to happen, to *all* of these people doing your kind of job or business. And whether competition among all of you is getting tougher or slacker, or staying about the same. Above all, it asks you to think if there is any chance there may be too many of you competing for the same jobs or business in the future.

Is Competition Going to Get Tougher?

Not only is there always competition but industry participants usually believe the competition to be tough. This is true even in near monopolies. Microsoft may have cornered the world market in personal computer operating systems, but it hasn't been an easy ride. Competition has been fierce and will only get tougher in the future.

The only thing we know about the future is that it will be different.—Peter Drucker

What you need to think about is whether competition is actually going to get *tougher*. Whatever your competitive situation today, it results in you making a profit or earning a salary of however many thousand dollars a year. But that's today. What your backer needs to know is what's going to happen *in the future*. Will the competitive environment enable you to continue to make that income or grow it in line with your plans in three or five years' time?

Again, Remember the Chunks

As for market demand in Chapter 2, you need to concentrate your efforts on assessing competitive intensity in your most important business chunks.

In the case of Leila, she and Chuck will look at competition in providing aromatherapy and reflexology services to stay-at-home moms, and reiki and reflexology services to businesspeople. They don't have to assess competition in providing, for example, shiatsu services to businesspeople; this chunk is too small.

Likewise, Elizabeth and Chuck will look at competition in providing admin and market research services to both senior and junior staff at ConsultCo. They won't need to look at competition, for example, in providing typing services.

Who's the Competition?

First, you will be clear about who your competitors are. Think about when you provide a particular service to a particularly good customer of yours. Who else could she have gone to? Think about all your services to all your customers. What other names frequently crop up—who do they go to, or who could they have gone to? They are your competition.

Life is nothing but a competition to be the criminal rather than the victim.—Bertrand Russell

Next, you should find out all you can about your competitors. If you're self-employed, this shouldn't be too difficult. How big are your competitors relative to you? How big were they a few years ago? How fast have they grown? Faster or slower than you? How long have they been around? How long have they offered this competing service?

What sort of service do they offer? What quality, price? Similar to yours? More upmarket, pricier? More downmarket, cheaper?

Do you know what financial resources your competitors have? If they needed to expand, could they do it from their own (or spouse's) pocket, or would they need a backer? What are their plans? Do they intend to broaden their service offering, reach out to a new customer group? Or are they likely to be content carrying on doing what they do now?

One complication can often be catchment area. How far afield must you look to include competitors? The answer lies in the first paragraph of this section. If you offer a service to local residents, but many of your clients are prepared to travel some distance to another provider, then that person is as much a competitor as the provider down the road.

Who are Leila's competitors? She knows that some of her stay-at-home moms also go to other providers in Notting Hill or in neighboring villages, but few go to aromatherapists in Central London. It's a 10-minute cab ride away, or longer on the bus, and the journey acts as a disincentive unless the trip is combined with shopping or some other purpose. She doesn't regard her peers in Central London as direct competitors in this business chunk.

It's different with her business clients. They have a choice of going during their lunch hour or after work to a reiki practitioner near their workplace, some rather luxurious compared to Leila's front room. Or they can visit Healing Hands in the evenings or at weekends. These Central London providers are direct competitors to Leila in this business chunk and need to be taken into consideration.

Who's the Competition for Employees?

It's a little more tricky, but it can be quite revealing to figure out who your competitors are if you're an employee. Your competition is not just your fellow employees who do the same job as you. It's also your fellow employees who could and would like to do the same job as you.

It's also independent contractors who could be engaged by your boss to do the job you do temporarily. Or they could be engaged on a longer-term basis should your employer decide to outsource your job.

Finally, it's all those in your marketplace who are doing similar jobs at other companies, or who would like to do similar jobs at other companies, who would apply for your job if they knew there was a vacancy. Or who might apply on spec anyway even if there were no vacancy. These are all your competitors!

It's important that you as an employee consider all sets of competitors, direct and indirect, current and potential. Your backer has to understand the labor market in which you work, both within your company and—should you have to leave your employer—outside your company.

May the Five Forces Be With You!

There's no better tool to assess the competitiveness of a marketplace than the model of five forces developed by Professor Michael Porter of Harvard Business School in his seminal work, *Competitive Strategy: Techniques for Analyzing Industries and Competitors*. First published in 1980, it has formed the bedrock for the study of business strategy by countless thousands of students and business executives worldwide ever since, myself included. It was designed for business markets rather than labor markets, but the principles work just as well here.

Porter identified five main sets of forces that shape the competitive intensity of a marketplace, as shown in Figure 3.1. Here's a quick word on each of these forces.

Figure 3.1 **Five Forces Shaping Competition**

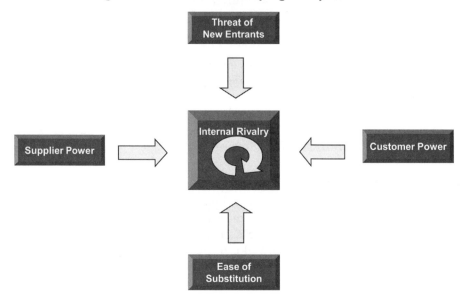

Internal rivalry

Internal rivalry for the self-employed (and remember that employees should think of themselves as self-employed here) is shaped by three main sub-forces: the number of players, market demand growth, and external pressures.

The number of players. The more players, the tougher typically the competition. Are there many players in your marketplace?

Market demand growth. The slower growing the market, the tougher typically the competition. How fast is your market growing?

Here's an example: Fast-growing, labor-scarce markets, such as plumbing (in the United States), tend to have less internal rivalry than slow-growing, labor-abundant markets, such as bus driving.

External pressures. External bodies, in particular government and the trade unions, have the power to influence the nature of competition in many workplaces. Whether this is through introducing (or raising) minimum wage, capping hours of work, toughening health and safety regulations, or imposing restrictive practices, competition can be greatly affected. In general, pressures from both government regulation and trade unions tend to reduce competition, although they are of course aimed at bringing about compensating benefits of other kinds. What external influences are there in your marketplace?

There are other factors influencing internal rivalry, which may be relevant in your workplace. One is high barriers to exit, where providers have little choice but to stay on competing when they should be withdrawing (for example, a restaurant with many employees, hence potentially high redundancy costs, or a shop with a long lease on the property that is difficult to offload). Another is seasonal or irregular overcapacity because of fluctuating levels of demand (for example, fruit picking).

How many providers are there in your marketplace? Too many? Enough? Too few (Great!)? How fast is the market for your services growing (Chapter 2)? What about the other factors? Put all these together and ask yourself how tough is the internal rivalry in your marketplace. High, low (Lucky you!), medium? And in a few years' time? Why?

> The trouble with the rat race is that even if you win you're still a rat. —*Lily Tomlin*

Threat of new entrants

The lower the barriers to entry to a market, the tougher typically the competition. In a labor market where there are low barriers to new entrants, such as for unskilled labor, competition in times of low market demand, say during economic recession, can be very tough. In a labor market where barriers to entry are very high, for example in medicine, law, or scientific research, competition is typically moderate—unless the regulating authorities have made a mess of long-term human resource planning.

Qualifications, training, and experience are the main entry barriers in most labor markets. But there can be others, such as:

➢ High investment costs to set up in business (for example, higher for dentists than for barbers, though higher for barbers than for cleaners)

➢ High costs of switching from one supplier to another (for example, higher for doctors than for restaurateurs)

➢ Reputation, or "brand equity" in business-speak (for example, higher for actors than for shop assistants)

How high are the entry barriers in your type of service? How serious is the threat of new entrants? High, low, medium? Is the threat going to get more serious over the next few years, less serious, or stay more or less the same? Why?

Ease of substitution

The easier it is for customers to use a substitute product or service, the tougher typically the competition. In labor markets, it is difficult for users to substitute for teachers or nurses, for example, but less difficult to substitute for cleaners (clever vacuum cleaners), TV or PC repair people (upgrade to a new model), or gardeners (drag Dad off the golf course).

How big is the threat of your type of service being substituted? High, low, medium? Is the threat going to get bigger over time? Why?

Customer power

The more bargaining power the customer has over the service provider, the tougher typically the competition. In labor markets, this is often a reflection of the number of providers in a particular marketplace, compared with the number of customers. The more choice of provider the customer has, the tougher the competition.

Customer power is also influenced by switching costs. If it's easy and relatively painless to switch suppliers, such as for your Realtor, competition is tougher. If switching costs are high, such as for your doctor, competition is less tough.

How much bargaining power do customers for your type of service have over providers like you? High, low, medium? And in the future? Why?

Supplier power

The more bargaining power suppliers have over the service providers, the tougher typically the competition. In labor markets, this force is not always so relevant. The main suppliers needed by most self-employed are their fellow self-employed, working as subcontractors. Thus the main supplier to a self-employed handyman could be his subcontracted apprentice, who should be readily replaceable if he were to move on.

In my own business of independent management consulting, I am often reliant on fellow independents to jointly provide the service needed by my clients. My associates can have strong bargaining power when they know they are ideally placed to do the work, whether because of their experience or because they just happen to be available at the right time.

How much bargaining power do your suppliers have over providers of your kind of service? High, low, medium? And in the future? Why?

Overall competitive toughness

These then are the five main forces shaping the degree of competition in a marketplace. Put them all together, perhaps as in the diagram above, and you'll have an idea of how competitive your marketplace is, compared to other marketplaces. How tough is your marketplace? High, low, medium? Is it set to get tougher? Why?

In terms of economic theory, these last few paragraphs are among the heaviest in the book. If you've survived them, well done! It's all downhill from here. If you've gotten a bit bogged down, some examples may make it clearer.

Some Examples for the Self-Employed

Leila at Healing Hands

Let's return to Leila. Market demand prospects, if you remember from the last chapter, seem promising. How does competition look over the next few years? Chuck and Leila have been through the Five Forces analysis, coming up with some interesting conclusions—see Figure 3.2.

They found that competition in massage therapy services in Notting Hill is low to medium overall. Since barriers to entry in many massage therapy services are rather low, however, competition could get quite a bit tougher.

Aromatherapy, Leila's initial offering, has a higher entry barrier than for her other therapies. Obtaining an accredited diploma in aromatherapy can take a year, covering training over

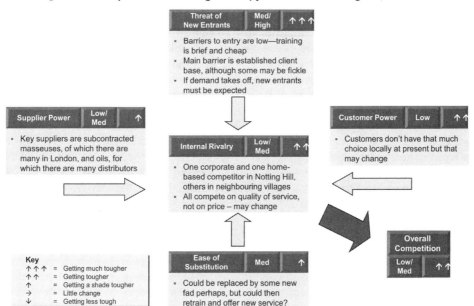

Figure 3.2 **Competition in Massage Therapy Services in Notting Hill, London**

12 to 20 weekends and costing the equivalent of US$4,500 to 6,000. This is what Leila did before she got started. Later she took a five-day intensive starter course in shiatsu for $600 and a three-day course in reiki for $450, which enabled her to get going in both these services. If she wasn't about to learn reflexology on the job with Ying, she could have done an eight-lesson correspondence course for just $300 to get started.

It doesn't take long or cost much to get started in many massage therapy services. Even in aromatherapy, Leila could have set up business without any formal accreditation and well before she had completed her diploma. It's a largely unregulated market, and there's little to stop anyone from setting up an aromatherapy business with little to no formal training—other, perhaps, than having read a book or two, practiced on a few buddies, and bought some massage oils. It may take a while for such a do-it-yourself aromatherapist to build credibility and business, but there's little to stop her having a go.

As a result, one of the Five Forces above may become a big issue for Chuck. The threat of new entrants to a market where demand is forecast to grow fast (reflexology) or steadily (aromatherapy) in a prosperous corner of London is high. Chuck and Leila will have to assume that competition in massage therapy in Notting Hill is going to get tougher. More masseuses will enter and start competing.

Leila secretly hopes, however, that what happened to Thai restaurants in Notting Hill won't happen in massage therapy. When she first moved to Notting Hill 12 years ago, there was one Thai restaurant in the village itself and two in nearby Bayswater. Their number mushroomed over a few years to 14 in Notting Hill and neighboring villages as Thai cuisine started to rival Chinese and Indian cuisine in popularity across London. But despite booming demand there just wasn't enough business locally to distribute among the 14 of them. Three had to close down and some of the remaining 11 have since been ticking along with modest profitability. Leila decides there's no need to inform Chuck about the local Thai restaurant experience!

It was largely because of the low barriers to entry in many massage therapy services that Chuck decided to bypass his rule about assessing competition for each business chunk and look at competition in massage therapy services as a whole. Providers of one massage therapy can diversify into other services to meet shifting demand with minimal time and expense. To have looked independently at competition in each of aromatherapy, reiki, and reflexology services would have been repetitive and added little to his findings.

Chuck has found, however, the first major risk to be factored into his Risk Jigsaw and ultimately his backing decision on Leila. It's by no means a deal-breaker at this stage, but by the time he comes to assess Leila's forecasts (Chapter 7) and weigh the balance of risks and opportunities (Chapter 8), one thing is for sure: The threat of new entrants into Leila's marketplace will loom large.

Carwyn the Carpenter

What about Carwyn, our other self-employed exemplar? Chuck finds that competition for carpentry services in Boston is also likely to heat up over the next few years but for very different reasons than for massage services in Notting Hill. Using the Five Forces model again, Chuck finds little threat from new entrants but a large rise in internal rivalry likely—caused by the forecast slowdown in market demand, itself affected by the impending tail off of the boom in loft conversions.

Over the next few years, Chuck suspects there could be too many carpenters chasing too few jobs in Boston. The ratio of applicants per vacancy is likely to rise sharply. It may only be temporary, since many of those who came to Boston during the boom years may return to where they came from. But some will have put down roots and may be reluctant to move, so the process of adjusting to a new level of demand could take a few years. Chuck hopes that Carwyn will be one of those likely to survive the adjustment process largely unaffected, but that's for Chapter 6.

Some Examples for Employees

Elizabeth at ConsultCo

Let's return to Elizabeth, remembering that Chuck has found that market demand prospects for market research services in Chicago are set to grow steadily, while at Elizabeth's employer, ConsultCo, demand is expected to grow quickly.

But will the competition get tougher? Chuck draws up his Five Forces model, as in Figure 3.3. He finds

Figure 3.3 **Competition in Market Research Services to ConsultCo Inc. and in Chicago**

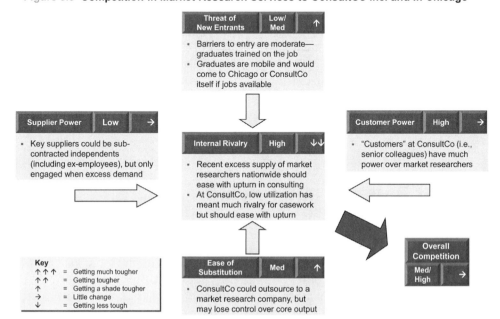

that competition in market research services to ConsultCo, and in Chicago as a whole, is pretty tough—medium to high—and likely to stay more or less that way. The recovery in the strategy consulting market should pick up the recent slack in market research work, resulting in a lowering of the applicants/vacancy ratio. There may be some new entrants, but they will be in response to job opportunities being created.

At ConsultCo itself, set to grow faster than the consulting market as a whole, jousting between colleagues over who can work on which market research assignments is expected to ease.

All in all, Chuck doesn't see anything

serious to worry about from competition in market research services in Chicago. The only niggle is whether ConsultCo may follow some of its peers and decide to outsource some of its market research work to a specialist third-party provider. The downside of this would be loss of control in a key component of the value ConsultCo delivers to its clients. But ConsultCo often gives advice to clients on outsourcing and should therefore be aware of its own outsourcing options. Chuck feels assured, however, that even if ConsultCo were to outsource its market research requirements, ConsultCo may well suggest that its dedicated market research team— largely Elizabeth —move to the chosen outsourcer.

Randy at Homes4U

Chuck didn't find the same rosy prospects for competition in Realtor services in Atlanta. Little threat of new entrants, perhaps. Some threat, perhaps, from internet-based Realtors. But the real threat will come from the huge intensification of internal rivalry should market demand crash. Realtors will lurch into the red. They'll start to compete on price—slashing their commission rates, rationalizing their office space and laying off staff. Some will close down. The remaining staff will have to work harder to justify their jobs. It may not be a bloodbath, but it could

well be nasty.

Chuck has found another serious risk in his deliberations over whether to back Randy. The first was the imminent downturn in market demand, and then there was the risk of transaction volumes overshooting downwards (both in Chapter 2). Now there's the related threat of widespread redundancies. His Risk Jigsaw is filling up unhealthily. For Chuck to consider backing Randy, Randy's going to have to emerge from Chapter 6's positioning assessment with flying colors. We'll see.

Market Balance and Pricing

With your analysis of market demand prospects (Chapter 2) and of competition (this chapter), you should now have a good idea of whether market demand and market supply are more or less in balance, now and over the next few years. This could have major implications for pricing prospects in your marketplace, hence on your earnings.

Suppose you're self-employed. If you conclude that you're in a balanced market and that market demand and supply are likely to remain balanced, then prices for your services may well carry on rising as they have done in the recent past—probably along with inflation, just above or just below.

If, however, your market is due to move from balance to oversupply—where supply exceeds demand—that will place a dampener on prices. You and your competitors will have to fight more fiercely for custom, and any planned price increases to meet rising costs may have to be put on hold.

If, conversely, the market is due to move from balance to undersupply (or excess demand), when more people want your type of service than there are services available, that's good news for you. You may be able to nudge pricing up above inflation.

Likewise, if you're an employee, it's unlikely that you and your colleagues are going to be awarded a significant salary increase when your company is facing a situation of oversupply in the market and not enough market demand. Conversely, in times of excess demand and your company has an overflowing order book, that's when you stand a good chance of pushing through a hike in salary or bonus.

What's likely to happen to market pricing is very important to your backer. This is because any extra dollar on the selling price of your service drops straight down to boost the bottom line. Conversely, every dollar off the selling price shrinks the bottom line.

There's a similar effect for employees. Let's take a simple example.

Ricardo, a bus driver in Calgary, Alberta, has wages equivalent to US$40,000 a year. He puts a regular $200 per month in a save-as-you-earn scheme and spends what's left after tax living a reasonable, sensible, nonextravagant life style. Suppose his company is facing recruitment difficulties, due to Calgary's booming oil-driven economic growth, and awards all bus drivers a pay hike of 7.5 percent. That's $3,000 per year extra pay gross, say $2,400 per year after taxes. Assuming Ricardo doesn't want or need to spend the extra cash on anything else, his monthly savings may now be $400 per month.

Doubt is not a pleasant condition, but certainty is absurd.—Voltaire

It's doubled! He hasn't had to work harder, put in more hours or look for extra work outside bus driving time, yet he's doubled his potential savings. The possibility of such a pay raise would be important information to Chuck.

Let's return to our main cast of four and see what Chuck has concluded about earnings prospects:

➢ In massage therapy services in Notting Hill, demand may outstrip supply for a short while, but new entrants are likely to rebalance the market. Overall, prospects for market pricing of these services seem favorable for Leila.

➢ In carpentry services in Boston, there's likely to be insufficient demand to fully utilize the current number of carpenters. Downward pressure on daily rates can be expected for Boston's subcontracted carpenters—including Carwyn.

> In market research services in Chicago, the current excess supply situation is likely to move to reasonable demand/supply balance, implying favorable prospects for salaries/bonuses for employees such as Elizabeth.

> In Realtor services in Atlanta, the impending fallout—with demand for real estate services likely to fall way below supply—means that for those Realtors who survive the squeeze times will remain hard. Bonuses will be the first to go and some firms may ask their employees to take a pay cut.

New risks are, therefore, added to Carwyn and Randy's Risk Jigsaws. In the case of Randy, Chuck is beginning to think that the task required of him in Chapter 6's positioning assessment is shaping up to be superhuman.

Competition and Pricing Risks and Opportunities

Now it's time to pull out all the main competition and pricing risks facing you and other providers of your services over the next few years. As you did in Chapter 2, it may be helpful to draw up a small table and highlight the most important risks and opportunities. You can find an example of such a table in Appendix A, Figure A.2.

These competition and pricing risks and opportunities are the second component of your Risk Jigsaw. Along with those on market demand (Chapter 2), U (Chapter 6), and your plan (Chapter 7), you'll be taking them into account when considering whether to back U in Chapter 8.

What Do Customers Need? 4

We dealt with market demand risk in Chapter 2 and market supply risk in Chapter 3. In Chapter 6 we move on from looking at the overall marketplace and look at you, at how you rate in your business or job in comparison with your competitors or colleagues. That's U risk.

But before we get there, we need to do some careful preparation and take another look at the marketplace as a whole. We need to work out what's common to all players in your business in the pursuit of success. What do you *all* need to do if you are to become successful?

To answer this, we have to address it in two parts. First, *what do customers need* from providers of your type of service? Or if you're an employee, what do your "customers"—your managers, or those to whom you report—need? That's this chapter. Then in Chapter 5 we'll ask: *What do you need to do to meet customers' needs and succeed in your job or business?*

How Are We Defining "Success"?

First, let's be clear about what Part I of this book is trying to do and what it's not. Here we're defining "success" as being able to bring home, with a reasonable balance of risk and opportunity, the kind of earnings you've envisioned in your business plan. It's a narrow definition, but it's the only one that's of interest or use to Chuck Cash.

Of course, this begs questions regarding job satisfaction and job fulfillment. These we'll return to in Parts II and III. For the time being, however, Chuck is not particularly interested in how spiritually meaningful your work is—*unless any dissatisfaction is going to impair your performance.* If this is so, as we'll examine in Chapter 6, then a major risk will need to be slotted into Chuck's Risk Jigsaw.

Remember the Chunks, Yet Again

We need to keep in mind yet again the most important chunks in your "business." The reason is simple: Not only do market demand prospects tend to be different in each chunk (Chapter 2), not only are some chunks more competitive than others (Chapter 3), but customer needs often differ from chunk to chunk. Some customers may be sensitive to price and will look around for the cheapest service available. Others may be sensitive to quality of service and are prepared to pay a premium to achieve that. Others again may be sensitive to time and will pay more for a service that is delivered promptly.

In Leila's marketplace, business customers for massage therapy may place a greater importance on punctuality than stay-at-home moms, who may be prepared to wait around for an extra quarter of an hour as long as they get what else they need from the service. Meanwhile, in Elizabeth's marketplace of ConsultCo, "customers" of market research services are likely to put greater importance on communication skills than will "customers" of admin services.

You need to assess customer needs in each of your most important business chunks.

What Do Customers Need From Providers Such As You?

What do customers need from providers of your type of service? If you're an employee, what do your managers need from you and your peers?

If you're self-employed

What are customers looking for when they buy your type of service in one of your business chunks? Are they looking for the lowest possible price for a given level of service? Are they looking for the highest quality service irrespective of price? Or, more likely, something in between?

Do customers have the same needs in your other business chunks? Do some customer groups place greater importance on certain needs?

What exactly do they want in terms of service? The most luxurious? Delivery on time? The most jovial camaraderie?

We're all customers of service providers. Depending on what we're buying, our expectations differ. Think of what you look for when you engage a gardener, a PC repairer, or a subcontractor for your business.

Different customer groups have different needs for different types of service. You, as a self-employed businessperson, need to know what each of your customer groups expects of you and your competitors. You need to know how they rank each need in order of importance.

If you're an employee

The same holds true if you're an employee. You need to know what exactly the people to whom you report—your "customers"—need from you in each of your business chunks. You need to know how important each need is in relation to the others.

The E2-R2-P2 of Customer Needs

In the business world, customer needs from their suppliers are referred to as customer purchasing criteria (CPCs). For companies that provide services to (or produce goods for) other companies, so-called business-to-business (or B2B) companies, CPCs typically include product quality, product range, delivery capabilities, pre-sale service, post-sale service, relationship, reputation, financial stability, and so forth. And of course, price. Elizabeth's employer, ConsultCo, is a B2B company.

For companies that provide services to the consumer directly, so-called business-to-consumer (or B2C) companies, CPCs tend to be similar, although typically with less emphasis on product range and financial stability. Depending on the service being offered, the consumer will place varying importance on quality, service, and price. Randy's employer, Homes4U, is a B2C company.

> Quality in a product or service is not what the supplier puts in. It is what the customer gets out and is willing to pay for. A product is not quality because it is hard to make and costs a lot of money…. This is incompetence. Customers pay only for what is of use to them and gives them value. Nothing else constitutes quality.
> —*Peter Drucker*

For self-employed people, CPCs, or more simply, customer needs, are again little different in nature. Except that customer needs can often pertain to the provision of services by *one individual*, not the collection of individuals that is a company. They can be grouped into six categories:

1. Needs relating to the *effectiveness* of the service
2. Needs relating to the *efficiency* of the service
3. Needs relating to the *relationship* with the individual service provider
4. Needs relating to the *range* of services provided
5. Needs relating to the *premises* (only applicable if the customer needs to visit the service provider's premises)
6. Needs relating to the *price* of the service

They can be conveniently remembered, with perhaps a faint redolence of a cult science fiction movie, as the E2-R2-P2 of customer needs.

Likewise "customer" needs of employees fall more or less into the same categories. Your managers expect from you the appropriate balance of service and price, that is, salary and benefits. But they provide the premises. Let's look at each in turn.

E1: Effectiveness

The first need of any customer from any service is that the job gets done. Not half-done, not over-done, just done. You want a crew cut. You go to the barber. He gives you a crew cut. You pay and go home. Job done.

You may have other requirements, like how long the haircut took, the interaction with the barber, whether he also offers a wet shave, how clean the barbershop is, or how reasonable his price. But the most basic requirement is that he is effective at giving you a crew cut. At getting the job done.

Suppose, however, that it's not a crew cut you want, but the cool cut sported by some celebrated movie actor? Now you start to get a bit more demanding with your requirements. You're going to want your barber, or hair stylist, to be competent technically at delivering such a haircut, to know about the pros and cons of living with such a haircut and to have done a few of these before. You don't want to be a guinea pig—not with your hair!

In other words, you as the customer will have certain expectations as to what constitutes job effectiveness. You'll have expectations in three areas: *skills, knowledge,* and *experience.* We'll take one at a time.

Skills

A skill is defined in dictionary.com as a "proficiency, facility, or dexterity that is acquired or developed through training or experience." It's not what you learned at school, it's what you were trained for in the world of work.

> Skill without imagination is craftsmanship and gives us many useful objects, such as wickerwork picnic baskets. Imagination without skill gives us modern art.
> —Tom Stoppard

Customers need different skills from different services. The dramatic skills of an actor are of little use if you need your swimming pool tiles relaid. Our exemplar Elizabeth's skills as a market researcher would be of little use to Randy's Realtor employers, although they might have used her typing and admin skills when market conditions were booming.

What skills does a customer expect from the service you offer? How important are these needs to your customers, relative to other needs? Are they of high, low, or medium importance?

Knowledge

"Knowledge" has six definitions, according to dictionary.com:
1. The state or fact of knowing
2. Familiarity, awareness, or understanding gained through experience or study
3. The sum or range of what has been perceived, discovered, or learned
4. Learning, erudition

5. Specific information about something
6. Carnal knowledge

Each of these definitions, leaving aside the last one, may add some understanding of what the customer may need from your service. Customers will expect you not just to have certain skills but to possess knowledge associated with those skills.

In many services, customers will expect you to have knowledge of the benefits to them from the provision of your services. Thus our exemplar Leila's stay-at-home moms may expect her not only to be skillful in aromatherapy massage, but to be able to explain how the therapy can be beneficial to their own particular needs—be they relief from muscle sprain, back pain, or stress.

What knowledge, general or specific, do your customers expect you to have in the provision of your service? How important are these needs relative to others? High, low, or medium?

Experience

"Experience" is defined in dictionary.com as "active participation in events or activities, leading to the accumulation of knowledge or skill." So it's an integral part of the concepts of both skill and knowledge. It appears in their definitions. They appear in its definition.

Yet it's wise to pull out experience as a specific customer need because it can sometimes be crucial. It may be important, but not as important as skill or relationship, for example, in selecting your physiotherapist. But what about in selecting your cardiac surgeon? No matter how well qualified she is, how adept she is with the scalpel, or how well you know her, if she hasn't had much experience in the precise surgical procedure that you need, would you opt for her?

It's not just in life-and-death situations where experience is important. It's important too in Elizabeth's market research services and in Carwyn's carpentry services.

The trouble with working in a career where experience is a major customer need is how to get started. The answer is in building it however you can. Think of Carwyn when he started out as a carpenter's apprentice. He barely earned enough to support himself, but he grew daily in experience. Sometimes we need to swallow our pride and work for free, or at a big discount, just to build the experience.

Do your customers require much experience from the providers of your service? How important a need is it relative to other needs? High, low, medium?

E2: Efficiency

We've looked at effectiveness, the most basic of customer needs for any type of service, and its three main components—skills, knowledge, and experience. The second distinct area of customer need is the second "E," efficiency. How long will it take to deliver this service effectively? How capable is this service provider in delivering one level of service in one space of time, another level in another space of time, and so on? In other words, how efficient is this service provider?

All customers place *some* level of importance on efficiency for all types of service. You may not care if your crew cut takes 10, 15, even 30 minutes, but you would care if it took all Saturday afternoon and you missed the big football game.

Different customer groups place different levels of importance on efficiency for the same service. Leila's stay-at-home moms are less concerned about punctuality and on-time delivery than her businesspeople.

Likewise, customer groups may place different levels of importance on efficiency for different services. ConsultCo consultants are more concerned at work that Elizabeth delivers her market research reports on time than they are at play when they hope that Leila will complete her reiki massage on time.

How much emphasis do your customers place on the efficiency of your service? How important a need is it relative to other needs? High, low, medium?

R1: Relationship

Your barber gives a good crew cut and he does it quickly. But do you like the guy? Is he the sort of guy you feel comfortable with having his hands on your head? Do you want your barber to chat or stay quiet? How do you want to interrelate? Does it matter to you if this guy seems bored and disinterested? Or would you prefer him to be interested and enthusiastic?

Never underestimate the relationship component in providing a service. A successful builder knows how to keep the homeowner as content as possible during the renovations. He'll try to ensure minimum disruption to everyday living—no wheelbarrows across the living room carpet—and be of good cheer and ready humor at all times. He knows that his business depends on personal referrals. If that spouse tells a prospective customer that he's not only a good builder but an okay guy to have around under trying circumstances, his chances of converting the next sale are much improved.

It's the same in the workplace. When the redundancy program comes along, it's not the boss's favorite who's first shown the door.

Dictionary.com defines relationship as "a particular type of connection existing between people related to or having dealings with each other." But it's useful to divide customer expectations of relationships in two: *rapport* and *attitude*. Rapport, defined as "mutual trust or emotional affinity," is the set of one-on-one relationships built up between your customers (or managers, if you're an employee) and you.

Attitude is best singled out. It's a major issue in this book. And it can often be a paramount factor in the provision of services. A positive attitude, conveying enthusiasm, cheer, conviviality, optimism, humor, energy, and other uplifting attributes, can leave the customer feeling she has received exceptional value from the service.

> It is not your aptitude, but your attitude, that determines your altitude.—*Zig Ziglar*

A negative attitude, conveying grumpiness, gloom, pessimism, misery, lethargy, and other down-spiriting attributes, can leave the customer feeling glad to be rid of the service provider.

A negative attitude may be the result of dissatisfaction with the job. If this is so for you, it may impinge on your competitive position (Chapter 6) and you may need to consider changing career—hopefully following your passion (Part III).

How much emphasis do customers place on personal relationships in your service? On rapport? On attitude? High, low, medium?

R2: Range

The second "R" and fourth area of customer need is the range of services provided. This is an area customers can find important for some services, even most important, and for other services of no importance at all.

Let's return to the example of a hair salon. No self-respecting hair stylist would offer any less than haircuts, perms, and colorings. But is that enough? Would customers prefer a salon that can also offer techniques such as relaxing, straightening, plaiting, and braiding? How important to the salon's target customer group is the range of services provided?

At the other extreme lies the functional barbershop. If most customers only want a crew cut, they're going to look for a barber shop that is effective and efficient, and where the barber is a good guy. If the barber were also to offer head massage, big deal! Yet to some customers, the head massage may the unique offering that draws them through the door.

How important a need is range to your customers compared with other needs? High, low, medium?

P1: Premises

This applies only to a small portion of the self-employed and not to employees. Many of the self-employed, such as tree surgeons, TV aerial installers, and professional speakers, don't need a storefront. Insurance brokers, travel agents, and shopkeepers do. Premises can be important, depending on how you are pitching your services.

Think about hair salons again. If you're aiming for the rich and famous, then you'll need a storefront on 5ᵗʰ Avenue, New York, or in Mayfair, London. And it had better be spectacular. If you're going for the middle-class, suburban housewife, you'll need a storefront on the local main street, and it should be clean and tasteful. The premises should be appropriate for the pocket of the customer.

Do you need a storefront for your type of service? What do customers expect of your premises? How important a need is it relative to other needs? High, low, medium?

P2: Price

This is the big one. Set your prices sky high, and you won't have many customers.

Think about the buying decisions you make regularly and the influence of price. For nonessential services, we tend to be more price sensitive. When your eight-year-old son's hair is flopping over his eyes, you look for a barber. He has little interest in his appearance (for the time being!), so you may look around for the cheapest. But how cheap are you prepared to go? Would you take him to a barber's that is (literally) dirt cheap, where the combs are greasy, the floor is covered with hair, and the barber is a miserable so-and-so? Probably not. You set minimum standards of service and then go for a reasonable price.

For essential services, we tend to be less fixated with price. When your central heating system breaks down in the middle of winter, will you go for the cheapest service engineer? Or will you call around your friends and acquaintances to find someone who is reliable, arrives when he says he will, fixes it with no fuss, and charges a price that is not exactly cheap but at least is no rip-off?

What are customers' pricing needs from providers of your type of service? How important a need is it relative to other needs? High, low, medium? Very high?

How Can You Find Out?

That's all very well in theory, you may ask, but how do you know what customers want? Simple. Ask them! Or if that is too embarrassing, ask a friend to ask them for you.

Your most unhappy customers are your greatest source of learning.—*Bill Gates*

It doesn't take long. You'd be surprised how after just a few discussions with any one customer group a predictable pattern begins to emerge. Some may consider one need "very important," others just "important." But it's unlikely that another will say that it's "unimportant"—unless perhaps for one out of a range of services provided. Customers tend to have the same needs.

The comprehensive way to find out customer needs is through "structured interviewing," where you ask a selected sample of customers a carefully prepared list of questions. (More on this in Chapter 6 and Appendix B.)

This is one of the steps in the *Backing U!* process that is much easier for the employee. Most employees have regular reviews with their managers, at least once a year when it's time to decide pay raises. Your boss will tell you what she needs from you and your colleagues. If she doesn't give you enough information on, say, the relative importance of each of her needs, probe her a bit further.

How Will Customer Needs Change Over Time?

While you're talking to your customers, or to your managers, you also need to find out how their needs are likely to change in the future. If they believe one need is highly important to them now, will it be as important to them in a few years' time? You need to know.

One factor that often tends to change over time is the emphasis a customer will place on price. Think of your laptop computer. Just a few years ago laptops were rather expensive, but when choosing between one of a half-dozen manufacturers to buy from, you might have paid a premium for a solid, well-known brand name. You may have been reluctant to buy a cheaper laptop and take the risk of it breaking down a year later (just as it came off warranty!). Now that the price of all laptops has come down (they are becoming "commoditized," in economics-speak), and the capabilities of so many manufacturers have greatly risen, you may be more prepared to take a punt on the cheaper machine—especially for the kids!

It's the same with services. When a service is new and innovative, customers may be happy to give it a go despite the seemingly high price. A few years later, when there are many other providers, customers will expect more reasonable pricing. Consider a spa vacation in the tropics. A few years ago you would have had to pay an arm and a leg to have them pampered in a five-star spa resort in the tropics. Now dozens of three-star hotels in Thailand offer excellent spa services. In a few years' time, some new angle on the spa theme will come out. It'll cost a bomb for a while, but if it's popular the price will soon come down.

It's similar for employees. Price may not be the most important consideration of prospective employers when there is a national or local shortage of people with your skills. They'll be prepared to pay top salaries and benefits to recruit employees who can do the job. But that won't last. Over time there will be new entrants and labor supply will come more into balance with demand. Employers will then pay more attention to price. Think of the pay packages offered to Internet-savvy software developers in the late 1990s dot-com boom. It couldn't last, and it didn't.

How are customer needs from providers of your type of service likely to change over time?

You've assessed customer needs, now and over the next few years. Let's see what customers need from our main cast of characters.

Some Examples for the Self-Employed

Leila at Healing Hands

What do customers need from massage therapy services such as Leila's in Notting Hill? To a certain extent, it depends on the type of customer. But Leila finds that all customers will expect to receive effective physical therapy from a therapist with a positive, enthusiastic attitude. They may also need, although perhaps of lesser importance, genuine experience from the therapist, understanding of the benefits of the therapy to customers, and a safe, hygienic, comfy environment. Stay-at-home moms, more so than business customers, also expect to be able to strike up a pleasing rapport with the therapist.

Where Leila's business customers are likely to differ most from the moms is in expectations over efficiency and price. Business customers will expect the therapy to start at the appointed time and for it to be completed by the right time. Moms may be more flexible over time, but they tend to place a greater importance on price.

It may help you, as it does me, to put this into a chart, as in Figure 4.1. The chart helps show which needs are most important and which differ (in bold italics) between groups of customers. It's also useful to add a column to show whether you think each customer need is going to gain or lose in prominence over the next few years. Leila and Chuck think that, as competition heats up, customer rapport and price will become more important to moms.

Figure 4.1 Customer Needs from Massage Therapy Services in Notting Hill, London

Stay-at-Home Mom Customer Needs		Importance	Change
Effectiveness - Skills	▪ Physical therapy	High	→
- Knowledge	▪ Understanding of benefits	Low/Med	→
- Experience	▪ Confidence in process	Med	→
Efficiency	▪ Effort	Low/Med	→
	▪ Timeliness	*Low**	→
Relationship	▪ Rapport	*Med/High**	↑ ↑
	▪ Attitude	High	→
Range		Low	→
Premises	▪ Safe, hygienic, comfy	*Low/Med**	→
Price		*Med**	↑

* Business customer needs are found to be the same as for stay-at-home moms, other than in timeliness *(High)*, rapport *(Low/Med)*, premises *(Med)*, and price *(Low)*

Carwyn the Carpenter

Chuck also finds out what customer needs are for carpentry services (such as Carwyn's) in Boston. Again, it depends to an extent on the type of customer, whether a building contractor, a maintenance manager or a homeowner. But most important to most customers, Chuck finds, are carpentry skills, efficiency and attitude. Price is taken as a given, because there seems to be an unwritten rate for the job, known to all players in the Boston marketplace.

Some Examples for Employees

Elizabeth at ConsultCo

What do Elizabeth's "customers" at ConsultCo (i.e, her managers) require from the market research services of colleagues such as Elizabeth, or indeed of external, subcontracted suppliers? Elizabeth believes that most important are a full understanding of the process, the unearthing of all relevant information, rigorous analysis, and a positive attitude.

Also important are the ability to meet time deadlines, the ability to write clear and coherent reports, and general knowledge of the economy and markets. Less important are clear oral communication and price (i.e., salary and benefits)—as summarized in Figure 4.2.

Elizabeth suspects, however, that her "customers" will increasingly expect market researchers to be able to present findings on their feet— not just to their fellow colleagues, but also on occasion to ConsultCo's clients. Communication skills will become more important over time. She also thinks that ConsultCo may start to take price more seriously. As ConsultCo continues to advise clients on the benefits of outsourcing, so too may it start to think more about outsourcing some of its own needs.

Randy at Homes4U

It doesn't take Chuck long to find out what his bosses, his "customers," in Homes4U expect of Realtor negotiators like Randy. They expect them to be able to win mandates from home vendors, sell the benefits of homes convincingly to would-be buyers, and close deals effectively between seller and buyer. Less but still important, they want their negotiators to be able to draw up sale leaflet particulars, understand what's driving the ups and downs of the market, and have some knowledge of required repairs and updating of homes, as well as their likely costs.

Chuck also finds that when the downturn comes, "customer" expectations of deal closure capabilities will become even more important.

Figure 4.2 "Customer" Needs for Market Research Services in Chicago and at ConsultCo, Inc.

"Customer" Needs		Importance	Change
Effectiveness - Skills	▪ Comprehensive info ▪ Rigorous analysis ▪ Coherent reporting ▪ Clear communication	High Med/High Med Low/Med	→ → → ↑
- Knowledge	▪ General knowledge	Med	→
- Experience	▪ Understanding process	High	→
Efficiency	▪ Effort ▪ Timeliness	Med Med	→ →
Relationship	▪ Rapport ▪ Attitude	Med Med/High	→ →
Range		Low	→
Premises	▪ *Not applicable*		
Price		Low/Med	↑

In this chapter, you've assessed customer needs for your type of service, now and over the next few years. In Chapter 5, we're going to look at what capabilities are needed from providers like you to meet those customer needs and perform your service successfully.

What Do You Need to Do to Succeed?

- ▶ **Introducing Key Kapabilities (K2s)**
- ▶ **Converting Customer Needs Into Service-Related K2s**
- ▶ **Converting the Customer Pricing Need Into Cost-Related K2s**
- ▶ **Some Self-Employed Examples**
- ▶ **Some Employee Examples**
- ▶ **How Important a K2 Is Management?**
- ▶ **How Important a K2 Is Market Share?**
- ▶ **Apply Weights to the K2s**
- ▶ **Don't Forget the Chunks!**
- ▶ **Just the One Example!**
- ▶ ***Attention!* Any Must-Have K2s?**
- ▶ **Is Attitude a Must-Have K2?**

In Chapter 4 you found out what customers need from your type of service if you're self-employed. Or if you're an employee, what those to whom you report need from your type of service. You rated each of these customer needs by degree of importance.

In this chapter, you're going to figure out what you and all other providers of your type of service need to do to meet those customer needs. Then you'll think about what else providers need to do in terms of managing themselves, as individuals, whether employed or self-employed, to provide a competitive service. Having done that, you'll be in a position to rate your own performance against all of these factors in relation to your peers. That's for the next chapter.

Introducing Key Kapabilities (K2s)

We define Key Kapabilities as what providers like you need to do to succeed in your type of business or job. They are what you need to get right to be able to meet customer needs *and* run a sound business (if self-employed).

In business-speak, they are called Key Success Factors (KSFs). They are what a company needs to get right to succeed in that marketplace. Typical KSFs are product (or service) quality, consistency, availability, range, and product development (R&D). Companies also need to get their service right, with such KSFs as distribution capability, sales and marketing effectiveness, or post-sale technical support. Other KSFs relate to the cost side of things, such as location of premises, scale of operations, state-of-the-art equipment, and operational efficiency.

The things taught in schools and colleges are not an education, but the means to an education.
—Ralph Waldo Emerson

But this book is about you as an individual, and many of these Key Success Factors will relate to the skills and attributes, or *capabilities,* required of *an individual person* providing your type of service. But not all. If you're self-employed, factors such as the range and skills of your subcontractors, or location and standard of premises, relate to your business, not to you as a person.

Knowledge comes, but wisdom stays.
—Alfred Lord Tennyson

We'll call them Key Kapabilities, or K2s for short. Not to be confused with the second highest mountain in the world, Mount K2 of the Karakoram range in the Himalayas, but the term may serve as a reminder of the peaks we may need to climb in order to succeed.

Converting Customer Needs Into Service-Related Key Kapabilities

The first thing we need to do is convert the customer needs we researched in the last chapter into K2s. In other words, we must work out *what you need to do in order to meet those customer needs.*

This is fairly straightforward for most customer needs. An associated K2 can often seem similar to, even the same as, a customer need. Suppose, for example, you as a customer want your hair stylist to be good at coloring. That's one of your needs. So she or he needs to be skilled at coloring. That's a K2.

But K2s generally tend to take a different perspective from customer needs. Here's an example. When you call up your Internet service provider technical help desk, you want the technician to fix the problem. You as a customer need someone who can understand and fix your problem. The associated K2s for the technician are an appropriate technical qualification and subsequent completion of relevant training and experience for handling this and similar problems.

Here's another: When you jump on the city tour bus in Acapulco, Rome, or Kyoto, you expect to be able to understand clearly what the tour guide is saying. The customer need is clarity of communication. The associated K2s are proficiency in the language of delivery and clear communication skills.

What do providers of your type of services need to do to meet customer needs? What are the associated K2s for each customer need in your business or job?

When converting a customer need, you may find that the associated K2 can sometimes be the same as you've already associated with another customer need. In other words, one K2 can sometimes be sufficient to meet two or more customer needs. Returning to the tour guide, for example, another customer need may well be rapport with the guide. Rapport will be greatly eased through fluency in the language of delivery. In this example one K2, language proficiency, serves two customer needs, namely (1) clarity of communication, and (2) rapport.

Converting the Customer Pricing Need Into Cost-Related Key Kapabilities

There's one customer need that needs special attention, and that's price. Customers of most services expect a keen *price*. The service providers need to keep their *costs* down. Price is a customer need; cost competitiveness a K2.

In a competitive service business like car repair, for example, middle-income car-owning customers tend to be sensitive to price, among other needs such as quality of work and integrity. The self-employed car mechanic will therefore try to keep his rental costs down by locating his garage well off the main street, perhaps on to some commercially zoned land alongside the railway line.

What importance rating did you give to price as one of your customers' needs in the last chapter? If you gave it a "low," lucky you. You can move on to the next section (after you let me know what your job is!).

For most of us, price is typically rated by customers as high importance or medium-high at best. In which case, we need to figure out how to keep costs down, or at least reasonable.

If you're an employee, this is all about your pay package. If you've rated price as highly important to your "customers," you and your peers need to be careful not to push too hard with your requests for a pay raise. Or you should think about offering your employer more flexibility within the overall package—lower basic, potentially higher bonus relating to performance, for example.

If you're self-employed, you typically have four main cost levers to play with if price is highly important: (1) cost of materials, (2) use of subcontractors, (3) overhead control, and (4) profit flexibility:

➢ There may be little you can do about the cost of materials or equipment. If you're a sole trader, you'll have precious little bargaining power over your suppliers. What you can do, though, is to keep as much control on material wastage as you can, be it paper and ink if you're desk-based, or copper piping if you're a plumber.

➢ Careful use of subcontractors may be a K2 in your line of business. A self-employed businessperson should only use subcontractors when she doesn't have the capability or the time available to do the work herself. But it's not always as easy as that. You may choose to keep your subcontractor happy and toss him some extra work, just to help him get by and stay in business, thereby being available to you when you really need him. It's a tradeoff.

➤ Control of overhead is usually an important K2 for the self-employed. If you need a storefront, then it should be appropriate to the market positioning of your business. If you need to advertise, it should be carefully targeted. And you may need to reconsider whether your business really needs its customers to be taken to so many lunches, dinners, and trips to the opera/baseball/Hawaii to succeed!

➤ Flexibility in profit level may be a K2. What's left of revenues after subcontractor and any other direct costs, and after overhead, is profit (pretax), the pay of the self-employed person. The ability to accommodate fluctuating profit levels, especially during market downturns, may be a K2. If you've leveraged up your lifestyle to an extent where a sharp fall in profits one year would put you and your family in financial distress, you are at a disadvantage to a competitor with greater personal flexibility. Acceptance of a long-term lower level of profit may also be a K2. If similarly competent competitors have come into your market prepared to work at lower levels of pay—for example, recent migrants—are you prepared to match their pricing?

One more set of cost-related K2s is important. There's not a lot you can do about it if you are an individual, self-employed person. But you should know about it because this is a source of competitive advantage that may lie with your larger competitors. Size may matter. Other things being equal, the larger the provider the lower their costs should be *for each unit* of business sold. This can be true for many overhead cost items, even for engaging subcontractors (the more work they're given, the lower the negotiated rate per day). These are "economies of scale" in economics-speak.

Two areas of overhead where these economies tend to be most relevant are in rental space costs and marketing expenses. Think of two hair salons competing against each other on Main Street. One has double the amount of space of the other and serves on average 80 customers a day, compared to the smaller salon's 40. They are thus similarly efficient, and they charge similar prices. But the larger one has lower rental costs *per customer* because of a discount negotiated with the landlord on the second commercial unit rented. The larger salon also pays lower marketing costs *per customer*, since advertising space in the Yellow Pages or in local glossy magazines costs the same per column inch for both salons, irrespective of how many customers the advertiser serves. These are economies of scale.

What are the main cost-related K2s in your business? Cost of materials? Use of subcontractors? Overhead control? Profit flexibility? Economies of scale?

Some Self-Employed Examples

Leila at Healing Hands

What are the K2s that providers of massage therapy like Leila need? To start with, the chart we've already drawn up on customer needs now comes in handy. We just need to add an extra column to put down the K2 that is associated with each customer need. Let's take a look at the marketplace in massage therapy services, first to stay-at-home moms—see Figure 5.1.

To succeed in this marketplace, Chuck finds, Leila and other massage therapists need to perform well in massage technique and enthusiasm, with communication skills another big advantage. Experience and cost competitiveness are also useful, more so than standard of premises and punctuality. Chuck also finds that two K2s—cost competitiveness and communication skills—are going to become more important in the future.

For the marketplace in massage therapy services to businesspeople, Chuck finds the same K2s but ranked in a different order. Efficiency leaps from bottom place to joint top, while cost competitiveness drops from middle place to bottom.

Figure 5.1 Associated Key Kapabilities for Massage Therapy Services for Stay-at-Home Moms in Notting Hill, London

Stay-at-Home Mom Customer Needs		Importance	Change	Associated Key Kapabilities
Effectiveness - Skills	• Physical therapy	High	→	• **Massage technique**
- Knowledge	• Understanding of benefits	Low/Med	→	• **Qualifications, diploma**
- Experience	• Confidence in process	Med	→	• **Direct experience**
Efficiency	• Effort • Timeliness	Low/Med Low	→ →	• **Work ethic** • **Punctuality**
Relationship	• Rapport • Attitude	Med/High High	↑ ↑ →	• **People skills (communication)** • **Enthusiasm**
Range		Low	→	• **Range**
Premises	• Safe, hygienic, comfy	Low/Med	→	• **Premises**
Price		Med	↑	• **Cost competitiveness**

Carwyn the Carpenter

Meanwhile, in Carwyn's marketplace of carpentry services in Boston, Chuck finds that K2s are, in order of importance, carpentry skills, efficiency, reliability, motivation, and cost competitiveness. As the market flattens out, cost competitiveness will become more important.

We'll see how Chuck rates the performance of Leila and Carwyn against each of their appropriate K2s in Chapter 6.

Some Employee Examples

Elizabeth at ConsultCo

At ConsultCo, Chuck adds another column to his chart on "customer" needs to derive associated K2s for market researchers, as in Figure 5.2.

Chuck finds that to succeed in this marketplace, Elizabeth and other market researchers need to perform well in interviewing skills and have direct experience of what needs to be done. They should also have sound analytical skills and be enthusiastic. Other factors such as structured writing skills and time management skills are also important, but not quite as important as those mentioned earlier.

Chuck also finds that two of these K2s, presenting skills and cost competitiveness, are likely to become more important over time. Market researchers at ConsultCo will have to sharpen their speaking skills and be more flexible in salary, bonus, and benefits.

Figure 5.2 **Associated Key Kapabilities for Market Research Services in Chicago and at ConsultCo, Inc.**

"Customer" Needs		Importance	Change	Associated Key Kapabilities
Effectiveness **- Skills**	• Comprehensive info • Rigorous analysis • Coherent reporting • Clear communication	High Med/High Med Low/Med	→ → → ↑	• **People skills (interviewing)** • **Analytical skills** • **Structured writing skills** • **People skills (presenting)**
- Knowledge	• General knowledge	Med	→	• **Good, relevant degree**
- Experience	• Understanding process	High	→	• **Direct experience**
Efficiency	• Effort • Timeliness	Med Med	→ →	• **Work ethic** • **Time management skills**
Relationship	• Rapport • Attitude	Med Med/High	→ →	• **People skills (communication)** • **Enthusiasm**
Range		Low	→	• **Range**
Premises		N/a		
Price		Low/Med	↑	• **Cost competitiveness**

Randy at Homes4U

Chuck now turns his attention to K2s for Realtors in Atlanta. What do Realtors need to perform well at to keep ahead of their colleagues/competitors? Again, a couple of telephone calls were all it took to confirm his views that the most important K2s are communication skills and selling/closing skills. Others are experience, house maintenance knowledge, and general education. With the local market crash imminent, selling/closure skills will become even more important.

How Important a K2 Is Management?

So far, we've derived two sets of K2s from the set of customer needs set out in Chapter 4: service-related K2s and cost-related K2s. There are two more sets to be considered, especially for the self-employed: management and market share.

Management-related K2s may be very important in your business. As a one-man-band, a freelancer, a self-employed individual, you have to do every job, play every role in your business. You're chairman of the board, chief executive officer, chief finance officer, chief operating officer, sales director, marketing director, IT director, even company secretary, all rolled into one. You may even have to act as HR director when you contemplate what training course you should go on and then discuss with the CEO (you again!) whether the business can afford your absence.

All of this might sound glamorous. Not so fast! You also have to do the un-glam jobs. You're the gofer. You go to the post office to mail your packages, you lug the PC to the repair shop, you answer the phone, you make the coffee. You do the bookkeeping. This requires discipline and time management, attributes that everyone struggles with and none more so than the self-employed. Trust me, I know. Especially when running your business coincides with the soccer World Cup (as I write!) or the Wimbledon tennis championships (next week!) on TV.

How important a K2 is management to your business? Scheduling customers? Bookkeeping? Cash collecting? Keeping lines of communication open through land line, cell phone, and email?

Above all, how important is sales and marketing to your business? Many self-employed or small businesses fail not because the individuals aren't competent at the service they offer. Quite the contrary. Very often they're the best and that's what gave them the confidence to break out on their own in the first place.

They fail because no one knows they're there.

Selling and marketing are the lifeblood of the self-employed person. If prospective customers don't know you're a player, or if they don't know how good you are, you have no business. And if you don't like selling and marketing, or if you're no good at it, then you'd better find a partner who can.

How important is management to your business? High, low, medium?

How Important a K2 Is Market Share?

There's one final K2—an important one—that we need to take into account that isn't directly derived from a customer need. This is the size of your presence in a particular business chunk—in other words, your share of that particular market. The larger the relative market share, the stronger should be the provider.

A high market share can manifest itself in a number of different competitive advantages. One such area is in lower unit costs, but we've already covered this under economies of scale in cost-related K2s, so we must be careful not to double count.

Market share is an indicator of the breadth and depth of your customer relationships and your business reputation. Since it is more difficult to gain a new customer than to do repeat business with an existing customer, the provider with the larger market share typically has a competitive advantage—*the power of the incumbent.*

For example, if your hair stylist fulfills all your customer needs—excellent hair styling, relaxing premises, rapport (aka gossip!), and a reasonable price, the fact that one or two of your friends are chatting about the excellent new stylist who has just set up further down the street will not necessarily tempt you away from your usual provider. Why switch? Your stylist would be most upset, especially when she has done nothing to deserve such disloyalty. This is the power of the incumbent. Customers don't like switching, unless they are sorely tempted (the pull factor) or forced to move through deficient service (the push factor). Keep the service levels high, and your customers will tend to stick with the service they know.

It can even be costly to switch, for example, if your service provider offers you loyalty discounts. Sometimes it's costly in terms of time to switch. For example, if you change Internet service providers, you face the hassle of having to notify all your contacts of your new email address. Sometimes it's costly in emotional terms to switch, as we saw with the hair stylist. The higher the switching costs, the greater the power of the incumbent.

It's similar with employees. If your boss has found someone who looks like he could do your job a helluva lot better than you can, then you might find yourself being shifted sideways or even out the door. But if your boss finds someone who could do your job better, but not that much better, than you, then she's going to think twice about taking on the hassle of dealing with your disappointment, let alone risk falling foul of employment law, by edging you out.

Incumbency tends to rise in importance as a K2 where customers rely on their service provider for historical continuity. It's less of a wrench to change your shoe repairer, even your hair stylist, than to change your psychiatrist or your accountant. The latter two have built up useful knowledge about you, whether it's your mind or your double-entry books. Switching to another provider may mean him taking a long time to build up the relevant understanding of you as an individual or business.

How great is the power of the incumbent in your job or business? How important is market share as a K2? High, low, medium?

Apply Weights to the K2s

You've now worked out which are the most important factors for success, the K2s, in your business or job. Each one has been ranked as being of high, medium, or low importance, presently and in the next few years. Now you need to weight them. This is where some readers may choose to part company. They may want to leave the ranking as it is—low, medium, high, and so forth. That's fine. Different strokes for different folks. It'll make the rating of competitive position a bit more subjective in Chapter 6, but the outcome should be the same.

Over the years, however, I've found that a reasonably quantitative approach works best. Don't worry; you won't have to work out whether a particular K2 has a weighting of, for example, 14.526 percent. That would be horribly spurious accuracy. But it's useful to derive a percentage for the weighting, whether to the nearest 5 percent or even 10 percent, so that in Chapter 6 you'll have a way of rating your *overall* competitiveness relative to your peers.

So that 14.526 percent would become simply 15 percent. No more accuracy than that is needed. How to do it? There are two ways: methodically or eyeballing.

If you want a systematic approach, take a look at the text box. If you want to eyeball it, so you can get a rough-and-ready answer, start from the ready check shown in Figure 5.3.

What level of skills is required for your job or business? Generally speaking, the higher the skill level required, the higher the weighting on relative market share and the lower the weighting for cost factors. In other words, the more skilled you are the more difficult is it typically for a competitor to dislodge you from a customer relationship. And the less likely your customer is going to desert you on grounds of price.

Figure 5.3 A Starting Grid to the Weighting of Key Kapabilities by Job Skill Level

Key Kapabilities	Unskilled	Semi-Skilled	Skilled	Professional
Relative Market Share (Incumbent Power)	10%	10%	15%	20%
Cost Factors (Overhead control, scale economies, etc.)	35%	30%	25%	20%
Management Factors (especially Marketing)	0%	5%	5%	10%
Service Factors: Effectiveness—Skill	5%	15%	15%	5%
Effectiveness—Knowledge	10%	5%	5%	10%
Effectiveness—Experience	15%	10%	10%	10%
Efficiency	10%	10%	10%	10%
Relationship—Rapport, attitude	10%	10%	10%	10%
Range	5%	5%	5%	5%
Premises (perhaps 5 to 10%, if applicable)	0%	0%	0%	0%
Total	100%	100%	100%	100%

A Systematic Approach for Deriving K2 Weightings

(WARNING! ONLY FOR THE MATHEMATICALLY INCLINED!)

Here's a step-by-step systematic approach to weighting K2s:

➤ Use the starting grid to derive a first cut weighting for *relative market share.*

➤ Use judgment on the relative power of the incumbent to amend, if appropriate, and settle on a weighting for relative market share of i percent.

➤ Revisit the importance of price to the customer. If you judged the customer need of medium importance, give *cost competitiveness* a weighting of 20 percent. If low, 10 percent. If high, 30 percent. Pro rata for in-between. Settle on c percent.

➤ Think on the importance of *management* issues to the success of your business, especially marketing. Settle on m percent, typically within a 0 to 10 percent range.

➤ You've now used up a total of (i + c + m) percent of your available weighting.

➤ Revisit the list of K2s relating to *service issues,* excluding price, which has already been covered previously. Where you've judged a factor to be of low importance, give it a K2 score of 1. Where high, 5. Rate pro rata for in between (for example, medium/high would be a 4).

➤ Add up the total score for these service-related K2s (excluding price) = S.

➤ Assign weightings to each service K2 as follows: weighting (percent) = K2 score * (1—(i + c + m))/S.

➤ Round each of them up or down to the nearest 5 percent.

➤ Adjust further, if necessary, so the sum of all K2 weights is 100 percent.

➤ Eyeball them for sense, make final adjustments.

➤ Check that the sum is still 100 percent.

There are so many exceptions to this, however, that these weightings should only be treated as a starting point. *There is no substitute for judgment.*

Having selected your weightings for relative market share and cost factors, the next step is to allocate what's left, typically around 50 to 60 percent between the various service-related and management-related K2s. Since there are usually around six or so of them, the easiest place to start is by giving each of them a weighting of 10 percent. The total probably won't add up to 100 percent, but hold that concern for the time being. Take a look at the level of importance you gave earlier to each K2 and start tweaking its weighting. One K2 with high importance gets nudged up to 15 percent, another with low importance drops to 5 percent. One on medium importance stays at 10 percent. And so on. They almost certainly still won't add up to 100 percent. Try some more tweaking. After two or three iterations, you should have a reasonable weighting system and the total will (must!) add up to 100 percent.

That's the quantitative approach to weighting. But again, if you don't like numbers, don't worry. You'll see in the next chapter that a nonquantitative approach should derive the same conclusions. Instead of percentage weightings, you can choose to weight your K2s with ticks, words (for example, high, low, medium), blobs, or whatever you choose! But you must weight them in some way because the K2s are not equal. Some K2s are more important than others.

Don't Forget the Chunks!

Once you've eyeballed the weightings in general, you need to assess to what extent these weightings differ for each of your business chunks. In particular, different customer groups can often place a different emphasis on price, so cost competitiveness may be more of an issue in some chunks than others. Other customers in other business chunks may be more concerned about the effectiveness or the efficiency of the service.

Have you now worked out some weightings for the K2s in your business or job? For further clarification, let's just take the one example. How should Leila and Chuck weight the K2s of providing massage therapy services in Notting Hill?

Just the One Example!
Leila at Healing Hands

Leila initially used a ticks method to remind herself which were the more important K2s. Then she converted them to percentages using a gut-feel, right-side-of-the-brain eyeballing approach. Chuck used his standard analytical approach.

They agreed to give a weight of 15 percent to relative market share, typical of a semi-skilled occupation. Leila had earlier wanted 20 percent, arguing that because of the more personal nature of the service, switching costs were higher than for, say, a carpenter or decorator. But later on they found it difficult to get the running total of 105 percent down to 100 percent, so they decided to lower market share to 15 percent.

They took the weighting for cost factors at 20 percent for stay-at-home moms but just 10 percent for businesspeople, who were clearly not as concerned over price. They felt that marketing was a big management issue. If Leila couldn't make her customers aware of her services, she wouldn't have many. So they gave that 10 percent.

The weighting allocated to the service-related factors came with little debate. It was just a question of allocating the 55 percent balance (for stay-at-home moms, 65 percent for businesspeople) in line with the importance levels already assessed for each K2. Chuck, of course, worked it all out systematically on his Excel spreadsheet, using the technique shown in the text box. Leila did it off the top of her head. Both approaches gave more or less the same results, which made them both feel comfortable. Their combined results are displayed in Figure 5.4.

They found that another significant difference between stay-at-home mom and business customers came in the efficiency K2. They agreed that raising its 5 percent weighting for moms to 15 percent for businesspeople seemed both reasonable and instructive.

Figure 5.4 Weighting of Key Kapabilities in Massage Therapy Services in Notting Hill, London

Key Kapabilities in Massage Therapy in Notting Hill	Weighting	
	Stay-at-Home Moms	Business-people
Relative Market Share	15%	15%
Cost Factors: Overhead control, scale economies	20%	**10%**
Management Factors: Marketing	10%	10%
Service Factors: Effectiveness—Massage technique	15%	15%
Effectiveness—Qualifications	5%	5%
Effectiveness—Experience	10%	10%
Efficiency—Work ethic, timeliness	5%	**15%**
Relationship—Communication skills, enthusiasm	10%	**5%**
Range	5%	5%
Premises—safe, secure, comfy	5%	**10%**
Total	100%	100%

Note: Where different, K2 weightings for businesspeople highlighted in bold

Attention! Any Must-Have K2s?

There is one final wrinkle. But it may be crucial.

Is any one of your K2s so important that if you don't rank highly against it, you shouldn't even be in the business or job? You simply won't begin to compete, let alone succeed? You won't win any business, or you won't be able to deliver on the business you win? In other words, it is a *must-have* K2, rather than a mere *should-have* K2.

Let's take an extreme example. Suppose Chuck Cash is thinking of backing Mr. Fayque, a locally respected psychotherapist working out of his smartly converted front room in a fashionable suburb of Tulsa, Oklahoma. Chuck has found that the most important K2s are psychotherapy techniques, communication skills, and experience. Qualifications are not regarded by most customers as important in their buying decision since "they all have the same diplomas."

Chuck finds that Mr. Fayque rates highly against all the major K2s. His customers feel comfortable in his grasp of techniques, he's immensely personable, and he has years of experience. There's just the one problem: He's not qualified. Chuck stumbled upon

> Weakness of attitude becomes weakness of character.
> —*Albert Einstein*

this entirely by chance when talking to a friend of a friend who went to the same school at roughly the same time as Mr. Fayque. She knew him all right, but she also knew that he'd dropped out of school in a haze of drug-fuelled hedonism. She wasn't aware he had ever returned. A couple more calls, and Chuck discovered that the framed certificate in pride of place in Mr. Fayque's front room was a fake. He had been practicing under false pretences.

In this case, qualification was a must-have K2. Mr. Fayque didn't have it. He shouldn't have been practicing, no matter how well he met all other K2s.

Are any of the K2s in your business or job must-haves? Keep a note of them before we assess your rating against all K2s in the next chapter.

Is Attitude a Must-Have K2?

In the Introduction to this book, the results of two surveys were shown that found half of all employees are dissatisfied with their jobs. That you are reading this book suggests you may be one of them.

In the next chapter you'll need to think about whether any dissatisfaction has affected your attitude to your work. Are you as enthusiastic as you should be to perform your work well? Do you perform it as well as your colleague who is far from dissatisfied with her work, rather she is irritatingly upbeat about it?

But before we do that, let's first assess how important attitude really is. Is it one of many should-have factors or could it be a must-have factor?

We've all seen it before: the best restaurant in town, exquisite cuisine, fine wines, conducive décor, pleasing ambience—yet surly, miserable, down-spiriting servers. Why, oh why, we wonder, does the manager put up with these guys? The answer is that he doesn't need to do anything about them. His tables are full, the cash rolls in daily. Courteous service is a customer need, and one of a number of K2s for every restaurant owner. In most restaurants, it's a must-have K2. Without it, people wouldn't come back. Regrettably it doesn't seem to regarded as a must-have K2 in some of the best restaurants.

Think of other places where you may have come across those same miserable faces, or heard those same miserable voices—insurance claims personnel, immigration officers, local government officials, medical receptionists, product return desk staff, and so on. Attitude is no must-have K2 there.

If you can't change your fate, change your attitude.
—Amy Tan

Then think of summer camp. Imagine dropping off your 12-year-old daughter at a summer camp in the Rockies and meeting a couple of camp staff wearing those same miserable faces. You'd stuff your daughter back in the car, do a u-turn, and head for home. An enthusiastic, cheerful attitude is a must-have in the summer camp business. Likewise in most leisure, travel, and entertainment businesses—think how many people would carry on watching *American Idol* on TV if Simon Cowell never cracked a toothy smile after one of his pompous but telling putdowns!

Attitude is a must-have in Leila's massage therapy business. Without a cheerful, enthusiastic, even passionate approach to her job, customers wouldn't come back. Period. It should also be a must-have for Randy's Realtor employers. Yet I suspect we've all come across the occasional Realtor with a bored, you're-wasting-my-time-cuz-I-bet-you-can't-afford-it attitude. Think how much more difficult it would be to make up your mind on buying a condominium if Randy droned, "As you can see, the condo ain't that big, it needs gutting, and it's darned noisy, so I don't know why the seller's asking so much for it."

How important is attitude in your job or business? Is attitude a must-have K2?

How Do *You* Measure Up?　6

▷ **Who Are Your Peers?**
▷ **How Do You Rate Against Each K2?**
▷ **What's Your Overall K2 Rating?**
▷ **What Does the K2 Rating Mean for the Self-Employed?**
▷ **What Does the K2 Rating Mean for Employees?**
▷ **How Can You Find Out?**
▷ **How Does Your K2 Rating Compare by Chunk?**
▷ **How May Your K2 Rating Improve Over the Next Few Fears?**
▷ **Some Examples for the Self-Employed**
▷ **Some Examples for Employees**
▷ **Any Chance You Won't Get Past First Base?**
▷ **Is It Your Attitude?**
▷ **Risks and Opportunities for Your K2 Rating**

This is the easy part. You've done the hard part in the last couple of chapters, paving the way for the show-down of this chapter.

It may also be the fun part. You may be pleasantly surprised at how well you rate against your peers.

But it may also be the shocking part. You may find that you're poorly placed to compete or even survive in the competitive arena in which you play. Your backer may back *off*, rather than back *U!*—in which case, you may need to move swiftly to Part III of this book!

In this chapter you'll assess how you perform against each of the Key Kapabilities (K2s) you identified in Chapter 5. Taking into account each K2's weighting, you'll then add up the ratings and see how your overall K2 rating, your "competitive position," compares to your competitors (or colleagues, if you're an employee).

You should do this for each of your main business chunks, since your position in one may be very different from that in another. Then you should consider how your position is likely to change over the next few years and what you can do to improve it over time.

Finally, you need to do a reality check. Do you rate poorly against one of the *must-have* K2s we highlighted in Chapter 5? If so, that may mean you don't get past first base. You shouldn't be in this job or business. Could it be your attitude?

Who Are Your Peers?

The first thing to decide is to whom you should compare yourself. Sometimes that seems a no-brainer. Often it requires a little more thought.

If you run one of three hair salons on a busy suburban street, the comparison may seem obvious: You judge yourself against the other two. But some of your potential customers may have their hair done in the city during lunch breaks. Others may have their hair done when they do their weekly grocery shopping at the out-of-town supermarket. They should be included as competitors too.

Don't be stingy. If you think another provider is serving customers who could potentially be yours, rate her too. Remember, this chapter is the easy bit. It takes just a few minutes to have a first shot at rating each competitor.

If you're an employee, you can compare yourself with those who do the same job, who serve the same "customers." Think too about those who *could* do your job by moving sideways or upwards, even downwards, in your firm.

Don't forget also to include the external supplier, which is what you could be if your job were outsourced. Consider how competitive she would be if your boss asked her to take over your job or aspects of your job while you were away on, say, maternity leave.

How Do You Rate Against Each K2?

Here you rate yourself against each of the K2s drawn up in the last chapter. But first you need to decide on a method for rating.

People have different preferences on how to rate things. Some like to do it in words, such as "strong," "not so hot," "simply the best." Then they'll run their eyes down the list of ratings, taking into account their weightings of high/medium/low, and conclude with a final K2 rating of something like "okay."

Real knowledge is to know the extent of one's ignorance. —Confucius

That's fine, if that's what you're comfortable with. The exercise remains valid. You'll have taken into account in your own way how you perform against K2s of varying levels of importance. And you'll have highlighted where you do well against your peers and where there's room for improvement.

Some like to rate with ticks. Two ticks against a K2 where they rate strongly, one tick where they do okay, a question mark where they're iffy, and a cross where they're not so good. Again that's fine, valid, and useful.

I've found over the years, however, that a numbers approach gives a more reliable and less biased result. Here's why. Suppose you rate yourself very highly on skills and experience, but know that you're not great at marketing or relationships; you may be tempted to overstate your overall K2 rating. Subconsciously, you may count your strong points more than your weak points because you yourself value them more (unlike, perhaps, your customers).

A numbers approach reduces the scope for such subjective fiddling of the result. If you're strong in one K2, fine. If you're weak in another, tough. The final K2 rating will take both your strength and your weakness into account objectively, in proportion to the numerical weighting it merits and which you've already specified.

How's it done? Simple. Rate yourself on a scale of 1 to 5. If you perform about the same as your peers against a K2, give yourself a score in the middle, a 3 (*good, favorable*). If you perform very strongly, a 5 (*very strong*). Poorly, a 1 (*weak*). If you perform not quite as well as most others, give yourself a 2 (*okay-ish*). Better than most, a 4 (*strong*). It's as easy as that.

Now do the same for each of your competitors against that K2. Who's the best performer against this K2? Does she merit a 5, or is she better but not *that* much better than everyone else, for a 4?

And so on against each K2.

What's Your Overall K2 Rating?

Your overall K2 rating is the result of taking into account both your rating *and* the weighting given to each K2. It is a measure of your competitive position.

Your competitive position will hopefully turn out to be good, preferably strong. It may even come close to very strong. Hopefully it won't come out as weak. The result should be the same whatever method you've used, whether words, ticks, or numbers.

If you've used the numbers approach, the overall K2 rating literally falls out at the bottom of the spreadsheet—if you use Excel. For the first 25 years of my career, I had to do it by hand—either by doing the math in my head or using a calculator if I was feeling lazy. For youngsters today, that must be difficult to imagine!

Excel makes things so much easier. The old manual approach is okay the first time you add things up, but the problem is that you may find yourself changing your mind again and again. And that's good. When you see your strengths and weaknesses so starkly highlighted against your peers, it's important to think, rethink, and have another think later. It just makes it a bit of hassle having to redo the calculations manually.

> Natural ability without education has more often raised a man to glory and virtue than education without natural ability.
> —*Cicero*

Here's a tip, again drawn from long experience. If you want to use the numbers approach and you're not familiar with or don't have access to Excel, just do the calculations by hand once and see what the answer comes to. Then think again. If you make any changes, don't bother to redo the calculations! Wait until the next day and think again with a fresh perspective. Have some further thoughts the following day, make any final tweaks, and *then* recalculate the overall rating!

Whether you do it by hand or use Excel, the calculation is the same. Your overall rating is the sum of each rating (r) against each K2 multiplied by the percentage weighting (w) of the K2. If there are n K2s, your overall rating will then be (r1 * w1) + (r2 * w2) + (r3 * w3) + ... + (rn + wn). As long as the percentage weightings add up to 100 percent, you should get the right answer. For those who aren't into algebra, a "cheerful" example should do the trick.

Annie is a cheerleader for her high school football team. Let's suppose there are just three K2s in the cheerleading "business": appearance, personality, and dance skills. Annie has a chat with her coach and concludes that these K2s should be weighted 25 percent for appearance, 30 percent for personality, and 45 percent for dance skills. She rates herself favorable, a 3, in appearance (no Angelina Jolie but no King Kong either), a 2.5 in personality (she's still a bit on the shy, retiring side compared to many others in the squad, one or two of whom would rival Paris Hilton in extrovertism), but boy, can she dance!—maybe not yet a Beyonce, but surely worth a 4?

Her overall K2 rating is then (3 * 25%) + (2.5 * 30%) + (4 * 45%) = 0.75 + 0.75 + 1.80 = 3.3. That's 3.3 out of a maximum 5. A pretty good rating, showing that she's in a "favorable" competitive position in the cheerleading business.

Of course, we could have come to the very same broad conclusion if we'd used alternative approaches, such as words or ticks, as demonstrated in Figure 6.1.

The main problem of the nonnumerical approaches is that assessing the final result in words or ticks becomes trickier if there are more than three K2s *and* the same number again of weightings to take into account. Try doing it for 10 K2s!

Another advantage of using numbers rather than words is being able to compare your overall position more precisely. If you use words or ticks, it can be difficult to fine tune between "good" and "a little better than good," or one tick and "one and a bit ticks." With numbers, the final K2 rating should be able to produce a clear ranking between the competitors—although you have always to be on guard for spurious accuracy!

In the cheerleading example, the words and ticks methods show that Annie, Billie, and Charlie are rated as good—or one tick—cheerleaders. Perhaps that's all you need to know. Debbie's the best, the others are all good. But suppose there are only two spaces left in the squad and you'd like to know how to rank each of the four. The words and ticks methods won't provide an immediate answer, but the numbers method shows the order quite clearly: Debbie, Annie, Charlie, then Billie.

There's even a bigger gap in K2 rating between Annie and Billie (0.6),

Figure 6.1 Annie's K2 Rating in Cheerleading

In Numbers

Key Kapabilities	*Weighting*	Annie	Billie	Charlie	Debbie
Appearance	25%	3	2.5	3	4.5
Personality	30%	2.5	4	3	5
Dance Skills	45%	4	2	3	2.5
K2 Rating	100%	3.3	2.7	3.0	3.8

Or

In Words

Key Kapabilities	*Importance*	Annie	Billie	Charlie	Debbie
Appearance	Med	Fine	Fine	Fine	Fit
Personality	Med/High	Bit shy	Outgoing	Fine	Extrovert
Dance Skills	High	Great	Iffy	Fine	Okay-ish
K2 Rating		Good	Good	Good	Very Good

Or

In Ticks

Key Kapabilities	*Importance*	Annie	Billie	Charlie	Debbie
Appearance	Med	✓	✓	✓	✓ ✓
Personality	Med/High	✓	✓ ✓	✓	✓ ✓ ✓
Dance Skills	High	✓ ✓	?	✓	✓
K2 Rating		✓	✓	✓	✓✓

who are both rated in the words method as good, than there is between Debbie, who's very good, and Annie, who's good (0.5). Extra snippets of analysis such as this, gained from the numbers method, could be useful in gaining the confidence of your backer.

What Does the K2 Rating Mean for the Self-Employed?

The main use of a K2 rating for your backer is to give him some idea of how your business is likely to fare over the next few years *in relation to the market as a whole.*

Your K2 rating is a measure of your competitive position. If it turns out to be around 3, then, other things being equal, he'll expect you to be able to grow your business in line with the market over the next few years. In other words, he'll expect you to hold market share.

If your K2 rating is around 4 or above, he'll expect you to be able to beat the market to gain market share. Suppose he's already worked out from Chapter 2 that the market is going to grow at 10 percent a year. With a K2 rating of 4, he's going to feel more comfortable if your plan is to grow business at, say, 12 percent a year.

If your K2 rating is around 2, however, your backer is going to be less confident about your business prospects. He may think that you'll underperform the market, and he'll be especially worried if your plans show you expecting to outperform the market! He's going to wonder if he's backing the right horse.

What Does the K2 Rating Mean for Employees?

The main purpose of the K2 rating for an employee is to give your backer comfort on whether you're going to be able to hold on to your job, thereby enabling you to achieve the earnings levels in your plan.

If your K2 rating is around 3, then your backer is going to think there's no reason why you should fare any worse, or better, than other employees in your firm over the next few years. If she's deduced from Chapters 2 and 3 that your firm's prospects are sound, that your firm is doing well in a growing, not-too-competitive market, then your competitive position rating of 3 may well give her sufficient comfort to back you.

If your K2 rating is around 4, or above, then even if your backer has found out from Chapters 2 and 3 that the firm may be facing some troubled times, she may still be interested in you. Other things being equal, if the firm has to cut back on staff over the next few years, they're less likely to start with you than those who are less well placed.

If your K2 rating is around 2, or below, your backer's going to be concerned. Even if she finds that the firm's prospects are promising, she's going to wonder if you're in the right job. She'll want to know what plans you have for strengthening your position. And if she's not convinced by those plans, she may recommend you to start looking elsewhere before you're forced to.

How Can You Find Out?

Finding out your K2 ratings is easy for employees. Ask your boss! Or wait until your next review comes along and ask her then. Ask her how you rate against each of the service-related K2s. You could even try asking her which of your peers she thinks rates most highly against each K2, although she might be a bit hesitant revealing this. Ask her how you should go about improving your performance against one or two of the K2s.

For the self-employed, the first step is to do it yourself. Over the years, or months if you've only just started, you'll already have had some occasional feedback from your customers: "Great piece of work" generally means you've done something right. "No way am I gonna pay you for that" suggests the opposite!

Have a go at rating yourself. Then stick a question mark against those ratings where you're a little unsure on how you perform. Investigate those ratings one or two at a time. Next time you're with a customer, throw in this line: "By the way, you know that job I did for you a couple of months ago. Were you happy with the turnaround time? Did you expect it to be quicker?" Gradually you'll be able to start removing the question marks and firm up your performance rating.

While rating your own performance, you should also be rating your competitors. All performance is relative, so if you give yourself a 3 against one K2, it will be relative to a competitor whom you rate as a 4, or another you rate as a 2. Do a first draft of rating your competitors at the same time as your own. Again stick in question marks against the numbers where you're unsure. Then start throwing in the odd question with your customers: "What about Joe? Does he turn things round as fast as I do?" Gradually the question marks on your competitors' ratings should also disappear.

The methodical way for the self-employed to find out their ratings is through *structured interviewing*. This is what business consultants do on behalf of their clients to derive their primary information when carrying out assignments on business strategy, marketing or due diligence. This is what Elizabeth, for example, does so well for ConsultCo.

A structured interviewing program differs from the more casual approach in two respects: You select a representative sample of interviewees, and you draw on a prepared questionnaire.

The advantage of a structured interviewing process is that it will in time give you all you need to know. There are two disadvantages: First, it takes up the time of your customers. There's a risk that you'll leave your customer thinking you've just wasted a quarter or half hour of her precious time. Second, you may be a bit sensitive about your customers knowing that you're doing a strategy review. You don't want them to think you may be moving on to bigger and better things, leaving them behind in your wake. You also may not want your customer to think too hard about your service compared to others, in case she suddenly realizes she'd be better off with a competitor!

These risks should, however, be containable as long as you prepare your story well in advance and try to make the experience beneficial for the customer, as well as for you.

For a more detailed description on how to conduct a structured interview program with your customers, please turn to Appendix B.

How Does Your K2 Rating Compare by Chunk?

We've talked this far as if there were only one business chunk. But most people work in quite a few business chunks. How do your ratings compare in each chunk?

You'll find that some ratings are the same, some are different. Take skills, for example. If the skills required for each chunk are the same, then your performance against that K2 is likely to be the same in each chunk. The weighting of that K2 may well differ by chunk but not necessarily your rating.

Other ratings may well be different. For instance, you may have years of experience in one chunk, but you've only just started in another. You may rate a 5 in the first, but only a 1 or 2 in the other. Or awareness. You may have loads of contacts developed over many years in one chunk, but you're finding it hard to get your name known in another.

Just as you've assessed market demand prospects and competitive intensity for each of your main business chunks in earlier chapters, so too you need to evaluate your K2 rating in each chunk. Then in Chapter 7 you'll be able to assess your business prospects in each chunk.

How May Your K2 Rating Improve Over the Next Few Fears?

So far the K2 rating analysis has been static. You've rated your current competitiveness. But that's only the first part of the story. What your backer is also going to need to know is how your K2 rating is likely to change over the next few years. He'll want to understand the dynamics. Is it set to improve or worsen?

The simplest way to do this is to add an extra column to your chart, representing you in, say, three years' time. Then you can build in any improvements in your ratings against each K2. These prospective improvements need, for the time being, to be both in the pipeline *and* likely to happen for your backer to be convinced. We're going to look in more detail in Part II of this book at how the analysis of these last three chapters can be a stimulus for you to *proactively and systematically* improve your K2 rating. How you can stretch your sights, identify the capability gap, and select a strategy to bridge the gap. But for now we'll just look at how your K2 rating seems set to change naturally over the next few years.

Whatever talents I possess may suddenly diminish or suddenly increase. I can with ease become an ordinary fool. I may be one now. But it doesn't do to upset one's own vanity.—Dylan Thomas

One obvious area where you may well improve your rating is in experience, since you will by then be three years' more experienced. If you already have 20 years' experience in a particular business chunk, then an extra three years won't make a difference. But if you've only had 20 months' experience to date, an extra 36 will make a big difference.

You've got to be before you can do, and do before you can have.—Zig Ziglar

Remember, though, that the experience K2 can work the other way. If you've been in the game for 20 years and your main challenger just three years, you may have an edge—maybe a rating of 5 to his 2.5. Three years' hence, however, you've been there 23 years and he six years. You're still a 5, but he's become a 3, possibly a 3.5. The gap has narrowed. Much may depend on the extent to which experience is judged by customers to be relevant to their buying decision.

Other areas where you may be able to improve your rating over time may be in skills or qualifications. If you're set to undergo any further training, that should be factored in. Your training may well be in an aspect of your job that will directly meet customer needs, such as in further skills or knowledge development. Or it may be in an area that improves your management-related K2s, such as a course in selling skills or public speaking.

Remember again, however, that improvement of K2 ratings is a double-edged sword. Your competitors too will have plans. This is where analysis of K2 dynamics gets challenging. It's easy enough to know what you're planning—but what about the competition?

Try adding a couple of further columns representing your two most fearsome competitors as they may be in three years' time. Do you have any idea what they're planning to do to improve their competitiveness in the near future? What are they likely to do? What could they do? *What are you afraid they'll do?*

By now you've added three columns, and the table may start looking a bit unwieldy. Perhaps you should draw up a new table altogether, representing the competitive situation in three years' time? You'll need to do this anyway if there are any significant changes likely in the K2s, or in their weightings. In that case, you can't use the current weightings to apply to future competitive position, so you'll need a new table.

Let's return to our cheerleader, Annie. There's not a huge amount she can or needs to do about her appearance, but she believes she's getting less shy by the month. In three years' time she figures she'll rate at least a 3 in personality. Meanwhile she's sharpening up her dancing skills all the time. She's been taking extra dance classes in streetdance, tap, and Ceroc, and she believes they're all contributing toward making her a better dancer all round, including for cheerleading. She thinks she could soon rate a 4.5 relative to the other cheerleaders.

Meanwhile there's going to be a change in manager, and the new manager has hinted that she's not interested in what her girls look like, as long as they can dance. The weighting for dance skills should increase, at the expense of that for appearance. In three years' time, Annie's K2 rating could have risen from its present 3.3 to 3.8 [= Appearance (3 * 20%) + Personality (3 * 30%) + Dance Skills (4.5 * 50%)], a huge jump—and perhaps even challenging Debbie for the number one slot!

But this assumes that the other girls stand still and make no attempt to improve their own rating, which is unlikely. Annie knows that Debbie and Charlie are also taking dance classes, so their competitive ranking should improve over time too. Annie does the calculations, and finds that she'll probably stay in second place, but only a shade behind Debbie's likely rating of 3.9.

How is your K2 rating likely to change over time? And what about your competitors?

Let's see how our main cast of characters measures up relative to their competitors.

Some Examples for the Self-Employed
Leila at Healing Hands

In Chapter 1 we looked at Leila's business and worked out which chunks really counted. In Chapters 2 and 3, we looked at market demand and competition in her main chunks. Then we paved the way for looking at Leila's competitive position by assessing customer needs in Chapter 4 and K2s and their weighting in Chapter 5. Now we're ready. How well placed is Leila in each of her main business chunks now and over the next few years?

It was easy for Leila to find out the ratings she was after. She didn't have to call any customers, they come to her. With her customers lying flat out on the couch, she can steer the conversation any which way. It didn't take her long to find out how she was rated, and more interestingly, how her competitors were rated.

She chose as her peers the two competitors she was most concerned about. At one extreme, the Kensington Wellness Centre (KWC) was a serious threat. Opened recently on the main drag, Notting Hill Gate Road, it offers the full range of holistic therapies, including aromatherapy and other services offered by Leila. Its minimalist entrance hall, hygienic clinics, and uniformed therapists offer a contrast to Leila's homely but rather bohemian and chaotic front room. Leila is concerned that her business customers may be undeterred by the higher prices charged by KWC.

At the other extreme, there's Suzi, who seems to be taking on Leila head-

Figure 6.2 Leila's K2 Rating in Massage Therapy Services for Stay-at-Home Moms in Notting Hill, London

Key Kapabilities in Massage Therapy for Stay-at-Home Moms in Notting Hill	Weighting	Healing Hands	Suzi	Kensington Wellness Centre
Relative Market Share	15%	3	1	3
Cost Factors: Overhead control, scale economies	20%	4	5	2
Management Factors: Marketing	10%	4	2	4
Service Factors: Effectiveness—Massage technique	15%	4	3	3.5
Effectiveness—Qualifications	5%	5	2	5
Effectiveness—Experience	10%	5	2	4
Efficiency—Effort, timeliness	5%	2	4	5
Relationship—Communications, enthusiasm	10%	5	5	3
Range	5%	3	1	5
Premises—safe, secure, comfy	5%	3	1.5	5
K2 Rating	100%	3.9	2.9	3.5

Key to Rating: 1 = Weak, 2 = Okay-ish, not too bad 3 = Good, favorable, 4 = Strong, 5 = Very strong

on. She's younger (late twenties), much less experienced (so far), not yet qualified (taking a long time), works out of the front room of her small home (shabby, one hears) in the relatively down-market area near the highway flyover. She deliberately offers a discount on Leila's prices of 10 to 15 percent. Leila's worried that some of her stay-at-home moms may be tempted to switch, especially as Suzi has a most jovial, entertaining (if crude, some say) personality. Leila has met her a couple of times and rather likes her.

After her unobtrusive interviewing of horizontally inclined customers and having filled in the K2 ratings, Leila reports to Chuck that she believes she is still the most competitive massage therapist to moms in the area. But she recognizes that she falls behind KWC in business customers. Her results,

with separate tables for the two main addressed customer groups of moms and businesspeople, are in Figures 6.2 and 6.3.

For all customers, Leila believes she rates highly in massage technique, better than Suzi, her customers say. KWC is variable—some of their therapists are good, others just okay. Just like their attitude—some are enthusiastic, like Leila and Suzi, some seem to be there just to do a job. Leila loses to KWC on range of services offered and standard of premises, but gains on cost competitiveness and hence price. She also scores poorly on timeliness, a weakness of which Leila has always been aware. Suzi has even lower costs and she oozes enthusiasm—but falls short on technique, qualifications, experience, range, and standard of premises.

Figure 6.3 Leila's K2 Rating in Massage Therapy Services for Businesspeople in Notting Hill, London

Key Kapabilities in Massage Therapy for Businesspeople in Notting Hill	Weighting	Healing Hands	Suzi	Kensington Wellness Centre
Relative Market Share	15%	2	0	5
Cost Factors: Overhead control, scale economies	10%	4	5	2
Management Factors: Marketing	10%	2	0	4
Service Factors: Effectiveness—Massage technique	15%	4	3	3.5
Effectiveness—Qualifications	5%	5	2	5
Effectiveness—Experience	10%	3	0	5
Efficiency—Effort, timeliness	15%	2	4	5
Relationship—Communication, enthusiasm	5%	5	5	3
Range	5%	3	1	5
Premises—safe, secure, comfy	10%	3	1.5	5
K2 Rating	100%	3.1	2.1	4.3

Key to Rating: 1 = Weak, 2 = Okay-ish, not too bad 3 = Good, favorable, 4 = Strong, 5 = Very strong

**Figure 6.4 Leila's Future K2 Rating in Massage Therapy Services
for Stay-at-Home Moms in Notting Hill, London
(With a More Experienced Suzi and an Experienced New Entrant)**

Key Kapabilities in Massage Therapy for Stay-at-Home Moms in Notting Hill	Weighting	Healing Hands	Suzi	Kensington Wellness Centre	Suzi in Three Years?	An Experienced New Entrant?
Relative Market Share	15%	3	1	3	2	1
Cost Factors: Overhead control, scale economies	20%	4	5	2	5	4
Management Factors: Marketing	10%	4	2	4	3	1
Service Factors: Effectiveness—Massage technique	15%	4	3	3.5	3.5	4
Effectiveness—Qualifications	5%	5	2	5	4	5
Effectiveness—Experience	10%	5	2	4	3	5
Efficiency—Effort, Timeliness	5%	2	4	5	5	5
Relationship—Comms, Enthusiasm	10%	5	5	3	5	5
Range	5%	3	1	5	2	4
Premises—safe, secure, comfy	5%	3	1.5	5	2	4
K2 Rating	100%	3.9	2.9	3.5	3.6	3.6

Key to Rating: 1 = Weak, 2 = Okay-ish, not too bad 3 = Good, favorable, 4 = Strong, 5 = Very strong

Leila is overshadowed by KWC for business customers because of lower market share, less effective marketing, and a larger gap in experience. The greater emphasis by business customers on timekeeping and the lower emphasis on price both count against Leila and in KWC's favor. Suzi isn't really in this market, although she'd like to be.

Chuck was encouraged by Leila's findings; however, he was mindful of his findings concerning the likely intensification of competition in massage therapy services in Notting Hill over the next few years (Chapter 3). He and Leila put their heads together to imagine what her competitive position might look like in three years' time—see Figure 6.4.

They weren't sure if Suzi would still be around. It wasn't clear that she was making sufficient earnings to remain in the business, and she may be tempted to return to nursing. But

Chuck insisted on assuming that she would still be there, and if so, what her position would then be like. They found that she could well have improved her position from a tenable 2.9 to a pretty strong 3.6, making her a more serious competitor to Leila—assuming Leila didn't manage to improve her timekeeping and remained on 3.9.

Chuck also wanted Leila to look at the possibility of an experienced therapist moving into the area, possibly because competition had become too tough in her own area. How effective a competitor would such a new entrant be to Leila? Assuming she was as technically proficient, qualified, experienced, and enthusiastic as Leila, but possibly with an even broader range and snazzier premises than Leila, let alone being as time efficient as Suzi, this new entrant could have a K2 rating of 3.6. Even though she would be a virtual unknown in the area, she could still be a serious competitor and over time possibly a formidable one. This is a concern to Chuck and an undoubted risk to Leila's business prospects.

Before we leave Leila, let's just take a quick look at how she could have derived her K2 rating if she and Chuck had used a nonquantitative approach—see Figure 6.5. Would Chuck's conclusions have been any different?

The difficulty of the nonnumerical approach is in judging the overall K2 rating, the bottom line. It's not easy looking at the chart to judge, for example, whether Suzi's overall K2 rating should be a good, an okay-ish/

good or even a good/strong. But if you worked out (correctly) that it should be good, then it's easy enough to deduce that in three years' time her position would have improved to a good/strong, and likewise, that an experienced new entrant would also come in at a good/strong.

The nonnumerical approach should give Chuck the same conclusions as his numbers approach: Leila is strongly placed in her stay-at-home mom chunk, but her position is somewhat vulnerable both to Suzi hanging on in there and to an experienced new entrant.

Either approach should work.

Figure 6.5 Leila's Future K2 Rating (in Words!) in Massage Therapy Services for Stay-at-Home Moms in Notting Hill, London (with a More Experienced Suzi and an Experienced New Entrant)

Key Kapabilities in Massage Therapy for Stay-at-Home Moms in Notting Hill	Import- ance	Healing Hands	Suzi	Kensington Wellness Centre	Suzi in Three Years?	An Exper- ienced New Entrant?
Relative Market Share	High	Good	Weak	Good	Okay-ish	Weak
Cost Factors: Overhead control, scale economies	Very High	Strong	Very strong	Okay-ish	Very strong	Strong
Management Factors: Marketing	Med	Strong	Okay-ish	Strong	Good	Weak
Service Factors: Effectiveness—Massage technique	High	Strong	Good	Good +	Good +	Strong
Effectiveness—Qualifications	Low	Very strong	Okay-ish	Very strong	Strong	Very strong
Effectiveness—Experience	Med	Very strong	Okay-ish	Strong	Good	Very strong
Efficiency—Effort, timeliness	Low	Okay-ish	Strong	Very strong	Very strong	Very strong
Relationship—Communication, enthusiasm	Med	Very strong	Very strong	Good	Very strong	Very strong
Range	Low	Good	Weak	Very strong	Okay-ish	Strong
Premises—safe, secure, comfy	Low	Good	Weak +	Very strong	Okay-ish	Strong
K2 Rating		Strong	Good	Good/ Strong	Good/ Strong	Good/ Strong

Carwyn the Carpenter

When it came to Carwyn's competitive position as a subcontracting carpenter in Boston, Chuck got much of the information he needed over a beer and a sandwich with Carwyn's contractor,

the proprietor of loft specialists, Boston Heights. Carwyn was admired for his dextrous carpentry skills, and his reliability and motivation were beyond compare. His efficiency was not, however, what it used to be. It took him longer to get things done compared with his sprightlier self of just a few years ago and with most of his fellow carpenters. Nevertheless his overall K2 rating came out at a healthy 3.4.

The difficulty for Chuck was that time didn't seem to be on Carwyn's side. Over the next few years, there was no way that Carwyn's 3.4 rating was going to rise. Given the high weighting

of 15 percent against the efficiency K2 and Carwyn's knees likely to continue to decline, Chuck could see Carwyn's position sliding to 3.1 in three years' time. That might be okay if the market stayed buoyant but not so if the market took a dip—as indeed it was forecast to do.

Chuck considers this to be a serious risk for Carwyn's business prospects.

Some Examples for Employees

Elizabeth at ConsultCo

It was easy enough for Elizabeth to do a first draft of her K2 ratings. She'd been with the company for more than 10 years, she'd had countless reviews from a succession of managers over the years, and if she didn't know her strengths and weaknesses by now she never would. Chuck followed up with a brief meeting with one of her managers and found it matched Elizabeth's own assessment almost perfectly.

What intrigued Elizabeth was to see the methodology she used for advising her corporate clients being used on herself—see Figure 6.6. She was quite pleased with the result. She emerged as a favorable to strong provider of market research services to ConsultCo and in Chicago. What's more, she came out as no less strong a competitor as her extremely bright young colleagues, fresh out of the best schools and up against whom she sometimes felt the twinges of an inferiority complex. She found that her young consulting colleagues had far more impressive degrees than she, wrote up and presented their findings much better than she, and were capable of working 18-hour days if called upon. But some of her own strengths seemed to make up for these relative weaknesses. She had more experience

and was more business savvy than they, and crucially, she was a master of the telephone interview.

Chuck also asked Elizabeth to consider the relative position of an external consultant being called in on a specific assignment. A tad worrying, Chuck found that a good, qualified, experienced, hard-working, efficient, and enthusiastic external market researcher could be almost as competitive overall as Elizabeth—despite the extra cost and lack of "market share" within ConsultCo.

It was when Chuck and Elizabeth looked at prospective K2 ratings in a few years' time, however, that alarm bells began to ring. One definite trend that emerged in their interviews is that ConsultCo staff will need to do more presenting on their feet in years to come. This will not help Elizabeth's K2 rating. Presentation is the weakest of her skills. Public speaking makes her want to crawl up into a ball and roll out of the door.

When looked at in the round, however, this trend may not be too disastrous for Elizabeth. Even if the weighting on presenting and other skills were to go up from 15 percent to, say, 20 percent, Elizabeth's K2 rating would

Figure 6.6 Elizabeth's K2 Rating in Market Research Services to ConsultCo, Inc., and in Chicago

Key Kapabilities in Market Research Services to ConsultCo and in Chicago	Weighting	Elizabeth	Young Consultant	Externals
Relative Market Share	20%	3	2	0
Cost Factors: Pay package	20%	4	4	2
Management Factors: Internal marketing, self-promotion	0%	2	5	0
Service Factors: Effectiveness—Interviewing skills	10%	5	3	5
Effectiveness—Analytical/structured writing, presenting skills	15%	2	4	4
Effectiveness—Qualifications	5%	2	5	4
Effectiveness—Experience	10%	4	2	5
Efficiency—Effort, timeliness	5%	2	5	5
Relationship—Communication, enthusiasm	15%	4	5	5
Range	0%	3	4	2
Premises (not applicable)	0%	x	x	x
K2 Rating	**100%**	**3.4**	**3.6**	**3.2**

Key to Rating: 1 = Weak, 2 = Okay-ish, not too bad 3 = Good, favorable, 4 = Strong, 5 = Very strong

only drop from 3.4 to 3.3. She'd still be in a favorable position.

Another trend of some concern is the thinking going on at ConsultCo concerning outsourcing. Chuck is aware that the current cost disadvantage of using external suppliers on an ad hoc basis could be transformed into a cost advantage if a long-term outsourcing contract were drawn up. This could raise the K2 rating of external market researchers from 3.2 to 3.8. There are still the outsourcing disincentives to ConsultCo of availability and confidentiality to be taken into account, however, so Chuck isn't too worried.

Randy at Homes4U

Randy's first shot at drawing up his K2 rating proved overly modest. By the time Chuck had finished talking to his boss—this time over a breakfast cappuccino and almond croissant—Chuck was left with no doubt that he was looking at a star. Randy was the best salesman, the best negotiator, and the best closer at Homes4U. In time, he could well become the best business developer, but the winning of new sale mandates was usually done by more senior staff.

The only wrinkle in Randy's stellar performance was his writing ability. He struggled long and hard over drawing up the sales particulars on houses for sale, and his final draft usually needed heavy editing by colleagues. This K2 only had a minor weighting of 5 percent, however, and so his overall K2 rating emerged at a strong 4.2.

As the real estate downturn loomed, deal closure skills were going to become more important and that could only further strengthen Randy's competitive position.

There was one thing, however, that came up over breakfast that roused Chuck's curiosity. Randy's boss wasn't entirely convinced of Randy's commitment to remain in the business. This came as news to Chuck. How could a star at his job think about switching career? (And to plumbing, his boss had heard rumored!) Chuck resolved to have a quiet word with Randy about this.

Any Chance You Won't Get Past First Base?

In the last chapter, we introduced the concept of the *must-have* K2—without a good rating in which you cannot even begin to compete.

Did you find a must-have Key Kapability in any of your business chunks? If so, how do you rate against it? Favorable, strong? Fine. Okay-ish? Questionable. Weak? Troublesome? A straight zero, not even a 1? You're out. You don't get past first base.

And what about in a few years' time? Could any of the K2s develop into a must-have? How will you rate then? Will you get past first base?

And even though you rate okay-ish against a must-have K2 today, might it slip over time? Could it slide below 2, into tricky territory?

This may be a case of being cruel to be kind. It's better to know. The sooner you realize that you're in the wrong business or job, the sooner you can move on. Part III can help you with that.

The ironic thing about must-have K2s is that you can rate superbly against all the other K2s, but if you don't rate at least a 2 (okay-ish) against a must-have, you may be nowhere. You're in the wrong business or job.

We saw the example of Mr. Fayque in the last chapter. He was accomplished in each of the K2s, bar the one must-have: He wasn't qualified.

There is one issue that is nagging Chuck in Elizabeth's case. He has learned from her boss that staff preparing market research reports in the future may be expected to present them too, sometimes directly to ConsultCo's clients. Does this mean, Chuck worries, that presenting skills may need to be upgraded from a should-have K2 to a must-have?

If so, this would be bad news for Elizabeth. She is naturally shy and doesn't like talking at meetings, let alone having to stand up and present on her feet. And to a client?! Chuck has rated her as weak (a score of just 1) against this K2, but this didn't impact much on her overall competitive standing. If, however, presenting skills were to become a must-have factor, Chuck would have to conclude that Elizabeth is in the wrong job.

Chuck will need to take this major risk into account when he finally assembles the risk jigsaw in Chapter 8.

Is It Your Attitude?

Is attitude a must-have Key Kapability in your business? If so, do you have the right attitude?

If your job demands a positive, sunny, helpful attitude, without which you shouldn't be doing it, what's yours like? How does it compare with others?

Are there any signs that your attitude about your job is on the wane? Is there any chance your attitude will slip so far that your rating against this must-have K2 will fall below favorable?

As discussed in Chapter 5, there's a pretty good chance that you, the reader of a book such as this, may be among the 50 percent of employees who are dissatisfied with their jobs. The good news is that you are one of many. The bad news is that it may be affecting your performance. Worse, your attitude may make

> The greatest discovery of my generation is that a human being can alter his life by altering his attitude of mind.
> —*William James*

you less well equipped to do the job as time goes on. And if your attitude falls below threshold level for a must-have K2, you may even become incapable of doing the job satisfactorily. You may be among the first to go during the next shakeout.

Better to realize it now and take some affirmative action—see Part III of this book—than plod on until you're shaken out.

This is the concern Chuck now has about backing Randy. After hearing from his boss that Randy was unsure he wanted to remain in the real estate business, Chuck had a long chat with him. It turns out that Randy has been helping out his uncle on the weekends now and again for a couple of years, picking up aspects of the plumbing trade. He loves the job. He loves getting his hands dirty and relishes the challenge of physically fixing things.

Randy knows that a market downturn is on the way in the real estate business. He knows he's one of the best and he'd probably be one of the few to survive at Homes4U. It's just that he's not sure he wants to spend the rest of his life selling houses. He thinks he'd

> For the first year of marriage I had basically a bad attitude. I tended to place my wife underneath a pedestal.
> —*Woody Allen*

prefer to do what he enjoys doing, that's plumbing, and at the same time give his work mates a better chance at staying in their jobs at Homes4U.

Enthusiasm for selling is a major K2 in the real estate business. It borders on being a must-have K2. If Randy's enthusiasm is going to diminish over time, that's a worry for Chuck.

Risks and Opportunities for Your K2 Rating

In Chapters 2 and 3, you pulled out the main market demand and competition risks and opportunities facing all providers of your type of service. Now you can add those risks and opportunities that relate to you and your K2 rating over the next few years. Again it might be helpful to draw up a small table, using the example shown in Appendix A, Figure A.2.

You've now completed the third component of the Risk Jigsaw, the risks and opportunities concerning U! There's just one more to go, in the next chapter on meeting your plan. Then all the main risks and opportunities will be pieced together in Chapter 8.

Will You Make Your Plan?   7

We're approaching the end-game of Part I, where we find out if you're backable in your current job or business. Your backer now has plenty of information on you and your job or business. He knows where market demand is headed, whether competition is going to heat up, and how you measure up to your competitors today and over the next few years. What's more, he has this information for each of your main business chunks.

He's ready to pull it all together and assess if you're likely to achieve your plans. That's what we'll look at in this chapter. In the next, we'll look at how your backer assesses the risks of you not making your plans, as well as the opportunities of you beating them.

A Reminder of Your Plans in Each Chunk

In Chapter 1 you were asked to think about your plans over the next few years. For many readers, plans will be nonexistent. If pressed you'll say that you expect to be doing more or less what you're doing now—but hopefully with a pay raise or two.

That's fine. We'll assume that your "plan" is a steady improvement on what it is today. You can review that "plan" in just the same way as you can a rigorously prepared plan.

Many readers will have general plans, such as switching the balance of their work from one chunk into another. Like Elizabeth, who wants to move away from typing and admin and more into market research.

Other readers will have more specific plans, for example to venture into a new area—a new service, or a new customer group. Like Leila, who has plans to take on a partner and develop a new service offering, reflexology.

If your only goal is to become rich, you will never achieve it.—John D. Rockefeller

Some readers will have only one plan. They can hear the 1960s anthem of the Animals in the back of their minds: "We gotta get outta this place." This chapter may help explain why that is so. On the other hand, it may challenge whether you should get out. The grass may not be greener on the other side of the fence. You may be better off staying where you are.

Lay Out Your Plans in a Market Context

The secret to assessing whether you're likely to make your plans is to lay them out in a market context. This will give you a market-derived perspective on the achievability of your plan. It's a "top-down," market-driven approach. The "bottom-up" approach, where you look at all the specific initiatives and schemes you have for developing business in each of your business chunks, we'll look at in a later section.

Once you have mastered time, you will understand how true it is that most people overestimate what they can accomplish in a year and underestimate what they can achieve in a decade. —Anthony Robbins

The process for a top-down assessment of your business plan is straightforward, as long as you take one step at a time. You've already done virtually all the work, especially in Chapters 1, 2, and 6. All you have to do now is bring the strands together and review them from the perspective of your backer.

The flow set out below is a process of eight steps, each following logically from the previous step:

1. *Business chunks*—You look at one chunk at a time.
2. *Your revenues or pay*—What revenues (for the self-employed) or pay (share of total pay for employees) are you expecting to achieve in each chunk this year? If this year is untypical in some way, it would be sounder to put here your "normal" revenues or pay for the year. You already worked this out in Chapter 1.
3. *Market demand prospects*—How do you expect the market to grow each year over the next few years in each chunk? You can put here your forecasts in either numbers or in words, as you researched in Chapter 2.
4. *Your K2 rating*—How do you measure up relative to the competition in each chunk and how may this change over the next few years? Again, in either words or numerical rating, as you researched in Chapter 6.

5. *Planned revenues or pay*—What revenues (for the self-employed) or pay (share of total pay for employees) are you expecting to achieve in each chunk in three years' time? Again, from Chapter 1.
6. *Planned revenue or pay growth*—What growth in revenues or pay each year does that represent over the next three years?
7. *How achievable?*—This is where you look at your plans from the perspective of your backer. Would your backer think you are likely to achieve your planned revenues or pay in this chunk? His assessment will be based largely on how reasonable your revenue or pay forecasts seem in relation to market demand prospects and your K2 rating—see later.
8. *More likely revenues or pay*—What your backer thinks is a *more* likely forecast of your revenues or pay in each chunk in three years' time.

In this process, your backer puts your plans in a market context. He looks at how the market is likely to develop and whether you are likely to fare better, worse, or the same as your competitors. And *against that market background,* he judges whether your plans and forecast revenues or pay seem achievable.

> I am a slow walker, but I never walk backwards.
> —Abraham Lincoln

How Achievable Is Your Plan?

As is often the case, I find that this assessment process works best in a chart. Eight entries in the process flow—so, for me, eight columns! Not everyone likes charts, however, so please feel free to work through the process flow shown above without using a chart if you wish—but remembering to repeat the flow for *each of your main business chunks.*

For those who like to see the whole landscape set out in a chart, however, take a look at the eight columns of Figure 8.1.

The first six columns are easy to fill in—you've already done the work! Columns 1, 2, and 5 are taken from the work you did in the very first chapter of this book. There you allocated your current revenues (if self-employed) or pay (if an employee) into your most important business chunks, both now and in three years' time. All you need to add here in column 6 are the average annual growth calculations—see the text box in Chapter 2 if you need help on how to do it. Or if you don't like numbers, you can slot in some descriptive words, such as "flat," "steady," "fast," and so forth.

Column 3 summarizes the conclusions of Chapter 2 on market demand prospects for each business chunk. Likewise, column 4 summarizes all that hard work on customer needs, Key Kapabilities, and your K2 rating in Chapters 4 through 6.

Figure 7.1 Assessing How Achievable Are Your Planned Revenues or Pay

Your Business Chunks	Your Revenues or Pay ($000)	Market Demand Growth (% per year)	Your K2 Rating (0-5)	Your Planned Revenues or Pay ($000)	Your Planned Revenue Growth (% per year)	How Achievable?	More Likely Revenues or Pay ($000)
	This Year	Next Few Years	Next Few Years	In Three Years	Next Three Years		In Three Years
1	2	3	4	5	6	7	8
	Source: Chapter 1	Source: Chapter 2	Source: Chapter 6	Source: Chapter 1	Source: Chapter 1	Source: Here in Chapter 7	
A							
B							
C							
Others							
Total							

Note that you needn't bother filling in the totals for columns 3 and 4 in the chart. Can you think why? It's because the market and competitive analysis in Chapters 2 through 6 has been at the level of *each of your main business chunks*. Each chunk is represented in one row of the chart, and we work on one row at a time until we get right to the end of the row in column 8. Once we've worked on all the chunks/rows, we'll then add up column 8 to get a total of likely revenues (or pay) and compare that with the total for planned revenues in column 6. Finally, we'll be able to assess how achievable your overall plan is in the bottom row of column 7—as highlighted with the explosion box!

Only columns 7 and 8 are new to this chapter, on how achievable your plan is and what outcome is more likely. These two columns will form the backbone of your backer's decision, along with the risk assessment in the next chapter.

Arriving at a conclusion on the achievability of your planned revenues (or pay, if you're an employee) in a business chunk can sometimes be obvious. But often it can require a dose of sound judgment. Judgment comes with experience. I've made scores of such conclusions over the years—from businesses worth tens of millions of dollars to individuals worth a few tens of thousands. I can't expect you to share my experience, but I can give you a few tips. My limited aim is not to help you get it absolutely right but to help ensure *you don't get it absolutely wrong!*

The key to the assessment is *consistency*—whether your plans for the future are consistent with these two main areas of evidence:

➤ Column 3: Market demand prospects (as in Chapter 2)
➤ Column 4: Your K2 rating, now and over the next few years (as in Chapter 6)

There are other areas of evidence you should also bear in mind. These can be important and should arguably be included in the chart as extra columns. But a chart of a dozen or so columns becomes a tad unwieldy. They are:

> ➢ Competitive intensity in the marketplace over the next few years (as in Chapter 3), although this can sometimes be just the inverse of column 3's market demand prospects—in other words, the faster the market growth, often the less competitive the workplace, and conversely, the slower the market growth, often the more competitive the workplace.
> ➢ Your recent track record—your revenue or pay growth over the last couple of years in relation to growth in market demand over the same period (if you're self-employed) or in relation to fellow employees (if you're an employee).

Here's an example of consistency: If you find that the market in a business chunk is set to grow steadily, and you assess yourself as having a favorable K2 rating in that chunk, then all else being equal, you should be able to grow your business at the same pace as the market in that chunk. "All else being equal" may well include (a) your finding that the market isn't likely to become more competitive, and (b) the fact that you have a track record in recent years of being able to grow your business along with the market. If your plan over the next few years is merely to grow your business at the same pace as the market, then your backer should find it achievable. If, however, your plan is to grow way beyond that, he'll need to have convincing reasons on how you plan to beat the market.

Your backer won't necessarily be fazed by a high growth plan, as long as it's consistent. Suppose your K2 rating in a business chunk has been and should remain strong (around 4 on the 0 to 5 scale), and is demonstrated by your having outperformed the market in the past. If you're planning to continue to beat the market in the future, then your backer should find the assumptions consistent.

But suppose your K2 rating in a chunk is just okay-ish (around 2) and you've underperformed against the market in the past. Suppose too that your K2 rating isn't expected to show any significant improvement in the future. If your plans for this chunk show you *beating* the market in the future, your backer's eyebrows will be raised. Your plans are *inconsistent* with both your future K2 rating and your previous performance.

Suppose, however, you've underperformed against the market in the past, but you've recently taken steps to improve your K2 rating to favorable (around 3). If you're planning to grow with the market in the future, then your story will at least be consistent. All your backer will need to do is confirm that you have indeed sharpened up your act.

Let's take a simplified example to illustrate this last point. Ajit, a self-employed IT Mr. Fixit consultant working from home in a suburb of Seattle, has been struggling to make a decent living over the last couple of years. He knows he's a whiz at computers, but he just can't seem to get enough billable business. Many jobs take just a couple of hours to fix, then he may not have anything else for the rest of the day, and sometimes nothing at all the next day.

He's tried some advertising in the local newspapers and Yellow Pages, but he doesn't really know if any of them work. Then his wife, Hamida, has an idea. She has always been good at drawing and loves doodling and sketching cartoons. She comes up with an amusing sketch of a crazed man banging his head against his desktop monitor, with the caption: "PC Headaches? Call the PC doctor down the road!" They make this into a small, black-and-white leaflet, and with the help of his two young sons, he leaves one at each home in the 100 nearest streets.

The leaflet tangibly improves Ajit's business. Many neighbors become regular customers. His utilization jumps and his business concept as a self-employed IT consultant becomes viable. Before his discovery of a winning marketing technique, his K2 rating was 2.8. Afterwards, it rises to 3.1. More critically, he has improved his rating against a must-have K2—market awareness—to favorable.

An assessment, therefore, of Ajit's prospects based on his prior revenue performance and his prior competitive position may have been misleading. He's now better placed to grow with the market than before.

A Test on Achieving Plan

Let's take a set of examples where you can test yourself on assessing whether plans seem achievable, from a market-driven, top-down perspective. But remember that this will be a first cut only, subject to consideration of any *specific, bottom-up initiatives* in the next section.

You're thinking of backing Ms. Random, who runs a business with six main chunks. She seems to be a sound manager, but her forecasting skills seem somewhat erratic. You take it one chunk at a time, working your way across each row in Figure 7.2. You need to take a view on the likelihood of Ms. Random achieving her plans in each chunk. Which of the possible boxed answers should be slotted into the six cells of column 7?

The answers are shown under the table, upside down. How well did you do? The reasoning behind the answers is as follows:

> ➤ Taking chunk B to start with, Ms. Random plans to grow revenues at the same pace as the market, and she's favorably positioned. Her plan seems *likely*.
> ➤ Tracking back to chunk A, her K2 rating is the same, yet she plans to grow much faster than the market, which seems *unlikely*.
> ➤ In chunk C, her K2 rating is again favorable, but she plans to grow slower than the market. Her forecast seems conservative and *most likely* to be achieved.
> ➤ In chunk D, her positioning is only okay-ish, and yet she plans to outgrow the market, which seems *unlikely*.
> ➤ In chunk E, her K2 rating is set to improve to strong and she plans

Figure 7.2 **A Test: How Achievable Are Ms Random's Plans?**

Her Business Chunks	Her Revenues or Pay ($000) This Year	Market Demand Growth (% per year) Next Few Years	Her K2 Rating (0-5) Next Few Years	Her Planned Revenues or Pay ($000) In Three Years	Her Planned Revenue Growth (% per year) Next Three Years	How Achievable?	Which Answers Match Each Chunk?
1	2	3	4	5	6	7	
A	10	5%	3.0	16	17%		1. Most likely
B	10	5%	3.0	12	5%		2. Likely
C	10	5%	3.0	10	0%		3. Likely
D	10	5%	2.0	13	9%		4. Unlikely
E	10	5%	3.5 to 4.0	14	12%		5. Unlikely
F	10	-2.5%	3.0	15	14%		6. Most unlikely

Answers: A:4, B:2, C:1, D:5, E:3, F:6

> to outperform the market, which seems *likely.*
> ➤ In chunk F, market demand is set to decline and competition is likely to be tough. Ms. Random is favorably placed, yet she is planning to grow revenues strongly, beating the market by a wide margin. This seems *most unlikely,* even wild in the absence of robust supporting evidence.

This process offers a first cut at assessing achievability, nothing more. All the above answers are subject to a major warning. They assume that Ms. Random will continue to offer the *same* range of services to the *same* customer groups within the *same* business chunks in the future as she did in the past. This may not be so. She may have *specific initiatives* up her sleeve to justify her planned earnings in each chunk.

These represent discontinuities and can often be the big exception to the above market-driven, "top-down" process, as we'll see in the next section.

Don't Forget the "Bottom-Up" Approach

One main reason the "top-down" assessment of plan achievability may not tell the whole story is because of specific initiatives you may be planning *within* a particular business chunk. These initiatives can work in either direction, enabling you to either beat or fall behind the market in that chunk.

These "bottom-up" initiatives typically relate to a changed mix of services and/or customers within a business chunk. You may be set to broaden, or conversely narrow, the precise mix of services you offer within a chunk. Likewise you may be set to broaden (or narrow) your range of customers within that chunk.

Let's take Leila's original business chunk of aromatherapy to stay-at-home moms. Suppose she came across a set of oils from the Far East for which some of her customers were prepared to pay a premium. That could boost her future revenues from this chunk over and above what could have been expected from the top-down approach.

It could also work the other way. Suppose she had been using these oils for some time, but couldn't charge a high enough premium to justify the additional costs of using them, so she withdrew them. Then her future revenues in this chunk could fall below what could have been expected from the top-down approach.

Likewise there may be discontinuities on the customer side. Suppose she has always done well with moms from four out of the five schools in her catchment area but has never cracked the fifth. Then a good customer of hers has a child start at that fifth school and becomes an influential figure in the PTA. Same business chunk, but now her addressable customer base may undergo a step-change. This might enable her to grow faster than would otherwise be apparent from the top-down approach.

Another main area of discontinuity concerns changes in investment attention. You may feel that recent underperformance in a business chunk may have been because of relative underinvestment, whether in assets, marketing, product development, or training. So you are planning to invest more in that chunk over the next couple of years. Conversely, you may feel that, having invested heavily in a chunk over the last couple of years, it's time to ease off the throttle and reap some rewards.

These "bottom-up" initiatives, highly specific to each business chunk, need to be given careful consideration by your backer when assessing the achievability of your plans.

What About Capacity?

There's another good reason why you may not be able to grow your business along with the market, despite your favorable K2 rating. Your utilization (average number of paid hours work per day) may be getting so high that you may be approaching capacity. There just may not be enough hours left in the day for you to serve more customers.

If so, lucky you! But you may want to consider nudging up your prices. That'll soon give you some more slack! Or you could try "bottom-slicing." This is when you rank all your customers by how profitable each one is to you. Then you start phasing out the least profitable and gradually replacing them with more profitable customers.

Our gardener did that to us a few years ago. He used to come once a week throughout the year before I started to take a bit of an interest and do bits and pieces myself. After a while, I scaled him down to once every other week spring through autumn, and once a month in winter. A year or so later, he became so busy that he bottom-sliced us and quit, sticking with customers who gave him more frequent (and less arduous!) work. Serves me right. It took me ages to find a replacement as good as he!

What All This Means for Employees

If you're an employee, it's possible you've been skimming through the pages thus far and thinking what on earth all this has to do with you. Fair point. Especially if you've been in the same job, with more or less the same pay, for the last few years and seem set to remain in that job for the next few years.

Let's think this through with an example.

Whitney works as an administrator in a private Miami hospital. She believes she has only one business chunk: admin services to hospital management. Her pay over the last three years has grown slowly, from $47,000 to $51,000. Only 1 out of the 12 in her group will ever be promoted, and Whitney doubts it'll be she. She doesn't have a plan, but she figures she'll probably earn around $55,000 in three years' time.

The market for private hospitals has continued to grow strongly, driven by the aging population. Miami is certainly no exception to this trend, giving plenty of job opportunities for hospital administrators over the years and every expectation of more jobs to come. It's not a particularly competitive labor market.

Whitney believes her K2 rating is fine. She usually gets positive feedback from her manager, and she knows she does the job better than at least two or three of her colleagues.

She's not, however, particularly satisfied in her work. When pushed, she'd say she doesn't enjoy it. She's good with people and she'd like to be in a more front-line job, meeting and helping customers, rather than being stuck in a back office doing administrative work. It was because she was generally dissatisfied with her work that she picked up this book.

What use is this chapter to Whitney? Perhaps not much. The answer to her column 7 on how achievable are her "planned" earnings is "likely." The answer to column 8 on her likely earnings in three years' time is the same as her "planned" earnings, $55,000.

This may raise two questions. What use is this book to Whitney, and what use is this chapter to employees in general?

This book may be very useful to Whitney. Not so much this chapter, perhaps, but the next chapter. What are the risks faced by Whitney's backer? One serious hazard could be if her general dissatisfaction with the job starts to impact on her performance. Also Part II may be useful to Whitney. She may learn how to improve her standing in her current job such that she has a better chance at landing the promotion. Or Part III. She may be inspired to back her passion and move to a job where she regularly finds herself face-to-face with customers.

What use is this chapter to employees in general? It could be important if you're planning any significant *change* in one or more of your business chunks. Then your backer will need to assess how achievable your planned changes are. Suppose, for example, Whitney agrees with her boss that she can spend a couple of hours a day helping out at reception, greeting customers and escorting them around the labyrinth that is the hospital complex. Suppose too that she gets such rave reports that she gets reassigned to that role full-time. Great, but for one thing: It pays $10,000 per year less than what Whitney is currently earning in the back office. That's a risk and carries a financial impact Chuck needs to know about.

Later in this chapter, Chuck takes a similar look at Elizabeth, one of our two main employee exemplars, and her planned shift toward market research. And he'll be concerned at what he sees.

This chapter can also be useful to employees in highlighting any risk of losing their jobs over the next few years. If market demand is set to contract, if job competition is going to get tough and if your K2 rating is not so favorable, your backer may assess the chances of you making your planned earnings as unlikely. We'll see later in this chapter Chuck's views on Randy's upbeat pay plans as he and colleagues face a market crash.

Revenue or Profit Plans for the Self-Employed?

This section applies only to the self-employed. Employees can skip to the section on examples, unless you have plans to become self-employed!

So far, we've been assessing revenue performance and revenue prospects. This may not be sufficient for your backer if you're self-employed.

Much depends on your cost structure. If there are differences in your cost structure for each of your business chunks, then you may need to do a further stage of assessment. Many self-employed people won't need to. Their main cost is their time, and costs of materials or of subcontractors may be similar in each business chunk.

If, however, differences are significant, you'll need this second stage. Ultimately, your backer isn't that interested in what happens to revenues, your "top line." *It's what happens to profits, your "bottom line," that matter to him.*

This second stage is also best laid out initially in a market context. In the first stage, we focused on market growth prospects and changes in your K2 rating. In the second stage, we focus on change in competitive intensity. The assessment process flows like this:

1. *Business chunks*—Again, you look at one chunk at a time

   Revenues and profits*
2. *Revenues this year*—As for the first stage on assessing revenue plan achievability
3. *Profit margin this year*—What percentage profit margin will you make in this business chunk this year?
4. *Profit this year*—Revenue multiplied by profit margin

   Competitive environment
5. *Recent competitive intensity*—How tough is competition currently

in this chunk compared to other chunks? High, medium, or low (from Chapter 3)?

6. *Future competitive intensity*—Roughly how tough is competition in this chunk likely to be over the next few years compared to other chunks? High, medium, or low (also from Chapter 3)?

Your profit plan

7. *Planned profit margin*—What percentage profit margin are you planning to make in this business chunk in three years' time (also from Chapter 1)?

How achievable?

8. *How achievable?*—Here's the assessment of your backer on the achievability of your planned profit margin in this chunk, taking into account changes in the competitive environment, in a range from most unlikely through to most likely.

Your backer's forecasts

9. *Likely profit margin*—What your backer thinks is a more likely percentage profit margin for this business chunk in three years' time.

10. *Likely revenues*—What your backer thinks are likely revenues in this chunk in three years' time (from the first stage chart).

11. *Likely profit*—Likely revenues multiplied by likely profit margin.

(* We typically use "gross profit," which is revenues less costs of materials and other direct costs, such as subcontractors. Even better where you have data is to use "contribution to fixed overhead," which also takes into account variable overhead costs. In many self-employed businesses, marketing spend can differ greatly by business chunk. If that's so for you, then it can be useful to define your contribution as "revenues less costs of materials, other direct costs, *and* marketing costs.")

Again, this assessment process may work better for you in a chart. There are 11 entries in the process flow, so you'll find a chart with 11 columns in Figure 7.3. Most of the work needed to fill out this chart you have already done. In columns 3 and 7 you need to put in your profit margins by chunk, current and planned. In columns 5 and 6, you put in indicators of how intense competition is today and how that is likely to change over the next few years, work you've already done in Chapter 3.

So this stage just adds columns 8 and 9. How achievable are these profit margin forecasts and what is a more likely profit margin? Column 10 is lifted directly from the likely revenue forecasts from Figure 7.1 and column 11 falls into place.

There are three main factors that will determine how achievable your profit margin forecasts are, as follows:

1. Pricing pressures from competitive forces in the marketplace ("top-down")

2. Your initiatives to improve the cost effectiveness of your business ("bottom-up")

3. Any initiatives you may have to invest in strengthening an existing line of business or in launching another ("investment")

Figure 7.3 **Assessing How Achievable Are Your Planned Profits**

Your Business Chunks	Your Revenues ($000)	Your Profit Margin (%)	Your Profit ($000)	Competitive Intensity (Low-Med-High)		Your Planned Profit Margin (%)	How Achiev-able?	Likely Profit Margin (%)	Likely Revenues ($000)	Likely Profit ($000)
	This Year	This Year	This Year	This Year	In Three Years	In Three Years		In Three Years	In Three Years	In Three Years
1	2	3	4	5	6	7	8	9	10	11
A										
B										
C										
D										
Others										
Total										

As in the first stage, your backer is looking for *consistency* in the profit margin forecasts. If competition is going to get stiffer, pricing is likely to come under pressure, and he'll expect profit margins to be squeezed. If your plans show profit margins moving the other way—actually improving—you'll need to have some good "bottom-up" reasons why.

Conversely, if competition is set to ease up and your profit margins are planned to stay flat, or even shrink, your backer may think you're being rather conservative—unless there are "bottom-up" reasons why you feel the need to be adding cost.

You may have a number of bottom-up initiatives in mind to improve your cost-effectiveness over the next few years. These could include:

➤ Reduced reliance on subcontractors, doing more of the service delivery yourself

➤ More careful buying of materials, or buying in bulk to drive down unit costs

➤ Better negotiating techniques on all your purchases, both subcontractors and materials

➤ Tighter control of overhead, for example, shifting to other telecoms or electricity providers, moving to more economical premises, or more targeted marketing

We'll look more carefully at how to improve profit performance in Part II. The important thing at this stage is that whatever your plans for driving down cost and improving profit margin from the bottom up may be, they'll need to be consistent and convincing to your backer.

Finally, you may need to incur extra cost in investing in your business. This could be for strengthening your competitiveness in an existing business chunk, for example in a refit of your premises or updating your

IT capability. Or it could be for diversifying into an entirely new business chunk, as, for example, with our massage therapist, Leila, moving into new premises with her new partner to add reflexology to her range.

Either way, the investment will need to be justified by the prospect of suitably higher gross profits over the next few years—see Chapter 12 in Part II on techniques for assessing feasibility. And the annual provision to allow for that investment, so-called "depreciation," may have an impact on your operating profit margin (that's gross profit less overhead less depreciation).

> We can achieve what we want to conceive and believe.—*Mark Twain*

Hopefully some examples will make this more clear, and there's no better place to start than with Healing Hands.

Some Examples for the Self-Employed

Leila at Healing Hands

Chuck starts off by reviewing Leila's revenue plan. He knows he'll have to review her profit plan later, since Leila will have a markedly different cost structure in her new business initiative of reflexology. He starts with revenues.

Leila's revenue plans

Chuck has already found what he needed to know on the markets Leila operates in (Chapters 2 and 3) and how well placed she is in those markets (Chapter 6). He's ready to assess whether her plans seem realistic.

He finds that they're challenging—see Figure 7.4. They're more likely not to happen than to happen. But they're not too far out.

Chuck feels comfortable with Leila's forecast in her oldest and largest business chunk, aromatherapy to stay-at-home moms. Market demand prospects are slowing and competition may get a little tougher, but Leila is so strongly placed that Chuck thinks Leila's forecast is likely to be achieved. But there are still risks. Because of the low barriers to entry, there's a clear risk of an experienced therapist settling in the locality and gnawing into Leila's customer base. Similarly, if Suzi can survive the next year or two, she's going to become a more serious competitor.

But these risks are for the next chapter. They are possible, perhaps reasonably likely. What Chuck believes is more likely is that Leila will make her forecast in this chunk.

Likewise in Leila's other proven chunk, reiki to businesspeople. Despite Kensington Wellness Centre leading in this market, she's still well placed, and Chuck finds her forecast reasonable and likely.

It's in the new line of business that Chuck thinks Leila and Ying have been a bit optimistic. Chuck feels confident that reflexology will take off, but so too could the number of practitioners. Barriers to entry are lower in reflexology even than in reiki and shiatsu, and well below those in aromatherapy. Kensington Wellness Centre has already started to offer reflexology, Suzi may too, and one or two more new entrants could arrive. Chuck has traveled to the Far East on holiday and has seen for himself the proliferation of reflexology

Figure 7.4 How Achievable Are Leila's Revenue Plans in Massage Therapy Services?

Leila's Business Chunks	Leila's Revenues ($000)	Market Demand Growth (% per year)	Leila's K2 Rating (0-5)	Leila's Planned Revenues ($000)	Leila's Planned Revenue Growth (% per year)	Chuck's View: How Achievable?	More Likely Revenues ($000)
	This Year	Next Few Years	Next Few Years	In Three Years	Next Three Years		In Three Years
1	2	3	4	5	6	7	8
Aromatherapy to Stay-at-Home Moms	22	Steady	3.9	30	11%	Likely	25-30
Reflexology to Businesspeople	0	Fast	3.1 to 3.3	25!	n/a	Difficult	10-15
Reiki to Businesspeople	13	Slow	3.1 to 3.3	16	7%	Likely	16
Reflexology to Stay-at-Home Moms	0	Fast	3.9	15	n/a	Possible	10-15
Others	9	Steady	3.5	14	16%	Possible	10-14
Total	44			100	31%	Challenging	70-90

practitioners on almost every street corner.

Nevertheless Chuck has confidence that Leila will succeed in gaining a reasonable share of this market, which seems set for fast growth. He thinks she should be able to achieve a similar scale of business in reflexology to businesspeople as Leila already does in reiki, with sales to moms just a little lower.

Overall Chuck feels that Healing Hands should be able to achieve revenues of $70,000 to $90,000 in three years' time. This is below Leila's bullish forecast of $100,000, but it still represents a successful, thriving business.

Leila's profit plans

Chuck then turns his attention to Leila's profit forecasts, the second stage of his plan review. He knows that most of Leila's planned revenue growth is set to come from the new reflexology venture. Yet all of the therapy work in this area will be undertaken by her new colleague, Ying, who'll get 67 cents

from every dollar received by Healing Hands for reflexology services. Leila's gross profit margin in this therapy of 33 percent compares with the near 100 percent she can achieve when she gives a therapy herself and there are negligible material costs. This is not so in aromatherapy, where the essential oils are quite expensive and her gross profit margin is around 90 percent.

How is this likely to change in the future? Chuck sees no great changes imminent in massage therapy gross profit margins, only that some allowance should be made for inflating costs of essential oils—see Figure 7.5.

What is more revealing is the difference in likely growth between Leila's overall revenues and profits. Revenues are set to jump from $44,000 to $80,000 (midpoint in the forecast range) in three years. That's almost double. Gross profits meanwhile are forecast to grow from $42,000 to $58,000, a rise of only one half.

Growth in gross profits is slower because of Leila's planned shift in business mix toward lower margin business, namely reflexology. In other words, there's to be a large increase in subcontractor costs. But it's still healthy profit growth. And it's healthier growth than if she were to go it alone, without Ying as a partner. Leila will be getting an extra $8,000 a year through giving Ying access to space (at low cost to Leila) and to Leila's clientele (at zero cost to Leila).

The third stage for Chuck is to look at future changes in overhead costs. Leila and Ying are poised to move into the storefront just off the main street, which they'll have rent-free as long as they fix it up. Refurbishing is estimated

at $9,000 and from then on overhead bills for power, gas, water, and so forth won't be very different from what she's paying when working from home. The main difference will be payment of local government property taxes, which will cost around $2,000 per year. Total extra overhead may come to around $4,000 per year.

Leila's $9,000 investment should generate $4,000 per year of extra profit ($8,000 gross profit, less $4,000 extra overhead)—a payback of just over two years. This is looking attractive to Chuck, but what are the risks? They're for the next chapter.

Figure 7.5 **How Achievable Are Leila's Profit Plans in Massage Therapy Services?**

Leila's Business Chunks	Leila's Rev's ($000)	Leila's Gross Profit Margin (%)	Leila's Gross Profit ($000)	Competitive Intensity (Low-Med-High)		Leila's Planned Profit Margin (%)	Chuck's View: How Achievable?	Likely Gross Profit Margin (%)	Likely Rev's ($000)	Likely Gross Profit ($000)
	This Year	This Year	This Year	This Year	In Three Years	In Three Years		In Three Years	In Three Years	In Three Years
1	2	3	4	5	6	7	8	9	10	11
Aromatherapy to Moms	22	90%	20	L/M	Med	90%	Possible	85%	27.5	23
Reflexology to Business	0	n/a	0	n/a	L/M	33%	Most Likely	33%	12.5	4
Reiki to Business	13	100%	13	Med	Med	100%	Most Likely	100%	15	15
Reflexology to Moms	0	n/a	0	L/M	L/M	33%	Most Likely	33%	12.5	4
Others	9	100%	9	L/M	Med	100%	Most Likely	100%	12.5	12
Total	**44**	**95%**	**42**			**70%**	**Likely**	**72%**	**80**	**58**

Carwyn in Boston carpentry

Chuck's chart shows that Carwyn may need to do some serious rethinking of his plans—see Figure 7.6.

Carwyn has been operating in only one business chunk for the last few years, subcontracting to Boston Heights, but it's instructive for Chuck to include in the chart Carwyn's alternative business chunks as well—even though revenues in these chunks are zero at present. These include subcontracting to other contractors, direct contracting to households, or returning to being an employee—whether for a construction firm, or as Carwyn used to be, as one of a building maintenance team in a large organization.

The chart spells out starkly that for Carwyn to carry on with what he is doing is a risky option. Market demand for loft conversions is set to decline sharply, and competition is poised to get very tough. Boston Heights will find it hard to win business without slashing prices, and the proprietor will only be able to hang on to his very best people.

Carwyn remains reasonably placed, but time is not on his side. Carwyn may get less work or even no work in a year or two from Boston Heights.

Carwyn's alternatives as a self-employed carpenter don't look too good either. Competition will be tough in general subcontracting as the market flattens out, and in direct contracting to households, Carwyn has never been one for selling himself.

Chuck thinks Carwyn might be better off returning to being an employee. Age may again count against him if he were to apply to a construction company, but it may be less of a problem with an employer such as where he used to work, Harvard University. His previous experience there would stand him in good stead and his undoubted carpentry skills, honed over the years, would be broadly valued. Pay may not be that good, but job security would be improved and the more generous pension scheme could come in handy 10 years or so from now.

Figure 7.6 **How Achievable Are Carwyn's Revenue Plans in Boston Carpentry?**

Carwyn's Business Chunks	Carwyn's Revenues ($000)	Market Demand Growth (% per year)	Carwyn's K2 Rating (0-5)	Carwyn's Planned Revenues ($000)	Carwyn's Planned Revenue Growth (% per year)	Chuck's View: How Achievable?	More Likely Revenues ($000)
	This Year	Next Few Years	Next Few Years	In Three Years	Next Three Years		In Three Years
1	2	3	4	5	6	7	8
Sub-contracting to Boston Heights	55	Sharp decline	3.4 to 3.1			Most Unlikely	
Sub-contracting to other companies	0	Flat	3.3 to 3.0	50	-3%	Unlikely	40?
Direct contracting to households	0	Flat	3.1 to 2.8			Possible	
Employee at construction company	0	Flat	3.2 to 2.9	n/a	n/a	Most Unlikely	n/a
Employee in maintenance	0	Steady	3.4 to 3.2	n/a	n/a	Promising?	[40+?]
Total	55			50	-3%	Challenging	40

Carwyn agrees that his plan to keep his revenues at more or less the same level as today is going to be challenging. He'll get in touch with his old contacts at Harvard.

Some Examples for Employees

Elizabeth at ConsultCo

Chuck's chart for Elizabeth shows up immediately the riskiness of her plans—see Figure 7.7.

Elizabeth is planning to turn herself from a top PA who also does market research into a market researcher who can also do PA work. It's risky. Sure, demand for market research services is set to grow faster at ConsultCo than the demand for admin services, but Elizabeth is in a stronger position in admin work than in market research.

In market research, she'll always be striving to compete with the young, hard-working consultants, who may not have her interviewing skills but do have the upfront presentational skills. In this chunk, Elizabeth also runs the risks of presentational skills becoming a must-have success factor and of market research being outsourced to external vendors.

Conversely, in admin services, Elizabeth has the huge advantage of versatility, compared with other PAs. With her capabilities in market research coming on top of her relative parity in admin capabilities, she will remain strongly placed as a PA in the company.

Chuck finds that Elizabeth's planned pay over the next few years seems achievable, although from a different mix of business chunks. The prerequisite to achieving them, however, must be to continue her positioning as a PA-cum-market-researcher, not the other way around.

Figure 7.7 **How Achievable Are Elizabeth's Pay Plans at ConsultCo Inc?**

Elizabeth's Business Chunks	Elizabeth's Pay ($000)	Market Demand Growth (% per year)	Elizabeth's K2 Rating (0-5)	Elizabeth's Planned Pay ($000)	Elizabeth's Planned Pay Growth (% per year)	Chuck's View: How Achievable?	More Likely Pay ($000)
	This Year	Next Few Years	Next Few Years	In Three Years	Next Three Years		In Three Years
1	2	3	4	5	6	7	8
Admin to Senior Staff	15	Slow	3.8	10	Down	Probably Higher	20
Admin to Other Staff	22	Slow	3.8	10	Well down	Probably Higher	20
Research for Senior Staff	15	Fast	3.4 to 3.3	45!	Trebled!	Unlikely	25
Other (including typing)	8	Down	3.8	5	Down	Likely	5
Total	60			70	5%	Likely	70

Randy at Homes4U

Chuck's chart for Randy highlights how unrealistic his pay plans are—see Figure 7.8.

Randy wants to earn a lot more money in three years' time. He currently makes $50,000; he wants to make $80,000. Chuck's chart blows that myth.

Sure, Randy is the last salesperson Homes4U would want to walk out of the door. But they won't be able to afford to keep him if those are his pay aspirations. The real estate market in Atlanta is set to crash; Homes4U is going to find itself scrabbling for sale mandates and the company looks set for red numbers on its bottom line for two, possibly three years. Commissions and/or bonuses of that order, even to a super-salesman such as Randy, will be out of the question.

There's also the risk of Randy losing his enthusiasm for selling houses. If that happens, Chuck figures, Randy can kiss goodbye his current $50,000, let alone his planned $80,000. Chuck resolves to have a good long talk with Randy over this gleam in his eye called plumbing.

Figure 7.8 How Achievable Are Randy's Pay Plans at Homes4U?

Randy's Business Chunks	Randy's Pay ($000)	Market Demand Growth (% per year)	Randy's K2 Rating (0-5)	Randy's Planned Pay ($000)	Randy's Planned Pay Growth (% per year)	Chuck's View: How Achievable?	More Likely Pay ($000)
	This Year	Next Few Years	Next Few Years	In Three Years	Next Three Years		In Three Years
1	2	3	4	5	6	7	8
Selling Houses	50	Heavily Down!	4.2 to 4.4	80!	17%	Unlikely	45-55
Total	50			80	17%	Unlikely	45-55

Risks and Opportunities in Your Plan

You've already pulled out into three separate charts the main risks and opportunities relating to market demand (Chapter 2), competition (Chapter 3), and your K2 rating (Chapter 6). Risks and opportunities associated with plans for your business or job are the fourth and final element in the Risk Jigsaw.

Here, therefore, you need to add those major risks and opportunities that relate to what you plan to do in your business, or with your job, over the next few years. How likely are those risks to occur, and if they do, what sort of impact would they have on your plan? Likewise for opportunities. Again, you may find the chart in Appendix A, Figure A.2 helpful.

You've now filled out all four of the components in the Risk Jigsaw. In the next chapter, you'll bring these four together and pull out those most important. You'll pinpoint those key risks or opportunities that determine whether you are, or are not, backable in your current job or business.

How Risky?

8

In the last chapter, you assessed whether your plans are likely to work out. You're almost there, but for one final stage. *How risky are U?* How likely is it that one or two of the risks you've met along the way will blow your plans? What are the odds of one or two of those opportunities enabling you to beat your plans?

The Risk Jigsaw Is Complete

We summarized the main market demand risks and opportunities toward the end of Chapter 2. Likewise for those relating to competition in Chapter 3. In Chapter 6 we moved away from looking at the market as a whole and looked at the risks and opportunities around you, and your K2 rating. Finally, in the last chapter, we pulled together the main risks and opportunities associated with your business plan. The risk jigsaw is complete. Now we just need to view the assembled picture as a whole.

Once you've gathered them all together, you'll be able to see whether the opportunities outweigh the risks. You'll be able to ask yourself: Are U backable?

Meet the Suns & Clouds Chart

I first created the Suns & Clouds chart in the early 1990s. Since then I've seen it reproduced in various forms in reports by my consulting competitors. They say imitation is the sincerest form of flattery, but I still kick myself that I didn't think of copyrighting it way back then!

> When written in Chinese the word crisis is composed to two characters. One represents danger, and the other represents opportunity.
> —*John F. Kennedy*

The reason it keeps getting pinched is that it works. It manages to encapsulate in one chart conclusions on the relative importance of all the main issues debated thus far. It shows, diagrammatically, whether the opportunities (the suns) outshine the risks (the clouds). Or vice-versa, if the clouds overshadow the suns. In short, in one chart, it tells you whether you're backable. Or not.

The Suns & Clouds chart (Figure 8.1) forces you to view each risk (and opportunity) from two perspectives: by how likely it is to happen and by how big an impact it would have if it did.

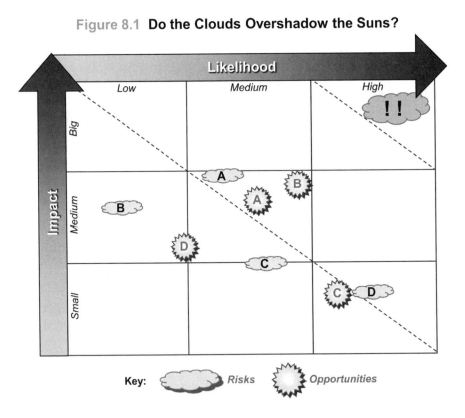

Figure 8.1 **Do the Clouds Overshadow the Suns?**

The great news is that you've done all the necessary work. Every bit of it. At the back end of Chapters 2, 3, 6, and 7, you drew up charts highlighting all the main risks and opportunities. In these charts, you didn't just list the risks and opportunities. You also filled in columns on likelihood and impact. All you have to do here is portray those findings graphically. As suns and clouds.

In the chart, risks are represented as clouds, opportunities as suns. The more likely a risk (or opportunity) is to happen, the further to the right you should place it along the horizontal axis. In Figure 8.1, risk D is the most likely to happen, and risk B the least.

The bigger the impact a risk (or opportunity) would have if it were to happen, the higher you should place it up the vertical axis. In the same chart, opportunity B would have the largest impact, opportunity C the smallest.

For each risk (and opportunity), you need to place it in the appropriate position on the chart taking into account *both* factors—its likelihood *and* its impact.

Don't worry if things don't make that much sense initially. This chart *always* changes with further thought and discussion. In some ways its greatest virtue is its stimulus to discussion. I have often given PowerPoint presentations of 100 slides or so, with no more than a couple of questions for clarification every now and then. Then when the Suns & Clouds chart comes up, toward the end of the presentation, it can remain on screen for a half-hour or more. It stimulates discussion and provokes amendment. The client may choose to debate for 10 minutes the precise positioning of one risk, or opportunity, *and why*.

Remember, there is no way you can be exact in this chart. Nor do you need to be. It is a pictorial representation of risk and opportunity, designed to give you a *feel* for the balance of risk and opportunity in your business.

What the Suns & Clouds Tell You

The Suns & Clouds chart tells you two main things about your backability: (1) whether there are any *extraordinary* risks (or opportunities), and (2) whether the overall *balance* of risk and opportunity makes you backable.

Extraordinary risk

Take a look at the top right-hand corner of the chart. There's a heavy thundercloud in there, with two exclamation marks. That's a risk that is both very likely *and* very big. It's a showstopper risk. If your backer finds one of them in your business or job, then that's it. You're unbackable where you are.

The closer a cloud gets to that thundercloud, the worse news it is. Risks that hover around the diagonal (from the top left to the bottom right corners) can be handled, as long as they are balanced by opportunities.

But as soon as a cloud starts creeping toward that thundercloud, for example to around where opportunity B is placed, that's when your backer starts to get itchy feet.

But imagine a bright shining sun in that spot where the thundercloud is. That's terrific news, and your backer will be falling over himself to invest in you.

It's not unusual for a backer to find a showstopper risk. There's an excellent weekly TV program on the BBC called *Dragon's Den,* where five millionaire "dragons" listen to a 10-minute presentation on a budding entrepreneur's plans and consider whether to back him or her. Most leave with no investment. Often it's just one risk that turns off the dragons. It may be incredulity that anyone would buy such a product or service. Or that the entrepreneur has been trying for so long or has invested so much, for such little result. Or the product is too costly to yield a profit. Each is a risk that the dragons see as highly likely and with big impact. Each is a top right-hand corner thundercloud, a showstopper.

Some risks are huge, but most unlikely to happen. That's not to say they won't happen. The unlikely sometimes happens. But these are not show-stopper risks. They are top left-hand corner risks. If we worried about the unlikely happening, we would never cross the road. Certainly no backer would ever invest a cent!

In fall 2001, my colleagues and I were advising a client on whether to back a company involved in airport operations. After the first week of work, we produced an interim report and a first-cut Suns & Clouds chart. In the top left-hand corner box, we placed a risk entitled "major air incident." We were thinking of a serious air crash that might lead to the prolonged grounding of a common class of aircraft. It seemed unlikely, but would have a very large impact if it happened. 9/11 came just a few days later. We never envisaged anything so catastrophic, so inconceivably evil, but at least we had alerted our client to the extreme risks involved in the air industry. The deal was later renegotiated and successfully completed.

The balance

In general, for most investment decisions, particularly for individuals, there's no showstopper risk. The main purpose of the Suns & Clouds chart will then be to present the *balance* of risk and opportunity. Do the opportunities outweigh the risks? Given the overall picture, are the suns more favorably placed than the clouds? Or do the clouds overshadow the suns?

The way to assess a Suns & Clouds chart is to look at the general area above the diagonal and in the direction of the thundercloud. Any risk (or opportunity) around there is worth noting. It's at least reasonably likely to occur and would have at least a reasonable impact. Or it's just very big. Or it's just very likely to occur. Whichever of these three possibilities, these risks and opportunities need to be given careful consideration.

Those risks and opportunities below the diagonal are less important.

They are either of low to medium likelihood *and* of low to medium impact. Or they're not big enough, or not likely enough, to be of major concern.

A backer will look at the pattern of suns in this general area above the diagonal and compare it with the pattern of clouds. The closer each sun and cloud to the thundercloud, the more important it is. If the pattern of suns seems better placed than the pattern of clouds, the backer will be comforted. If the clouds overshadow the suns, the backer will be concerned.

In the chart above, there are two clouds and two suns above the diagonal. The best placed is opportunity B. Risk A and opportunity A more or less balance each other out. Likewise risk D and opportunity C, although the latter is just below the diagonal. Opportunity B seems distinctly clear of the pack, with its nearest remaining challenger being risk C, which is well below the diagonal. The opportunities seem to surpass the risks. The business looks backable.

Some Exercises in Suns & Clouds

Here are some exercises to help you grasp the concept of the Suns & Clouds. In each exercise, I've relocated just the one risk or opportunity from the Suns & Clouds chart you've already seen. You'll see that just the one movement can throw the delicate balance in deciding whether to back a business.

Have a look at the following four exercises. On the basis of these charts alone, would you back these businesses?

In exercise I (Figure 8.2), risk A is moved into the top right-hand box. I hope you've concluded that you wouldn't touch this business with a 10-foot pole. Risk A is bad news. It's very likely to happen, and if it happens it's going to be big. It's bordering on a showstopper. Regardless of opportunities B and A, stay clear. Look elsewhere.

In exercise II (Figure 8.3), opportunity A is moved into the top right-hand box. Would you back this business? Sure you would. Opportunities A and B dominate the chart. If you find a gem of a business like this, just let me know!

In exercise III (Figure 8.4), all that has changed from the original is that opportunity B has dropped down to the diagonal. Would you back this business? Tricky. There's no clear preeminence of suns or clouds in this chart. They all seem to balance each other out. This doesn't mean that the business isn't backable. What it does mean is that this business seems rather predictable, dull even, with not much upside likely. And conversely not much downside to worry about.

This is a typical Suns & Clouds pattern for a mature business. A stable business for a banker to lend to but not an exciting prospect for an equity investor.

In exercise IV (Figure 8.5), risk A has been made a little more likely and with a little more impact. Again it's tricky. Just this slight move has greatly altered the balance of risk and opportunity. Risk A now cancels out opportunity B, though opportunity A still looks clear and overall the op-

Figure 8.2 **Exercise I: Would You Back This Business?!?!**

Figure 8.3 **Exercise II: Or Would You Prefer This Business?!**

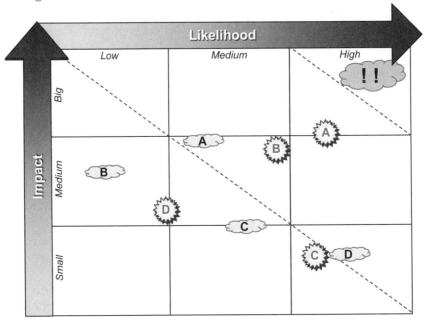

Figure 8.4 **Exercise III: But What About This Business?**

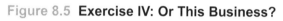

Figure 8.5 **Exercise IV: Or This Business?**

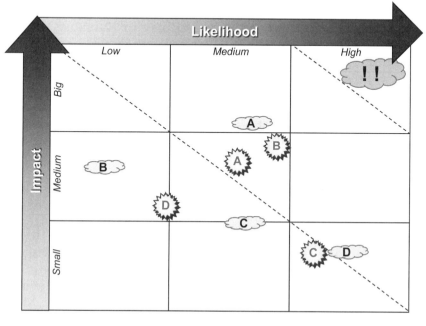

portunities may still just shade the risks. But if I were the backer I would want to know everything there is to know about risk A. It would worry me, and I would want to know what the business could do, if anything, to mitigate that risk.

You now understand how the Suns & Clouds chart works. Let's move on from the theoretical and try it on a real example. If you were a music producer at Parlophone in the first few months of 1962, would you have backed the Beatles?

Would You Have Backed the Beatles?

Let's have some context. In Britain of the early 1960s, Parlophone was a distinguished record company that had never backed any rock 'n' roll artists. At the time, there were dozens of young rock 'n' roll groups with persistent promoters doing the rounds of the studios. This particular group, the Beatles, had been turned down by all other recording studios.

Their leader, John Lennon, had been fronting groups for five years. He'd formed the Quarrymen in 1956, when he was 16, and within a couple of years fellow members had come to include Paul McCartney and George Harrison. They evolved into Johnny and the Moondogs and then, inspired by Buddy Holly and the Crickets, into Long John and the Silver Beetles. With Lennon's love of the pun, that soon morphed into the Beatles. (I am grateful to Suzanne Smiley's *A Brief History of the Beatles: From Their Humble Beginnings in Liverpool to the Birth of Beatlemania in America*, published in May 2000, for this interesting background.)

The group was one of many playing the Liverpool club scene. Their break came when they secured a gig to play in Hamburg, then a city crazy over U.S.–style rock 'n' roll. Their first trip proved short-lived. After a nightclub prank and a night in jail, they were packed off back home. Undeterred, they were back again the following year and it was there they made their first recording, a cover of a song called "My Bonnie." It was on their return that the curiosity of a Liverpudlian record store owner, Brian Epstein, became aroused. Three customers came into his shop in just a few days and asked for a copy of "My Bonnie." He had heard of the Beatles from the local music magazine, *Mersey Beat*, but had had no previous interest in seeing them. So he went to see them at the Cavern Club. He wasn't hugely impressed with their music but thought they had charisma. He signed up to be their manager, arranged for them to make a demo tape, and set off to hawk it around the record companies.

If you'd been George Martin, a producer at Parlophone, would you have backed these guys? You knew that one other record company, Decca, had shown some interest but had turned them down in favor of a group called Brian Poole and the Tremeloes. Decca executives also believed—in a now classic quote—that "guitar groups are on the way out." For your company's first venture into rock 'n' roll, would you have chosen these four lads from Liverpool? Let's look at their Suns & Clouds in Figure 8.6.

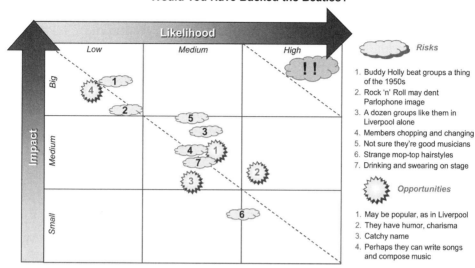

Figure 8.6 **Early 1962: If You'd Been at Parlaphone, Would You Have Backed the Beatles?**

It couldn't have been an easy decision for George Martin. On the one hand, there were so many wannabe groups around (risk 3) and the Beatles seemed unexceptional musically (risk 5). On the other hand, they seemed to have charisma and humor (opportunity 2). And they had built a loyal following among club-goers in Liverpool (opportunity 1). These may have been the four issues that stood out, two risks and two opportunities, above the diagonal.

No one would blame him, he must have thought, if he turned these guys down. Yet he had a hunch. They seemed to have something. Maybe they could improve their musical abilities. Maybe they could be marketed. He backed them. What would you have done?

How the Suns & Clouds May Change

The likelihood of a risk or an opportunity happening tends to change over time. Likewise, sometimes its impact, if it did happen, can get bigger or smaller. The Suns & Clouds chart can show this clearly.

There are two major areas of change that can be usefully depicted in the Suns & Clouds chart:
1. Things happening in the market as a whole, which you can do nothing or very little about
2. Things happening to you, your K2 rating, your initiatives, your plans to mitigate risks, and so forth, which are very much in your control to do something about

Change in the Suns & Clouds chart can be illuminated with arrows. The arrows will show you whether the risks are getting more or less serious, whether the opportunities more or less promising.

If the risk seems to be getting more serious over time, it can be useful to color-fill the arrow in red (or black, if you're working in black and white). If the risk is getting less serious, color-fill it in green (or white, if you're in black and white). Likewise, if an opportunity is getting more promising over time, color-fill the arrow in green, and if less promising in red. That way you'll get an immediate visual impression of whether the balance of risk and opportunity is moving over time in your favor or against you.

For risks and opportunities that are under your control to influence, as opposed to those that affect the market as a whole, you can use the same color code, but I recommend sticking a little target sign at the end of the arrow. That'll show you where to aim and that it's within your power to make that target. You can either improve the overall balance of risk, or you can leave it be. It's your call. You'll have no such choice with risks and opportunities that affect the whole market. They are beyond your power to influence.

If we return to our original Suns & Clouds example, let's see how things may change over time. Are any key risks or opportunities likely to change in importance over the next few years? How is the balance of risk and opportunity likely to change?

We see in Figure 8.7 that opportunity B seems less likely to happen over time. And that risk C may well get more likely *and* be of bigger impact over time.

We also see that opportunity A, one which the exemplar has in her

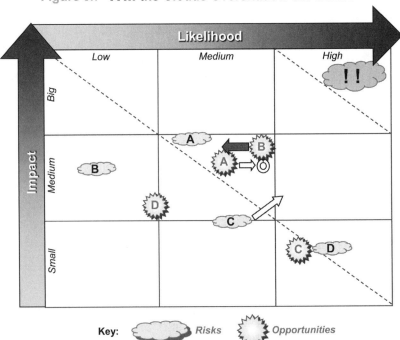

Figure 8.7 *Will* the Clouds Overshadow the Suns?

control to do something about, becomes more likely over time. On balance, she remains backable.

Again, a real example should help. When you were assessing the Beatles back in early 1962, you'd have thought about what you could do to improve their chances of success. You could have encouraged them to develop their own musical and songwriting capabilities. And to differentiate themselves further from other Liverpudlian groups—you might even have accepted that their mop-tops should stay, rather than revert to the rock 'n' roll pompadour. And that they should wear more distinctive clothing, even collarless jackets! You'd also have insisted, contractually, that they cut out the drinking and swearing on stage.

How would that have impacted the Suns & Clouds and your backing decision?

Figure 8.8 might have helped you. If you'd believed you could shift some of the key risks that were under your control to the left, the overall balance of risk and opportunity would have improved significantly. Risks 3 and 5 could have been nudged to the left, with risk 7 shifted contractually all the way to the left. Meanwhile, opportunity 4 might be able to be nudged to the right. The chart might have made your decision to back the Beatles a bit simpler.

Figure 8.8 **Early 1962: Thinking of Backing the Beatles, How Could You Have Improved Their Chances?**

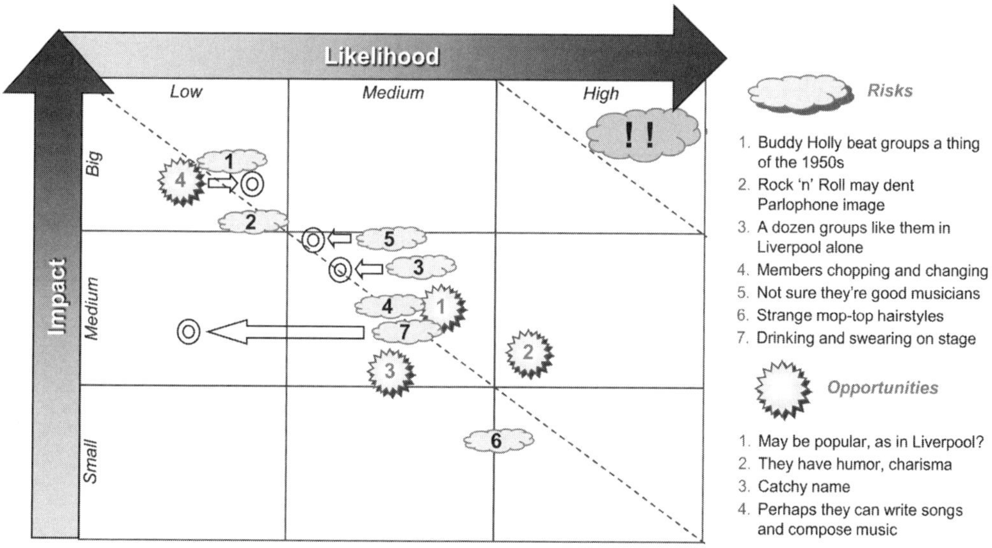

Would You Have Backed the Beatles *After* Their First Album?

As a postscript to this tale, let's see how the backing decision might have changed one year later. After the release of their first album, would you have backed the Beatles?

You know the answer, but it's fun to see how the Suns & Clouds chart may have changed.

One year later, the Beatles' first single "Love Me Do" had reached the U.K. Top 20. Their second single, "Please Please Me," and their first album, of the same name, were riding high as number ones in both the single and album charts. Was this a flash in the pan? Were these guys to come and go with little trace like many before them? You wouldn't know then that their album would stay at number one for 30 weeks, before being replaced by, yes, their second album! That their fourth single, "She Loves You," would become the biggest seller of all time, topping even hits by their role model, Elvis Presley, and would remain so for more than a decade.

What you did know was that you'd sure made the right decision the year before. You'd also greatly underestimated them as musicians. They could even write and compose catchy songs. The Suns & Clouds chart was transformed—see Figure 8.9.

Figure 8.9 **Spring 1963: Now Would You Back the Beatles?!**

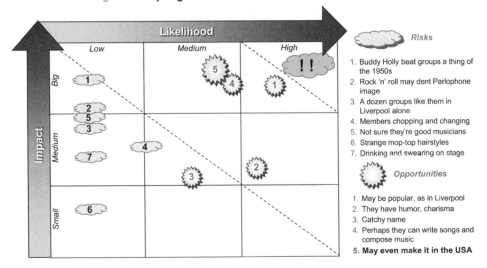

Risks

1. Buddy Holly beat groups a thing of the 1950s
2. Rock 'n' roll may dent Parlophone image
3. A dozen groups like them in Liverpool alone
4. Members chopping and changing
5. Not sure they're good musicians
6. Strange mop-top hairstyles
7. Drinking and swearing on stage

Opportunities

1. May be popular, as in Liverpool
2. They have humor, charisma
3. Catchy name
4. Perhaps they can write songs and compose music
5. **May even make it in the USA**

All the risks in the earlier Suns & Clouds chart had retreated leftward into insignificance. Even the risk of the four members splitting up was greatly reduced. Meanwhile the opportunities before the group were dazzling. Their popularity as performers had soared. Their potential as songwriters was astonishing. And to cap it all, a new, huge opportunity had arisen (number five). Could they conceivably become the first British singer or group to wow a U.S. audience?

Would you have backed the Beatles in the spring of 1963? The Suns & Clouds chart says it all. Would you play the lottery if you knew what number was coming up?

Would You Have Backed Oprah?

Here's one more example. This is an individual rather than a group and she's more contemporary. She is the phenomenon that is Oprah.

In 1983, Ms. Winfrey was a talk show host at a local TV station in Baltimore, Maryland. She had done well there and seemed to be on a steadily upward career progression. After graduating with a degree in communications at Tennessee State University, she went on to become the youngest and first black female news anchor at a local TV station in Nashville. She moved to Baltimore to present the evening news but later switched to a talk show slot.

This was a young woman who was going places. And yet her early years had hardly been promising. Born in Kosciusko, Mississippi, to unmarried, teenage parents, her mother was a housemaid, her father a soldier turned coalminer turned barber. She was raised initially by her grandmother in modest rural environs and then by her welfare-dependent mother in an inner city neighborhood in Milwaukee. She has stated that she suffered abuse there from the age of nine. She rebelled. She became pregnant at 14 but lost the child soon after birth. She was sent to her father in Nashville, where his strict attention to schoolwork helped her to gain a scholarship to Tennessee State University.

Suppose Oprah now needed some backing, and she came to you, an investor like Chuck Cash, to tell you she had been offered a job in Chicago to host WLS-TV's low-rated, half-hour, morning talk show, *AM Chicago.* Suppose she needed cash to pay off, say, credit card debt incurred in Baltimore or to put down a deposit on a two-bedroom apartment in a trendy part of downtown Chicago.

She was optimistic that this show would do well. It had slipped down in the ratings in recent years and needed some new vigor. She thought she had what it needed: warmth, humor, vitality, and empathy with both interviewee and audience. She was confident that she could raise ratings in Chicago, maybe compete with the doyen of daytime talk shows, *Donahue.* She thought her formula could even one day go national. Would you have backed her?

You may not have. Oprah's Suns & Clouds would have looked none too promising—see Figure 8.10. Successful talk shows were hosted by white, middle-class males, many with years of experience in journalism and/or TV reporting. They had interviewing skills that were seen as integral to the talk show format.

Oprah was black, female, working class, and overweight. She had little foundation in journalism or reporting; she was primarily a presenter. These were big risks, with high likelihood, high impact.

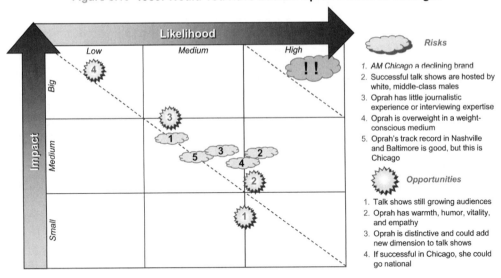

Figure 8.10 **1983: Would You Have Backed Oprah's Move to Chicago?**

Risks

1. AM Chicago a declining brand
2. Successful talk shows are hosted by white, middle-class males
3. Oprah has little journalistic experience or interviewing expertise
4. Oprah is overweight in a weight-conscious medium
5. Oprah's track record in Nashville and Baltimore is good, but this is Chicago

Opportunities

1. Talk shows still growing audiences
2. Oprah has warmth, humor, vitality, and empathy
3. Oprah is distinctive and could add new dimension to talk shows
4. If successful in Chicago, she could go national

On the other hand, you may have seen something in Oprah when you met her. Her prospects on paper may not have looked very good, but there was clearly something quite exceptional about her personality. She—her vitality, her empathy—may have been the big opportunity.

You may have backed her.

If you had, it would have been a good call. Within months, her show went to the top of the Chicago talk show ratings, surpassing *Donahue*. It was relabeled under her name and extended to one hour. Opportunity 3 in the chart had shifted far to the right. Three years later the show went national, shifting opportunity 4 into the top right-hand box.

The rest is history. She's the highest paid entertainer on TV ever and the first black female billionaire. She's also a leading philanthropist. She has donated hundreds of millions of dollars to charity and has fronted fundraising campaigns to raise yet more. She has been rated as one of the most influential women in the world.

How Risky Are Your Plans?

Back to reality and your own job or business. It's time for you to position *your* suns, *your* clouds.

You already know what the main risks and opportunities facing you are. You've already pinpointed them for your backer in Chapters 2, 3, 6, and 7. All you need to do now is place each of the main risks or opportunities appropriately in the Suns & Clouds chart.

The policy of being too cautious is the greatest risk of all.—Jawaharlal Nehru

Is there a showstopper risk? Is your backer going to run a mile? Hopefully not.

But is there any risk approaching the showstopper area? Will your backer have to think about it very carefully

122

indeed? Can you do anything to mitigate the impact of this risk? Would you be able to demonstrate this to your backer, with supporting evidence?

What about the overall balance of risk and opportunity? Do your suns outshine your clouds? To what extent can you shift any clouds to the left, or suns to the right?

Would you back U in your current business or job?

Take calculated risks. That is quite different from being rash.—George S. Patton

We have one final step to go before we can answer that question. In Chapter 9 we backtrack and examine the whole storyline, from Chapter 1 through to Chapter 8. The main conclusions, the key risks. That's for the next chapter.

Could Your Attitude Blow Them?

There's one more thing we need to check on before we leave this chapter. Is there any chance your attitude is, or could become, a showstopper risk?

We examined this in Chapter 6 (see Any Chance You Won't Get Past First Base? and Is It Your Attitude?). If you're reading this book because you're one of the 50 percent of people dissatisfied with their current job, your attitude may be a risk.

Let's remind ourselves of Zig Ziglar's quote, which we came across in Chapter 4: "It is not your aptitude, but your attitude, that determines your altitude." To what extent is your attitude getting in the way of your altitude? If your attitude is a risk, where should it be placed on the Suns & Clouds chart?

Is your attitude a minor factor in lowering your K2 rating in a job where attitude is nice to have but not a must-have? Fine. Then the risk of you losing your job (or promotion) because of your attitude is of low likelihood, high impact.

If, however, attitude is a must-have K2 and yours is not what it should be, is there any chance of you losing your job because of your attitude? Is there a strong chance? May you become unbackable?

If we return to the original Suns & Clouds example, suppose risk A represents the risk of you losing your job because of your attitude. Your attitude is not great but not dire, so you assess the current risk as of low likelihood, high impact.

But suppose that two things seem likely to happen. Your incoming boss sees things in a different light and wants to put customer service top priority, with attitude becoming a must-have Key Kapability for all his team members. Meanwhile, your enthusiasm for the job continues to wane and your attitude deteriorates.

Is the risk of you losing your job likely to grow over time, as shown in the arrow in Figure 8.11? If so, your attitude could become a serious constraint on your backability.

Figure 8.11 Could Your Attitude Become Too Great a Risk?

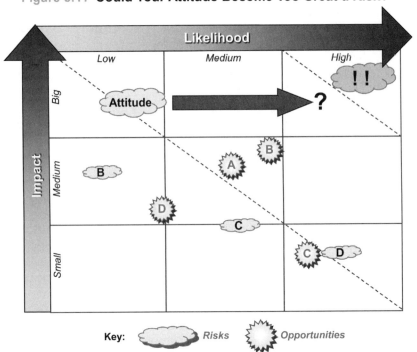

Key: Risks   Opportunities

Some Examples for the Self-Employed

Leila at Healing Hands

Chuck has drawn up so many Suns & Clouds charts in his time, he feels he could moonlight as a weather forecaster. He drafts one for Leila and they discuss it. Leila's already feeling pretty aggrieved that Chuck didn't buy into her revenue forecasts, so she's ready to fight for her views on risks and opportunities.

But she's pleasantly surprised. Chuck assures her it doesn't look all doom and gloom. Because he's assessing impact compared to his own view of Leila's prospects, rather than Leila's view, the risks don't seem so big. And overall the risks and opportunities seem reasonably balanced—see Figure 8.12.

Clearly the main risks center around competition—especially new entrants. Chuck has already allowed for the possibility of new entrants in reflexology, where barriers to entry are very low. That's why he scaled down Leila's forecasts. So the risks of his scaled-down revenue forecasts being driven down further (risks 3 and 4 in the chart) seem containable.

Chuck believes there are two further big risks. One that can be mitigated and one that cannot. First, Ying could quit (risk 6). If her reflexology revenues take off successfully, she may decide that she could do without paying Leila a 33 percent commission and set up on her own, taking customers with her.

Figure 8.12 **Risks and Opportunities for Healing Hands in Massage Therapy Services in Notting Hill, London**

Risks

1. Customers switch to new de-stress solution
2. Experienced competitor moves to Barnes and takes market share
3. New entrants in reflexology
4. New entrants drive down pricing
5. Kensington Wellness Centre slashes prices
6. Ying quits Leila and sets up on own

Opportunities

1. Reflexology takes off as in Far East
2. Suzi pulls out
3. Healing Hands' reflexology sales move towards Leila's expectations, if no new entrants

* Note: Over and above **Chuck's view** of likely profits in three years' time

But Leila can mitigate this risk. She could offer to reduce commission to 20 percent after an initial two years, once investment costs have been recouped. Or she could build in a three-month termination notice to her agreement with Ying, say bye-bye when Ying leaves, and bring in a replacement reflexologist. Some customers would follow Ying, others would stay with Healing Hands. The impact of Ying's exit would be lessened.

The other big risk, an experienced therapist moving into the area (risk 2), Leila can do nothing about. If it happens, it happens. In Chuck's research, he read about an investment banker quitting her job, training in aromatherapy, setting up in Chelsea, and not winning enough business to make ends meet. There were simply too many therapists covering that uber-trendy area of London. Suppose that this woman, or worse, someone more experienced than her, chose to relocate 2 miles north to Notting Hill? That, Chuck concludes, is a risk he'll just have to take.

Carwyn in Carpentry

Chuck already knew in the back of his mind what Carwyn's Suns & Clouds were going to look like. More Mississippi than Arizona, more Wales than England, he'd figured. He wasn't far wrong.

Chuck decided to assess the impact of risks and opportunities in relation to the prospect of Carwyn's revenues being able to hold flat. He found that most of the risks he had been chewing over fell just above the diagonal—see Figure 8.13. They were all serious. None of them showstoppers, perhaps, but cumulatively not good news for Carwyn.

The loft conversion market seemed set to dip. Activity at Boston Heights was likely to drop, and with Carwyn's

Figure 8.13 **Risks and Opportunities for Carwyn in Boston Carpentry**

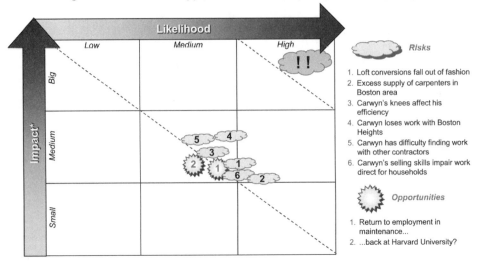

Risks

1. Loft conversions fall out of fashion
2. Excess supply of carpenters in Boston area
3. Carwyn's knees affect his efficiency
4. Carwyn loses work with Boston Heights
5. Carwyn has difficulty finding work with other contractors
6. Carwyn's selling skills impair work direct for households

Opportunities

1. Return to employment in maintenance...
2. ...back at Harvard University?

* Note: Over and above Carwyn's revenues *holding flat* at this year's level

knees, he would find it tough to hang on (risk 4). There would be an excess supply of carpenters, and Carwyn would find work with other contractors hard to secure. Carwyn wasn't much of a salesman, so selling direct to households would be tough.

All these risks were serious. They were offset to a certain extent by Carwyn's track record in the maintenance team at Harvard University and his willingness to start making inquiries there and elsewhere. But Chuck was going to need some evidence that a return to employee status was likely, preferably with a firm offer in hand, before he would back Carwyn.

Some Examples for Employees

Elizabeth at ConsultCo

Chuck had already figured out what the key risk to Elizabeth's job prospects was. It was when he saw her expectations of work mix, hence pay mix, that alarm bells had rung. That was in the last chapter. But would it be balanced by opportunities identified elsewhere?

Yes and no. Sure, the market was due to bounce back after a few years in the doldrums. Sure, Elizabeth's interviewing skills and experience would hold her in good stead. But Chuck was concerned that Elizabeth may try to risk all on doing market research. Fine in ambition, but risky when it was clear to Chuck that her value to ConsultCo lay in her being a PA who could do market research well, rather than vice-versa.

That was risk 4—see Figure 8.14. After much discussion, Elizabeth came to understand Chuck's concern and assured him she would strive to maintain a balance between market research and admin work. That assurance was enough to persuade

Chuck that the cloud could be shifted a bit to the left.

The other risk that had troubled Chuck was the possibility of presenting becoming a must-have K2 (risk 2), not just an important should-have K2. Chuck concluded that this was a low-medium risk and one that he, and Elizabeth, would have to live with and keep an eye on. In the meantime, Elizabeth must not abandon her admin work.

Figure 8.14 **Risks and Opportunities for Elizabeth in Market Research Services to ConsultCo, Inc., and in Chicago**

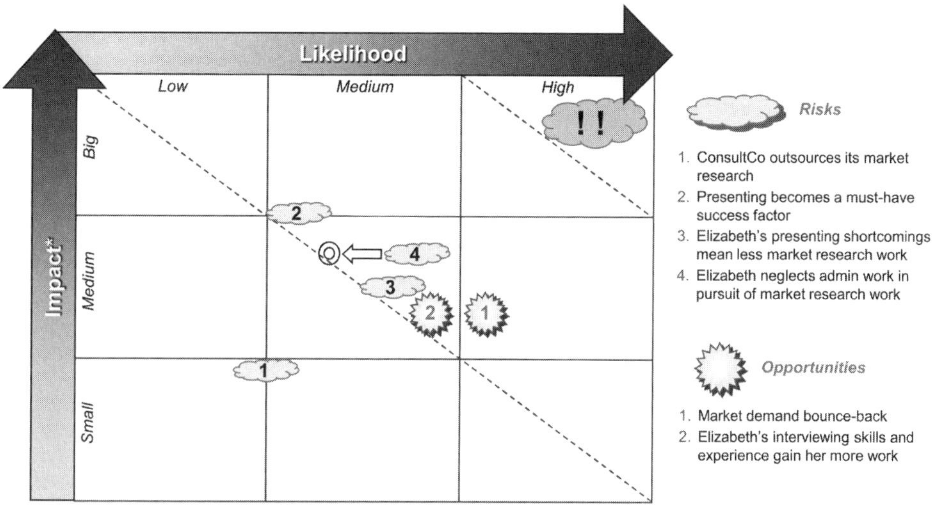

* Note: Over and above Elizabeth's pay expectations

Randy at Homes4U

It was the Suns & Clouds chart that sorted out Chuck's thinking on Randy. Randy was the top salesman at Homes4U. No doubt about that. He would probably be the last to be kicked out in the forthcoming market crash.

But Randy's income aspirations didn't match the difficult trading conditions Homes4U was likely to be facing over the next few years. And just how serious was Randy when he pondered over quitting and starting up as a plumber? Would the opportunities before this super-salesman outweigh the risks?

In Figure 8.15, Chuck relates the impact of risks and opportunities to his own flat forecasts of Randy's likely pay, not to Randy's expectations. If he had related them to Randy's forecasts, the chart would have shown clouds covering all the wrong places. And that wouldn't have helped Chuck in his backing decision.

Chuck found that the main opportunity facing Randy was overshadowed by the two main risks. The risk of Homes4U being badly hit by the market collapse was significant. But the greater risk concerned Randy's motivation—risk 5. If he really expected to grow his pay by 60 percent, in extremely difficult market conditions and with his enthusiasm possibly affected by his interest in plumbing, then Chuck would need to think very carefully about backing him.

Figure 8.15 **Risks and Opportunities for Randy in Realtor Services at Homes4U and in Atlanta**

Figure 8.15 **Risks and Opportunities for Randy in Realtor Services at Homes4U and in Atlanta**

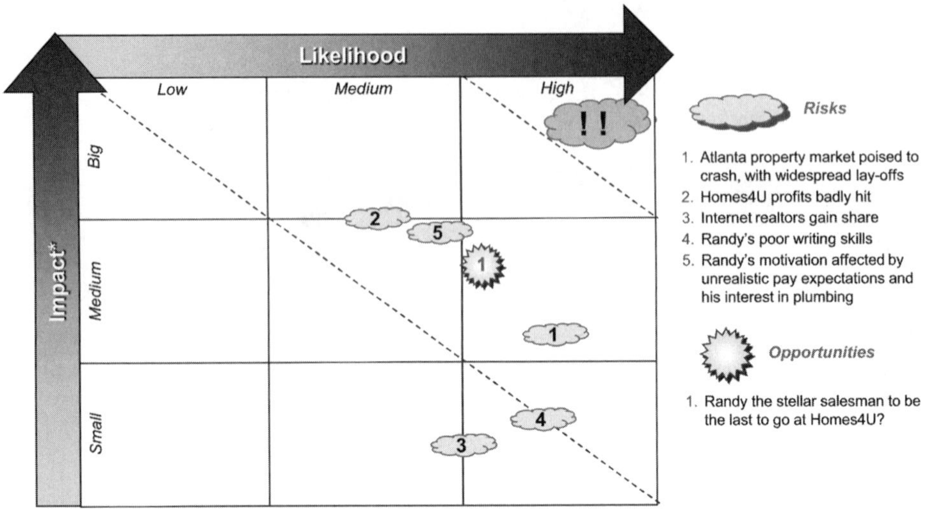

* Note: Over and above Randy's pay moving apace with inflation

The backing decision is almost made. You reviewed your plans in the last chapter and assessed risks and opportunities in this one. Let's move on to Chapter 9 for the final storyline.

Would You Back U?   9

In Chapter 8 you assessed whether the risks around achieving your business plan were surpassed by the opportunities of exceeding them. You're all but ready to conclude whether you're backable in your current job or business. All that's needed now is a simple storyline to underpin and justify your conclusion.

Putting It All in Context

This is the fun bit. All, yes, *all* the hard work has already been done. In each chapter you've had to do some serious research and thinking—about your markets (Chapter 2), your competition (Chapter 3), your K2 rating (Chapters 4 to 6), the achievability of your plans (Chapter 7), and the risks and opportunities around those plans (Chapter 8).

All you need to do now is take the headlines of your conclusions from each of those chapters and weave them into a coherent storyline. One that puts the backing decision in full context.

> It's not the size of the dog in the fight, it's the size of the fight in the dog.—*Mark Twain*

And that storyline will lead you to answer the key question behind Part I of this book: *Would you back U in your current business or job?*

Developing the Storyline

In this chapter you need to compose a series of conclusions, which when put together suggest the overall conclusion—the answer to the key question.

You should set the storyline out as follows.

The overall conclusion on why you are or aren't backable (in which you summarize the main findings from the headlines below):

➤ *Market demand prospects*—Your conclusions on what's going to happen to market demand, by key business chunk (Chapter 2).

➤ *Competition*—Your conclusions on whether competition is tough and going to get tougher, by key chunk (Chapter 3).

➤ *Your K2 rating*—Your conclusions on how you stack up to the competition, now and over the next few years, by key chunk (Chapter 6).

➤ *Your plan*—Your conclusions on whether your plans are achievable (Chapter 7).

➤ *Risks and opportunities*—Your conclusions on what main risks and opportunities are likely to affect your plan (Chapter 8).

This storyline must be concise. You must force yourself to get right to the point. *Each bullet point should be no more than one sentence.* It can have a couple of commas, with some backup qualifying phrases, maybe even a dash or a colon. But just the one sentence.

The more long-winded you make this storyline, the more difficult it will be to derive your overall conclusion—the answer. The answer itself should also be just the one sentence. The overall headline should address the question: *Would you back U?*

A Storyline for Sharon Stone Pre–*Basic Instinct*?

Let's take an example from the world of celebrity. It's 1992 and suppose our fictional Chuck Cash was thinking of backing a then little-known Hollywood actress, Sharon Stone. She has just been cast for the role of crime novelist Catherine Trammel in the planned movie *Basic Instinct*. Many of Hollywood's leading ladies have turned down the role, perhaps because of the risqué, occasionally violent sex scenes. Let's imagine that the funding Sharon is seeking from Chuck, perhaps for a move up the property ladder, depends on the success of this new movie.

Chuck's conclusions may have been along these lines.

Sharon seems set to shine in what could well be a high-grossing movie, enhancing her Hollywood marketability and enabling her to meet, even exceed, her plans:

➤ *Market demand prospects*—Demand for lead female actresses in Hollywood thrillers is buoyant, although hits in the steamy, femme fatale, *Body Heat* genre are infrequent.

> *Competition*—Competition for lead female roles gets stiffer by the year, but has been limited for this movie, with many stars turned off by its explicitness.
> *Sharon's K2 rating*—Sharon's career has been patchy, with forays into B movies, but this movie could make her highly marketable—her producers say her auditions were sensational, conveying smoldering sensuality and *sang froid.*
> *Sharon's plan*—Sharon's financial plans should be met if she acts on a par with her co-star, Michael Douglas, and greatly exceeded if the movie does well at the box office.
> *Risks and opportunities*—The opportunity for this movie to be a hit, with its blend of intrigue, lust and Californian splendor, seems to outweigh the risk of it flopping because of Sharon's current lack of star pull.

Note that each bulleted sentence represents the conclusion of one chapter, and that the overall conclusion, which sits firmly at the top, summarizes all the bullets below it. Based on that overall conclusion, would Chuck have backed Sharon? You bet!

After our excursion into the cosmos, let's get back down to earth.

Some Examples for the Self-Employed
Leila at Healing Hands

Is Chuck going to back Leila? Let's look at the storyline.

Leila is well positioned in the growing market of massage therapy services, with the major risk of an experienced new entrant seeming containable:

> *Market demand prospects*—Demand for aromatherapy services to stay-at-home moms should grow steadily, while reflexology to businesspeople could grow rapidly.
> *Competition*—Competition in massage services in West London is moderate at present, but entry barriers are low, especially in reflexology, and new entrants may well arrive as the market develops and if other areas get oversupplied.
> *Leila's K2 rating*—Leila is well placed in her moms market, less so for businesspeople, and her customer base would give her an edge against a well-trained new entrant.
> *Leila's plan*—Leila's plans in aromatherapy and reiki seem reasonable but challenging in reflexology, although Leila should achieve good growth overall in her business.
> *Risks and opportunities*—The major risks of an experienced therapist moving to the area and Ying quitting seem balanced by the opportunity of market demand taking off in reflexology.

The answer is yes. Chuck will back Leila. His investment is not without risk, but no investment ever is.

If you were Leila, would you back U in your current business? The answer should be the same—yes.

Carwyn the Carpenter

What about Carwyn? Will Chuck back him? Let's take a look at his storyline.

Carwyn's position in Boston carpentry is slipping and he is vulnerable to the imminent downturn in loft extensions—he needs to seek employment in maintenance *now*:

> ➤ *Market demand prospects*—Demand for carpentry in Boston is likely to be flat over the next few years, once the boom in loft extensions has abated.
>
> ➤ *Competition*—Competition will intensify as demand slackens off, although many non-Bostonian migrants may return to whence they came.
>
> ➤ *Carwyn's K2 rating*—Carwyn is still an excellent carpenter, but time may not be on his side as the labor market toughens.
>
> ➤ *Carwyn's plan*—Carwyn's plans

to maintain current revenues seem challenging, and he should consider returning to employment in maintenance.

> ➤ *Risks and opportunities*—Market and competitive risks greatly outweigh opportunities, the most promising being a return to maintenance employment.

The answer is no. Chuck is not going to back Carwyn at this point in time. It's just too risky. He's only reasonably positioned in a chunk of the market poised for contraction. And his position is heading south. Chuck will ask Carwyn to come back and see him once he has a job offer, preferably as a full-time employee in maintenance work for a stable, reputable employer.

If you were Carwyn, would you back U in your current business? Unlikely. It's time to look elsewhere, and the sooner the better.

Some Examples for Employees

Elizabeth at ConsultCo

Will Chuck back Elizabeth, the first of our two employee exemplars? Let's look at the storyline.

Elizabeth is distinctly placed at ConsultCo and should prosper there as long as she sticks to her core competencies of PA first, market research second:

> ➤ *Market demand prospects*—Demand for market research services is set to recover following the dot-com bubble burst, with ConsultCo likely to outpace the market.
>
> ➤ *Competition*—Competition is stiff among market research houses but should ease off as market demand recovers.
>
> ➤ *Elizabeth's K2 rating*—Elizabeth

is favorably placed in market research against the bright young consultants at Consult-Co, but may slip back if greater emphasis is placed on presenting skills.

> ➤ *Elizabeth's plan*—Elizabeth's financial targets should be achievable as long as she stays a PA who also does market research, rather than vice-versa.
>
> ➤ *Risks and opportunities*—The most serious risk is if Elizabeth neglects admin work in the single-minded pursuit of market research work.

The answer is a qualified yes. Chuck will back Elizabeth as long as she guarantees she will remain with her main job as a PA and not attempt to switch roles to that of a full-time market researcher.

If you were Elizabeth, would you back U in your current job? The answer should be the same—yes, as long as you recognize that your bread and butter resides in admin work, and your jam in market research.

Randy at Homes4U

Finally, will Chuck back Randy? What's his storyline?

Randy could hold his job in the teetering Atlanta realty market, but his income expectations are unrealistic and he needs to make up his mind on a career switch to plumbing:

> *Market demand prospects*— Demand for real estate services in Atlanta is poised for a nosedive, with Homes4U revenues set to shrink along with the rest of the market.

> *Competition*—Realtors will compete on price to hold up transaction volumes, many firms will plunge into the red, and widespread redundancies can be expected.

> *Randy's K2 rating*—Randy is an exceptional Realtor and could be the last to be let go, but his heart seems to be in plumbing.

> *Randy's plan*—Randy's income aspirations over the next three years are unlikely to be met, even if he held his job, although they could perhaps be met if he succeeded as a plumber.

> *Risks and opportunities*—Randy's

future motivation as a Realtor is as much a risk as that of market collapse, while plumbing seems an unproven opportunity.

The answer is no. Chuck won't back Randy until he makes up his mind. If he decides to stay in realty and accepts that he needs to tighten his belt over the next couple of years, fine, Chuck will rethink things. If he quits and tries his hand in plumbing, Chuck will ask him to come back and let him know how he has got on after a few months. He wishes Randy well, although behind his back he is fuming that Randy didn't tell him his mind was set on plumbing from the outset. It would have saved Chuck a good couple of days' work!

If you were Randy, would you back U in your current job? If you were honest with yourself, the answer would have to be no. You're in a job that you're darned good at, but it's not where you want to be. And with the forthcoming market downturn, it's not where you're going to make your numbers. Time to stop day-dreaming and start doing something about a career in plumbing?

A Storyline for Backing the Beatles

We saw in Chapter 8 a couple of Suns & Clouds charts that might have helped Parlophone producer George Martin finalize his decision on backing the Beatles in early 1962. Let's look at what may have been the full storyline.

The Beatles don't seem musically outstanding, but they have charisma and could extend their popularity beyond Liverpool:

> *Market demand prospects*—Demand for Buddy Holly–style beat groups seems set to remain and could reach a wider audience.

> *Competition*—There are a dozen or more beat groups in Liverpool alone, and countrywide it'll be difficult to differentiate one from another.

> *The Beatles' K2 rating*—The Beatles don't seem particularly musical, they look silly and behave badly, but their humor and charisma could extend their popularity beyond their home town.

> *The Beatles' plan*—Their financial targets aren't unreasonable and could readily be met with some hit covers—much more so if they could write their own tracks.

> *Risks and opportunities*—Risks seem to overshadow opportunities, but they've got something and may be worth a shot.

Should he have backed the Beatles? Yes. If you were Paul McCartney in early 1962, would you have backed U in your current business? Of course. You were in the right business. You knew you were good at it, you loved it, and the sky was the limit.

My Storyline: Why I Wrote This Book

In the next section, I am going to suggest that you write your own storyline to answer the basic question of Part I of this book: Would you back U in your current business or job?

It's only fair that I be prepared to do what I'll be asking you to do. In short, would I back *me* in my current business?

Let me briefly give you some background. I was an economist by training and spent the first dozen years of my career after university working as an economist in various idyllic tropical locations such as the British Virgin Islands, Borneo, Java, Thailand, and Fiji. I suspected that carefree times couldn't last forever, so I enrolled in business school and ended up incarcerated in a London investment bank. I belatedly escaped, and after a brief foray into politics, worked with a terrific U.S.–based management and technology consulting firm for 10 years. Sadly, it went under, and now I'm an independent consultant, working with a network of fellow freelancers under the banner of Vaughan Evans & Partners (VEP). I specialize in advising companies and financiers on the risks and opportunities of investing in businesses, typically small- or medium-sized. This work is similar to what you find here in Part I of this book, and it's called strategic due diligence (SDD).

Here's the storyline I developed in 2005, having applied the *Backing U!* tools on myself:

VEP's offering is distinctive, but leads to fluctuating utilization, so downtime needs to be better used to diversify into areas such as writing:

> *Market demand prospects*—Demand for SDD recovered in 2005 after its deep recession of 2002–2004 and should remain buoyant over the next few years. (Yes, I too failed to spot the looming credit crunch!)
> *Competition*—Competition has intensified greatly in the 2000s, with top-tier providers more aggressive on pricing and low-cost providers upping their game.
> *VEP's K2 rating*—VEP's SDD offering (top-tier quality @ low overhead pricing = exceptional value added to client) is distinctive, but lack of critical mass constrains regular flow of work.
> *VEP's plan*—VEP's SDD activity levels and revenues fluctuate widely, so downtime needs to be used more productively to assure financial targets.
> *Risks and opportunities*—VEP is overly exposed to the volatility of SDD work and needs to diversify into areas such as writing and speaking.

And that's why I'm writing this book. Would I back *me* in my current business? Tricky question. My revenues from SDD go up and down like a yo-yo. One quarter they're hot, next quarter they're not. They're like London buses—none comes for ages, then three arrive at the same time (and you can only jump onto one!). Spread over the year, they're okay, but Chuck would prefer less volatility, more predictability. It took me a while to recognize that the VEP model could only ever be like that. If I were to better use downtime to diversify earnings—for example, through writing then speaking about this book—then I might back me.

What's Your Storyline?

I've done it. Now it's your turn. It may not be pretty. The fact that you're reading this book means you may harbor some doubts on your backability.

> You never achieve real success unless you like what you are doing.
> —*Dale Carnegie*

There's one thing I've learned. It's better to be honest and *dispassionate* in assessing your own backability. When I launched my consulting business a few years ago, my analysis was crammed throughout with wishful thinking. Perhaps it served a purpose in boosting my confidence—it can be lonely working from home. But I was fooling myself.

Worse, it pushed back the dawn of realization by a couple of years. It then took two years (of downtime) to write this book, and plus another two (interminable!) years for publishing, so my diversification arrived much later than it need have done.

So try to be totally objective. Think what Chuck Cash would conclude.

Not what you'd want him to conclude. Develop a fair and balanced storyline, but make sure it's independent, hard-hitting, and conclusive.

Would You Back U in Your Current Business or Job?

Once you've developed your storyline, that's almost it. Would you back U in your current business or job? *Yes,* or *no.* Or perhaps, *yes, if...* Or even, *no, but ...*

Only those who dare to fail greatly can ever achieve greatly.—Robert F. Kennedy

If the answer is *yes,* or *yes, if...,* then you should find Part II helpful. This shows how you can set about performing even better in your current business or job.

If the answer is *no,* or *no, but...,* then you should turn to Part III (see Figure 9.1). You need to find a business or job where you stand a better chance of succeeding. Part III will show you how to find a career where you aspire to be, a career that inspires you.

It will show you how to back the passion in you.

Figure 9.1 **Moving on to *Backing U!* Part II or Part III?**

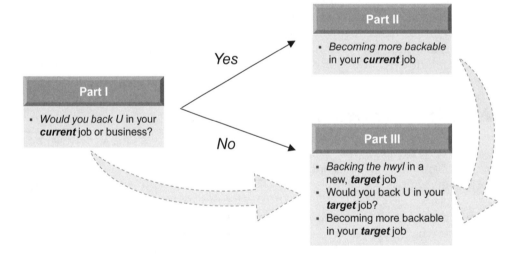

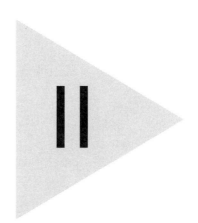

Becoming
More Backable

Introduction

Part II is for you if you concluded in Part I that you would back U in your current job or business. Your earnings target is likely to be met. Opportunities seem to outshine the risks in your current field.

If you were dissatisfied with your job before reading Part I, perhaps you are a trifle less so now? Were you perhaps suffering from the human tendency to see the grass as greener on the other side? Has the grass on your own side started to turn a shade or two greener? I hope so.

All that is human must retrograde if it does not advance.—Edward Gibbon

Part II builds on the work you have already carried out in Part I. It shows you how to improve your prospects in your current field, shortening the odds on success, and making yourself more backable.

Part II does this in a sequence of steps. These are similar to those used in drawing up an ambitious strategy for a business, large or small, and are readily applicable to drawing up an ambitious personal development strategy, whether for an employee or the self-employed. They are:

➤ Envision the capabilities of the ideal provider (Chapter 10)
➤ Stretch your sights and identify the capability gap (Chapter 11)
➤ Select your strategy to bridge the capability gap (Chapter 12)

Chapter 10 envisions the future and the ideal provider of the type of services you offer. It encourages you to think "out of the box" about how things may evolve in the markets and companies you serve. It pushes you to think more creatively than you may have done in Part I on the future of your marketplace in each of your main business chunks. It suggests that you build scenarios ("What if such-and-such happens?") about the future and consider what would be the capabilities of the ideal provider of services under each scenario. You then deduce what capabilities would be common to these providers in all or most of the scenarios. These could become target capabilities for which you aim.

Chapter 11 starts by reviewing your overall strategic position by means of the Strategic Bubble Bath chart. You'll map how well placed you are in your main business chunks, ranked by how attractive each chunk is. You can then reconsider where you aim to be in three to five years' time. If your plans in your current business do indeed seem achievable, as concluded in Part I, are you sure you have set sufficiently challenging goals for yourself? Should you stay with these business chunks or venture into new ones? Should you be aiming to become the ideal provider in your type of service? Should you be stretching your sights and making your plans more ambitious? Should you be "going for goal"?

The chapter then suggests that you revisit the assessment of your strengths and weaknesses in Chapter 6 for each of your main business chunks. You'll do this in the light of the scenarios you've developed and your newly reset sights. This will lead you to identify the shortfall between your current capabilities and the capabilities to which you aspire—the K2 gap.

Nothing is harder on your laurels than resting on them.
—Anonymous

In Chapter 12, you'll select a strategy on how to bridge the K2 gap. You'll be introduced to the three main generic strategies, which we call *Stand Out!, easyU!,* and *Sharpen Act!* We look at Madonna's distinctive and highly successful strategy. You'll be shown how to develop your strategic options, which may include investment in marketing and training if you're an employee, possibly self-financed. If you're self-employed, further areas of investment may include premises, equipment, staff, or partnership. You'll be shown how to evaluate these options and how to build a realistic action plan.

In Chapter 13, we look at the possibility of you as an employee becoming self-employed. One alternative that may have emerged in Part I is for you to carry on doing the same job, initially for your same company, but independently, running your own business. In other words, you outsource yourself. Your form your own company, typically called NewCo in the world of corporate finance, and in this case UCo. This chapter sets out the main pros and cons of going independent. And it offers a host of tips, especially in the crucial area of sales and marketing, where so many of the newly self-employed founder.

Chapter 14 reviews where you could end up having followed the initiatives set out in Chapters 10 through 13. Having envisioned the ideal provider, reset your sights, identified the gaps, built on your strengths and worked on your weaknesses, and possibly having launched UCo, you should now be better placed against your peers.

How would that impact on your K2 rating of Chapter 6? To what extent will your Suns & Clouds chart of Chapter 8 have become sunnier? Will the balance of risks and opportunities have shifted in your favor?

Will U have become even more backable in your current job or business? That's the intention. First, let's do some brainstorming.

Envision the Capabilities of the Ideal Provider

> **Envision Future Scenarios**
> **Profile the Ideal Provider in Each Scenario**
> **Identify Common Capabilities**

Chapter 10 envisions the future marketplace and the ideal provider of the type of services you offer. It suggests that you build scenarios about the future and consider what the capabilities of the ideal provider of services under each scenario would be. Then you can deduce what capabilities are common to these providers in all or most of the scenarios. These could then become the minimum target capabilities for which you can aim.

Envision Future Scenarios

The first step in making yourself more backable is to envision the future of the marketplace in which you work. Will it be more competitive? Will customers have different expectations? Will providers need to develop different capabilities?

To do this, it helps if you can do some brainstorming. Brainstorming may conjure up images of smart, flashy yuppies pacing around the conference room table fixing yellow stickies to flipcharts, while nibbling on their Brazil nuts and dried apricots and sipping Perrier. Perhaps—and fine if that's you—but there are plenty of other ways of brainstorming.

I am enough of an artist to draw freely upon my imagination. Imagination is more important than knowledge. Knowledge is limited. Imagination encircles the world.—Albert Einstein

What you do need to do is try to think a bit more creatively and laterally than you may have done in Chapters 2 through 4. You need to go beyond those chapters. You need to get the right-hand side of the brain working.

Different folks have different strokes for thinking laterally. Some think most creatively in bed, some in front of a log fire, others in a place of worship. Some visualize, some meditate, others soak in a flotation tank. Me? I walk. The setting has to be green, preferably with plenty of blue. The cliff paths of the West Wales coastline are perfect, with fields, hedgerows, and baaing sheep to one side, the Cambrian Sea, rocks, and squawking cormorants to the other. If I can't be there, a park or a golf course will have to do, preferably with a lake or pond, and some wildfowl waddling around.

Do not quench your inspiration and your imagination. Do not become the slave of your model.
—*Vincent van Gogh*

Wherever and however you do it, you need to stimulate those gray cells to think creatively. In Chapter 2, you looked at market-demand drivers in each of your main business chunks and how they may change, thereby influencing demand for your services in the future. In essence, you were more or less extrapolating the past into the future.

Seven, eight, nine times out of ten, perhaps, such extrapolation should suffice. The most likely tends to happen. But what if the unexpected happens? To one or more demand drivers in a business chunk? What if a previously unconsidered driver becomes important? What if demand lifts off in a related chunk? What if market demand in one of your chunks should start to blur with that in another chunk? Perhaps one where you are worse (or better) placed than in the initial chunk?

Likewise for competition and customer needs. To what extent did your thinking in Chapters 3 and 4 reflect an extrapolation of the past into the future? Sure, you had to come up with the most likely developments in the competitive environment, the most likely developments in customer needs. That's what Chuck needed to know. But what about other less likely but possible developments?

Try to brainstorm a range of scenarios on what may happen in your marketplace. Venture beyond the more likely outcomes; you've already drawn those up. Think of those that are less

Every child is an artist. The problem is how to remain an artist once he grows up.
—*Pablo Picasso*

expected but still *quite* likely to occur. Stay clear of fanciful outcomes with only a remote chance of happening. Go for scenarios that could actually happen. Apply the reasonability test: "Is it reasonable for me to assume that such-and-such an outcome could take place over the next five years? Sure it may be less likely to happen than the other outcome, but looking back five years from now would I be surprised that it actually happened?"

If this whole brainstorming thing is not really for you, don't worry. There's a shortcut. In truth you've probably already identified the most important of the scenarios in Part I. And you've probably already translated them into risks and opportunities in your Suns & Clouds chart of Chapter 8. You can use them. You may need to develop them a bit further, but that shouldn't be too troublesome.

For those of you happy to press on with brainstorming, it's likely that one or two of your chosen scenarios will still be lifted from your Suns & Clouds chart. This is inevitable. In that chart you pulled together all the main risks and opportunities you had identified in the preceding chapters. Some of these, whether for good or bad, could readily be developed into scenarios.

Other scenarios, especially on the opportunity side, could be new. They'll be incremental to those shown on your Suns & Clouds chart. They should hopefully reflect the "out of the box" nature of your brainstorming. They may steer you in a new and promising direction.

> The man who has no imagination has no wings.
> —Muhammad Ali

Settle on *two to four scenarios*. Give each a name, something that brings the scenario to life.

An Example: Leila at Healing Hands

Let's take as an example Leila, our aromatherapist, who has just been backed by Chuck Cash. He has advised her that she should build on the work they did together in Part I of this book. All that research and analysis can be used as a foundation toward making Leila even more backable.

Leila is in the alternative health business and she knows exactly how to relax. Among her other capabilities, she's a yogi. So she puts aside a whole morning and clears her appointments diary. She does all her routine warm-up exercises, then embarks on a prolonged yoga session. She lets her mind float around what her markets and customers may look like in five years' time.

Her starting point is what she and Chuck concluded as being most likely in her two main business chunks. They'd found that demand by stay-at-home moms for aromatherapy is likely to be steady, while demand by businesspeople for reflexology should grow rapidly. On the competition front, they'd acknowledged that there was a threat from a similarly qualified practitioner setting up in Leila's catchment area. On customer needs, they'd found that rapport with the masseuse and price would become more important needs over time. What could reasonably happen beyond that?

In her long yoga session, Leila envisions the future. She doesn't confine her thinking to issues specifically concerning market demand, competition, or customer needs. She lets her mind float freely among all three areas. She comes up with four scenarios, as follows, each appropriately and catchingly named:

➤ *Foot-ure*—Businesspeople may be more interested in Thai foot massage than reflexology.

➤ *Soma-therapy*—Local moms may be interested in higher value healing oils for use in aromatherapy, or color therapy oils, such as aurasoma.

➤ *Wonderwoman*—A well-qualified, highly experienced therapist may move into Notting Hill to escape a more competitive area, such as Mayfair or Chelsea.

> *Gong*—Ying leaves to set up a reflexology business on her own.

Neither of the first two scenarios was directly factored into Chuck's backability analysis. Neither is highly likely to happen in the next five years, but each of them, it seems to Leila, is reasonably likely to happen. The Wonderwoman and Gong scenarios, on the other hand, were specifically recognized by Chuck as the biggest risks facing Leila's business—as shown in her Suns & Clouds chart in Chapter 8. No envisioning of the future could be credible without considering those two scenarios.

If You're an Employee

If you're an employee, you need to follow the same brainstorming process as for the self-employed. But remember that you need to do the thinking at two different levels, just as in Part I. Where might market demand for your type of services be heading *in general*, and more specifically where might demand for your type of services be heading *within your company or organization?*

Likewise for the competition. How is competition for your type of services shaping up in your town, region, country? And how is it shaping up in your company?

And for customer needs. How are the needs of users of your type of services changing in your town, region, country? And how are the needs of your "customers"—your colleagues—in your company changing?

An Example: Elizabeth at ConsultCo

Let's see how successful our PA-cum-market-researcher Elizabeth was with her brainstorming. Like Leila, she's just been backed by Chuck and has received the same advice on building on the work done in Part I to make herself more backable.

The trouble is that Elizabeth is not really one for free flowing thinking. She regards herself as a highly practical person. She gets on with the job at hand, whether at the office or at home. She's more a doer than a thinker, and when she does pause to think, it tends to be of the straight-line variety.

Nevertheless she has a go. It seems a shame not to, after all that hard work getting Chuck to back her. She treats herself to a quality bottle of Napa Valley cabernet and spoils herself with lengthy, hot, candle-lit baths two nights in a row. That seems to do the trick, and she comes up with three scenarios:

> *Copycat*—Another PA at ConsultCo decides to follow Elizabeth's lead and help out on market research assignments.
> *Bite the Bullet*—Presentation and communication skills for market researchers become essential.
> *Eventful*—Given the business pickup at ConsultCo, Elizabeth has heard that more marketing events are likely to be held and the

slimmed-down marketing team may need some extra help in organization.

The first of these scenarios wasn't factored into Chuck's backability analysis. Indeed, Elizabeth didn't mention to Chuck that one of her PA colleagues, Irene, had asked Elizabeth in passing how she managed to get started in market research work. Copycat wasn't that likely to happen, but it could and no one would be entirely surprised if Irene, or even the rather pushy Jane, followed Elizabeth's example.

> Think left and think right and think low and think high. Oh, the thinks you can think up if only you try!—*Dr. Seuss*

But it was the presentation skills scenario that plagued Elizabeth most. It was the most severe market risk she and Chuck had found. In the Suns & Clouds chart, they had placed it as low to medium likelihood but high impact. Perhaps there was just no way round it. If her senior managers were going to expect their market researchers to stand up and present their findings to the client, then she may have to prepare for it. She may have to bite the bullet.

The third of these scenarios would be a new chunk, one that had some appeal to Elizabeth. She got on well with the people on the marketing team. They were an outgoing bunch and enjoyed pressing flesh at the marketing events they arranged. But they found the pre-event organization rather tedious. Elizabeth liked arranging and organizing things and thought she'd make a good fit.

Profile the Ideal Provider in Each Scenario

You already had a go at assessing the Key Kapabilities (K2s) required for providers of your type of services to meet the needs of your customers—see Chapter 5. Now you should consider what K2s are required to meet possibly changed future customer needs under each of the scenarios you have envisioned. Some K2s may differ in importance, and weighting, compared to before. Some may be brand new. The new and re-weighted K2s need to be drawn up for each scenario.

The ideal provider in any scenario will be the person who rates highly against each of the K2s for that scenario. Some examples may help.

Leila has developed four scenarios that are reasonably likely to happen: Foot-ure, Soma-therapy, Wonderwoman, and Gong. She believes that the ideal provider under each of these scenarios will need these capabilities over and above those set out in Chapter 5 during Chuck's analysis:

➢ *Foot-ure*—A qualification, preferably a certificate, in Thai foot massage, backed up by experience and reinforced by sound technique. Hygiene may increase in importance.

➢ *Soma-therapy*—Knowledge and experience of the benefits of different healing oils, and in the case of aurasoma, perhaps a qualification from an appropriate institute.

➢ *Wonderwoman*—A greater emphasis on customer rapport and

marketing capabilities, reinforced perhaps by an effective customer loyalty scheme.

> *Gong*—No specific extra capabilities in this scenario—just good managerial skills in managing Ying's expectations at Healing Hands.

Elizabeth meanwhile believes that the ideal provider under her three scenarios will require these capabilities over and above those set out in Chapter 5:

> *Copycat*—A greater emphasis perhaps on internal marketing and self-promotion to colleagues.
> *Bite the Bullet*—A greater emphasis on presenting skills, given its possible conversion to a must-have K2.
> *Eventful*—No new skills, just plenty of enthusiasm for working on basic organizational tasks for marketing events.

Each of these scenarios may happen, or none may happen. If one of them does happen, it might have implications for Leila's or Elizabeth's K2 rating. In the next chapter, we'll see what they need to do to prepare for and address such an eventuality.

Identify Common Capabilities

Having determined the required extra capabilities for each scenario, the final step in envisioning the ideal provider is to identify what capabilities are common to each of the scenarios. These could become target capabilities on which you can set your sights.

You must not forget here your original, most likely scenario, the one developed in Part I. The capabilities that were identified and weighted there remain the most important, since they are the ones most likely to be needed. Those you are now adding or reconsidering may represent just the icing on the cake.

Lack of commonality doesn't necessarily mean that isolated K2s are unimportant. But it does mean that, in the next chapter, you may choose not to take a particular K2 into account. You won't have the time or resources to prepare for every eventuality. Choices will have to be made. You'll need to formulate a strategy and pursue it.

Let's see whether there are any common extra capabilities needed for the ideal providers under each of Leila's scenarios. At first sight, there doesn't seem much overlap. They are:

> Training in Thai foot massage
> Training in aurasoma
> Hygiene
> Customer loyalty scheme
> Managerial skills

The only two that have any commonality with the K2s developed in

Chapter 5 are hygiene and managerial skills, where they were already considered important and given a reasonable weighting. But perhaps they should be given greater emphasis in Leila's plans.

In the next couple of chapters, we'll see what strategy Leila develops in response to her envisioning the future. Will she pursue a new business chunk, whether Thai foot massage or color healing? Remember that this would be in addition to her and Ying setting forth in the new chunk of reflexology. Will she stick to the plans she set out for Chuck, but work on some sort of customer loyalty scheme? Will she be flexible in sharing revenues with Ying? She'll need to set her sights and choose her strategy.

Elizabeth also didn't at first see much commonality between the extra capabilities required by the ideal provider under each of her three scenarios. They were:

➢ Internal marketing and self-promotion
➢ Presentational skills
➢ Organizational skills

Yet upon further inspection there was a common thread. The first two scenarios, although not the third, seemed to require someone with a forceful, self-assured personality to succeed in them. This gave Elizabeth food for thought as she set out to ponder her strategy in Chapter 11.

What scenarios do you envision in your marketplace? What extra capabilities will the ideal provider require in each scenario? Which capabilities are common? How may they influence the K2s needed to succeed?

You're drawing a picture of the ideal provider in your marketplace over the next few years. In the next chapter, you'll ponder to what extent you should aim to acquire the capabilities of the ideal provider.

Stretch Your Sights and Identify the Capability Gap

11

- ▶ **Do Your Sights Need Stretching?**
- ▶ **Set Out Your Strategic Position**
- ▶ **How Close to the Ideal Provider?**
- ▶ **Identify the K2 Gap**
- ▶ **An Example for the Self-Employed**
- ▶ **An Example for an Employee**

Chapter 10 envisioned the future marketplace and the ideal provider of the type of services you offer under various scenarios. You drew up some capabilities that may be needed to compete in your marketplace over the next few years.

This chapter starts by mapping your strategic position—how well placed you are in your main business chunks, ranked by how attractive each chunk is. It then asks you to reconsider where you aim to be in three, five years' time. If your plans in your current business do indeed seem achievable, as concluded in Part I, are you sure you've set sufficiently challenging goals for yourself?

Should you stay with these business chunks, or should you venture into new ones? Should you be aiming to become the ideal provider in your type of service? Should you be stretching your sights and making your plans more ambitious? Should you be "going for goal"?

Hide not your talents, they for use were made. What's a sundial in the shade?
—Benjamin Franklin

You then revisit the assessment of your strengths and weaknesses in Chapter 6 in the light of the scenarios you've developed and your newly reset sights. And you identify the shortfall between your current capabilities and the capabilities to which you aspire. This is the K2 gap. In the next chapter, you'll set out to select a strategy on how realistically to bridge this gap.

149

Do Your Sights Need Stretching?

Where do you want to be in your current job or business in three, five years' time? What's your vision of yourself? Do you envision being more or less where you are today, doing more or less the same things, serving more or less the same customers?

Only those who will risk going too far can possibly find out how far one can go—T. S. Eliot

If the answer is a yes, or a rather less committal "I suppose so," that's fine. You're backable anyway. That's why you're reading Part II of this book.

If, however, you're of a more ambitious nature, you may want to raise those sights. Sure, you're backable now, but how about becoming more backable? How about raising the bar on your potential achievements? How about raising the return on your investment in yourself?

If you're an employee, try thinking of yourself as a business. Chuck Cash has already agreed to back you in your current career. He figures he'll get an acceptable rate of return from you. But think how pleased he would be if you managed to give him an annual rate of return 1 percent, 2 percent, even 5 percent higher than what he'd expected? And if he's going to get a higher return, think how much higher yours would be!

That's just one side of the coin, I know. The other side is the nonmonetary, which may, of course, be much more important to you. Especially if your financial circumstances seem reasonably under control. Caring for or helping other people may be your main driver of job satisfaction, letting the money side of things hang. That's fine and admirable. But the bills need to be paid.

Achievement is largely the product of steadily raising one's levels of aspiration... and expectation.—Jack Nicklaus

However you take these nonmonetary factors into account, you may still benefit from coming up with an answer. Where do you want to be in your current job or business in three or five years' time? Do your sights need raising?

There are three main aspects of setting and possibly raising your sights:

1. Which business chunks should you address? The same as now, or promising others?
2. In which business chunks should you become more competitive and improve your K2 rating?
3. How close to the ideal provider should you become in the chunks of your choice?

Deciding on the first two of these can be facilitated with the *Strategic Bubble Bath* chart. For the third, we'll meet the *Going for Goal* chart.

Set Out Your Strategic Position

In Part I you declared yourself backable in your current career. That's why you're reading Part II. This implies that the main business chunks you address are in at least reasonably attractive markets (Chapters 1 through 3) and that you are at least reasonably placed in those chunks (Chapter 6).

In setting your sights for the next few years, however, would you like to reset them to address another business chunk (or chunks) that are in *more* attractive markets than the ones you currently address? If so, do you have grounds for believing that you would be at least reasonably placed in this new chunk? Or that you could readily become reasonably placed?

Meanwhile, are there any business chunks where the markets are less attractive from which you should consider withdrawing? Or where your K2 rating is not that good?

Furthermore, isn't it time we redefined what we mean by an attractive business chunk? In the business world, the definition is relatively straightforward. Market attractiveness is typically taken to be a blend of these four factors:

1. Market size
2. Market demand growth
3. Competitive intensity
4. Market risk

These factors remain valid for an individual as well. But they're not sufficient. They make no allowance for the soul, for the subjective—something that's often treated as irrelevant in the corporate world.

We need to add at least a fifth factor, which we can term *enjoyment* (or *fulfillment*, if you prefer). This should give the definition of attractiveness a better balance.

If you're thinking of resetting your sights to address a more attractive business chunk, you should look before you leap. Just do a wee check on why you think the new chunk might be more attractive. You can either do it in your head, or like me, you may choose to draw up a simple table. As usual you can choose to populate each cell with words, ticks, or numbers. I prefer numbers, since they enable you to calculate a simple average, yielding a useful pecking order for the chunks.

Figure 11.1 shows an example of someone who is in four business chunks and is contemplating getting into a fifth. Chuck has backed her, so she must already be in reasonably attractive chunks.

Chunk D emerges as the most attractive, followed by new chunk E. B is rather unattractive. In assessing overall attractiveness, she has gone for a simple average of the ratings against each factor. She could instead have opted for a weighting system, yielding a weighted average. Or she could, say, have double-counted one of the factors, say enjoyment. More accurate, perhaps, but she went for simplicity.

Figure 11.1 **Attractiveness of Business Chunks: An Example**

Business Chunks	Market Size	Market Growth	Competitive Intensity	Market Risk	Enjoyment	Average Attract-iveness
A	3	1	2	3	5	2.8
B	2	2	2	3	2	2.2
C	2	3	3	4	4	3.2
D	3	5	4	2	4	3.6
E (New)	3	4	5	2	2	3.2

Key to Rating: 1 = Unattractive, 3 = Reasonably Attractive, 5 = Highly Attractive
[For competitive intensity, remember that the more intense the competition, the *less*
attractive the market. Likewise for Market Risk: the riskier the market, the **less** attractive]

One word of warning! When assigning a rating to competitive intensity, remember that the more intense the competition, the *less* attractive the chunk. A highly competitive chunk would get an attractiveness rating of 1 (not 5!). It's the same for market risk. The riskier the market, the *less* attractive it is, so the lower the rating. The other factors are more straightforward—the larger the market, the faster it's growing or the more enjoyable it is for you, the higher the rating.

The next step is to pull out the K2 ratings she would have drawn up in Chapter 6 for each of her main business chunks. For example, she may have assessed a K2 rating of 4.0 for chunk A, 2.6 for B, 3.4 for C and 3.7 for D. E is a new chunk, but she figures she could become reasonably competitive within a year and achieve a rating of 3.0.

She's now ready to draw up a Strategic Bubble Bath chart. Each business chunk is represented by a bubble. Its position will reflect her K2 rating (along the bottom of the bath) against the attractiveness of the chunk (up the side of the bath). The size of each bubble should be roughly proportional to the scale of revenues she currently derives from the chunk.

In a strategic bubble bath, the closer your chunks float to the top right-hand corner the better placed you are. Above the top right dotted diagonal, you should be thinking of investing further in that chunk. Should your bubble sink to below the bottom left dotted diagonal, however, you should seriously consider getting out of that chunk.

The strategic position shown in Figure 11.2 is sound. It shows reasonable strength in the biggest and reasonably attractive chunk, C, and an excellent position in the slightly less attractive chunk A. Chunk D is highly promising and demands more attention, given the currently low level of revenues. Chunk B should perhaps be exited—it's a rather unattractive chunk, and she's not that well placed. The new chunk E seems reasonably promising.

Figure 11.2 **Strategic Bubble Bath: An Example**

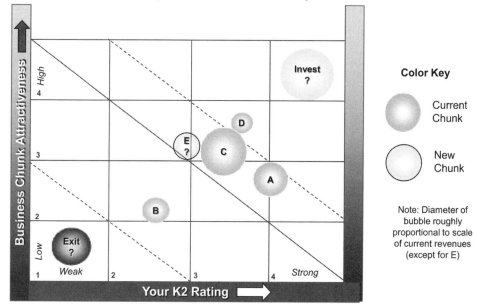

In setting her sights, this exemplar may consider the following worth pursuing, subject to evaluation of her strategic options in the next chapter—see Figure 11.3:

> ➤ Continued development in chunks A and C.
> ➤ Investment in chunk D (see arrow showing the resultant improved K2 rating).
> ➤ Entry to chunk E (with her K2 rating improving with experience).
> ➤ Exit from chunk B (see the cross).

Try setting out your own strategic bubble bath. It should look good. You found that you were backable in Part I, so your strategic position should be sound. Your *main* chunks, from which you derive most revenues, should find themselves positioned above the main diagonal.

Do you have any new chunks in mind that you are thinking of moving into? How attractive are they? How well placed would you be?

Are there any chunks you should be thinking of getting out of?

Which chunks are so important that you would derive greatest benefit from improving your K2 rating? Where should you concentrate your efforts?

Those are your sights. Should they be stretched? How close to the ideal provider of services in one or more of those key business chunks do you aim to become?

Figure 11.3 Strategic Bubble Bath and Sight Setting: An Example

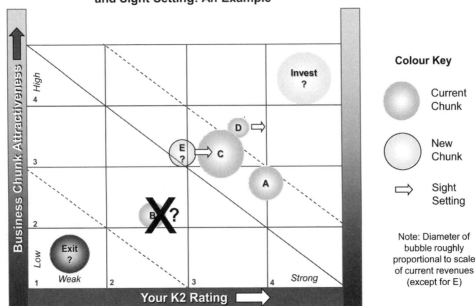

How Close to the Ideal Provider?

In Part I, you identified your strengths and weaknesses and rated them against the Key Kapabilities required to compete in each of your main business chunks. You found that there was a gap between your overall rating and that of the ideal provider, who realistically would have gained a rating of between 4 and 5 against each K2.

In the last chapter, you envisioned scenarios where new K2s may be required or existing K2s gain in prominence. These could further widen the K2 gap—if you were to sit still.

> If you want to be successful, find someone who has achieved the results you want and copy what they do and you'll achieve the same results.—*Anthony Robbins*

Where do you want to be in tomorrow's marketplace? Are your sights currently set on bridging the K2 gap found in Part I? Or should you consider raising your sights toward bridging the possibly wider K2 gap of Chapter 10?

Do you want to become a good player in tomorrow's marketplace? A strong player?

Or do you want to go for goal and *lead* in tomorrow's marketplace?

Do you want to get as far as you can toward becoming Ms. (or Mr.) Ideal Provider Tomorrow?

Why not? The fact that you're reading this book indicates you're serious about self-development. Why not stretch your sights the whole way and go for goal?

If so, however, remember that the goal-posts may well have shifted by the time you're ready to shoot. Time moves on, and the ideal provider in five years will have a different mix of capabilities to her equivalent today. Perhaps only with slight differences in nuance, perhaps radically different. You may find the Going for Goal chart in Figure 11.4 helpful.

Think of yourself as on the threshold of unparalleled success. A whole clear, glorious life lies before you. Achieve! Achieve!
—Andrew Carnegie

Figure 11.4 **Going for Goal**

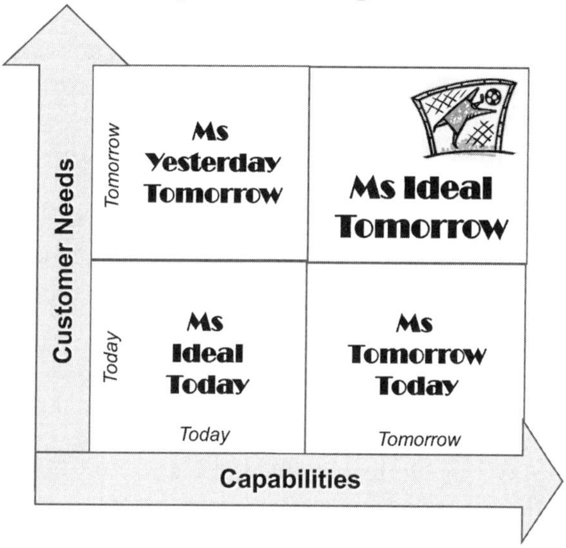

The Going for Goal chart highlights three important points:

➤ It's fine being Ms. Ideal Provider today, but today lasts only one day.
➤ If you don't develop the extra capabilities required to meet the customer needs of tomorrow, you'll become Ms. Yesterday Tomorrow.
➤ There's little point in developing extra capabilities today unless customers need them, or you'll become Ms. Tomorrow Today.

If you've raised your sights to the very top and are aiming to become Ms. Ideal Provider Tomorrow, you need to plan carefully how you are going to bridge the K2 gap—and when.

Identify the K2 Gap

In Chapter 6, you set out your ratings against the K2s you assessed in Chapter 5 for each of your main business chunks. These K2s were in turn largely based on customer needs you identified and ranked in Chapter 4.

Your Chapter 6 work was not a purely static exercise. You were encouraged to take a dynamic perspective. You looked not just at customer needs and K2s today, but how they might change over the next few years. You also considered how you might improve your standing against one or more of the K2s over the next few years. *And* you gave some thought as to how your competitors could enhance *their* standing in the future.

You need to revisit those charts. You need to track whether customer needs, K2s, your K2 ratings, or your competitors' K2 ratings have changed as a result of change in:

➢ The external marketplace, given the scenario development you undertook in Chapter 10.

➢ Your aims, given the resetting of your sights earlier in this chapter.

You can now identify the K2 gap. You've revisited the K2 ratings in your main business chunks, set your sights on which new chunks you may choose to enter, and established to what extent you wish to bridge the gap with the ideal provider. In the next chapter, you'll develop a strategy on how to bridge this gap.

Some examples may help clarify. Let's start with the simplified example of Annie, the cheerleader we last met in Chapter 6. We found that her dancing skills were currently sufficient to place her second in the team, behind the glamorous, vivacious but less coordinated Debbie. Over the next few years, we found that she should narrow the gap through gradually shedding her shyness and further developing her dancing range. Furthermore, a new manager was expected to place less emphasis on looks and personality and more on dancing skills. This would be to Annie's benefit.

Suppose Annie does some brainstorming and scenario development. Britney on her MP3 player in her bedroom-cum-den is how best Annie chills out. She suspects that it's not just the new manager who will place less emphasis on looks; it could be the whole of society as it becomes more politically correct. Over time the weighting placed on dance skills could become yet higher.

She also does some resetting of her sights. She realizes that she's driven to become as close to the ideal cheerleader as she is capable of. Certainly she wants to surpass Debbie. But how to get there? There's not much more she can do about her appearance. She's already working on becoming a better dancer. That leaves the shyness. That's her main K2 gap.

Annie sets her sights on being no more shy than the average 18-year-old girl by the time she graduates from high school. She's not sure how she's going to do it (that's for the next chapter!), but that's her goal and she's going to go for it.

Figure 11.5 **Annie's K2 Rating Target in Cheerleading**

Today

Key Kapabilities	Weighting	Annie	Billie	Charlie	Debbie
Appearance	25%	3	2.5	3	4.5
Personality	30%	2.5	4	3	5
Dance Skills	45%	4	2	3	2.5
K2 Rating	**100%**	**3.3**	**2.7**	**3.0**	**3.8**

Tomorrow

Key Kapabilities	Weighting	Annie	Billie	Charlie	Debbie
Appearance	20%	3	2.5	3	4.5
Personality	30%	3?	4	3	5
Dance Skills	50%?	4.5?	2	3.5?	3?
K2 Rating	**100%**	**3.8**	**2.7**	**3.3**	**3.9**

Tomorrow with Sights Set

Key Kapabilities	Weighting	Annie	Billie	Charlie	Debbie
Appearance	15%	3	2.5	3	4.5
Personality	30%	3.5?	4	3	5
Dance Skills	55%?	4.5?	2	3.5?	3?
K2 Rating	**100%**	**4.0**	**2.7**	**3.3**	**3.8**

She then reworks her K2 rating on her Excel spreadsheet, and finds that she could indeed surpass Debbie if she succeeds in conquering her shyness and bridging her K2 gap—see Figure 11.5.

This is a simplified example, with only the one business chunk and just the three basic K2s. But it's good to keep things simple. In identifying your K2 gap, try to follow the example of Annie and keep it simple. Stick to your most important business chunks. Settle on those K2s that need to be worked on seriously.

Let's return to our two main exemplars, Leila and Elizabeth, who are each in a number of business chunks.

An Example for the Self-Employed

Leila enjoyed mapping her strategic bubble bath. It seemed to sum up for her just why Chuck found her so backable. It was clearly her core business of aromatherapy to stay-at-home moms that gave Chuck so much comfort. It was an attractive chunk, and she was really well positioned in it. Its bubble (A) stood out confidently on her chart—see Figure 11.6.

Leila decided to keep the chart simple, and so she left out less important chunks, such as shiatsu. They were small, but there was no question of exiting them. There was no need to. She had done the training, and they incurred no extra cost. They were good to keep in her portfolio since they offered her customers a choice of therapies.

Leila also decided that she might as well make the bubbles proportional to future revenues, not current revenues, since she was definitely going ahead with her investment in the reflexology business. But she was careful to make the bubbles proportional to Chuck's concluding views on year five revenues (Chapter 7), not her own original forecasts.

Leila also built into her bubble bath the new chunk opportunities she identified during her brainstorming, namely Thai foot massage and soma-therapy. It was difficult to size these or indeed to rank them for attractiveness at this stage. But she had a feeling Thai foot massage may turn out to be a more attractive segment than soma-therapy.

Leila then thought more about what she'd learned from her brainstorming exercise. The most worrying scenario was Wonderwoman, the possibility of a highly trained masseuse coming into her patch of West London. Given some grim stories of oversupply coming out of other parts of London, such as in nearby Chelsea, Leila knew she'd better be prepared for it.

Figure 11.6 **Leila's Strategic Bubble Bath and Sight Setting**

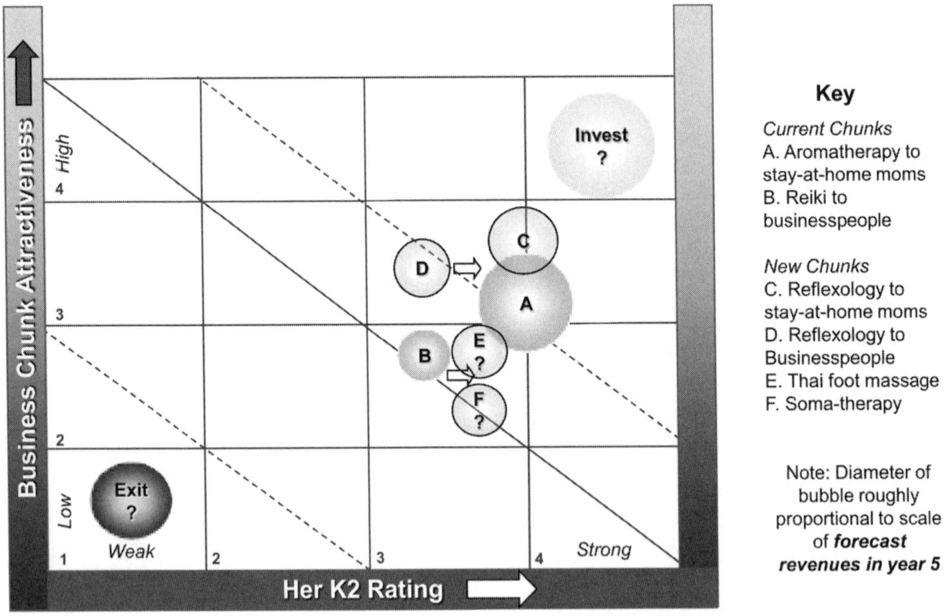

Leila decided to raise her sights. She was going to develop Helping Hands to such a level that any serious new entrant would find it very difficult to gain a foothold. Leila was going to "go for goal," to become as close to the ideal massage therapist as she could conceivably become. She was going to be the undisputed number one in her area. She was going to develop a position where she would have no fear at all of the Wonderwoman scenario.

Looking at her strategic position, it was clear that the greatest room for improvement was in her services to businesspeople. To meet her raised sights, this situation had to improve. She inserted some arrows onto the chart.

Then she returned to the K2 rating she'd drawn up with Chuck (Chapter 6). Her most serious weakness was in her timeliness, but there was no sense in working on that. That was Leila. It was too late for this leopard to change her spots. Anyway, some of her business customers seemed to like her rather disorganized approach. But there were other areas she could work on to improve her competitiveness, not just with businesspeople, but with all customers—like the range of services offered and the standard of her premises.

Leila then updated her K2 rating table to take into account the target capabilities she'd identified while undertaking the scenario development exercise. In particular, she gave greater prominence in the K2 weightings to factors such as hygiene, marketing, and managerial skills.

Leila finally identified her realistically achievable K2 gap as follows:

➢ Standard of hygiene, if not glossiness of décor, to be on a par with that of Kensington Wellness Centre.
➢ More attention to management issues, especially in managing Ying's expectations.
➢ Greater focus on marketing— including possibly a customer loyalty scheme.
➢ Further broadening of range of services offered, including Thai foot massage and soma-therapy within the next few years.

All Leila had to do now was to develop a strategy on how to bridge this K2 gap over the next few years.

An Example for an Employee

Elizabeth also enjoyed doing her strategic position mapping. Sometimes she felt she had little confidence in herself. Her deficiencies tended to overwhelm her and make her feel inadequate, assuming an importance out of proportion to their relevance.

The strategic bubble bath seemed to put things in perspective—see Figure 11.7. She was really rather well placed overall. Pretty strong in admin, credible in market research. There also seemed no rush to withdraw from other services such as typing. And there was a potential new chunk, thrown in by her scenario development exercise, of helping out the marketing team with their organization.

There was no doubt, however, that the results of her scenario planning were, on the whole, worrying. There was a distinct possibility that either the Copycat scenario (an admin colleague follows her into market research) or the Bite the Bullet scenario (presenting skills become a must), or both, could

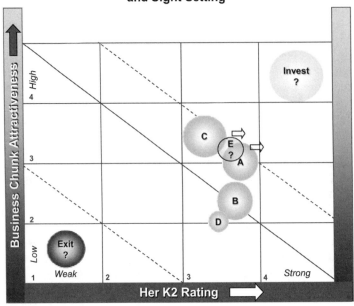

Figure 11.7 **Elizabeth's Strategic Bubble Bath and Sight Setting**

happen.

Elizabeth decides that the only way she is going to be able to sleep well over the next few years is to raise her sights. She too is going to "go for goal." Sure, she'll never in a million years become the ideal market researcher, but she sure as hell is going to narrow the gap.

If she could somehow get over her phobia of standing up in front of people, she would be able to defend herself against both scenarios. She resolves that she will do what it takes to improve her public speaking and presentational abilities.

Just for completeness, Elizabeth reworks the K2 weightings and her K2 ratings that she undertook with Chuck to build in the implications of the scenario development. Just as she thought, her weaknesses in presentational skills and internal marketing stand out even more starkly than before.

She recognized those weaknesses before she met Chuck. Chuck advised her to be wary of abandoning her position in the admin chunk to the market research chunk, where she was reasonably placed but vulnerable. Her subsequent scenario development reinforced the need to either become more competitive or to accept withdrawal from market research. She had now stretched her sights. She was going to go for it. She wanted to stick with market research and so she'd just have to bridge the K2 gap in:

> Presentational skills
> Communication skills

She wasn't sure how she was going to do this, but she resolved to research the options available to her. She wasn't to know it, but the solution to her problem was on her doorstep, so inexpensive as to be virtually free and a huge amount of fun to boot. And it's available to you too. We'll find out more in the next chapter.

You've reviewed your sights, and possibly raised them. You've identified the K2 gap. All you need is to select a strategy to bridge it. That's for Chapter 12.

Moderation is a fatal thing. Nothing succeeds like excess.—*Oscar Wilde*

Select Your Strategy to Bridge the Gap

12

In the last chapter, you identified the K2 gap—the shortfall between your current capabilities and those you aim to have. In this chapter, you'll select a strategy to bridge this gap. You'll be introduced to the three main generic strategies, and you'll be shown how to develop your strategic alternatives. These may include investment in training (or marketing if you're an employee)—possibly self-financed. If you're self-employed, other areas of investment may be in premises, equipment, staff, or partnership. You'll be shown how to evaluate these alternatives and how to build a realistic action plan.

> Vision is not enough, it must be combined with venture. It is not enough to stare up the steps, we must step up the stairs.—
> *Vaclav Havel*

What's Your Strategy?

First, what *is* a strategy? There are many definitions. It was originally a military concept, taken from the Greek *stratos* (army) and *ago* (to lead). An early military strategist was General Sun Tzu, a contemporary of Confucius in 6th century B.C. China. One of the oft-repeated verses from his treatise, *The Art of War*, remains highly relevant today, not just for the military but in business and self-development: "So it is said that if you know your enemies and know yourself, you will win a hundred times in a hundred battles. If you only know yourself, but not your opponent, you win one and lose the next. If you do not know yourself or your opponent, you will always lose."

That could do as a starting definition for the purposes of this book: *Know yourself, know the competition.*

The following quote from management guru Keniche Ohnae's book, *The Mind of the Strategist: The Art of Japanese Business,* builds on that definition: "What business strategy is all about; what distinguishes it from all other kinds of business planning—is, in a word, competitive advantage. Without competitors there would be no need for strategy, for the sole purpose of strategic planning is to enable the company to gain, as effectively as possible, a sustainable edge over its competitors."

I'm an economist, however, so I feel the need to bring the word "resources" into the definition. Just as economics can be defined as the optimal allocation of a nation's scarce resources, so too can a company's—or indeed an individual's—strategy be defined thus: Strategy is how you deploy your resources to gain a sustainable advantage over the competition.

Strategy is how you deploy your resources to gain a sustainable advantage over the competition.

What resources do you have? You've already examined them in Chapter 6 when you were assessing your capabilities and your K2 rating. And again in Chapter 11 when you were identifying the K2 gap. You've already done most of the groundwork needed to draw up your strategy.

When a company formulates its strategy, it considers how best to allocate its available resources to meet its goals. These resources are essentially its assets—its people, its physical assets (for example, buildings, equipment, and inventory), and its cash (and borrowing capability). It has to decide on how it should allocate—or invest—these resources to optimal effect.

For an individual, it's no different. You need to deploy your resources to their most telling effect. Except that the number of people involved is often in the singular. It's you! The most obvious of your resources are *your* capabilities, *your* physical assets (if any), and *your* cash (and/or overdraft potential).

Your most precious resource, however, may be time. And that could be your secret weapon. You may be able to find time during working hours where you could invest in training to improve your skills. Or you may have to think about carving a chunk out of leisure time.

"Time is money" is an old cliché, but that makes it no less valid. It's especially true if you're intent on making yourself more backable, as presumably you are since you're reading Part II of this book!

If you're self-employed, a day off for training could mean the loss of a day's earnings. If you're an employee, and you can't get your employer to agree it's in the company's interests as well as yours, it could mean the forfeiting of a day's vacation. Any day invested in self-improvement tends to have both an *actual cost*, what you have to pay out in cash (although this may be free, like a day in the public library), and an *opportunity cost*—the forfeiting of what else you could be doing. That could well be time spent on pursuing an alternative strategy. Or it might just be the sacrifice of your leisure time. That has an opportunity cost too—it's time that could otherwise be spent with the kids, on the golf course, or with your feet up.

In summary, you need to develop a strategy to bridge the K2 gap. A strategy is the allocation of available resources to meet your goals. That strategy will exploit your capabilities and will typically entail investment in cash and time.

> We shall either find a way or make one. —*Hannibal*

Robert M. Grant, in his excellent book on business strategy, now in its fifth edition and a must-read for business school students, *Contemporary Strategy Analysis,* introduces readers to business strategy by inviting them to think about how strategy is relevant also to the individual. He cites the extraordinary case of an entertainer in her mid-forties at the time with the family name of Ciccone but known to many across the world by her Christian name alone: "In the summer of 1978, aged 19, Madonna arrived in New York with $35 to her name. After five years of struggle she landed a recording contract... 'Madonna' [her first album, 1983] ultimately sold 10 million copies worldwide... .Twenty years later, Madonna was still the world's highest earning female entertainer and one of the best-known women on the planet."(Blackwell Publishing, Malden, MA, 2005, page 6)

Grant wonders how on earth this unprecedented feat has been possible, given the entertainer's evident limitations: "What is the basis of her incredible and lasting success? Certainly not outstanding natural talent. As a vocalist, musician, songwriter, or actress, Madonna's talents seem modest. Few would regard her as a natural beauty."

> The people who get on in this world are the people who get up and look for the circumstances they want, and, if they can't find them, make them.—*George Bernard Shaw*

One answer, according to Grant, has been the clarity of her ambition, her going for goal: "her dedication to a single goal: the quest for superstar status." She also possesses "relentless drive" and has been adept at "drawing on the talents of others—writers, musicians, choreographers, designers." But he spies one consistent strategy throughout her career: "Most striking has been her continuous reinvention of her image—from the street-kid look in the early 1980s, to hard-core sexuality in the 1990s, and the spiritual image that accompanied motherhood."

There is one further element to her strategy that has been key to her success: "As a self-publicist, she is without equal. In using sex as a marketing tool, she has courted controversy through nudity, pornographic imagery, suggestions of sexual deviance and the juxtaposition of sexual and religious themes. But she is also astute at walking the fine line between the shocking and the unacceptable."

Only a diehard fan would disagree with Grant's assessment. Madonna is an entertainer of unexceptional musical or dramatic resources, yet successful to an astonishing and unprecedented degree. She has been an inspiration not just to her natural successors, like Kylie and Britney, who can also sing and dance a bit, but to countless other pop music and reality TV wannabes. Many of the latter possess plenty of Madonna's resources of determination and self-publicity, but seem blissfully unaware that talent is needed upon which to base the marketing hype.

We know that Madonna's goal was to be a superstar. What was her strategy? How did she allocate her available resources to meet that goal? In one sentence, which is what a strategy should fit in, how about this? *Madonna's strategy has been to build on her capabilities in the performing arts through sustained investment of cash, time, and energy in image reinvention and self-publicity.*

We'll come back to Madonna later in this chapter. But what's your strategy? How are you going to allocate your available resources to meet your goals? In one sentence?

First, let's take a look at some generic strategies.

Consider the Generic Strategies

There are three main generic strategies for an individual to select to achieve his or her goals. The first two are based on generic business strategies. To develop a sustainable competitive advantage, and to enjoy profitable growth, companies generally follow one of two generic strategies: (1) a differentiation strategy, or (2) a low-cost strategy.

To simplify, they either do something distinctive and well, or do more or less the same as the others but at lower cost. What they would be well advised *not* to do is the same as most other companies, the so-called *me-too* recipe for lack of success.

For an individual, whether employed or self-employed, these generic business strategies are directly transferable. Let's call the differentiation strategy the *Stand Out!* strategy, since we can all get a handle on the importance of standing out, being special to someone or some group of people (customers). It's making your offering different, special, distinctive from the next provider. It's Madonna's strategy.

For the low-cost strategy, let's call it the *easyU!* strategy. European readers will be familiar with the astonishing success of the low-cost airline easyJet (similar to the success of Southwest Airlines in the United States), which later diversified into a range of other low-cost offerings in other sectors, such as easyCar, easyMoney, easyMobile, and so forth. If you're going to make your offering the lowest cost on the market, then easyU! just about sums it up.

But for individuals, there's a third generic strategy that is hugely important. That is where circumstances combine to constrain your pursuit of the other two strategies. You may not be able to differentiate sufficiently, you may not choose to become the lowest cost provider, but you *do* need to improve your competitiveness, your K2 rating, or you may find yourself in trouble. We'll call that the *Sharpen Act!* strategy.

To summarize, there are three generic strategies for individuals to achieve their goals:

➤ Stand Out!—differentiate for success
➤ easyU!—become low cost for success
➤ Sharpen Act!—improve your competitiveness for partial success

Let's take a look at each in turn.

Stand Out!

Think about how well-known, successful companies differentiate themselves. Rolls Royce in the majesty of car design, Dell in custom-built laptops, Sony in high-quality graphics on game machines. Or on a less lofty plane, McDonald's in burger quality consistency, Ben & Jerry's in homemade ice cream, Quizno's (or Prêt-A-Manger in Britain) for fresh, quality ingredient sandwiches.

In each case, this differentiation will come at an extra cost. But that will be more than made up by the volumes of business sold, and typically, the extra grand, dollar, or even dime able to be added to pricing over and above competitors' offerings because of the differentiation.

It's the same with individuals. Madonna has been around for over 20 years, yet her concerts have become no cheaper to get into. Likewise for the Rolling Stones, whose differentiation (the bad boy image, created from the very start and painstakingly maintained through the decades) has kept them a premium act for closing on half a century.

> If the three keys to selling real estate are location, location, location, then the three keys of selling consumer products are differentiation, differentiation, differentiation.
> — *Robert Goizueta*

Think of comedians. All successful comedians, in whatever country, have readily recognizable persona. Charlie Chaplin had perhaps the most identifiable differentiation in Hollywood history: a tramp in an ill-fitting suit with a bowler hat and an umbrella. Chaplin fell into that role while auditioning as a drunk. It went down well enough to land the role and the rest is history.

I'm not suggesting you go down to the nearest charity shop and buy a suit three sizes too small and a silly hat. But it is worth considering in what ways you differentiate yourself from other providers of your services.

You have, of course, looked at many aspects of your differentiation in earlier chapters, namely Chapter 6 on your K2 rating and Chapter 11 on your K2 gap. But it's worth having a rethink because it may influence your choice of strategy.

Differentiation is all about building on your strengths. It's taking what you're good at, those K2 ratings where you're doing well, and doing them even better. It's typically not about working on your weaknesses, which is more associated with the third generic strategy, Sharpen Act!

As we'll see in our example later on, our massage therapist Leila adheres to the Stand Out! strategy. So too does Madonna. Hers is a strategy of image reinvention and self-publicity. Interestingly, though, even Madonna has not shirked from applying aspects of the Sharpen Act! strategy over the years. Can you think what they are? What weaknesses has she worked on over the years? We'll return to these questions when we look at the Sharpen Act! strategy in a few paragraphs.

The Stand Out! strategy is essentially that promoted by Marcus Buckingham and Donald O. Clifton in their stimulating bestseller, *Now, Discover Your Strengths.* The thesis behind their book is that organizations that over the years have encouraged us to iron out our weaknesses in order to become stronger have been misguided. They have failed to encourage us to identify our unique pattern of strengths and build on them.

The authors worked with the Gallup Organization for many years. In one large survey they quote, employees were asked this question: "At work, do you have the opportunity to do what you do best every day?" They found that those answering "strongly agree" to this question worked in business units with higher customer satisfaction ratings, greater productivity, and lower employee turnover. Yet the "strongly agree" respondents were only 20 percent of those surveyed. If only a fraction of the remaining 80 percent could be encouraged to work to their strengths, the authors argue, just imagine the uplift in productivity and profitability, let alone employee satisfaction.

The authors identify two principles they believe guide the world's best managers: (1) Each person's talents are enduring and unique, and (2) each person's greatest room for improvement is in the area of his or her greatest strength. The book then shows how you as an individual can capitalize on your strengths, and how you as a manager can manage the strength-building process of your employees and of the organization as a whole.

Buckingham and Clifton perhaps exaggerate to make a point, certainly a forceful point. Differentiation through playing to your strengths can for sure be a route to success and is almost certainly the best route. But the low-cost strategy is also well proven. And their dismissal of what we call here the Sharpen Act! strategy is not wholly fair. As we shall see later, individuals may not find themselves in the right circumstances to play wholly to their strengths. They may have little practical choice but to work on their weaknesses. This may not yield them stunning success, but it could well enable them to keep their jobs and improve their lot. It could make them more backable.

easyU!

It's easy enough to visualize how the likes of JetBlue in the United States and Ryanair in Europe have been successful. These low-cost airlines have grown rapidly and profitably, despite seeming to give away so many of their tickets. The trick is in load factor. Their planes are usually full. And if a passenger only contributes to the costs of landing charges and taxes, that's still preferable for the airline to an empty seat.

How can this apply to an individual? How can an easyU! strategy work for you?

Simple. It's all about utilization. If you're self-employed, your earnings are typically a reflection of your charges on the one hand and your utilization on the other. If your time charged is low, there's no point in having high charges. Your earnings at the end of the year will be low.

easyJet makes money because of high utilization. Perhaps you could too?

I can think of many examples locally of artisans who apply this philosophy. Frank, who comes now and again to chop back the jungle we call a garden, needs to be booked weeks in advance. He's so well liked and his rates so reasonable, everyone wants him. Same with John the decorator, Eric the electrician, and Ken the plumber. Yes, a plumber with reasonable rates! Beggar's belief, I know, but we've known Ken since he was an apprentice and spent a whole day taking to pieces and rebuilding our ancient boiler. It still didn't work too well, and he was reluctant to accept payment, but we insisted. Many years later, he still charges reasonable rates and he's incredibly busy, but he'll still find time to squeeze in a loyal customer with a leaking tap.

> The man who will use his skill and constructive imagination to see how much he can give for a dollar instead of how little he can give for a dollar is bound to succeed.
> —Henry Ford

But for every good 'un, there are many rogues. They charge you the earth, knowing full well you won't call them back again. Like the TV aerial installer guy, who will remain nameless. Do these guys reach sufficient utilization with such poor customer retention? I doubt it.

It applies at both ends of the pay scale too. One of my former management consulting colleagues retired as a director, but wanted to keep his brain active. So he offered to continue to work for the company on a freelance basis at a much discounted daily rate—a fraction of what the company could bill out the client for his time. Suffice it to say he found himself busier in "retirement" than he had been in full-time employment!

Is this a strategy that could work for you? If you're an employee, the strategy could apply too. Would you be prepared to take a pay cut, and tighten the belt at home, in order to retain your job? You may have no option if your company is restructuring. But even if it isn't, is it worth considering this strategy to secure your position in the company?

If you're self-employed, how's your utilization? How price sensitive are your customers? Would your utilization be improved if you shaved your prices? Would that improve your profit?

Sharpen Act!

We've discussed the differentiation strategy and the low-cost strategy. For individuals there's a third generic strategy to be considered. It's not the optimal, perhaps, but it could well be better than no strategy at all. It's the Sharpen Act! strategy. It's where you build on your strengths to the extent that you're able to in the circumstances, but meanwhile you work on some of the weaknesses that are holding you down. You set out to improve your K2 rating.

This is a strategy that Buckingham and Clifton (mentioned previously) may not approve of, but you may have little choice. Individuals are not like companies. In a market economy, companies can buy or sell business units; open or close down production units; hire or lay off personnel; outsource operations, possibly to offshore, low-cost economies; or relocate headquarters to lower cost towns. They play to their strengths, whether following a differentiation or a low-cost strategy. They deploy their resources to maximize shareholder value.

Individuals can't necessarily do that. They have other commitments. To their children, perhaps, in continuity of schooling. To caring for their aged parents. To the needs of their spouse. To their communities—the other people, societies, charities, and organizations they support. These commitments impose constraints, very often welcome ones, on freedom of action.

Individuals also have financial commitments. To the mortgage provider. To the credit card company. To the health insurer. To the private school. These commitments also impose constraints, typically less welcome than those above, on freedom of action.

Individuals also have desires. Suppose they desire to be doing some form of work that they're really not that well placed to address? Should they play to their strengths—stick to the work they're good at and abandon their dreams? Or should they improve on some of their weaknesses and have a go? It's surely an option, a possible strategy.

The Sharpen Act! strategy is essentially that deployed by Elizabeth, our PA-cum-market researcher, and we'll discuss that further later in this chapter. As noted earlier, however, there are some elements of the Sharpen Act! even in Madonna's strategy. Her overriding strategy is of course one of Stand Out!, but over the years she has also worked on some of her weaknesses and sharpened up her act. For example:

> Voice training, improving her pitch, range, and control to the extent that she was able to audition for, and win, the role of Eva Perón in *Evita,* the movie based on the musical by Tim Rice and Andrew Lloyd Webber.

> Body toning, famously, through harsh yoga regimes and even

CHAPTER 12 SELECT YOUR STRATEGY TO BRIDGE THE GAP

giving consideration in recent interviews (*Sunday Mail,* October 2006) to going under the knife: "Never say never! I sure don't rule it out, although I don't want to be made up of silicone, plastic and man-made fibre."

Does the Sharpen Act! strategy apply to you? Either on its own, or in conjunction with Stand Out!? Or does easyU! make more sense? Let's look at the alternatives you may choose to consider within these generic strategies.

Develop Strategic Alternatives

You know where you want to get to. You know how you want to travel there. But which route do you take? The answers are, of course, as many and diverse as getting from your home to the office, from London to Timbuktu, or from Las Vegas to heaven!

There are any number of possible strategic alternatives. Any number of permutations of investment in time, effort, and cash. Your challenge is to narrow down the universe of alternatives into those two or three most strategically consistent and viable.

If you're self-employed, there are perhaps six main areas you may need to invest in, namely marketing, training, equipment, premises, staff, and partnering. If you're an employee, the latter four are unlikely to be relevant. For employees, investment in training is likely to be the most important, but investment in marketing should not be dismissed. Let's take a look at these two first, since they apply to all of us.

Investment in marketing

There are hundreds of thousands of self-employed people out there, like—I have to admit—myself, who don't devote enough time, effort, and cash to marketing. Then we complain when the phone doesn't ring.

It's just not where our interest lies. We prefer to spend our time doing our job, not selling ourselves to potential customers. We'll take a deeper look at this in the next chapter on the pros and cons of setting up your own business.

Suffice to say that if no one knows you're there you won't get any business.

Every dollar, pound, or zloty spent on marketing is an investment. Not all will be well spent. Some will turn out to be lousy investments. But you won't know until you try. And some spending may pay big dividends.

Not so long ago I met up with a former contact I had lost touch with over a roast beef sandwich, a beer, and a coffee. It set me back around US$60. I saw it as a networking investment. I had no expectations of any direct work, but I thought he might give me some tips on what was going on and who was doing what. And maybe a referral or two. I was wrong. His company was contemplating changing its policy on the use of outside consultants. Two months later I landed my first contract with them. A handsome return on investment.

Would that other lunches, coffees, letters, phone calls, and emails were as productive! In truth, you just don't know. The vast majority are dead ends. But you don't know that at the time. You've just got to keep at it.

Does your business need further investment in marketing as one component of your strategy to achieve your goal?

What if you're an employee? Is investment in marketing applicable? Very much so. Again, you're not going to get far being good at your job if no one in your organization knows about it. Much as you may dislike it, especially if you're a modest character, you do need to let your boss—and his boss too—know how you're contributing to the company's success.

> The fact is, everyone is in sales. Whatever area you work in, you do have clients and you do need to sell…. You need to sell you and your ideas in order to advance your career, gain more respect, and increase your success, influence and income.—*Jay Abraham*

This doesn't mean you have to be a creep. We've all seen them at the office. They time their visits to the water cooler to coincide with the boss's. They laugh uproariously at the boss's feeble jokes (think of the atrocious David Brent character in the BBC sitcom *The Office*, or Michael Scott in the U.S. adaptation). If the boss is a fan of the New York Yankees or Liverpool Football Club, guess what? So are they!

Such creeps sometimes win through. I've known some who have got to the very top. Good luck to them. But good managers generally see through such creepery. Of course, they'll appreciate an employee being courteous, even humorous, but most of all they want to know that the job is being done well. And it's up to you to let your boss know just that. That may require a conscious and sustained effort in self-promotion. An investment in marketing.

Investment in training

This is often the key investment option for the employee. You know where you want to be in five years' time. You know what the K2 gap is. You know that yours is primarily a Sharpen Act! strategy, with a touch of Stand Out!. And you know that further training will be the key to bridging that K2 gap and meeting your goal.

Training can be on-the-job or dedicated. It can refine your skills or develop new, related skills. It can aim at a modest honing of capabilities, or at developing new, life-changing capabilities. It can be anything from a one-day blitz in speed-reading to a two-year MBA course.

Whatever the training options you as an employee consider, they should satisfy two fundamental criteria:
  ➢ They should be consistent with your strategy.
  ➢ They should be a sound investment.

The first criterion is self-evident. We're talking here about training for the workplace. Training in cooking skills is fine, but unless you're a chef, it's beyond the scope of this book. If you're training for work, it should be consistent with your strategy of investing your available resources to bridge the K2 gap assessed earlier in Chapter 11.

The second criterion is more intriguing. As an employee, there should be areas of training available to you provided by your company. The HR function in larger organizations has become highly sophisticated over the last couple of decades. There is typically a provision made for each grade of employee for some element of training each year. This is not always the case with smaller companies.

But what if what the training courses provided by the company don't coincide with the K2 enhancement needed to achieve your personal goals? Then you have three choices. You can try to persuade your boss that it is in the company's interests for you to broaden your capabilities through undertaking this training. Or you can leave the company for a similar company where that training will form part of the employment package. Or you can finance it yourself.

> The problem is the average person isn't tuned in to lifelong learning, or going to seminars and so forth. If the information is not on television, and it's not in the movies they watch, and it's not in the few books that they buy, they don't get it.
> —*Jack Canfield*

If you do have to finance the training yourself, then you should be reasonably confident it will prove a sound investment. The investment option may need to be evaluated, as we'll see in the next section.

If you're self-employed, training can be just as important. You may need further training in your field of specialization or to diversify into a related field. You may need some serious training or coaching in an area of deficiency, such as selling skills.

But for the self-employed, any cash costs for training are usually to your account. There's no boss for you to persuade. You're the boss and you've got to convince yourself. The training investment will need careful evaluating, and it had better yield a good return.

There may be occasions when you can get your customers to cover the costs of training. This is not an unethical suggestion. Now and again, you may pitch for work where your current capabilities cover most of the work required but not all. If the customer cannot find a provider who has the full range of capabilities, she may be willing to contract you on the understanding that you will upgrade your capabilities during the course of the engagement to complete the work satisfactorily. Your customer won't pay for any cash costs of training, but she's effectively covering them by paying you for the work you'll carry out during and after training.

> Outside of a dog, a book is a man's best friend. Inside of a dog, it's too dark to read.
> —*Groucho Marx*

Investment in premises or equipment

If you're self-employed, investment in premises or equipment may be required to bridge the K2 gap identified in Chapter 11.

There is never just the one solution to such investment. Think of buying a house. You develop your criteria for the ideal house: four bedrooms, three baths, two-car garage, fenced backyard, a green and peaceful neighborhood, and located in a particular school district. You'll find plenty of houses that fit some of these criteria but few that fit all. One or two may fit the criteria so well they'll be outside your price range.

It's similar with selecting business premises. You'll need to select your criteria carefully, screen and rank the available options, and narrow them down to a manageable two or three.

Think too of buying a digital camera or an MP3 player. You'll have your criteria, but there are so many to choose from, each differing in specifications, design, and price, that you despair of ever being able to make up your mind! It can be almost as daunting with business equipment. Which laptop? Which drill? Which pick-up? On the plus side, the range to choose from is typically narrower than in consumer goods. On the minus side, business equipment is generally more expensive, so it's important to make the right decision.

Again, you need to select your criteria carefully, screen the options available, and narrow it down to those most promising.

Investment in staff

This is potentially the most exciting of the investment options available to you. If you're a self-employed business person, investment in an employee tends to mean one thing: You're growing! It means that you're making the transition from being self-employed to an employer. There's no halfway house. You're either an employer in the eyes of the tax authorities, or you're not. If you employ one person today, you could be employing half a dozen tomorrow. Or a dozen? Two dozen? One hundred?!

Again, you need to ensure that the engagement of staff is consistent with your strategy for bridging the K2 gap and has every chance of achieving a sound financial return. In general, you'll need to feel comfortable that the extra revenues you'll be able to generate with an employee on board are greater than the total extra costs incurred from engaging the employee—including wages, benefits, social security, insurance, and extra overhead. This may not always be the case, however. You may choose to engage an employee to take some of the load off you, make life more tolerable, and acknowledge the tradeoff between extra cost and improved quality of life.

Investment in partnership

This is another exciting investment option. Again it implies growth, although partnerships can sometimes be used as a defensive measure to ward off aggressive competition.

Partnerships among the self-employed can range from the wholly informal to the contractually formal. At the least formal end of the scale, it can mean a simple arrangement of mutual referral. You as a plasterer are asked if you know a good electrician, so you offer the name of your "partner," using the word in its broadest sense. He'll do the same for you. Similarly with carpenters, plumbers, and roofers in whom you have confidence. No formal contracts, no sales commissions. Just an understanding: You scratch my back, I'll scratch yours. And a pint or three of beer in the pub later on!

Partnerships can be made more formal for the benefit of all parties. This is especially true where a joint investment in premises or equipment, or both, needs to be made. A partnership shares the risk. Many professional practices are partnerships, whether lawyers, doctors, dentists, vets, alternative therapists. As we've seen in Part I, our massage therapist Leila has plans to form a semi-formal partnership with the reflexologist, Ying.

Formal partnerships are a means of reducing the financial risk of an investment, but they introduce an entirely new area of risk, namely dependence on others. Before signing on the dotted line, it's crucial to minimize that risk by finding out as much as you can about your prospective partners. One word of caution: Try to make sure your partners share the same core values, ethics, and horizons as you. These, more so perhaps than compatibility of skills and experience, are what will hold the partnership together. And make the parting tolerable when the partnership splits up, as regrettably, most do.

Marketing, training, equipment, premises, staff, and partnering are the main areas of strategic investment for you to consider, within the context of one of the three generic strategies discussed above.

You now need to develop two or three strategic alternatives. Each will represent a defined and coherent strategy for bridging your K2 gap. They may reflect investment in one area alone, or investment in a combination of areas. Alternative A, for example, may involve further training in marketing skills, while alternative B may be more ambitious, involving relocation of premises and partnership with someone with proven marketing skills.

Let's look at how you should set about evaluating which of these alternatives should best be pursued to achieve your goals.

Evaluating the Alternatives

You have some strategic alternatives. But you can't do both or all of them. How do you choose which to pursue?

Let's ask Chuck Cash. He often has to do this for those whom he backs. He seeks the alternative that gives him, and his client, *the highest return for the lowest risk.*

Chuck projects future cash flows under each alternative, assesses their value in today's money (NPV, or net present value) and computes the return on investment under each (IRR, or internal rate of return). He then tweaks the assumptions underlying each alternative to see how sensitive the NPV and IRR are to things not working out as expected.

But Chuck may not be around. And this is no business school course in finance. Let's try to keep things simple while still being useful. There are three things to understand about evaluating investment alternatives.

The first is the nature of making an investment. It usually means a cash outlay today that should give you cash, or other benefits, coming in for years to come. Investment tends to be a one-time, upfront cost, leading to recurring annual benefits.

The second thing to remember is what's called "sunken costs." When you're comparing the viability of strategic alternatives, any cash you've already spent has to be forgotten about. Tough, but it's gone. It's history. You must only take into account what *extra* cash you need to spend on an alternative from this day forward to generate the benefits expected.

The third and final thing is the difference between money of today and money of tomorrow. Which would you rather be given: $1,000 today, or $1,000 in five years' time? A no-brainer. You'd take the cash today, which you could spend, bank, or invest. If you banked it, you could see it grow through interest (and after tax) to around $1,150 after five years. If you invested it in the stock market, you would hopefully see it grow to much more than that. On the other hand, it could crash to below $1,000. That's the risk you knowingly take on when playing the stock market, but in general, you could not unreasonably expect it to grow to, say, $1,500.

What would you do if you were offered the choice of $1,000 today, or say, $1,250 in five years' time? Not so straightforward. You'd have to feel reasonably confident that you could invest the $1,000 well enough to build it to more than $1,250 over five years.

In short, money invested today in a strategic alternative has a higher value than money you may generate in future years as a result of that investment.

Here's a simple* way to evaluate a strategic alternative. Work out the cost of the investment, say $I. Assess the annual benefits from the investment, or the difference between the extra cash inflow (from revenues) and the extra cash outflow (from expenses) generated each year as a result of the investment. If the annual benefits are different each year, take their average over the first five years, $B/year. Divide B into I, and this gives you the "payback," the number of years taken for the cash costs of the investment to be recouped.

* Technical note: Simple or simplistic? The payback approach to evaluating investments has its drawbacks. It doesn't properly take into account the time value of money, nor the possible lumpiness or risk of annual cash flows, and it ignores cash flows beyond the payback period, thereby favoring investments with short-term returns. But it's the easiest approach to explain in lay terms.

If payback is *four years* or less, that could well be a sound invest-ment.** But don't jump on it. Work out the payback on the other strategic alternatives as well. Who knows? They may have an even lower payback.

**Technical note: That is equivalent to a 9 percent per year rate of return over a five-year period, assuming—conservatively—no benefits beyond five years.

If you believe your investment is going to give you a longer-term ad-vantage and could last all of ten years, then an investment with a longer payback may still be beneficial. You might give serious consideration to an investment with a payback of six to seven years. It'll be riskier, of course, because all sorts of things could happen to your competitive situation over that time period.

Next you need to work out the "net benefits" of the strategic alternative. Here, strictly speaking, you should discount the value of benefits received in later years, because of the time value of money discussed above—es-pecially if annual benefits in, say, year five are much larger than in year one. But for many investments made by individuals, as opposed to those by companies, it should be a good enough first approximation to assess net benefits by adding up the sum of the annual benefits in the first five years and subtracting the investment costs.

If your strategic alternative represents an investment with a much longer-term horizon, such as enrolling in an MBA program, then you'd be strongly advised to work out net benefits properly, using the discounted cash flow method—which, of course, you'll learn all about at business school!

The above assumes that benefits are readily measurable. Often the benefits will be more obscure. The main benefit of a strategic alternative may, for instance, be an improvement in your K2 rating, making you more competitive and better placed to respond to competitors' initiatives. The trick then is to compare the *with* and *without* scenarios. The *with* scenario is what your earnings would be if you make the investment. The *without* scenario is what your earnings would be if you do nothing. The difference in annual benefits between the two scenarios can then be attributed to the investment.

There are, however, other elements that have not been taken into ac-count. The above has focused on one side of the story, the financial ben-efits, whether readily measurable or not. What are the other, nonfinancial benefits of pursuing one alternative compared to the others? A greater sense of fulfillment or higher status in the community, for example? Are there any negatives in pursuing the alternative, such as a more stressful peer group, longer working hours? All these need to be factored into the evaluation.

Finally, and crucially, as ever in this book, there's risk. Each alterna-tive will be more or less risky than the other. The alternative that promises the highest returns for the lowest investment outlay may be unacceptably risky. Another alternative that offers modest payback for a modest outlay may be virtually risk-free. How risky are your proposed alternatives?

Now you're ready for the evaluation itself. It may be helpful for you to lay out the strategic alternatives in a table, along with their investment cost, annual benefits, payback, net benefits, nonfinancial benefits, and risk, as shown in Figure 12.1.

Figure 12.1 **A Simplified Approach to Evaluating Strategic Alternatives**

	Unit	A	B	C
Financial Benefits Investment Costs = I	$			
Average Annual Benefits = B	$/Year			
Payback = I /B	Years			
Total Benefits (over 5 years) = TB = B x 5	$			
Net Benefits = TB - I	$			
Risk	L/M/H			
Nonfinancial Benefits		➤ .... ➤ .... ➤	➤ .... ➤ .... ➤	➤ .... ➤ .... ➤ ....
Nonfinancial Dis-benefits		➤ .... ➤ .... ➤	➤ .... ➤ .... ➤	➤ .... ➤ .... ➤ ....

The table will guide you on which of the three alternatives is the most *financially* beneficial. It should be the one with the highest net benefits and with an acceptable payback. *And* with acceptable risk. Note that the alternative with the fastest payback is not necessarily the best—net benefits may be too small, even though they are the most rapidly achieved. But if the alternative with the fastest payback is not mutually exclusive with the one that has the highest net benefits, perhaps you could do both?

!!!WARNING!!!
Investment appraisal can be complex. If you are uncertain of the evaluation methods or unclear about the results of your evaluation, you should seek professional advice!

The most financially beneficial alternative may not, of course, be the most beneficial to you overall. You need to compare the financial benefits in the table with the nonfinancial benefits. This is highly subjective. One alternative may be the most financially beneficial, but it may have the most negative implications on your quality of life. That's when evaluation becomes tricky. At the end of the day, it's up to you how you balance your earnings aspirations with other aspects of your life. There's always a tradeoff.

It's up to each of us to figure out for ourselves the work-life balance that best suits us.

Build an Action Plan

So you've selected the most appropriate strategy to narrow the K2 gap and achieve your goals. That's the easy bit! The tricky bit is in carrying it through, in implementing the strategy.

For that you'll need to draw up an action plan. This will be a chart of all the actions you need to undertake achieving your strategy, including a start date and a target completion date. Figure 12.2 shows a format you might find useful.

The key to getting things done is to revisit your action plan regularly, say, once a month. Chastise yourself if you've fallen behind. Insist on giving yourself sound, supportable reasons if you have.

If you wait until all the lights are green before you leave home, you'll never get started on your trip to the top.
—Zig Ziglar

The problem with implementing a strategy is that if you fall behind with one action, it often has a bearing on another. If you're not careful, you may find you're unable to launch one strategic thrust because of delay in another. Prolonged delay can mean having to abandon that thrust. You may even have to trash the whole strategy.

What's going to be in your action plan? When should each task start? By when should you have finished it? How realistic is that? Will you really

Figure 12.2 **Drawing Up an Action Plan**

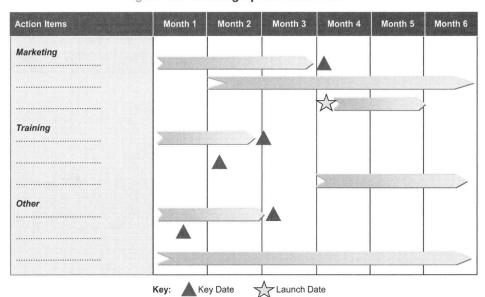

Key: ▲ Key Date   ☆ Launch Date

be able to do that task by the end of that month? Make it as realistically achievable as you can. Then go out and achieve it.

You now have a strategy and an action plan. It's time to return to our two main exemplars, Leila and Elizabeth, and see how they drew up their strategic alternatives, evaluated them, and then prepared their action plans.

A Strategy Example for the Self-Employed

Let's recollect where we are. Leila has done her brainstorming, scenario envisioning, and sketching of the ideal provider. She has drawn up her strategic bubble bath, reset her sights, decided to go for goal, and identified the K2 gap. All she needs to do is decide on a strategy for how to achieve her new goal, which is to become the undisputed number-one massage therapist in the Notting Hill area.

Leila decides that her strategy needs to be a blend of Stand Out! and Sharpen Up!. She's going to build on her strengths, as well as address some of her perceived weaknesses, such as hygiene, management, and marketing. As you may remember from Chapters 1 and 7, Leila already has plans to move

into new premises, a back room of a barber's shop set off the main street. It's going to be rent free, but she and her partner Ying will have to do it up. Chuck estimated a payback on that investment of just two years.

Leila figures that this should be the basis of her strategic alternative A. The strategy will include new premises, partnership with Ying, upgrading of hygiene, tighter management, and more innovative marketing, including a customer loyalty program.

But is this strategy ambitious enough? After all, this was her strategy before she met Chuck, before she did her brainstorming, before she reset her sights. Would this alternative be sufficient for her to achieve her stretched

Figure 12.3 **Evaluating Leila's Strategic Alternatives**

	Unit	A: Off-Main St	B: Main St
Financial Benefits Investment Costs = I	$	8,000	20,000
Average Annual Benefits = B	$/Year	4,000	8,000
Payback = I /B	Years	2	2.5
Total Benefits (over 5 years) = TB = B x 5	$	20,000	40,000
Net Benefits = TB - I	$	12,000	20,000
Risk	L/M/H	Low/Med	Med/High
Nonfinancial Benefits		➤ Hygienic, professional ➤ More status ➤ More space at home	➤ Very hygienic, professional ➤ Higher profile, yet more status ➤ Cover for Leila ➤ Raised entry barriers
Nonfinancial Dis-benefits		➤ Dependence on Ying ➤ Less flexible than at home ➤ See less of daughter	➤ Dependence on both Ying and new employee ➤ See even less of daughter

goals? Perhaps not, Leila thought. To become the number one massage therapist in the area, she couldn't stay hidden away out of sight. She did some snooping around at potential alternative sites. It wasn't long before she came across what seemed to be the ideal spot. It was on the main street, sandwiched between a French-style café and a plus-size boutique—venues frequented by many of Leila's current and potential clientele. Currently configured as a charity shop, she heard that the landlord was prepared to listen to any reasonable offer.

Leila spoke to the landlord, received an encouraging response, and did the math. The premises were bigger and would cost more to do up nicely. Revenues would need to be a lot higher to cover the rent, which, although reasonable, was well above the zero she would be paying in the room behind the barber's. She would need to hire another masseuse to generate the extra profits and to provide cover during lunchtime and when engaged in management matters.

Leila evaluated the two alternatives and summarized her findings in Figure 12.3. There was no debate. Alternative B generated higher net benefits and had a good payback of two and a half years (although not as impressive as the two years for alternative A). She had stretched her sights and only alternative B could fully meet them. Highly qualified new entrants would be deterred from coming into the area if this alternative was successful.

But it was riskier. No getting away from that. She would now be dependent not just on Ying, but on an employee. There was more cash needed up front. There were much higher monthly operating costs to be covered by higher revenues. But it seemed worth it. It was a big challenge, but she was highly confident she could make a go of it. Now for another wee chat with Chuck.

To prepare for that meeting, Leila drew up an action plan for alternative

Figure 12.4 **Leila's Option B Action Plan**

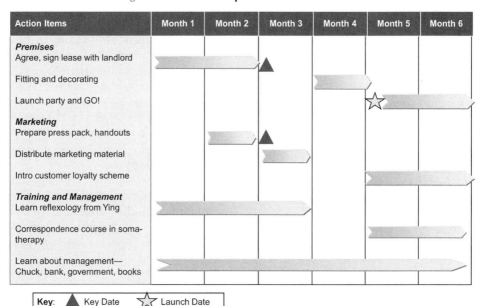

Action Items	Month 1	Month 2	Month 3	Month 4	Month 5	Month 6
Premises Agree, sign lease with landlord						
Fitting and decorating						
Launch party and GO!						
Marketing Prepare press pack, handouts						
Distribute marketing material						
Intro customer loyalty scheme						
Training and Management Learn reflexology from Ying						
Correspondence course in soma-therapy						
Learn about management— Chuck, bank, government, books						

Key: ▲ Key Date   ☆ Launch Date

B (Figure 12.4). Leila figured it would probably take four months before launch. The key dates would be the signing of the lease with the landlord, the finalization of the promotional press pack and marketing literature, and the launch day itself. Leila wanted a big splash for that. Some of her customers were involved in local press, business, and government, and she was sure she could enlist their help to make it an occasion to remember.

First, however, she needed to sharpen her pencil and ensure that the new business plan, the financial forecasts, the risk assessment, and the action plan measured up to the demanding standards she had learned were set by Chuck.

A Strategy Example for an Employee

In the last chapter, we found that Elizabeth had also decided to go for goal. She was going to become as competent a market researcher as she could be, while reinforcing her known strengths in admin work. But Elizabeth recognized that her strategy was going to be more akin to Sharpen Up! than Stand Out!. She was determined to work on her weaknesses and bridge the capability gap in presentational and communication skills.

Elizabeth was reticent about asking her boss for help. As far as she knew, he was largely unaware of how diffident Elizabeth was at presenting. He may not even have thought much about how important presentational skills could become in years to come. He simply had too many other things to think about, like where the next big piece of business was going to come from. She feared that if she alerted him of her need for training, he may realize that, yes, Elizabeth wasn't really that hot at presenting and perhaps he should use one of those super-confident youngsters next time. On the other hand, he might be delighted that Elizabeth was seeking to improve her capabilities on behalf of the firm. It was a close call. On balance, Elizabeth didn't feel like taking the risk.

Elizabeth decided she had to do this on her own in her spare time. If necessary, she'd take some time off work. She investigated her strategic alternatives. They seemed daunting. A few minutes of Googling and she found a one-week residential course in presentational skills and public speaking for $3,999. The country club setting sounded lovely, but that seemed more like the sort of course companies should pay for to train their employees. She also found a two-day, nonresidential course in downtown Chicago for $1,950 and a one-day course for $650. Finally, she uncovered a seemingly more cost-effective, ten-week, one-evening-per-week course at a local further education college for $289.

She figured that the one- or two-day courses were probably going to be a waste of time. She might learn what she was supposed to do, but there would be little chance for her to practice. So she decided to try the local college for a few weeks (alternative A), and if that didn't help much then she might have to bite the bullet and invest in the country club course (alternative B).

A couple of days later she caught up with some of her old girlfriends from high school for the reunion they held every few years. It was great to see the girls again, but she couldn't get over how Susan had changed. She used to be so shy that you'd have to pry open her mouth to get an answer. Yet there she was, holding everyone's attention with amusing stories of her family and holidays.

Sharing a cab on the way home, Elizabeth remarked to Susan how talkative she had become. She heard that Susan had joined a public speaking and communications club a couple of years ago. It met once a fortnight and had transformed Susan's confidence. Would Elizabeth like to come along to a meeting as a guest and see whether she liked it? If she did, she could join. It would set her back all of $16 for the joining fee, then a mere $3 a month in membership dues!

It sounded too good to be true, but Elizabeth went along. It was just as Susan had said. From the moment she walked into the room, she felt the club reach out and embrace her. Everyone was applauded and cheered,

made to feel good. Every speaker was evaluated in an amazingly positive and encouraging way—nothing at all like the carping criticism one received after presentations at work. The speakers were learning in a fun and astonishingly supportive environment. Elizabeth signed up that evening, but it took her a further four meetings before she summoned the guts to stand up and speak. And she completely mucked it up. But so what? Her evaluator told her that most newcomers did the same, including he, and look at them now!

Elizabeth didn't have to bother with the further education college, and certainly not with the country club. Alternatives A or B? For the trash can! She'd found the solution. It had been on her doorstep all the time. And it was all but free!

A Word on Toastmasters International

What was this extraordinary organization that Elizabeth discovered? Does it exist in reality? Indeed it does and it's called Toastmasters International. In Elizabeth's Chicago area alone, including Du Page, Lake, McHenry, and Cook counties, there are more than 60 such clubs. As of September 2007, there were around 11,300 Toastmaster clubs in 90 countries across the world, with 220,000 members. Three in five members are in the United States, with a further one in ten in Canada. Half of them are female, half male. Seven in ten are aged from 35 to 50, and eight in ten have a college degree. You can find Toastmasters clubs from Alaska to Alabama, Barbados to Brussels, Costa Rica to China.

I've been a member since 1990, a founder member of London's second oldest club, London Corinthians Toastmasters. Over the years, I've seen scores of people transformed. I've seen petrified speakers learn to control their nerves and ultimately, incredibly, enjoy performing. I've seen dull speakers come alive. I've seen good speakers become captivating.

Presentational and public speaking skills are initially like cycling or typing skills. They're not inherited, they can be learned. They're difficult at first to grasp, easier over time. Once learned, they become more like the golf swing—best kept tuned up through regular practice. Lack of practice can allow faults to creep in—whether swiping from the top in golf, or putting hands to the face in speaking. Toastmasters is the ideal forum for such practice. There are hundreds—thousands—of real-

I was late, of course. I poked my head through the door and the elegant woman standing at the front of the group said immediately: "Hi. You must be Vaughan?" "That's me", I said. "Well, welcome to Corinthians," she enthused, and the whole room burst into applause! Just for walking through the door! I almost did an about-turn. Had I stumbled into an undercover branch of Alcoholics Anonymous?

Ten minutes later I was on my feet for a one-minute impromptu speech. I was given a peach of a topic, a holiday misadventure. I spoke about how I had been robbed at knife-point in South America in the 1970s. I can talk for hours on that story, riddled with embellishments, naturally, but I dried up completely after 30 seconds and could think of no more to say. I returned to my seat, in abject shame, yet the whole place applauded again! Wow, I thought, that feels better! I felt the warmth, I felt the support. This clap-clap approach seemed to work!—*Vaughan Evans (extract from a speech on the occasion of the 18th anniversary of London Corinthians Toastmasters, November 2007)*

life Elizabeths whose work and social life has been uplifted by Toastmasters clubs across the world.

A chance dinner with her old classmates meant that Elizabeth didn't need to evaluate her strategic alternatives. She didn't even need an action plan. It was all too obvious. She just needed to turn up every other Thursday evening and her communications skills would improve, steadily and surely. Irreversibly. She pursued a strategy where the investment costs were not far off zero, the risks negligible, the payback immediate, and the returns astronomical.

For those readers who aren't members of Toastmasters, let me leave you with this thought. You're reading a book on career development, perhaps career change. You're clearly interested in self development. There's no more effective program for self-development worldwide than Toastmasters International. Type the word Toastmasters and the name of your town or county into Google, find the nearest club, and go along as a guest. You have nothing to lose. You'll come across a bunch of like-minded souls. At worst, you'll have a good evening's entertainment. For free.

At best, it'll transform your life.

13

Backing UCo?

- ▷ **The Self-Employed Workforce**
- ▷ **The Issue of Credibility**
- ▷ **Going It Alone: Pros and Cons**
- ▷ **What's Your Service?**
- ▷ **It's All About Selling and Marketing**
- ▷ **Seven Tips on Selling Yourself**
- ▷ **Some More Tips**
    Don't forget the delivery
    Then there's the admin
    Stash the cash!
    Where's your support?

In Chapter 11 you were encouraged to stretch your sights and reset your goals. This may have led you to consider a radical strategic alternative in Chapter 12 of going it alone, of quitting your job to carry on providing more or less the same services, but under your own banner.

This chapter is for those who are currently employees, but are considering the option of becoming self-employed. You'll form your own company, typically called NewCo in the world of corporate finance, but for you, UCo. You'll set out to sell your services independently, perhaps initially to your former colleagues, now your customers, and subsequently to new customers. Or you may be entering into competition, whether direct or indirect, with your former company. What are the pros and cons, the pitfalls, the risks, the opportunities, of UCo? Read on.

The Self-Employed Workforce

When I was at business school in the early 1980s, there was much academic debate on what the workforce would look like at end of the century. Many believed that the nature of work was fundamentally changing. One of my lecturers, Professor Charles Handy, a spellbinding communicator and author of many ground-breaking books on the nature of organizations, envisaged that the workforce would become more atomized (see *The*

Age of Unreason or *The Elephant and the Flea*). Technology—and this was largely the telephone, the answering machine (then with magnetic tape technology), and the fax machine, well before dial-up Internet, email, and later, broadband—would enable people to work either independently from home or in loose networks of like-minded individuals. The need for large organizations, for large companies of people, would diminish.

It hasn't quite turned out like that. Sure, we all know lots of self-employed people working out of small offices or from home (the so-called *soho* workforce). We probably all know self-employed people who work within networks, usually informal. Think of Ken the plumber, whom I mentioned in Chapter 12, and who will refer his customers to any tradesman who meets his standards. I too work as an independent, based in my soho (that is, my loft) and with my own offering in management consulting reinforced by a network of associates. They too are fellow independents, all with complementary areas of specialization.

Yet the proportion of the self-employed in the U.S. workforce has stayed strangely flat. Growth has been negligible. They represent around 10.5 percent of the nonagricultural workforce (half of the agricultural workforce is self-employed), within just one decimal point of the rate in the mid-1980s (10.4 percent).

The self-employed are mainly male (roughly 13.5 percent of the male workforce, compared with 8 percent for women), white (12 percent of the white workforce, compared to 11 percent for Asian, 7 percent for Latino and 5.5 percent for blacks), and experienced (18 percent of 55- to 64-year-olds, compared with just 2.5 percent of 25- to 34-year-olds). (Data from "Self-Employment in the United States: An Update," *Monthly Labor Review*, July 2004.)

After farmers, the self-employed are found mainly among those in management, business, and financial occupations (22 percent); construction (21 percent); other services (20 percent); and sales (16 percent). In "other services," highest rates of self-employment are in personal care (barbershops, hair salons, nail salons) and household repairs and maintenance. In professional services, self-employment is generally low (9 percent), but with higher rates in fields such as health care, design, education, landscaping, and child daycare. But the highest rates are for artists (47 percent), writers (47 percent), musicians and singers (43 percent), and photographers (38 percent).

Why haven't these rates grown over the last two decades? The answer is complex and may lie within some large-scale trends in the workplace. On the one hand, globalization and transnational mergers have led remorselessly to larger and larger corporations worldwide. On the other hand, the generally applied corporate strategy of sticking to what you are good at and selling off or outsourcing noncore activities has served to restrain employment growth in larger organizations.

The trend to outsourcing does not, however, seem to have had much impact on the self-employed. When a large company outsources, it tends to do so to a specialized outsourcing provider, typically a company, not an individual. Outsourcing has propelled the growth of thousands of small- and medium-sized businesses, but it seems to have had little effect on the self-employed. The industries and occupations where self-employment rates are high are little different from what they were 20 years ago. Some exceptions spring to mind, such as IT services, and film and TV production services, but they are relatively few and have yet to make a major statistical impact.

The Issue of Credibility

One major constraint limiting growth in self-employment is credibility. When a reasonably large organization buys services, it needs to feel comfortable that the service will be delivered to the appropriate standard and on time. If that doesn't happen, it may want the supplier to face some sort of penalty. In the worst case, this could be court action. If the provider is an individual, the organization may be reticent to impose a penalty, let alone sue her.

Thus the buyer of that service within the organization is taking on an element of risk that would not be present if he bought from a company. Should things go wrong, his boss could well turn round and ask him why he used this individual. What was so distinctive about her offering that made it worth taking on the risk that she would not perform? Why did he take the risk?

Take a simple example. The manager of a medium-sized insurance broker's firm decides that the offices are looking a bit drab. Some carefully selected greenery should brighten things up. Rather than request each department to put up its own plants, he asks his PA to contract a plant display provider to design, install, and look after the lot. The PA has three main options. She could either go to a nationally or regionally branded plant display firm, to a local firm, or to an independent, self-employed individual specializing in the field, like Pansy.

The advantages to the PA of going with Pansy's Plants are significant. She's likely to be more conscientious, enthusiastic, and committed, since this is her livelihood. She will also be cheaper since she has few corporate overheads. But there may be perceived disadvantages. The PA will be reliant on Pansy and her alone, not just for regular maintenance, but for sorting out the paperwork. And what happens when Pansy's on holiday, or sick? What happens if she gets so busy that she can't show up when she's needed?

Some of the PA's concerns would be addressed if Pansy had a partner. The two of them would be able to stagger their holidays and cover for each other when sick. When it comes to the final decision, the PA may choose Pansy, and more likely perhaps if Pansy had a partner, but she may conclude that life would be simpler if she went with Office Greenhouse, the local firm that many other companies in the office block tended to use. That way it would all be less personal and more commercial, and there would always be a receptionist available to call when something needed sorting out.

Thinking back to our analysis in Part I of this book, guarantee of supply is typically an important customer need (Chapter 4) and credibility often a Key Kapability (Chapter 5). It may or may not be a must-have factor, depending on the nature of the service provided.

> Nobody talks of entrepreneurship as survival, but that's exactly what it is and what nurtures creative thinking.—*Anita Roddick*

The issue of credibility is seldom one of competence in doing the job. For the self-employed, the issue can often be one of *being available* to meet the needs of the client at the precise time the client wants those needs met. It is this issue that may offer a partial explanation as to why the economy-wide trend to outsourcing has led to such little growth in the rate of self-employment.

This issue applies primarily in business to business, or B2B, services. It applies less in B2C, or business to consumer, services. The householder often prefers an independent plumber or gardener to an employee of a small plumbing or gardening firm. Many householders value the one-to-one relationship, and yes, it usually works out to be cheaper.

Going It Alone: Pros and Cons

For a chapter about setting off on your own and forming UCo, you may think the above section comprises a rather gloomy start. Credibility is going to be an issue, especially in B2B work, it says. And the rate of self-employed has barely changed since the 1980s.

Good. It's just as well to take such an important step with your eyes open. I'm self-employed, and it ain't easy. If any reader thinks otherwise, you're in for a rude awakening. Self-employment can be rewarding. It can help you achieve the work-life balance you seek. But don't make the mistake of thinking it's going to be easy.

Let me give you more of the bad news, then I'll balance that with some good. Here are six reasons why setting up UCo will be tough:

1. It's not easy to win business.
2. You have to do everything yourself.
3. There ain't no security.
4. Work blurs into home time.
5. It can be lonely.
6. Don't do it for the money.

Then there's the balance—four big reasons why UCo could well be good news:

1. You're your own boss.
2. You'll grow *your* business.
3. You can select your own free time.
4. You'll see more of the family.

Let's first face up to the bad news. These are some of the arguments against.

⇩ It's not easy to win business

Most newly self-employed people have little experience of winning business. At their former company, they may have been handed work to do on a platter. Business won would have been promoted by the marketing team and clinched by the sales team, with the company having a brand that conferred some degree of credibility in the sales process. You may not have been on either team. You helped deliver the business after it had been won.

The newly self-employed person may have come out of government or some other nonprofit-making organization. In this case, she may have even less idea of what it takes to market and sell a successful enterprise. One with no brand name and no track record other than your own résumé.

There are thousands of self-employed people out there offering a service that too few people know about. That's unfortunate, but a few choice tips in the next section (*It's All About Selling and Marketing*) may help.

⇩ You have to do everything yourself

When you're self-employed, who do you ask to type a letter? Then post it? Or answer the phone? Make the coffee? Keep the books? Wine and dine a key client? Chat up the local journalist? Design the business cards? Write the brochure? Provide content for the website? Choose the laptop? And the ISP? Delete the spam? Fix the abominable pop-ups? Slot in a new ink cartridge to the printer? *And* having done all that, provide the service and do the job?

The answer is scary: U!, U!, U!

You're not just the CEO. You're also the GIC—gofer-in-chief.

If you're going to back U in UCo, face it. You'll have to do most everything yourself. Much of it will be fun. Some of it will be pure grind. All will need to be done. And the buck stops with U!

Time allocation is a key prerequisite of a successful self-employed person. There are so many tasks to be done. How to fit it all in? Again there will be some tips later in the chapter (*Then There's the Admin*).

⇩ There ain't no security

If you're an employee and you're feeling dreadful, with the flu or perhaps something worse, what do you do? You call the boss and suggest, croakily, that you stay home for the day. You'll still receive your salary. Likewise if one of the kids is unwell, your spouse is unavailable, and you need to take the child to the doctor, your bank account will still be credited at the end of the month.

Sure, we've all come across ogre bosses who can be unsympathetic, or downright heartless, but most managers accept the situation and cause little fuss—as long as they feel that the employee is genuinely trying to keep time away from work to a minimum.

Likewise, when you're on holiday. For an employee, it may be quite comforting to think of your paycheck landing in the bank while you lie spreadeagle on a Caribbean beach on New Year's Eve. You may even contemplate the contribution your company is making to your pension fund as you sip your rum punch and think about having a turn at the limbo.

Above all, an employee feels she has some sort of job security. Not as much these days as in earlier decades, perhaps. Not so much in the United States as in Britain. Not so much in Britain as in continental Europe. But some. It's human nature. No matter how easy it is to make staff redundant, no manager likes doing it. No more than they like firing employees for incompetence. As long as you're doing your job conscientiously, and as long as the company is ticking over profitably, you have a reasonable degree of job security.

> A real entrepreneur is somebody who has no safety net underneath them.
> —Henry Kravis

There's none of that when you're self-employed. None at all. When you're sick, or when you have to care for sick relatives, there's no pay. Same when you're on holiday. The cost of the holiday is not just what you pay to the tour operator, but the earnings you are foregoing by being there. There's no pension, other than what you take out from profit and pay into your own personal pension fund.

And there's no security when the market gets tough. Unlike for an employee, who may hold on to the job and hopefully salary as the company tightens its belt, the self-employed have to take the revenue downturn on the chin. For the self-employed, you eat what you catch. You are as we all once were: a hunter-gatherer.

⇩ Work blurs into home time

Another disadvantage self-employed people admit to when pressed is that there becomes a finer distinction between when work stops and play starts. Work can infiltrate leisure time.

This is especially true if you work from home. It can be difficult to turn off the laptop or put down your tools and play with the kids when there's work remaining undone.

Take the most extreme example of this, the politician. I was a full-time politician for a couple of years in the early 1990s. I loved it, but it put huge pressure on my then young family. The work is never-ending. Political issues pay no heed to the time of the day. There's as likely to be an issue arising at 9 P.M. as at 9 A.M. The pressure starts at dawn when you need to be prepared to answer calls from the local (or national) radio or TV stations. And after attending whatever events you need to in the evening, work finishes only after you've caught the news reviews late into the night.

The diary in between will be filled to the brim by your agent and activists. Slots have to be consciously set aside for the family, but even when you manage to make these slots your mind can be, sadly, elsewhere. And that's assuming no crisis. When there's a political emergency of any kind, and they are frequent, all diary events are rubbed out, and the needs of the family again put on hold.

Sure, the politician's life is a grotesque extreme of the pressures of the home-based self-employed, but I've known some to be so obsessed with their businesses that they too live a version of this lifestyle. Fine if that's their sole goal. But some only realize the impact on their family after it's too late.

There will be further tips on how to counter this disadvantage later in *Then There's the Admin.*

⇩ It can be lonely

As CEO of UCo, you're likely to be pretty isolated for much of the time. That comes with the territory. Worse, when things go badly, it can be lonely.

When I worked with an international firm of management consultants, it was always a blow when the team lost a pitch for a coveted piece of business. Fortunately, the winning happened more frequently than the losing and so it was relatively easy to shake off the bad news. The team would retire to the pub, have a quick post-mortem, get it out of the way, down a beer or two, crack some jokes, and go home. The next day, we'd move on to the next challenge.

Things are different when you're self-employed. Bad news such as a lost pitch can be hard to take. It gets more personal. It's not your company the client is rejecting in favor of another provider. It's you. It's your skills, your track record, your storyline, your pricing, your personality, your face, your armpits (?!), your everything. In a word, *you*. It can be tough. That's when it can be lonely. (Ironically, while drafting this section—literally today—I've just lost the largest piece of business I've pitched since being self-employed. I've been working to land this on and off for over six months. It's a body blow. I feel dispirited, drained of confidence, lonely. Again. But it could have been worse. I didn't lose to a competitor. That's when it really hurts. On this occasion, the company just seems to have changed its mind, maddeningly, about going ahead with the project. At least I can now spend more time writing this book!)

But again that comes with the territory. A self-employed person *will* receive bad news now and again. Whether it's a lost pitch, a demanding client, a disappointing subcontractor, a prolonged delay, a dispute in payment, bad times will happen. You need to develop a support network to see you through the bad times. There are some tips later in *Where's Your Support?*

⇩ Don't do it for the money

It's a common fallacy that self-employed people make more than employees. It's not generally the case.

It's easy to see how the misconception arises. When you look at the hourly or daily rate charged by a self-employed service provider it often seems high. Multiply by eight hours a day, five days a week and 52 weeks a year, and the hourly rate seems extortionate. But once you build in a factor to allow for her utilization, you'll find that the annual takings come crashing down. Depending on the type of business, she'll be doing well if she can sell three days per week, very well indeed if she can average four days per week, after allowing for marketing, pitching, admin, and sheer down time. And who's going to pay her when she's on holidays or sick with the flu?

Then think of all the extras she'll have to pay for herself, benefits that employees often take for granted. There are pensions and insurances (for example, life, health, dental) that may have to come out of her takings, expenses that could account for 10 to 15 percent of her revenues.

Then there's another factor, especially for those of us in B2B services. Some clients seem to begrudge paying the self-employed the kind of daily rate we feel we need to pay our bills. Why? Because they feel we have so many benefits from working from home. We don't have to pay an office rental or other overhead; we don't have to tolerate a stressful commute every day; we can supposedly take time off whenever we feel like it for a round of golf—so why should they pay us a commercial rate? Most have no comprehension of the trials of self-employment. Nor should we expect them to have.

A word of advice: If you're contemplating launching UCo because you see it as a way of making more money, think twice. That may turn out to be the case; if so, lucky you. But when you present your plan to someone like Chuck Cash, be aware that he won't expect you to make more money. He'll look very carefully indeed at your assumptions on pricing and utilization.

Phew! So much for the disadvantages, now let's try to redress the balance. Here are some of the main advantages of being self-employed, of being the head honcho of UCo!

⇧ You're your own boss

This is the most obvious advantage. No reporting, no asking for permission, no annual reviews, no internal politics, no need to account to anyone but U! To those of us with little patience for bosses of limited capability other than playing the corporate game of snakes and ladders, this is a big plus.

⇧ You'll grow *your* business

Each time you win a new customer, that's *your* precious customer. Each time you receive payment, that's *your* bank account you'll be dropping the check into. Each time you prepare your annual accounts, hopefully you'll be tracking the growth of *your* company, *your* enterprise, *your* initiative, *your* energy. *Your* baby. It feels good.

⇧ You can select your own free time

This is the flipside to the disadvantage above of work slipping into leisure time. Leisure can also slip into work time more easily when you're self-employed. You're bashing away at the laptop, and the lad comes home from school. "Dad, how long are you going to be?" "Oh, just a couple of hours, son." "But, Dad, you're always working. And look, it's sunny outside. It might rain later on. And you know how you like me to do more exercise. Oh, come on, Dad, let's go to the park *now?*" Why not?!

What is this life if, full of care, there is no time to stand and stare?—William Henry Davies.

Ask a London taxi driver what he likes about his job. He'll tell you it's the flexibility of the hours. That's why so many golf courses in the counties around London are full of taxi drivers in the middle of the week. "Once I've made my numbers, I head off for the course," said one to me recently. I bet his doctor approves of that attitude for life!

It's easy to get distracted, however. We all have our weak spots. I'm particularly vulnerable when the Wimbledon tennis is on the TV. Or the Ryder Cup. Or West Indian cricket. Fortunately, Welsh (or Fijian) rugby tends to be on weekends. Likewise, Liverpool (or Brazilian) soccer. Otherwise temptation would be overpowering. It's just as well I can't fathom what's going on in American football, baseball, or basketball. I'd never get any work done!

The self-employed person needs time discipline, for sure (see *What About the Admin?* later on). But the opportunity now and again to be able to break out, without having to answer to anyone other than your own self and your own business, is to be treasured.

⇧ You'll see more of the family

Few self-employed people have long commutes. Many work from home or from nearby offices, maybe on the main street down the road. Many visit other people's homes within a reasonable radius of theirs. Time saved in commuting should mean more time with the family. When you see both parents of a child at an after-lunch performance of the school's jazz band, what's the betting that the working parent is self-employed?

So there you have it. Some fantastic advantages to being self-employed, balanced by some rather grim disadvantages. It's a lifestyle choice. Over to you!

If you do decide to go for it, here are some tips on how to make UCo a success.

What's Your Service?

What service do you offer? This may sound rather obvious, but you need to be clear about what service you intend to offer as UCo, and to whom.

There are four typical situations where an employee makes the transition to self-employed:

1. *Outsourced*—She works for a company (or nonprofit organization), providing clearly defined services within the company, and she leaves to supply the same services to her former company, and perhaps to other companies as well, but as a self-employed contractor.
2. *Competing for clients*—He works for a company that supplies services to other companies (B2B) and he leaves to compete with his former company in providing those services to the same and other clients.
3. *Competing for custom*—She works for a company that supplies services to consumers (B2C) and she leaves to set up a business supplying the same or similar services to consumers, perhaps in competition with her former company or perhaps targeting other consumers (for instance, in a different area).
4. *A fresh start*—He works for any company and leaves to start his own business, little or nothing to do with his former job or his former company.

It's important to be clear as to which of these routes applies to you. Your sales and marketing strategy—in the next section—will depend on it.

In Part I of this book, where you assessed whether you were backable in your current job, some consideration was given to the possibility of the first route above, of becoming outsourced. Thus Chuck considered whether the PA-cum-market researcher Elizabeth should outsource herself and provide her services to her former employer, ConsultCo, and advised against.

The second and third routes also require much forethought. Will you be competing against your former employer? How will you rate against the required K2s? How will you handle the credibility issue? Or will you be dodging direct competition and targeting a niche where your former employer has little interest? The latter may be more attractive to a backer.

Or is yours the fourth of the routes, a fresh start? Like Part I's Leila, a former flight attendant who set up as an aromatherapist. Or Randy, the Realtor who is intent on becoming a plumber? If so, you need to be sure that the market demand for your new offering is buoyant, that competition is not becoming tougher, and that you'll have the requisite K2s. This will be very much the theme of Part III of this book.

Another way of looking at the fresh start route is to consider whether your intended offering addresses some "unmet needs" in the marketplace. This is one of the secrets to a new venture's success highlighted by William Bridges, a leading authority on organizational transitions, in his esteemed work *Creating You & Co.* He suggests that an "unmet need" could be uncovered by spotting signs such as a missing piece in a pattern, an unrecognized opportunity, an underused resource, a signal event, an unacknowledged change, a supposedly impossible situation, a nonexistent but needed service, a new or emerging problem, a bottleneck, an interface, or other similar signs.

It's All About Selling and Marketing

I said it earlier, but I'll say it again because it can't be emphasized enough. Believe me, I've found out the hard way (and I'm still learning). Here it is. If no one knows you're there, you won't get any business. No matter how good you are at what you do.

If you come from a sales background, you'll have a head start on forming UCo. Even if there are others out there much better at executing the work

If no one knows you're there, you won't get your share.

than you, you could well do better than they. You'll know how to make customers aware of your offering and how it differs from the others.

One of the most successful professional speakers in Britain is Frank Furness (www.frankfurness.com). When he started out, he readily admits that he wasn't the most charismatic of speakers. But he had been in sales and marketing all his life and he set about applying all this experience on himself and his business. Through a strategy of relentless marketing, coupled with a sideline bootcamp business in coaching starter speakers to do the same, he has built a thriving business worldwide—and meanwhile has developed into a speaker capable of delivering inspirational content.

If, however, you're like most of us who have gone it alone, and you've had very little experience in selling and marketing, then please take one thing away from this section: *Seek help!*

Consider postponing any plans you may have had to further develop your offering. Learn instead how to sell. It'll open your eyes. Learn the most effective ways to market your type of service.

Next to doing the right thing, the most important thing is to let people know you are doing the right thing.
—*John D. Rockefeller*

The first step is to buy some books. What? Too expensive? Not enough time to read them? You're kidding! You're thinking of becoming self-employed and you're not prepared to invest in some learning?!

You've already invested a few bucks on this book. That's just the start. You should invest in two or three books on how to sell and market your service as well. Some of them may be fat and pricey. Buy them anyway.

You don't have to read every word. Skim through, hunt for the bits that seem appropriate to your situation. If there's *one tip* in that book that helps you make *one sale,* your investment could be recouped many times over.

Here are a couple of books that have helped me. *Getting Business to Come to You*, by Paul and Sarah Edwards and Laura Clampitt Douglas, is a comprehensive guide. They show you how to stand out from the crowd, through focusing, niching, and demonstrating why you're the best provider. And how to create a winning marketing message and develop a promotional package. Finally they help you to select marketing methods that are tailor-made for you. It's all in there, in almost 700 pages.

Slimmer is *Get Clients Now!* by C. J. Hayden, a book that's tailored to management consultants and professionals. That's the business I'm in, and it's more relevant to me than other more general marketing books. She shows how to develop a marketing strategy and features a 28-day marketing program aimed at locating, landing, and keeping clients.

Try putting your occupation and the words "sales, marketing" into Google or Amazon and see what's been written that's targeted directly at your business. There probably won't be many, but buy one or two. They may not be brilliant, but there may be a nugget or two in there that could justify the purchase price a hundred fold.

Another small book I found useful is *Rapid Referral Results* by Roy Sheppard, which highlights the importance of referrals, one of the key tools in the armory of the self-employed—see below under *Don't be shy about asking for referrals.*

If reading these and similar books doesn't do the trick, consider enrolling on a course. There are plenty around, whether at local further education colleges, business schools, or ad hoc seminars by sales professionals. The latter can be quite expensive, so look carefully for someone who's experienced in your field and do thorough web research on her before you pay up and attend.

Seven Tips on Selling Yourself

Here are some tips I've learned along the way. They may not be comprehensive, such as what you might find in larger tomes on sales and marketing, but do these and you'll be well on the way:

1. Perfect your elevator speech.
2. Reinforce your message.
3. Try 10-touch marketing.
4. Pick up that phone.
5. Don't be shy about asking for referrals and testimonials.
6. Don't be greedy.
7. If you have to, use an agent.

Perfect your elevator speech!

You need to be absolutely clear about what it is you offer and why it delivers distinctive benefits to your clients. All in one simple sentence. It should be able to be delivered, if necessary, when meeting a stranger in an elevator between the first and third floors!

Here's an example. Pansy visits many office blocks and frequently finds herself giving her elevator speech, literally. Not surprising, really. Her elevator companion will be dressed for the office, whether suit and tie or smart casual, depending on the office dress code. But Pansy will be in her usual baggy green T shirt, with her logo of Pansy's Plants embossed in yellow, and her denim cutoffs. She looks different and intriguing and this often sparks a chat. Here's her line: "I'm Pansy, and I run my own office plant display company. I'm passionate about how the right plants can create a sense of well-being in an office environment." Short and sweet, it communicates what she does and focuses on a feel-good benefit to a potential customer.

Reinforce your message!

Don't just send a client a letter, a leaflet, or a business card. Certainly don't just zap her an email. Call her. Knock on her door. Get yourself in a newspaper or journal talking about your business and its benefits. Bump into her at networking events. Get your clients to speak highly of you to her.

Let her receive a simple message by hearing it from many different sources.

The message can be further reinforced if she hears from these varied sources at around the same time. If in the space of a week, she has met you at a conference, read about you in a journal, and been recommended to you by a peer, your message will be that much greater than the sum of the three individual messages. This is the Holy Grail of the PR world: simultaneous bombardment of the client with a simple message from multiple sources.

Try 10-touch marketing!

I can't remember where I heard this from, probably from some surfing on the web, but it lodged in my mind and I find it most helpful—if only to remind me how my own woeful marketing efforts fall way behind target every year. You need to develop a 10-touch marketing campaign for your key clients, every year. In other words, your client needs to be reminded of your existence and your message 10 times during each year—that's more or less once a month, excluding the summer holidays. The touches can range from sending a Christmas card to a two-hour PowerPoint presentation, from a catch-up call to a liquid lunch on a Friday, from an email with an interesting attachment to a piece of business. But try to make it a 10-touch year for each key client.

Think of your message as a Post-it note. At the first contact, you slap it on her shoulder. After a while it starts to lose its stickiness. It needs another slap, most effectively from a different angle, another source. And so on. Your goal is to have that Post-it sticking on her shoulder week in, week out, so when the moment arrives that she needs your kind of service, she reaches up to her shoulder, extracts the Post-it, and calls you first.

Don't let the client forget about you. Don't let the competition sneak in behind you because you fail to get in touch with a client for three, six months. Don't lose work without even being asked to pitch. That really sucks! Keep slapping that Post-it! Try 10-touch marketing.

Pick up that phone!

Why are so many self-employed people so shy of picking up the phone? Like me. I would do anything rather than call a client and ask him how business is going (and— hint—whether there's any opportunity for me to be of help). I'll suddenly discover that bills need to be paid, letters written, computer scanned for viruses, garbage taken out—whatever, other than pick up the phone. I'd prefer to have a tooth pulled or make a speech in front of a thousand people with my pants down.

The problem is that we know only too well how much we hate receiving unsolicited telephone calls ourselves. Late Sunday afternoon and the phone rings. No, not your mom, sister, or a family friend, but some hapless caller from an overseas call center trying to get you to upgrade your cell phone. Or worse, a tape recording congratulating you on winning some phony timeshare vacation. We worry that our client may find our call no less an annoyance.

Too bad. We have to do it. Especially for those of us in B2B services. Phoning is much more effective than the cop-out of emailing. An email can get buried in a client's inbox in minutes. If you hate calling as much as I do, here are some tips that have helped me:

> *Prepare your pitch*—Have your pitch on a piece of paper in front of you, with the opening line or lines typed out, word for word, and the rest in bullet points.

> *Psych yourself up*—It may be 11 A.M. and the phone has been silent all morning. You haven't opened your mouth since the kids went out of the door at 8:30. Clear your throat. Look at your achievements around the office. Assert your right to make contact by telephone. Remember, you're great! A friend of mine who is a self-employed life coach has a Post-it note on his telephone on which he has written in red ink: *You're the dog's bxxxxxks!** It seems to work!

* Note: This is a humorous, British slang expression, referring to a prominent part of a dog's anatomy and meaning "simply the best," or the "bees knees." It (perhaps rudely, for which I apologize) illustrates the point that you should find your own way of boosting your confidence before you pick up the phone.

> *Stand up!*—If there's one thing to remember, it's this. You will be

communicating only with your voice. Your face, your eyes, your hands, the other main tools for communication, are unseen. Your voice will carry so much more conviction, authority, and *energy* if you're standing. Imagine going to the theater and seeing all the actors deliver their lines seated. You'd soon be yawning. It's the same with the phone. Stand up. Don't let your client nod off!

> *Don't waste her time*—Have something of interest or use or amusement to discuss with her, something she's going to remember once the phone has been put down. Give her some tidbits on what's happening in the market, for example, on what her competitors are up to. Don't just call her and ask if there's any work for you.

> *Remind her of what you have in common*—From previous meetings, hopefully you'll have found something, anything, that you and she have in common—live in the same part of town, brother went to same school, mutual friend, worked for similar companies, kids the same age, share the same hobby, support the same team, whatever. Try to tap into that commonality every time you speak to her. The personal touch is often remembered longer than the impersonal, no matter how articulate or informative the pitch.

> *Angle for a follow-up*—Try to steer for some follow-up action, enabling you to contact her again the next day or week. You may refer her to some interesting article during the conversation, then email it to her later.

Another thought: Find a partner. If you're on your own, it's so much more difficult to get the difficult things done, especially client calling. With a partner, he'll give you no choice. Likewise, you'll give him no choice. The clients have to be called, so call them you will. You'll split them between the two of you. And you'll compare notes at the end of the day. That's partner pressure to perform.

One final tip about the phone. Invest in a high-quality answering machine cum speakerphone. The hands-free speakerphone can be invaluable when you need to speak and make notes at the same time, although it's best not to use it when cold calling, when you should be standing up. The answering machine (or voicemail, if you prefer) is a godsend. You make a call, you get your client's voicemail, and you await the call back. Finally it comes, right at the end of the day. The kids are back from school; you've had a long, unrewarding day; you're tired, a little down. *Don't take it!* Leave it to your chirpy answering message.

Then you have two choices. You can either go through the whole process again—psyching yourself up, checking your script, standing up—and call her back. Or you can wait until you're feeling less tired, more affirmative, and more optimistic the following morning. The answering machine gives you the option.

Don't be shy about asking for referrals and testimonials!

There is no better way of getting an introduction to a new prospective client than being referred to him by an existing, satisfied client. That's a referral, and it's the lifeblood of the self-employed. Best of all is when your client will actually call up the new client, or mention you next time he sees him. Next best is when your client suggests you should contact this prospective client and gives you an agreed testimonial about your capabilities. This you can put into a letter and follow it up with a phone call a few days later. Still good is when your client just says "Sure, you can use my name" and you call the prospective client, saying, "So-and-so suggested I give you a call."

Right now we have a problem with a smelly drain. The emergency drainage guy has been here and told us that it's definitely not a sewerage problem, that all seems to be working fine. It's probably an old surface water drain that wasn't closed off properly when the garage was converted to a side extension by the previous owner five years ago. The laminated floor boards will have to be ripped up, so it's a job for a builder with a sound understanding of drainage and who's not too heavy handed in the carpentry department. Who to go to? We have no idea. If only someone could refer us to someone who'd be just right for sorting this out. If only we had a referral.

It's the same with your clients. They always have a choice of provider. That's the marketplace. But they'd feel a lot more comfortable using a provider that's been recommended to them by someone they know and trust, rather than taking potluck with the Yellow Pages. They'd feel safer using a referral.

Don't be shy asking for referrals. You should ask every client for them. Here's a tip from Roy Sheppard's book. He recommends you try something like this: "Referrals are the lifeline in our business. That means we have to work so much harder ensuring clients like you are totally satisfied with our work. That way you'll hopefully recommend us to others."

Your client should agree with that. He'll like the fact that you are trying harder for his benefit. Then you can nudge the conversation on to some actual referrals—who else should you be talking to, would he be prepared to contact them, could you use his name, and would he be prepared to give you a testimonial?

Don't be greedy!

This is a simple tip in completing the sale. When you realize you're in pole position to win a piece of work, don't blow it by being greedy. Remember it's better to be utilized and earning something than unutilized and earning nothing. It's as simple as that.

I fell into this trap early in my self-employed career. I contacted a former client about an opportunity I thought he might be interested in, and where an associate and I were unusually well placed to help him. He emailed me back with just two words: "How much?" This client has deep pockets. I knew he could opt for a top-tier consulting firm and get similar advice, but at twice, even thrice, my price. So I thought I'd go halfway, at 50 percent above my usual rates. Bargain for him, bonus for me. Wrong again. He didn't reply. I was underutilized for the next couple of months. I could have done 10, maybe 20, days' work for that client at my usual rate, or even at 10 to 15 percent above. Instead I blew it. I hope I've learned that lesson.

Don't blow business by being greedy. Give good service at a good price. That'll be doubly good value to the customer. And he'll use you again.

If you have to, use an agent!

If you've read the books on sales and marketing, been to a seminar or two and tried out some of my tips above, and you still aren't selling as much as someone of your capabilities should be delivering, try an agent. Find someone who's a professional salesperson and well placed to help you. Someone with some good contacts, preferably. Someone with plenty of energy and a passion for selling. Such people do exist! Payment of 10 percent, even 15 percent commission on sales should more than repay itself, compared with the alternative of you remaining underutilized.

> The definition of insanity is doing the same thing over and over again and expecting different results.
> — *Albert Einstein*

The final word on selling and marketing yourself should rest, perhaps slightly out of context, with the inimitable Ms. West.

> It's better to be looked over than overlooked.—*Mae West*

Some More Tips

Sales and marketing will be the most important function in UCo. But it's not the only one. You also have to deliver the goods, run a tight, profitable business, and stash the cash. And you need to build your support network. Here are some more tips.

Don't forget the delivery

It goes without saying that you must be especially good at your job if you're going to be self-employed. Unlike for an employee, there's no one to hide behind. You're on your own, totally exposed.

Ideally, you'll be demonstrably better at your job than most employees at competing companies. Unlike them, you'll have no brand name when you start up. Unless you're going to compete on cost, you'll have to offer a better or a distinctive service to win custom. Like Leila, our aromatherapist.

Although you must certainly place most of your emphasis in the early days on selling and marketing, don't forget to keep sharpening your tools in delivering the service.

It may be a timing issue. If you're thinking of leaving your company in six months' time and launching your own business a couple of months later, you should think about whether you need to get in any further training or development *now*, rather than wait until you leave your present company.

Ideally you'll be ready for top-notch service delivery from the day you launch. Then all you need to do is bring the business in and deliver quality work.

Then there's the admin

Unfortunately there's more to running your own business than selling, marketing, and delivering. Remember, you're not just managing director, sales and marketing director and operations director. You're also finance director, receivables manager, bookkeeper, and clerk.

UCo, like all small businesses, will have its fair share of red tape. Are you going to set up a company or a partnership, or just put your earnings through you? What bank accounts should you use? Will you need to apply for a sales tax license? You should get advice on these and other startup financial decisions from an accountant.

Then there's also the regular admin work. You'll need to learn about book-keeping, filling in your sales tax forms and 101 other things needed to keep the business ticking over. It's your responsibility, for example, to pay the electricity bill on time, thereby saving the embarrassment of being cut off while serving the client. Imagine you're a hair stylist and the power cuts off when your client is in curlers under the drier!

You may find some government-sponsored courses in your area focusing on the red tape of running your own business. Go to them. They may be dull, but they could save you grief later on.

Some companies set aside time for employees to catch up with their expenses and other admin, termed "laundry days," say one Monday morning each month. That's fine, it you like things scheduled. Personally, I like to stagger things. I know that I have to set aside two or three days each October to do my annual accounts and tax return. And an hour or so each quarter for my value-added tax return. The rest I tackle when the inbasket pile rises above 6 inches!

However you address it, admin work must be kept under control, yet it mustn't eat into too much of your work time. It's a delicate balance, one that will come with experience—and the odd mistake.

Stash the cash!

There's one admin task, however, which takes precedence over all others. Revenue on your P&L account is great, profit even better. But that's all paperwork. Profit doesn't go into the bank. Only cash does, and it needs collecting. By you.

Cash management is often quoted in surveys as one of the main reasons why most small businesses fail. Entrepreneurs are so busy selling and managing the delivery of work, they fail to pay sufficient attention to the building up of receivables (trade debtors). Meanwhile they often have little choice but to meet their payables (trade creditors) on time or they won't be able to deliver. If they're not careful, they'll run out of cash.

No matter how marvelous the market, how brilliant the business concept, how excellent the entrepreneur, if she runs out of cash, the business is bust.

It can be difficult for a small businessperson to insist that a customer pays up on time. You don't want to make too much fuss because you want his business again. Tough. You have no choice. You have to explain to your customer that whatever service you provide does not include acting as his banker.

Ken Blanchard, Don Hutson, and Ethan Willis, in their excellent little book, *The One Minute Entrepreneur,* remind us that "making it in business requires three very important things...CASH, CASH, CASH." You'd do well to bear all three of them in mind.

Where's your support?

We saw earlier that lack of support of colleagues is a major disadvantage of being self-employed. So we self-employed must have some support system in place to compensate. What will yours be in UCo?

Consider these situations. I had a pretty good start to 2004 and set off with the family for a long summer holiday contentedly ahead of budget. By the middle of October I was still feeling good about the year. I had eight "leads" in my pipeline, one or two of which were surely bound to land in the final quarter, I thought, so sealing a good year. I was wrong. In the space of seven days, seven of the leads evaporated. One I lost in a fair fight with a competitor and in each of the others my clients were unable to proceed, or chose not to. It was rough. The eighth lead floated away a week later. It wasn't until early December that I picked up another piece of work.

So between August and November 2004, I earned not one penny. The highest earning member of my household was my 15-year-old daughter, who'd been doing two hours every Saturday morning teaching little ones at math class! And that was on minimum wage!

It could have been worse. Another freelance consultant I know, Dick, managed to sell just 15 days' paid work in 15 months. He went weeks without the telephone going. Imagine not just a silent morning or a silent day, but a silent week. Imagine a silent month. It wasn't just disheartening, it was morale-sapping and confidence-shattering. Dick persevered, however, and is now thriving with the very same business proposition he was offering during that awful year. In retrospect, he seems to have gone through just a prolonged bout of bad luck.

Suppose such hard times were to happen to you. How would you cope? What would be your support mechanism? Mine, when I went through those wretched couple of weeks of vanishing business, was my family. Less work meant more time to play with the lad, so that couldn't be a bad

Always look on the bright side of life.—*Eric Idle*

thing, I reasoned.

Dick also relied on his family for support, along with sympathetic fellow freelancers. But he also had one other form of support that I believe is essential to maintaining sanity if you're self-employed. He had a bank balance that was robust enough to be able to withstand *one year's worth of zero business*. It's a sound philosophy to have. No one enters the world of self-employment expecting to earn nothing for a whole year. But if you know that if everything goes wrong, if work dries up for a full 12 months and yet you can still survive, that can be a huge dose of comfort during the bad times. It can help you sleep at night.

I wanted to be an editor or a journalist. I wasn't really interested in being an entrepreneur, but I soon found I had to become an entrepreneur in order to keep my magazine going.
—*Richard Branson*

My advice? Before launching into self-employment, make sure you have your lines of support teed up. They include not just your family, friends, and associates, but also your bank account, or a bank manager prepared to extend adequate credit.

Still thinking of UCo? Be aware that's it's not a bed of roses. But then nowhere is. UCo, on balance, is the place for me. How about U?

14

- ▷ **Things Look Sunnier?**
- ▷ **Would You Have Backed the Early Madonna?**
- ▷ **After *Sex*?**
- ▷ **Would You Back Richard Branson's Virgin Galactic?**
- ▷ **How a New Strategy May Impact Suns & Clouds**
- ▷ **A Self-Employed Example**
- ▷ **An Employee Example**
- ▷ **Are U Now More Backable?**

In Chapters 10 through 13, you envisioned the ideal provider, reset your sights, and identified the capability gap. You built a strategy to bridge it, possibly focused around the launching of UCo, and developed an action plan. Has your Suns & Clouds chart of Chapter 8 become sunnier? Will the balance of risks and opportunities have shifted in your favor? Will U have become even more backable in your current job or business?

The answer, hopefully, should be a resounding *yes!* That, after all, has been the purpose of Part II.

Things Look Sunnier?

The strategy you developed in Chapter 12, which set out to address the K2 gap you identified in Chapter 11, originated from the brainstorming and scenario development you undertook in Chapter 10. This in turn took as its starting point the risks and opportunities you assessed in Chapter 8 of Part I.

> Small opportunities are often the beginning of great enterprises—*Demosthenes*

Hopefully, therefore, your strategy will have been centered around either reducing the likelihood and/or the impact of the risks identified in Part I, or improving the likelihood and/or the impact of the opportunities.

Take a look at the risks and opportunities you assessed in Part I. How will they have changed as a result of your new strategy, assuming it is implemented successfully? What if your strategy is implemented with only partial success?

Are some of the risks now less likely? Or if not, then with lower impact? Have new risks been introduced by pursuing your new strategy? If so, are they containable?

What about the opportunities? Hopefully some identified in Chapter 8 may now be more likely. Or if not, then with higher impact? Has your new strategy identified new opportunities? How likely? How big? How promising?

How has this impacted your Suns & Clouds chart? Are the risks and opportunities now better balanced? Is your chart sunnier? It should be. That's what your strategy was designed to do.

Would You Have Backed the Early Madonna?

In Chapter 8 we looked at how the Suns & Clouds chart may have helped a prospective backer of the Beatles back in early 1962. Then we saw how that chart would have been transformed into blazing sunshine one year later. Sticking to the pop music theme, we took in Chapter 12 Madonna as an example of someone whose crystal clear strategy has propelled her to the top of her industry's earnings league year after year. Let's see how that strategy may have affected her Suns & Clouds chart over time.

Let's suppose you're a prospective investor, like Chuck Cash. It's 1982, and you show up at a grubby studio in downtown Manhattan to meet a young woman with grandiose aspirations of stardom. Ms. Ciccone is a dancer who can sing a bit. She's a hard worker, but she's hard up. She's been scraping a living in New York City for five years, through a succession of low paid jobs, including modeling in the nude (as subsequently featured in glossy magazines).

She has, however, made some progress as an entertainer. She has worked with a number of modern dance companies, been a backing dancer on a world tour and played vocals and drums with a rock band, the Breakfast Club. She has written and produced a number of solo disco and dance songs. These brought her to the attention of Sire Records, with whom she signed a singles deal. Her first single, "Everybody," written by herself and for which she received $5,000, has just come out and is proving a hit on the dance charts and in the clubs. However, it has made no impact on the Billboard Hot 100.

Suppose she needs backing, whether for personal reasons or to invest in some promotional activity. She thinks an album deal is imminent. And stardom just around the corner. You see her as high risk. Figure 14.1 shows Madonna's Suns & Clouds as you may have seen them in 1982.

Would you have backed her? On the basis of the Suns & Clouds alone, possibly not. Music trends seemed to have been moving in other directions. "Everybody" was successful only in the small niche of club music. She might have followed that up with another single or two, even

Figure 14.1 **Would You Have Backed Madonna in 1982?**

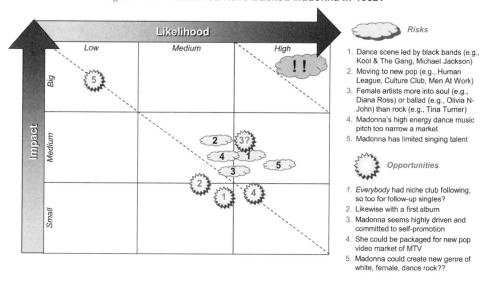

Risks

1. Dance scene led by black bands (e.g., Kool & The Gang, Michael Jackson)
2. Moving to new pop (e.g., Human League, Culture Club, Men At Work)
3. Female artists more into soul (e.g., Diana Ross) or ballad (e.g., Olivia N-John) than rock (e.g., Tina Turner)
4. Madonna's high energy dance music pitch too narrow a market
5. Madonna has limited singing talent

Opportunities

1. *Everybody* had niche club following, so too for follow-up singles?
2. Likewise with a first album
3. Madonna seems highly driven and committed to self-promotion
4. She could be packaged for new pop video market of MTV
5. Madonna could create new genre of white, female, dance rock??

an album. But they too might have found just a niche following. She was a good dancer but a rather screechy singer. She dressed and looked sexy but so did loads of other dancers.

But you may have seen something else. One opportunity (sun 3) might have had an impact beyond the obvious. You would have spent some time with her and may have witnessed what many later came to recognize. A relentless drive, evidenced perhaps by her life over the previous few years as she painstakingly built up her performing experience. A steely professionalism. An extrovertism bordering on the exhibitionist, with a readiness to blend her very person with her image. Boundless ambition. This was special. You may well have decided to back her.

One year on and her Suns & Clouds (in Figure 14.2) will have changed out of recognition. Her first album, *Madonna*, reached the top 10 on the U.S. album charts and five of its singles became hits. One of them, "Holiday," went on to sell 12 million copies. The main risks concerning the breadth of her appeal would have evaporated. The main opportunity—of her being able to carve out a new genre of white, female dance-rock music with huge popular appeal—was now looking not just conceivable but likely.

If you hadn't backed her the year before, you wouldn't be able to afford to now. Opportunities before her were unbounded.

After *Sex*?

Madonna's Suns & Clouds would have stayed more or less like that through the 1980s. Albums such as *Like a Virgin, True Blue,* and *Like a Prayer* kept her at the top of the charts. Meanwhile she also received critical acclaim in the movie, *Desperately Seeking Susan,* although roles in other movies didn't earn such plaudits.

Figure 14.2 **Would You Have Backed Madonna in 1983?!**

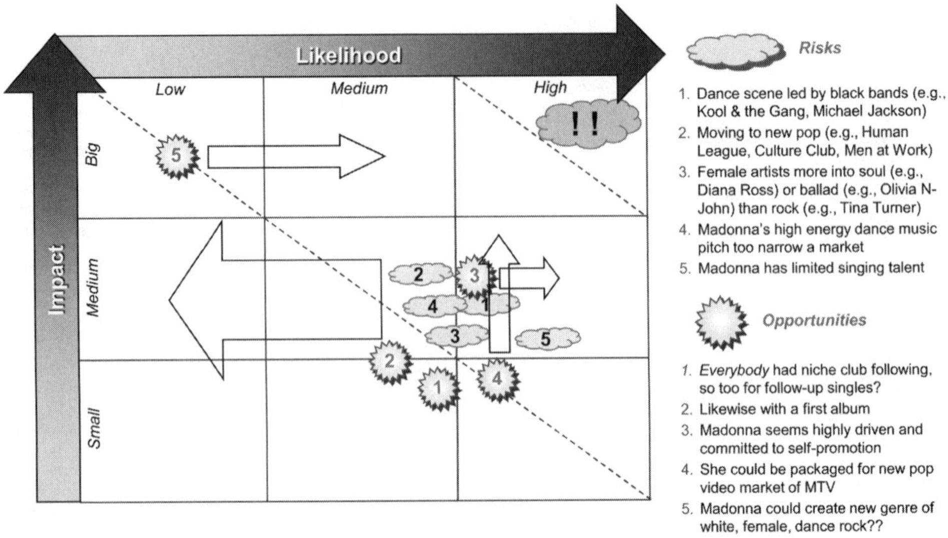

Risks

1. Dance scene led by black bands (e.g., Kool & the Gang, Michael Jackson)
2. Moving to new pop (e.g., Human League, Culture Club, Men at Work)
3. Female artists more into soul (e.g., Diana Ross) or ballad (e.g., Olivia N-John) than rock (e.g., Tina Turner)
4. Madonna's high energy dance music pitch too narrow a market
5. Madonna has limited singing talent

Opportunities

1. *Everybody* had niche club following, so too for follow-up singles?
2. Likewise with a first album
3. Madonna seems highly driven and committed to self-promotion
4. She could be packaged for new pop video market of MTV
5. Madonna could create new genre of white, female, dance rock??

Then in 1992 came *Sex,* an extraordinary, coffee table book of photographs featuring Madonna in an array of sexually explicit poses. The book was largely damned by the media as being narcissistic, some said pornographic. It was followed by an album called *Erotica,* which was met with similar criticism. The video accompanying the (successful) lead single was withdrawn from MTV. Not long afterwards, Madonna took the leading female role in a movie, *Body of Evidence,* a smuttier take on *Basic Instinct.* The movie flopped, further denting Madonna's appeal. Had she blown it? Had her star waned? Were these ventures into sexual explicitness just a sad, final fling for an entertainer who had passed her sell-by date?

Suppose she had needed some backing then. Sure, she already had her millions of dollars stacked away in property and investments. But suppose she wanted more. Suppose she needed cash to buy another spectacular property, a virtual palace for $25 million? Would you have backed her? Would you have thought her capable of continuing to generate the kind of multimillion dollar income stream every year she had achieved in the 1980s?

Back in 1993, would you have thought that Madonna would recover from such a critical mauling, from an apparent obliteration of her fan base? That she would have gone on to produce further platinum-selling albums (like *Ray of Light* in 1998)? To star in a top-grossing movie (like *Evita* in 1996)?

You may well have done. For all the risks, the dominant feature in Madonna's Suns & Clouds would have been her *consistent strategy.* Her drive for self-publicity and capacity for self-reinvention may well have convinced you that, just as she dragged down her celebrity star rating in 1992, so too could she yank it up again in years to come. And perhaps she may have learned some lessons from 1992 and be a trifle more circumspect in her future reinventions. In 1993 her chart may have looked like Figure 14.3.

Figure 14.3 **Would You Have Backed Madonna Again in 1993?**

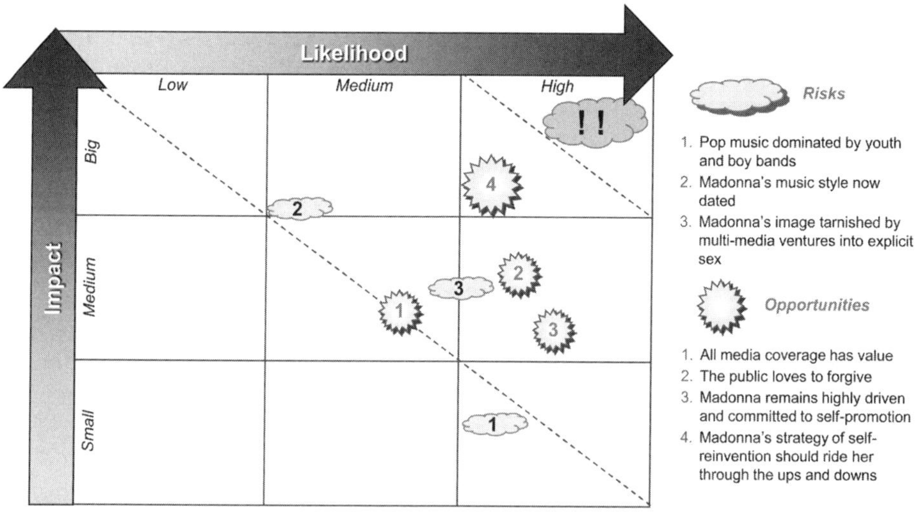

The one thing you know for sure in the world of entertainment is that an entertainer needs to keep her name in the headlines, her face on the front covers of magazines, whether in praise or condemnation. Any news is good news. No news is obscurity. You're aware that in her year of sexual exhibitionism, Madonna had been even more in our faces than before. You may have figured that all she had to do was to continue to reinvent herself, preferably into something entirely different—into an Argentinean folk heroine, perhaps, or an Eastern mystic, or an all American girl, or a devoted mother, or a lady of the manor, whatever—and she could postpone her sell-by date indefinitely. The strategy seemed brilliant. You would surely have backed that strategy and would have been pleased that, 13 years later, in 2006, her *Confessions* tour, still controversial with its provocative deployment of a crucifix and crown of thorns, became the highest grossing global tour by a female artist ever.

Would You Back Richard Branson's Virgin Galactic?

Let's take one more example of a consistently successful *Stand-Out!* strategy. Richard Branson is an entrepreneur the like of whom has seldom, if ever, been nurtured in Britain. He has launched successful new ventures in areas of activity as diverse as music and money management, mobile telephony and airlines, all under the brand name of *Virgin*—the name of his first business after leaving high school in 1970. This was a mail order record business, and he soon followed this with a small record shop on London's Oxford Street. He later opened a recording studio and had a stroke of luck when his first artist produced a first song that sold 5 million copies. Branson didn't look back, and both his recording and retail businesses took off.

In 1984 he made an extraordinary detour, venturing into the airline business. He knew it was risky: "We started the business in 1984 and almost all my colleagues at Virgin said I was completely mad to go into the airline business. The newspapers said calling an airline Virgin was mad." (Source: www.virgin.com) Airlines are indeed notoriously risky enterprises and many investors won't touch them with a 10-foot pole. History is littered with airlines that have gone under. Remember Pan Am? Eastern? Laker Airways, the original no frills, cut-price, trans-Atlantic carrier? Yet all of these companies were run and backed by people who knew about airlines, not by music entrepreneurs!

Would you have backed Branson in his Virgin Atlantic venture? You can imagine the Suns & Clouds chart. A fearsome agglomeration of thunderous dark clouds blowing ominously toward the top right-hand corner. With one sun shining defiantly in their midst.

This sun would have been a phenomenal brand name, associated not just with quality, value-for-money service provision and a perception of the little man fighting against the global goliaths. But one also suggestive of excitement and glamour. This was raised to a new level following the airline launch. Branson embarked on a series of world speed record attempts to keep the brand in the headlines, usually involving Branson himself. In 1986 his boat, *Virgin Atlantic Challenger II*, broke the record for crossing the Atlantic Ocean. A year later he did the same in the hot air balloon, *Virgin Atlantic Flyer*. He later achieved the same feat flying across the Pacific Ocean, before making several attempts to circumnavigate the globe in a hot air balloon. Foiled by weather, these attempts proved unsuccessful, though not so in terms of publicity.

Aided no doubt by this high-profile marketing strategy, Branson's airline has been an astonishing success. It has held its own both with its rival British Airways and with American transatlantic carriers. It has survived two severe downturns in the air industry without government subsidization or resort to Chapter 11.

Branson has now moved on to the new travel frontier: space tourism. His new venture, *Virgin Galactic,* plans to launch six paying passengers at a time (plus two crew) into space from a spaceport in New Mexico. They will be flown to a suborbital altitude of around 60 miles, where they will be allowed to unstrap and experience weightlessness for about six minutes. Would you back him?

You may ask why this question is relevant to this book? Virgin Galactic is a business venture and this is a book about backing you as an individual. The answer is that a business, certainly a new venture, is often little more than the aggregate talents and experience of the entrepreneurs behind it. In this case, you'd be backing Branson.

What would the Suns & Clouds for Virgin Galactic look like? Some would argue that this venture makes even Virgin Atlantic look like a safe bet! At least the backers of a new airline understand its basic economics (and sensitivity to fuel prices). They understand the technology and appreciate the risks of technical failure or sabotage.

But for space tourism, technology is unproven and still developing. Investors will be all too aware of the sad demise of space shuttles *Challenger* and *Columbia*. There may also be health risks since space tourists won't have the preflight conditioning and training of astronauts. And the economics are uncertain. How many flights per year per spacecraft? How much will people be prepared to pay (once the rich have been there and back)? How many competitors with how many spacecraft?

These risks will shape some formidable clouds in Virgin Galactic's Suns & Clouds. But the one outstanding sun found in the Virgin Atlantic chart will still be shining for Virgin Galactic. The brand name remains stellar. And Branson himself is hot on the marketing trail again with plans for him and his family to be on board for Virgin Galactic's maiden voyage in 2010. You can imagine the fanfare and media coverage.

Branson's Stand-Out! strategy, like Madonna's, remains consistent. It hasn't always worked—Virgin Trains hasn't been a runaway success—but more often than not it has. Would you back Virgin Galactic?

Back, literally, to this planet....

How a New Strategy May Impact on Suns & Clouds: A Self-Employed Example

In Chapter 12 we saw how Leila planned to embark on a more ambitious strategy than the one Chuck had backed her on. She was going to move into Main Street premises with Ying, do them up to smarter, more hygienic specifications, recruit an employee masseuse, and move to full-time working herself.

She knew that this was a riskier strategy, but she also knew that this was what she wanted to commit herself to. She felt that she'd had a good ride being the laid back aromatherapist working out of her front room. But this made her vulnerable to both new entrants at the lower end of the range like Suzi and to a prospective highly qualified new entrant at the top of the range. Now was the time to be bold.

What would be the impact of the new strategy on her Suns & Clouds chart?

Figure 14.4 starkly shows the gamble Leila would be taking. Her new strategy introduced the severe new risk (new cloud 7) of higher fixed costs—both of premises and the new employee. This was balanced by the extra revenues (new sun 4) she hoped to achieve from the new strategy. The new strategy also had the effect of shifting the risk of a

Figure 14.4 **Risks and Opportunities Facing Healing Hands' New Strategy in Massage Therapy Services in Notting Hill, London**

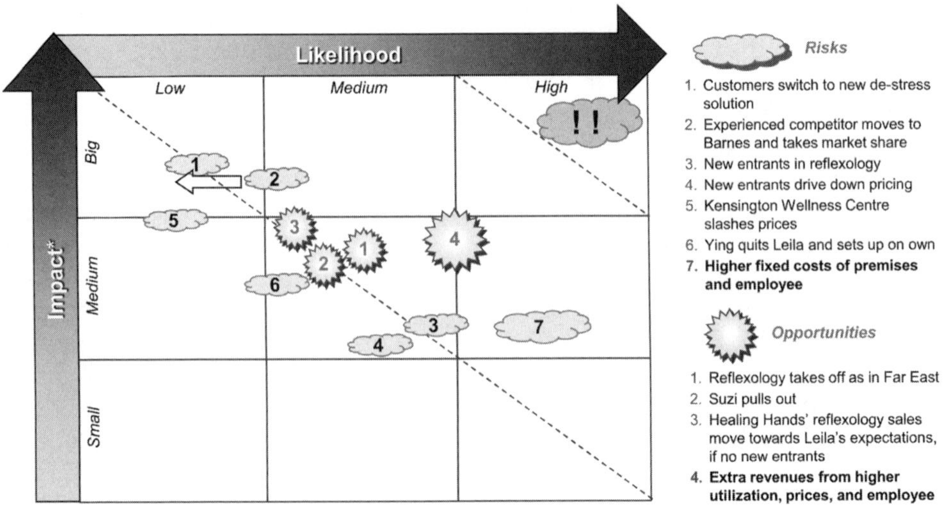

Likelihood
Low
Medium
High
Impact*
Big
Medium
Small
!!
Risks
1. Customers switch to new de-stress solution
2. Experienced competitor moves to Barnes and takes market share
3. New entrants in reflexology
4. New entrants drive down pricing
5. Kensington Wellness Centre slashes prices
6. Ying quits Leila and sets up on own
7. Higher fixed costs of premises and employee
Opportunities
1. Reflexology takes off as in Far East
2. Suzi pulls out
3. Healing Hands' reflexology sales move towards Leila's expectations, if no new entrants
4. Extra revenues from higher utilization, prices, and employee

* Note: Over and above ***Chuck's view*** of likely profits in three years' time

prospective highly qualified new entrant (old cloud 2) to the left.

It was clear that Chuck's decision on whether to back this new strategy would be based on the positioning of sun 4. There was an inevitability around cloud 7. The fixed costs of the premises, on rental, local taxes, utilities, insurance, and so forth, could be readily assessed. Likewise the fixed costs of the employee, including her benefits.

The uncertainty would be around the extra revenues, sun 4. Leila would have to make a highly convincing case on where these extra revenues would come from and why. She saw them coming from three sources:

- Putting in more time herself, now full-time.
- A slight rise in pricing—she felt her customers would understand that the spic and span new premises justified an extra pound or two.
- Her employee's services, which would be charged at a discount to Leila's initially, but nevertheless at a rate covering costs by a healthy margin.

Leila was convinced that there would be sufficient demand from stay-at-home moms, businesspeople, and others in west London to justify these revenue assumptions. She drew up the numbers. They looked good. All she had to do was convey that conviction to Chuck.

How a New Strategy May Impact Suns & Clouds: An Employee Example

In Chapter 11 we learned that Elizabeth had decided to go for goal and improve her skill set as a market researcher. In Chapter 12 we found that her ideal strategic alternative would be to join Toastmasters International and improve her public speaking and communications skills.

Will this strategy have made her more backable? How will it have impacted on her Suns & Clouds chart?

If successful, the strategy will transform Elizabeth's backability—see Figure 14.5. The risk of presenting skills becoming a must-have K2 (cloud 2) is still as likely, but it will have a lower impact on Elizabeth's positioning, given her improved presenting skills. Meanwhile, the likelihood of Elizabeth losing market research work because of her presentational shortcomings (cloud 3) will have been significantly lowered.

The two most prominent clouds in Elizabeth's former chart have been blown away. There are now no clouds left above the diagonal. Just two suns, shining happily on their own, with a new third one (helping the marketing team with admin work) not far off. She has become more backable, thanks to Toastmasters.

The Toastmasters strategy came about only after Elizabeth had followed a rigorous process, which it may be useful to recall:

➤ She envisioned the future and developed three scenarios, CopyCat, Bite the Bullet, and Eventful, for which she needed to be prepared.

➤ She profiled the ideal provider under these scenarios and identified common capabilities, in particular presentation and communication skills.

➤ She mapped out her strategic

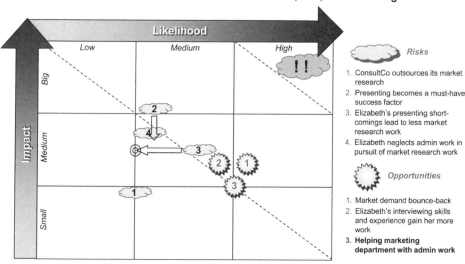

Figure 14.5 **Risks and Opportunities Facing Elizabeth's New Strategy in Market Research Services to ConsultCo, Inc., and in Chicago**

bubble bath, stretched her sights, decided to go for goal, and identified the K2 gap, especially in presentation and communication skills.

➢ She recognized that her strategy was going to be more akin to Sharpen Act! than Stand Out!

and developed three strategic alternatives to bridge the K2 gap.

➢ The most beneficial and yet by far the cheapest strategic alternative was to join Toastmasters International.

➢ This strategy made her more backable.

Are U Now More Backable?

Hopefully the strategy you've developed will have made you too more backable. Your Suns & Clouds chart should have been improved, possibly even transformed, like Elizabeth's. Or your strategy may have made your chart riskier, as for Leila, but with potentially much higher returns.

> I believe the true road to pre-eminent success in any line is to make yourself master in that line. I have no faith in the policy of scattering one's resources, and in my experience I have rarely if ever met a man who achieved preeminence in money making…who was interested in many concerns.—*Andrew Carnegie*

Let's recap where you are. In Part I, you concluded that you were backable in your current business or job. You may not have been wholly satisfied in your work before reading Part I, but afterwards you felt better about it. You proceeded to Part II and followed some techniques on how to make yourself more backable. Hopefully you now are more backable, or are setting out to become so.

If, however, you were not absolutely convinced in Part I of your backability in your current job or business, and if in Part II those doubts were not laid to rest, then perhaps you should move on to Part III. Part III is primarily aimed at those who found that they were not backable in Part I and are thinking of switching to a new career, one that they feel passionate about.

Could that be of interest to you too?

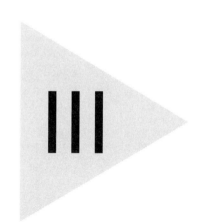

Backing the *Hwyl!*

Introduction

If you concluded in Part I that you would not, or probably would not, back U in your current job or business, then Part III helps you to find a field where you would back U. It shows you how to back the *hwyl*, the Celtic concept of passion, fervor, spirit, which can lift you to extremes of success. (By the way, don't be disheartened by the apparent absence of vowels in *hwyl*! The word actually contains two vowels! There are seven vowels in the Welsh language, the familiar five as in English plus "w" and "y." *Hwyl* is pronounced as in *who-yl*.)

> Ask not what the world needs.
> Ask what makes you come alive… then go do it. Because what the world needs are people who have come alive.
> —*Howard Thurman*

There are many excellent books that can guide you on finding the right job from the bottom-up—identifying your interests, values, transferable skills, and then finding jobs that match them. You can do no better than to read the classic but still peerless *What Color Is Your Parachute?* by Richard N. Bolles (referred to later as just *Parachute*). Or the lucid and methodical *Changing Careers for Dummies* by Carol L. McClelland. Or the energetic *I Don't Know What I Want, but I Know it's Not This* by Julie Jansen. Or if you're thinking of setting up your own business, *Creating You & Co.* by William Bridges. Part III doesn't decry these approaches. On the contrary, they have helped thousands of people make life-enhancing career changes.

This book merely sets out an alternative. It suggests that you try putting similar faith in a *top-down* approach, a *demand-driven* approach, a *hwyl-driven* approach: starting from where you want to be, where the passion lies, and then assessing just how realistic your chances are of succeeding in that field—and what you can do to shorten the odds.

As for Part II, Part III takes as its building blocks some of the approaches and techniques already laid out in Part I. The market assessment techniques of Chapters 2 and 3, and the K2 rating techniques of Chapters 4 to 6 will be revisited sketchily in Chapter 16, and in greater depth in Chapter 17. There too you'll find again the Suns & Clouds chart of Chapter 8, already revisited in the last chapter, as you assess your backability in your short-listed jobs with *hwyl*. Chapter 18 meanwhile returns to the techniques developed in Part II and shows you how to develop a strategy for improving your chances of success in your preferred field.

Part III starts, however, with the discovery of passion, or *hwyl*. Chapter 15, Wherein Lies the *Hwyl?*, asks you to find the field of work where your passion lies. Whose job, or business, do you most covet? If you were in that business, you would be so fired up, so full of *hwyl*, that work wouldn't seem like work at all. It doesn't matter at this stage whether you believe you could actually do this job, run this business. The important thing is to imagine what you would love to be doing during the day job. You'll be given some tips on how you can come up with plenty of jobs with *hwyl*. Then you'll be shown how to pull out a dozen or so of those jobs with the most *hwyl*, ready to be screened in the next chapter.

The purpose of Chapter 16, Screening for Reality, is to screen the long list down to a short list of three or four jobs that not only have *hwyl* but also where you could be successful. You'll take a first cut at assessing how attractive the markets are for these jobs and how well placed you would be to get in and succeed in them. You'll be introduced to the *Hwyl* Star chart. Many of the longer-shot, more aspirational jobs in your long list will be screened out, and it's possible that you won't have enough left to make a short list. That's no problem. This should be seen as an iterative process. You'll return to the full list of the previous chapter and bring forward a new long list of a dozen or so jobs, drawn from the next level down of your *hwyl* rating. You'll repeat the screening process, you may even have to do it once again, before finally ending up with your short list of jobs that not only have *hwyl* but offer sound prospects of you getting in and succeeding at them.

Twenty years from now you will be more disappointed by the things that you didn't do than by the ones you did. So throw off the bowlines. Sail away from the safe harbor. Catch the trade winds in your sails. Explore. Dream. Discover.— *Mark Twain*

Chapter 17, Where Best to Back?, will guide you through the work you must now undertake to narrow your field further. You'll need to do further research, especially on the most promising job or business. You'll need to speak to people who do that job and their "customers." The tools introduced in Part I should now be redeployed in detail. You need to understand where the market is going, how tough is the competition, how well placed you would be, whether you will make your earnings plan, and how risky it would be to back U. You'll be able to firm up the placement of these short-listed jobs on the *Hwyl* Star chart and conclude which you should back, and which should be kept in reserve as a plan B.

Chapter 18, Shortening the Odds, can be crucial. Depending on your timescale, you may be able to improve your prospects of getting into and succeeding in your target job. You need to consider whether some of the tools deployed in Part II can be of help. Do you need to build on your strengths or work on some weaknesses? Which of the Stand Out!, easyU! or Sharpen Act! strategies would shorten the odds of success in your target job? How would that improve its positioning in the *Hwyl* Star chart? If you were to do the same or similar to prepare for other short-listed jobs, would that change their relative positioning? By the end of this chapter, you will have planned how to go about improving your chances of success in your target job or business.

In Chapter 19, Now Back the *Hwyl!,* we'll look at some key steps you need to take to start your own business with *hwyl* or go for the job with *hwyl* identified in Chapter 18. It will not be comprehensive—that's for specialist manuals on the job-hunting process, for example, Daniel Porot's *The PIE Method for Career Success: A Unique Way to Find Your Ideal Job.* But this book will divulge some tips, such as on interviews, that have been learned by the author along the way, with examples and anecdotes.

Part III will show you how to find the right job or business with *hwyl* and improve your prospects of getting in and succeeding there. Hopefully it will inspire you to get out and back your *hwyl*!

15

This chapter helps you to find the field of work where your passion lies. Whose job, or business, do you most covet? If you were in that business, you would be so fired up that work wouldn't seem like work at all. The job would fill you with *hwyl*, the Celtic concept of *passion, fervor, spirit,* which can lift you to extremes of success. No matter at this stage whether you think you could actually do this job, run this business. The important thing is to imagine what you would love to be doing during the day job. You'll be given some tips on how you can come up with dozens of jobs with *hwyl.* Then you'll be shown how to pull out a dozen or so of those jobs with the *most hwyl,* ready to be screened in the next chapter.

> Life is to be lived. If you have to support yourself, you had bloody well better find some way that is going to be interesting.
> —*Katherine Hepburn*

First, however, let's do a quick review of the traditional, bottom-up, and yes, well-proven approaches to career change.

The Bottom-Up Approach to Career Change

There are some excellent books on the market for guiding you through a bottom-up process on career change. Let's take it from the top.

Here's an example of the potentially awesome force of *hywl*. My father took me to my first Wales versus England rugby battle in Cardiff in 1967. Wales had lost every international that season and this was their last chance to salvage some pride. Incredibly, they selected an 18-year-old schoolboy, Keith Jarrett, to play at fullback, a pivotal position. There was one problem. The lad was a center and hadn't played at fullback since he was in the Under-16s! Undaunted, he played as a man possessed, uplifted by the *hwyl*, by the mournful hymns and arias emanating from 60,000 Welsh voices in the stadium. He scored 19 points in a Welsh victory of 34–21. Visiting teams often say that the Cardiff *hwyl* is worth 10 points for the home team. On that day of my initiation, the *hwyl* was historic.

What Color Is Your Parachute? by Richard N. Bolles

Bolles's *Parachute* should be your first stop if you're embarking on a job search. It's a classic. Revised annually since 1970, it's packed with advice, experience, anecdotes, and wisdom.

Bolles differentiates between job searches that are mechanical and those that are life-changing. A mechanical job search is one where you submit your résumé to a range of prospective employers and you seek employment based largely on what you have achieved in your career to date. You are planning on doing more or less the same as you have been doing thus far, except of course with hopefully improved terms or conditions of service and prospects for advancement. A life-changing job search, on the other hand, is one where you plan to switch to a career which is in harmony with your values, interests, and skills, one that enhances your life in every way. Bolles provides the full range of tools to help with both.

For a life-changing job search, which is what Part III of this book is about, Bolles suggests you build your own personal flower. This represents a picture of the job of your dreams. There are six petals surrounding the core, each representing an influencing factor. These are listed as follows:

- ➢ Where the job should be located
- ➢ Which field the job should be in (defined by your favorite interests or fields of fascination)
- ➢ What type of organization (taking into account your favorite people environments)
- ➢ What values the organization should have
- ➢ What working conditions you would expect
- ➢ What salary and level of responsibility you would expect

At the core of this flower are your favorite transferable skills. The dream job will not only enable you to apply your favorite skills, but will also satisfy your desires for location, interests, culture, values, working conditions, and service terms. You then attempt a match with reality. You live with your flower, take it around with you, and show it to friends and people whose opinion you respect. Hopefully a picture of the ideal job will begin to emerge. The book then helps you set out to secure it.

Parachute is valuable not just in getting you to the destination but for the journey itself. For what you learn about yourself and your desires, ambitions, and beliefs along the way. Bolles's approach is primarily from the bottom up. You carefully work out what you are good at, what you want, what you believe in, and methodically derive the job that fits you. *Backing U!* takes a different approach, a top-down approach, a *hwyl*-driven approach. Here we start by looking at jobs to which you aspire and *then* see whether they fit you.

There are many other good books on career change, on moving to the job of your dreams. They too offer a primarily bottom-up approach. Here are some of the best that I've come across.

Changing Careers for Dummies by Carol L. McClelland

This book starts on similar territory to *Parachute*. You're encouraged to set the stage for career change by considering your personality or temperament, your values, your health, your hobbies and interests, your desired location and the impact of your family on your work. It then seeks to find out what your ideal work environment would be in terms of schedule, type of organization, terms of service, and type of colleagues.

The book shows you how to search for your hidden treasure—your passion. It starts by asking you to identify your "skills that make time fly." Here it borrows from Howard Gardner's *Frames of Mind: The Theory of Multiple Intelligences* and asks you to consider which of these innate talents or intelligences is most applicable to you:

➤ Do you think in words?
➤ Do you think in a logical, organized fashion?
➤ Do you connect well with others?
➤ Do you have a good eye?
➤ Do you have a good sense of your body?
➤ Do you appreciate nature and its creatures?

The book asks you to identify your favorite topics, processes, internal drivers, tools, industries, client group, and meaning in work. These are all assembled to record your "hottest interests and passions." Each becomes one in a deck of cards, and you're asked to deal yourself a succession of hands of four cards each. This technique is used to brainstorm a range of new careers, each grounded in your very own passions.

This is in some ways a similar approach to *Parachute's* flower. But the next part of the book moves on to become a highly informative career guide. Each of the innate intelligences listed above is given its own chapter, and you are given creative guidance on what career choices may be available to you within each of those intelligences. Under each type of intelligence, you are given both standard and "out of the box" options on career choice and advice on where to look next. This book is both a stimulating *and* practical contribution to career change.

I Don't Know What I Want, But I Know It's Not This by Julie Jansen

This is a different type of book. It's written in a more chatty style, and it's stacked on each page with examples of people who have tried this, done that. It asks you to consider in Part I what your work situation is before tailoring Part III of the book to each of five generic work situations, which she describes as:

➢ Where's the meaning
➢ Been there, done that, but still need to earn
➢ Bored and plateaued
➢ Yearning to be on your own
➢ One toe in the retirement pool

For each work situation, she offers a three-step process: complete the self-assessment, explore roadblocks and opportunities, and create an action plan.

Part II of the book covers familiar territory. She asks you to think about where you want to be by evaluating your values, attitudes, and readiness to change in one chapter, and your personality preferences, interests, and skills in another. It's the bottom-up approach again, applied innovatively to the five work situations in Part III of her book.

Creating You & Co. by William Bridges

We've come across this distinctive book earlier, in Chapter 13 on *Backing UCo!* The meat of Bridges's book is a clever variant on the bottom-up approach to career change. He suggests that you should find and then mine your DATA, an acronym that refers to your desires, abilities (talents you were born with), temperament (and vocation), and assets (qualifications and experience). It's a thought-provoking take by a leading academic in organizational and individual transitions. The final part of the book is a useful look at turning your DATA into a business—finding an opportunity, creating a product, and running a micro-business.

Other books you may find useful include the following:

➢ *How to Get a Job You'll Love* by John Lees—A leading British careers coach gives his take on values, interests ("your house of knowledge"), skills, personality, and intelligences (again using the Gardner approach). Through a "field generator," Lees guides you on how to identify suitable fields of work.
➢ *Do What You Are: Discover the Perfect Career for You Through the Secrets of Personality Type* by Paul Tieger and Barbara Barron-Tieger—These experienced trainers help you identify your personality type and find the job that best suits it. The authors provide career advice and highlight the strengths and pitfalls of each personality type with real-life examples.
➢ *The Pathfinder: How to Choose or Change Your Career for a Lifetime of*

Satisfaction and Success by Nicholas Lore—The founder of a career counseling network sets out techniques for designing a new career direction to fit your talents, personality, needs, goals, and values, and "how to deal with the *yeah but* voices in your head that keep you going back to the same ill-fitting job, day after day."

➤ *Build You Own Rainbow: A Workbook for Career and Life Management* by Barrie Hopson and Mike Scally—Experienced British career counselors lead you through a workbook based on their long running workshops on career and life management. The book is in six sections, addressing these questions: Who am I? Where am I now? How satisfied am I? What changes do I want? How do I make them happen? What if it doesn't work out?

My advice to you is simple—and enjoyable. Take yourself off to a good library, or to one of those super bookstores with sofas and lattes, and skim them all. They are all good. Each has its own distinctive take. Any one of them could be of huge help to you. Select the two or three that suit your own preference for approach and style of writing. Then borrow or buy them, dig in, learn, and enjoy!

A Top-Down, Demand-Driven, *Hwyl*-Driven Approach

This book suggests an alternative to the bottom-up, skills-driven approach. It suggests a top-down, demand-driven, *hwyl*-driven approach. Instead of starting bottom-up from what your values, interests, and skills are, it starts top-down with where you'd like to end up.

What job would you love to have? In which job would you be happy?

Which job can you think of where work would no longer be "work"? You would be so fired up that it wouldn't seem like work at all. You would rush to work in the morning and you wouldn't want to leave in the evening.

Who would you most like to be? Whose job, or business, do you most covet? If you were in his or her job, would you consider that you had the dream job?

In which job would you be consumed with *hwyl*? You would feel such passion, such fervor, such spirit about the job that you would be uplifted to extremes of success.

> You can have anything you want, if you want it badly enough. You can be anything you want to be, do anything you set out to accomplish, if you hold to that desire with singleness of purpose.—
> *Abraham Lincoln*

That's the top-down approach. It's demand driven, in that it seeks to pinpoint those jobs that attract you to them, that draw you toward them. Rather than supply pushed, where you steer yourself toward a job that suits your values, interests, and skills

And it's driven by *hwyl*. The job will entice you with its promise of *hwyl*.

How to Know Where the *Hwyl* Lies?

You'll know when you've found a job with *hwyl*. Just thinking about it is exciting. It'll make your thoughts race. It'll wake you at five o'clock in the morning, and you won't want to go back to sleep.

It'll fill you with drive. To do something about it. To pick up the phone, knock on a door.

Above all, you'll know you've found the *hwyl* when you speak about the job. When people talk about something they're passionate about, the voice changes. The pace quickens. The pitch rises. The volume gets turned up a notch or two.

As an extreme example, take a teenage girl in two situations. Imagine her mother or father asking her how school went that day. The answer comes back monosyllabically, monotonously, ponderously. Then the telephone goes and her best buddy's on the line. The voice undergoes a metamorphosis. Suddenly it's animated, rapid, rich in variety of tone, pitch, and volume. Punctuated throughout with laughter. Whatever the two teenagers are talking about, it's surely something that fires them. And it's reflected in the voice.

It's the same in public speaking. I've belonged to a public speaking and communications club for many years (see Chapter 12 on Elizabeth's new strategy and her discovery of Toastmasters International). At every meeting four or five people stand up and deliver a prepared speech for five to seven minutes on a topic of their choosing. All speakers are advised to choose a topic they are interested in, preferably one they are passionate about. As a result, and this is extraordinary given the range of backgrounds and talents of all these amateur speakers, it's very seldom that we hear a dud speech. Whatever the topic, the speaker's enthusiasm for the topic will be conveyed to the audience through above all her *voice*. No matter how inexperienced the speaker, no matter whether she has learned any of the tricks of vocal variety, the speech will be a winner if the topic brings out the *hwyl* in her.

If you want to know whether the *hwyl* lies for you in a particular job, try talking about it to a friend. Talk about its daily routines, the kind of people who work there, their ambitions, their achievements. Talk about the pros and cons. Talk about it in relation to other jobs where the *hwyl* may also lie. Talk about how it differs from ordinary jobs, why it inspires you more than your current job. Ask your friend to observe how you talk about these jobs. When you speak of this particular job, does your voice become faster, more animated, more impassioned?

Or join Toastmasters! Speak about the job to a small audience. Ask your evaluator beforehand if he'll note any difference in your vocal variety on this speech, compared with previous speeches. Will the speech convince him too that the job is fascinating?

The *hwyl* will be reflected in the voice. If you speak about a job where the *hwyl* is, your voice will confirm it.

But how to find such a job?

Some Tips on Finding Where the *Hwyl* Lies

The problem with the top-down approach, I can hear some argue, is in getting started. Suppose you have never heard of or come across the ideal job for you! How can you envision it and then work out whether you're suited for it?

You can't! They're right! This will be the case for some people. In which case, please, please revert to the bottom-up approach. Read *Parachute* and fill in the flower. Geography: North America. Interests: beekeeping and honey. People environment: people who help others. Values: mutual support. Working conditions: outdoors. Salary: at least average earnings. Transferable skills: accounting and (favorite) beekeeping. Then, after the job search, *Eureka!*, you find it: a vacancy for a new commune member of the Honey Cooperative in Moose Jaw, Saskatchewan—a job you previously didn't know existed!

These cases I suspect may be uncommon. In the majority of cases, the top-down approach should work too because *you already know of*, or you can get to know of, the kind of work you would like to do. That's not to decry the bottom-up approach, of course. It's proven. It works.

How to find the ideal job for you? How to discover where the *hwyl* lies? If you don't already know, and many of you do, here are some tips.

Whose jobs do you admire of those you know?

Think of your family. Your friends. Your old school friends. Your colleagues. Your former colleagues. Your kids' friends' parents.

Are any of them in a job or running a business that would inspire you? Have they been in the past? Are they thinking of switching to one?

Take one further degree of separation: What about the family, friends, and colleagues of your family, friends, and colleagues? Do they have jobs that would inspire you?

Take a piece of paper (or open up a Word table on your laptop) and make three columns. In the left-hand column, write down all the names you've just thought of. In the middle column, write down the kind of work these people do, or did. Then in the right-hand column, indicate to what extent the work would inspire you. Try ticks. Or a cross for a job that does nothing for you. One tick for an okay job. Two ticks for a good job. Three ticks for a great job.

Then give four, five, or however many ticks you can fit across the column for the jobs that would truly inspire you—the jobs where the *hwyl* lies.

What jobs do your fellow interest-sharers do?

Do you belong to any clubs, societies, voluntary groups, political groups? Your fellow members in these clubs share at least one thing in common with you, their interest in the purpose of that particular club/society/group.

All of you in that group like, for example, golf, or books, or ballroom dancing. Or you are all prepared to help out on the stalls at the school's summer fair. Or you all derive satisfaction from helping elderly people in the neighborhood with their shopping.

Might there be something else you have in common with these people, other than the one common interest through which you know each other? Might you have work interests in common? Are any of them in a job that would inspire you? And what of their friends and family?

Take out your sheet of paper and add to it some jobs of your fellow interest-sharers.

Do you know a dozen people who found the *hwyl*?

Who do you know who has changed careers successfully in their lives? Not many? I bet that's not so. I'm sure you could list a dozen or so with ease. Have any of these career switches been of interest to you? Inspired you?

I can think off the top of my head of a dozen people I know who've made successful career changes. Here they are (names changed, of course):

➢ Eleanor, an accountant who couldn't abide the tedium and switched to her passions of life coaching, color therapy, and percussion workshops.

➢ Rhys, a bus driver who found the London traffic too stressful and passengers too awful, went to evening classes in gardening and then set up on his own as a gardener.

➢ Calum, a corporate financier who tired of the greed culture and moved into his passion of garden design.

➢ Julia, a solicitor who found the work unfulfilling and became a music teacher.

➢ Carmel, a private equity director and mother of three who retrained as a mathematics teacher.

➢ Paul, an actor and singer in London West End musicals who set up as a children's party entertainer, later extending the brand into related entertainment services.

➢ Lisa, an architect who found herself laid off during a construction recession and retrained as an osteopath.

➢ Kay, a former university lecturer who after some years as a full-time mom retrained as a stress management counselor.

➢ Anthony, Graham, Marcus, and Martin, all former consulting colleagues who moved into areas of inspirational self-employment, respectively starting a horse-riding school, livestock farming, managing a hotel at an Alpine ski resort, and classical singing.

Now that I've started, I can readily think of a further dozen. Can you rattle off a dozen people you know who've made interesting career changes? And then another dozen? Have any of these changes been inspirational for you? Would you have liked to have done the same?

Ask your friends, family, fellow club/society members to rattle off a dozen examples likewise. You could soon have well over a hundred exemplars! Any inspiration there?

Again, take out your sheet of paper and add to it the jobs of people you've known, or people your friends and family have known, who've found the *hwyl*.

Who do you know of whose work inspires you?

So far you've looked to people you know for inspiration. Now take a look at people you don't know, but you know *of*. Think of people you've read about in books who have inspired you. Think of people you've looked at and read about in newspapers, in the supplements, in magazines.

Think of people you've seen on TV. In documentaries, in reality shows, in sports, on the news. People who've inspired you in some way.

Think too of fictitious people. People in novels, in movies, in the theater, in dramas or soaps on TV. People whose imaginary lives have come alive for you through fiction or drama.

Yet again, out with the paper and add in the names of those you know of who've found the *hwyl*, their jobs and to what extent (the ticks) you would share the *hwyl*.

Even celebrities can change careers

I'm not sure how useful you'll find this section because celebs exist in a world of their own, cocooned from the real world by their property, wealth, fame, paparazzi, and bodyguards. But celebrities do sometimes change careers, moving into fields beyond those in which they gained their fame.

Think of Hollywood actors who have moved successfully into politics, such as President Ronald Reagan, Governor Arnold Schwarzenegger, and Mayor Clint Eastwood (all initially standing in California!), or Glenda Jackson, Member of Parliament. Or those who've been active in political pressure groups, such as Brigitte Bardot, Jane Fonda, and Vanessa Redgrave. Or sportspeople who have moved into broadcasting, like John McEnroe, or into acting, like Vinnie Jones. Or actresses who have moved into pop singing, like Kylie Minogue and Jennifer Lopez.

Think too of celebs who have moved into the world of business, such as Paul Newman and his natural food line, Linda McCartney and her vegetarian cuisine, Elle Macpherson and her lingerie line. Or think of dozens of celebs and their perfume launches, from Britney and Paris to famous-for-being-simple Jade (a British *Big Brother* phenomenon!).

For most celebs, it's their very celebrity that gives them the launch pad for their career change. But in thinking of the career switches of celebrities you've followed, perhaps some of those on the B or C Lists, you may find some inspiration.

Broaden your reading for inspiration

If you're still short of inspiration, then you may need to read around a bit more. You could try making a conscious effort to dedicate your leisure reading time to discovery of types of work. There's an abundance of material available to help.

In the *Sunday Times* magazine in Britain, there's an amazing one-page feature at the back that has run for years called *A Life in the Day Of*. Each week it features one person whose life is typically ordinary but extraordinary. The subjects chosen can range from a movie star to a chambermaid, a political campaigner to a factory worker, a top lawyer to an asylum seeker. All they have in common is their individuality. Read them and similar features in other magazines and discover who inspires you, why and what job they do.

There are also books you can read for inspiration. You could start with *What Should I Do With My Life?* by Po Bronson, an astonishing collection of stories of ordinary people who "had unearthed their true calling, or at least those who were willing to try." From the investment banker who became a catfish farmer to the chemical engineer who became a lawyer in his sixties, these are stories of "individual dilemmas and dramatic gambles," not always successful. The tales of the author's subjects are interesting, and at times, inspirational.

Or you could try one of Barbara Sher's books. She's a therapist, motivational speaker, career counselor, and prolific author. You could browse through a range of her books in a bookstore and see which one inspires you. Or read the reviews on Amazon.com. Her bestselling books include *I Could Do Anything If I Only Knew What It Was: How to Discover What You Really Want and How to Get It*.

Then there's the mega-selling phenomenon of the *Chicken Soup for the Soul* series, Jack Canfield and Mark Victor Hansen's moving compilation of extraordinary stories about ordinary people. One story might strike a light for you.

There's also a wealth of examples in the career change books referred to earlier in this chapter, especially in Julie Jansen's book.

Again, pull out your list and add more names, jobs, and ticks.

Consult a list

We're starting to scrape the barrel a bit here. If you haven't found inspiration from any of the above sources, it's unlikely that a dry, factual, unemotional list of (thousands of) occupations is going to inspire. But you never know.

There are lots of sources. No need to invest serious cash when the Internet is around. The best place to start if you live in the United States is the Bureau of Labor Statistics website (www.bls.gov). Once in you can click through to the Occupational Outlook Handbook, which is updated every other year. It's a mine of information. You can search for any occupation that you're interested in, or browse from a menu of occupations, drilling down to the ones of interest. For each occupation, there's information on the nature of the work, working conditions, training and qualifications, employment, job outlook, earnings, related occupations, and sources of further information.

There are also regular reports and tables produced by the Bureau, which you can download. One fascinating table you might find useful is of the "Fastest Growing Occupations covered in the Occupational Outlook Handbook" and can be found on www.bls.gov/news.release/ooh.t01.htm. In the 2006–2007 handbook, the fastest growing occupations likely over the period 2004–2014 include home health aides, network systems and data communications analysts, medical assistants, computer software engineers, dental assistants, preschool teachers, post-secondary teachers, and computer systems analysts. The table gives the number of jobs likely to be created, the percentage increase in employment for each occupation and the level of training required. One of these in-demand jobs may have your name on it.

Similar sites are available on the Internet in most countries. In Britain, you can find whatever labor statistics you need from the website of the Office for National Statistics, www.statistics.gov.uk. A very useful website for graduates is www.prospects.ac.uk, which provides a treasure trove of information on every graduate job conceivable. Under each job you get information on the job description and typical activities, salary and conditions, entry requirements, training, career development, typical employers, sources for vacancies, case studies of real people working in the field, and contacts/resources for further information.

Have you found any occupations of interest that you had not uncovered earlier? If so, add them, along with the appropriate ticks, to your list.

Take a career test

I'm a bit reluctant to recommend this last route. It really belongs to a bottom-up approach, and I've already referred you to a bunch of good books that will guide you through that process.

Nevertheless, there are some well-established career tests around, many of which can be accessed on the Internet. Some may charge a few bucks, others are free. Your best bet is to latch on to www.jobhuntersbible.com, the website of Dick Bolles, author of *Parachute*. Then click through to Tests and Advice, and then Career Tests.

You should now be on www.jobhuntersbible.com/library/counseling/ctests.php. Bolles will walk you through the merits of the various tests on offer, including the *Princeton Review Career Quiz*, the *Self-Directed Search* by John Holland, the *Career Key,* and the *Career Interests Game*, developed originally by Bolles from Holland's work (as the *Party Exercise*) and found in *Parachute*, but adapted by the University of Missouri and available on their website www.career.missouri.edu. It's a fun game and well worth playing.

Any more jobs and ticks to add to your list?

How Martha Stewart Found the *Hwyl*

We discussed the career changes of celebrities earlier on. But some became celebrated only after they had switched from a previous career. Sean Connery was a body-builder, Catherine Zeta-Jones a dancer, and Kelly Clarkson worked as a telemarketer and cocktail waitress in a small town in Texas before having a shot at *American Idol*.

Then there's the phenomenon that is Martha Stewart. A part-time model during her university days at Barnard, studying history and architectural history, Martha Kostyra became a successful stockbroker. She quit in her early thirties to become a full-time mother while undertaking a major restoration of an early 19th century farmhouse. It was from its basement that she started a catering business with a friend from college. Within a couple of years, she had produced a cookbook, *Entertaining*.

The rest is history. The book became a bestseller and over the next few years she produced more books, including *Weddings*, wrote articles, made TV appearances, and launched her own housewares line at K-Mart. In 1990 she became editor of the magazine *Martha Stewart Living*, which would peak in 2002 with a circulation of 2 million. In 1993 she appeared in a TV show named after her, initially a half-hour a week, then an hour a week, then daily.

All the things I love is what my business is all about.
—*Martha Stewart*

In 1997 Martha Stewart secured funding to purchase all the print, TV, and merchandising activities associated with her name and consolidated everything into a company, *Martha Stewart Living Omnimedia*. The company was floated on the New York Stock Exchange a couple of years later, making her a billionaire on paper.

Millions were lopped off the company value when she was accused, then convicted, of insider trading, on a deal where she had saved a mere $45,000. But the conviction and her subsequent serving of a short prison sentence did not halt the Martha Stewart express. More lines at K-Mart, more books, more TV programs, the brand has extended even further into the building of Martha Stewart houses.

All this from a former model-cum-stockbroker. She discovered the *hwyl* in her own basement kitchen. She went on to radiate that *hwyl* to the U.S. public in print and on TV. She became a brand and the brand went stratospheric.

What *hwyl* could you uncover in your kitchen? Your study? Your backyard?

How Ralph Smedley Found the *Hwyl*

It won't surprise you to learn that not all who find the *hwyl* go on to become billionaires! Nor would many of us choose to. Fulfillment can come in many forms other than material. For many it comes from helping others. Or in creating structures to be able to help others.

Ralph C. Smedley is an amazing example of this. After graduating from Wesleyan University in Bloomington, Illinois, in 1903, he took a job as director of education at the local branch of the Young Men's Christian Association. There he soon realized that older boys would benefit from some training in communications skills, so he started a public speaking club.

He called it the Toastmasters' Club because the activities resembled a banquet with toasts and after-dinner speeches. The boys enjoyed taking turns to make speeches and evaluating them, as well as presiding at the weekly meetings.

Smedley's Bloomington club blossomed, but soon he was promoted to general secretary of the YMCA and transferred to Freeport, Illinois. After his departure, the club folded. Over the following years, Smedley set up other Toastmasters clubs wherever he was transferred. In Freeport, he invited businessmen and other professionals to join the meetings, but to no long-term avail. The club thrived while Smedley was there but disappeared once its founder moved on. Subsequent clubs in Rock Island, Illinois, and San Jose, California, suffered the same fate.

Smedley must have despaired of ever seeing his creation blossom into a self-sustaining organization. "I observed a tendency among my fellow secretaries at the YMCA to regard The Toastmasters Club as a sort of peculiarity—an idiosyncrasy of mine," he later said. "Perhaps it was not altogether orthodox as a 'Y' activity."

Finally, Smedley arrived in Santa Ana. Yet again he started up a Toastmasters club, but in Southern California's optimistic climate the concept at last caught on. Men (yes, it was all male in those days, but certainly not now) from neighboring communities sought out the group and liked what they saw. Smedley helped them organize their own Toastmasters clubs and these clubs united in a federation.

Smedley had found his *hwyl*. As he turned 50, he resigned from the YMCA to concentrate on developing Toastmasters. He opened a tiny office in a downtown Santa Ana bank with a desk, typewriter, telephone, and second-hand answering machine. He hired a secretary to handle the correspondence, while he wrote materials for the club's use. The organization grew.

Smedley remained involved with Toastmasters until shortly before his death in 1965 at the age of 87. By then, Toastmasters International had grown to a membership of 80,000. It had moved into its own large office building in Santa Ana, and Smedley himself took part in the dedication ceremonies. It must have been an emotional occasion, a tribute to one man's vision and drive.

The organization now has 220,000 members in 90 countries. The Santa Ana Toastmasters Club, since renamed as the Smedley Number One Club, still reserves a chair for him at every meeting. It is placed alongside the lectern and carries his photograph and the original club charter.

Ralph Smedley found the *hwyl* and he lived it, to a grand old age.

(I am grateful to *Toastmasters International* for permission to reproduce part of its biography of Ralph C. Smedley.)

Your Long List of a Dozen Jobs with *Hwyl*

Back to the mundane. No offense, but let's face it. Very few of us will turn out to be a Martha Stewart or Ralph Smedley, let alone a Bill Gates or Nelson Mandela. But we do owe it to ourselves to make the most of our time while we're here, preferably benefiting many, not just ourselves. And the first step in this process is to find the *hwyl*.

The time has come to review your list. Take out your sheet of paper and see what you've come up with. Hopefully you have by now jotted down plenty of names, jobs, and ticks. All those with ticks will inspire you to a certain extent. You've looked at people you know, people you've read about, and people you've seen on TV, and thought about those whose jobs could inspire you. You may also have looked at lists or taken a career test. You may have gained inspiration from thinking about successful people who found the *hwyl* with a career change.

You may have before you a list of two, three or more dozen jobs that could inspire you to varying degrees. Now the list needs to be made more manageable.

You need to rearrange the full list (easier if you've typed it out on your laptop) by grouping the jobs by the number of ticks received. At the very top group together all those jobs that gained five or more ticks. Then those with four, three, and so on. Last, and least, should be those with crosses.

Now you weed out those with the fewest ticks. Obviously, you'll start with all the crosses. Then you'll move on to the single ticks. Carry on this process until you have only a dozen or so jobs left. Hopefully these final dozen will each have received at least three ticks.

> And in the end, it's not the years in your life that count. It's the life in your years.
> —*Abraham Lincoln*

No more than a dozen jobs are needed at this stage. You can always return to the list if you have to. A dozen is a reasonably sized list to be taking into the next chapter on screening. This is your *long list* of jobs with *hwyl*.

To reiterate: at this stage, it doesn't matter whether you could do these jobs well, or if indeed you could even qualify to do them. The important thing is to derive a manageable long list of jobs that inspire you, ranked *purely* by the extent to which they will fill you with *hwyl*.

An Example: Wherein Lies Randy's *Hwyl*?

We last came across Randy in Chapter 9. Chuck has declined to back him, since he's not really sure what he'd be backing. Randy is a super Realtor and would be the last to be let go once the market downturn takes hold in Atlanta. But his heart is not in it. He wants to be a plumber. Chuck has asked him to get his act together and come back when he's made up his mind as to what he's going to do next.

Randy is a brilliant salesman, a natural, yet what he really loves is getting his hands dirty and fixing things. He's pretty sure that plumbing is where the *hwyl* will lie for him. But he's going to need to convince Chuck. So he decides to follow the Backing U! process rigorously.

Randy thinks of all the people he knows, and the people they know, and the people he knows of, and he comes up with a good list (see Figure 15.1).

He finds himself giving most ticks to jobs where he can use his hands to fix things.

He doesn't have a problem putting down plumbing or pipefitting, and giving them five ticks. But he can't really see the point of putting down legends like Hank Aaron and Carl Lewis, since they excelled at jobs he knows he'll never be able to do. Sure he played football and competed in the athletics events at high school, but there were plenty of other boys better at those sports. Basketball was his game. Chuck reassures him and begs him to be patient. The important thing at this stage, he reiterates, is to capture the *hwyl*. If Randy was in that job, would he feel the *hwyl?* Of course, duh, thinks Randy!

Randy then converts the full list to a long list of those jobs that rated four or more ticks (see Figure 15.2).

Randy begins to see Chuck's

Figure 15.1 **Randy's Full List of Jobs with *Hwyl* [1]**

Who	Job	Hwyl
Randy, now	Realtor—salesman and negotiator	✓✓✓(✓)
His dad	Air conditioning engineer, self-employed	✓✓✓✓
His uncle	Plumber, self-employed	✓✓✓✓✓
His grandfather	Painter/decorator, employee	✓✓
His brother	Professional footballer (Atlanta Falcons reserves)	✓✓✓✓
His brother's friend's brother	Trainee manager, Worldspan (airline reservation system)	✓✓
His sister	Dental technician	✓✓
His neighbor A	Plasterer	✓✓
His neighbor B's ex-partner	Computer software developer	✓
His neighbor C's cousin	Car repairer	✓✓✓✓
High School buddy A	Accountant	x
High School buddy B's neighbor	Insurance salesman	✓✓
High School buddy C's grandfather	Air Force pilot	✓✓✓✓
His teacher's father	Vending machine service and repair	✓✓
His dad's friend A	Glazier	✓✓✓
His dad's friend B's brother	Scaffolder	✓✓
His mom's friend	Food manufacturing plant worker	x

Figure 15.1 **Randy's Full List of Jobs with *Hwyl* [2]**

Who	Job	Hwyl
His boss	High school teacher in geography (formerly)	✓
His colleague's father	Policeman	✓✓
Buddy A	Cab driver	✓✓
Buddy B's elder brother	Wall Street trader	✓✓✓✓
Buddy C's uncle	Advertising	✓✓✓
Buddy D's dad's friend	Pipefitter, gas turbine power plant	✓✓✓✓✓
Basketball buddy A	Unemployed	x
Basketball buddy B's cousin	Character actor in Hollywood	✓✓✓✓
His girlfriend	Nurse	✓✓
His girlfriend's brother's friend	Firefighter	✓✓✓✓✓
Ex-girlfriend's ex	Market research	✓✓
Michael Jordan	Professional basketball player	✓✓✓✓✓✓
Hank Aaron	Professional baseball player (Atlanta Braves)	✓✓✓✓
Carl Lewis	Professional athlete	✓✓✓
Will Smith	Movie actor	✓✓✓✓
BoneCrusher	Rapper (Atlanta)	✓✓✓✓
Barack Obama	President	✓✓✓

Figure 15.2 **Randy's Long List of Jobs with *Hwyl***

Job	Hwyl
Professional basketball player	✓✓✓✓✓✓
Plumber, self-employed	✓✓✓✓✓
Wall Street trader	✓✓✓✓✓
Pipefitter, gas turbine power plant	✓✓✓✓✓
Firefighter	✓✓✓✓✓
Air conditioning engineer, self-employed	✓✓✓✓
Professional footballer	✓✓✓✓
Car repairer	✓✓✓✓
Air Force pilot	✓✓✓✓
Character actor in Hollywood	✓✓✓✓
Professional baseball player	✓✓✓✓
Movie actor	✓✓✓✓
Rapper	✓✓✓✓

point. Sure, nothing would give him greater inspiration than being a top pro basketball player, but the list shows that being a plumber, a pipefitter, a trader, or a firefighter aren't so far behind. Knocking on the door of those would be jobs such as an air-conditioning engineer, like his dad, a football player, a pilot, or a rapper. Plumbing is in good company.

Wherein Lies My *Hwyl?*

At this stage, I could have drawn another character, typically a largely fictional, part real character, to use as a final everyman example.

But I've asked you to do it, so you'd be perfectly within your rights to ask me to do the same! Also it just so happens that I did this very exercise a few years ago! I realized then that I didn't want to be a management consultant forever. Many would argue that it's a young person's game. To succeed, you need terrific energy and drive. The working hours can at times be grim. I was then in my early fifties, and I wondered how much longer I'd be able to keep up the pace.

> If you do work that you love, and the work fulfills you, the rest will come…You know you are on the road to success if you would do your job, and not be paid for it.
> —*Oprah Winfrey*

There was no question of early retirement. I had a young family, with hefty bills for housing and education, so I needed the income. And I had no pension to speak of. What should I aim to be doing in five years' time? Something that provided enough income to pay my bills, some contribution to a pension, and above all, filled me with *hwyl*. I wanted to be like Ralph Smedley, still enjoying my contribution to society into my eighties.

I looked at all the people I admire, whether I knew them or knew of them, whether real or fictional. I looked at the jobs they did, the businesses they ran. I thought deeply about whether such a job would inspire me, to what extent I would be consumed with *hwyl* when I woke up on a Monday

Figure 15.3 My Full List of Jobs with *Hwyl* [1]

Who	Job	Hwyl
Me (now), Aymen, Greg, Simon, Andy, Maurice, Andrew, Nathalie, Lucy, Mike	Management consultant, independent, self-employed	✓✓✓(✓)
Stephen L., David G., Stephen W.	International management consulting group, director	✓✓
Philip S., Tariq K., *Leo Bloom*	Consulting arm of Big 4 accounting groups, director	✓
Mike P., Ian K., Alex C.	Specialist, niche management consulting group, director	✓✓✓
Ian H., Mark B., Martyn K.	Economic consulting group, director	✓✓✓
Jonathan D-E., David W., Caroline C.	Private equity, venture capital, director	✓✓
Richard S., Peter W., Robin T.	Development economics/finance agency, director	✓✓✓
Stephen U., *Gordon Gekko*	Corporate/project finance, capital markets, director	✓ (x)
Bill Gates, Terry Matthews, Robert S.	Big business, e.g. director of strategy	✓✓
Michael Heseltine, Anita Roddick	Medium-sized business, director/shareholder	✓✓
J. D. Ivor Evans, Richard H. Jones	Established small business, owner/manager	✓✓✓
Tony Wheeler, Levi Roots	Business start-up, owner/manager	✓✓✓
Sian & John M., Peter & Amanda B.	Travel & tourism business start-up, owner/manager	✓✓✓
Kamontip E., *Basil Fawlty*	Country hotel/stress management retreat owner/manager	✓✓✓✓
John Harvey-Jones	Portfolio of nonexecutive directorships	✓✓✓✓
Patsy Stone, Edina Monsoon	Sales, marketing, advertising, PR	✓

Figure 15.3 **My Full List of Jobs with *Hwyl* [2]**

Who	Job	*Hwyl*
Peter Lampl, Gerard Morgan Grenville	Charity or nonprofit organization, founder	✓✓✓✓
Maude Jones, C.B.E.	Charity or nonprofit organization, director	✓✓
Lissie E., Nancy C., Nick S.	Architect, surveyor, real estate developer	✓
Margaret & John G., Gordon N.	Farmer	✓
Gwyneth Jones, Terry Burns	Civil servant, or adviser to civil service	✓✓
Tom Watts, Daniel J. Evans, *007*	Sailor, soldier, airman, spy	✓(✓)
Col. Krai Chanyaem, *Philip Marlowe*	Policeman, private eye	✓
Dalai Lama, *Geraldine Granger*	Preacher, *pregethwyr*	✓✓
Paul Marsh, Charles Handy, Mon C.	University lecturer in business, finance or economics	✓✓✓✓
Peter Gladstone, Fred Hall, Sarah L.	High school teacher in mathematics or economics	✓✓✓
David Lloyd George, James Callaghan	Politics☐ cabinet minister	✓✓✓✓✓✓
Gandhi, King, Mandela, Suu Kyi	Politics☐ democratic revolutionary	(✓✓✓✓✓)
David Penhaligon, Vince Cable	Politics☐ Member of Parliament (UK, EU or *Cymru*)	✓✓✓✓✓
Helena L., Doreen F., Geoff D.	Politics☐ local government councillor	✓✓✓
John Simpson, Martin Bell	Newscaster or reporter on TV or radio	✓✓✓✓
Day, Snow, Humphrys, Paxman, Neil	Presenter on current affairs TV or radio show	✓✓✓✓✓

Figure 15.3 **My Full List of Jobs with *Hwyl* [3]**

Who	Job	*Hwyl*
Simon Jenkins, Arianna Huffington	Journalist/columnist☐ current affairs	✓✓✓✓✓
A. A. Gill, Jeremy Clarkson	Journalist/columnist☐ features, arts, sports	✓✓✓
Michael Wills, John Lloyd	Independent TV producer	✓✓✓
Mike S., Mark W.	Media manager	✓✓✓
Richard Burton, Paul Newman	Screen actor	✓✓✓✓✓
Anthony Hopkins, Diana Rigg	Stage actor	✓✓✓✓
Peters Brook & Hall, Michael Winner	Stage or screen director	✓✓✓
Ray, Paul, Mick, Tom, Jimmy, Freddie	Rock musician, singer, songwriter	✓✓✓
Julian Grant, Katherine Jenkins	Classical or jazz musician, singer, composer	✓✓✓
Cherie Blair, *Horace Rumpole*	Law☐ barrister	✓✓✓
Evan Ll. Jones M.C., Robert D-E.	Law☐ solicitor: family, corporate	✓✓
Frances, Trevor, Megan & Tom C.	Doctor☐ family, hospital	✓✓
Chimamanda Adichie, Robert Harris	Writer☐ fiction	✓✓✓✓
Bill Bryson, Andrew Marr	Writer☐ nonfiction: self-help, travel, history, current affairs	✓✓✓✓✓
Dylan Thomas, Benjamin Zephaniah	Writer☐ drama, poetry	✓✓✓
Bill Russell, Aileen Bennett	Speaker	✓✓✓✓✓

morning. At this stage I made no attempt at assessing whether someone with my age and background would have a chance of getting in to such a job or starting such a business, let alone prospering once in. All I set out to do was compile a list of jobs that would inspire me. Some seemed more inspirational than others, one or two promised genuine *hwyl.*

Here's the full list I drew up, unranked as yet—see Figure 15.3. (Fictional names are in italics.) I've axed one or two jobs that would be too embarrassing (or "sad," as my kids would no doubt say) to lay out here—such as playing wing forward for the Welsh rugby team!

One interesting observation from the list was the relatively low number of ticks—three/four—I accorded my present job, independent management consulting. I have always thoroughly enjoyed the consulting itself—the travel, teamwork, management meetings, strategic analysis, report writing, presentations—but the marketing and selling can be tiresome. Other fields, with perhaps greener grass, seemed more meritorious of four or more ticks.

The full list then needed weeding. The jobs with crosses came out quickly, so too those with one, two, and even three ticks. More than a dozen jobs remained standing after the weeding, each registering four ticks or more—see Figure 15.4.

These were the jobs that passed through to the next part of the process, on screening the long list to produce a short list of achievable jobs with *hwyl.* That's for the next chapter.

Figure 15.4 **My Long List of Jobs With *Hwyl***

Job	Hwyl
Politics—cabinet minister	✓✓✓✓✓✓
Politics—Member of Parliament (UK, EU or *Cymru*)	✓✓✓✓✓
Presenter on current affairs TV or radio show	✓✓✓✓✓
Journalist/columnist—current affairs	✓✓✓✓✓
Screen actor	✓✓✓✓✓
Writer—nonfiction: self-help, travel, history, current affairs, arts	✓✓✓✓✓
Speaker	✓✓✓✓✓
Portfolio of nonexecutive directorships	✓✓✓✓
Charity or nonprofit organization, founder	✓✓✓✓
Country hotel/stress management retreat owner/manager	✓✓✓✓
University lecturer in business, finance, or economics	✓✓✓✓
Newscaster or reporter on TV or radio	✓✓✓✓
Stage actor	✓✓✓✓
Writer—fiction	✓✓✓✓

Screening for Reality 16

In the last chapter, you derived a long list of a dozen or so jobs or businesses you would love to do. Careers with *hwyl*. Some of these jobs you may stand little chance of getting into, let alone succeeding in them. It's a shame, but that's life. Others you may do well in. The purpose of this chapter will be to derive a short list of three or four jobs. These will not only be jobs with *hwyl* but also jobs in which you could succeed.

You'll do very little extra research in this chapter. That's for the next chapter. Here you'll take a first cut at assessing how attractive the markets are for each of these jobs and how well placed you would be to get in and succeed in them. You'll effectively be doing a quick and dirty assessment of how backable you'd be in each job. You'll be introduced to the *Hwyl* Star chart—an adaptation of one that my small business clients have found useful over the years—to help derive your short list of achievable jobs with *hwyl*.

Many of the more aspirational jobs in your long list will be screened out, sadly, but at least they'll have come and gone without you wasting any serious time on researching them, let alone pursuing them. It's possible so many jobs will be filtered out that you won't have enough left to make a short list. That's no problem. You should see this as an iterative process. You'll return to the full list of the previous chapter and bring forward a new long list of a dozen or so jobs, drawn from the next level down of *hwyl* rating—for example three ticks, rather than four. You'll repeat the screening process, you may even have to do it once again, before finally ending up with your short list of achievable jobs with *hwyl*.

In the next chapter, you'll do some serious research on these short-listed jobs. But first let's get on with the screening.

Screening for Backability

The first thing to realize is that the screening process has to be objective and dispassionate. The aim is not to provide you with a clearer ranking of which job you'd most like to do and where the most *hwyl* is. It's to find out in which job you could be *backable*. Out of all those jobs with *hwyl*, where would a backer consider you worth a punt?

Follow your own particular dreams. We are handed a life by peers, parents and society, you can do that or follow your own dreams. Life is short, be a dreamer but be a practical person.—Hugh Hefner

This aim has implications for the criteria we'll use in ranking the jobs. Typically, when people are thinking of a career change, they'll list criteria such as pay, working conditions, values, culture, location, type of colleague, status, and so forth. Then they'll use these criteria to rank possible careers for relative attractiveness.

This is all highly valid. But it's not for here. It's for the next chapter, *after* we've screened the long list for backability.

There is little point in spending loads of time doing further research on a career where it's highly unlikely that you'll be backable to a real-life Chuck Cash.

These jobs first need to be screened for hard-nosed, economic, competitive factors. Is the market for these jobs growing? Are there more job-seekers than jobs available? With your skills and experience, would you stand a reasonable chance of getting in and succeeding?

You can't always get what you want.—The Rolling Stones

Let's aim to deliver a realistic short list. The long list is the dream list. What gets through the screen and into the next chapter needs to be a short list of achievable, backable jobs with *hwyl*.

How Attractive Are the Markets for These Jobs?

The first thing we need to consider from the perspective of a prospective backer, as in Part I, is how attractive are the markets for these jobs.

In Chapter 2 we looked at how to assess market demand prospects, risks, and opportunities. Then in Chapter 3 we looked at the supply side and assessed prospects for competition, and whether there would be balance in labor supply and demand for these jobs over the next few years.

At this stage there's no need for you to do any research on assessing these markets. Only if the job gets through the screening process is it worthwhile doing serious research.

Gut feel is what's needed at this stage. You need to rank your long list by what you feel. You already have a vague notion of market demand and competition for these jobs, because you know something about them. These are jobs to which you aspire, where you believe the *hwyl* lies. Let your gut feel provide these preliminary estimates.

You need to rank each of the long-listed jobs or businesses by four criteria:

  ➢ *Number of people engaged in this job or business*—Are there many people working in this field, compared to the numbers engaged in other fields?
  ➢ *Growth in jobs or businesses*—Is this a field where there will be growing demand for people over the next few years? Or is demand more likely to stay flat, or decline?
  ➢ *Competition for jobs or among businesses*—How ferocious is the competition to get these jobs? To what extent does the supply of people wanting to do these jobs exceed vacancies available? If this is a business, how intense is the competition between businesses? To what extent is it intensifying?
  ➢ *Job market risk*—How risky is this job or business, compared to others?

As usual, the ranking can be done in words, ticks, or numbers, whatever your preference. Mine, as ever, is for numbers, and Figure 16.1 shows an example.

The chart shows a rough market attractiveness ranking of someone's long list of eight jobs or businesses. B seems to be in the most attractive

Figure 16.1 Rough Market Attractiveness of Long-Listed Jobs: An Example

Long-List of Jobs and Businesses	Number of Jobs	Growth in Jobs	Competition for Jobs	Job Market Risk	Market Attractiveness
A	5	4	3	2	3.5
B	4	4	4	3	3.8
C	4	3	3	2	3.0
D	2	1	2	3	2.0
E	3	3	2	4	3.0
F	5	2	4	3	3.5
G	3	1	4	3	2.8
H	4	2	4	3	3.3

Key to Rating: 1 = Unattractive, 3 = Reasonably Attractive, 5 = Highly Attractive
(For competition for jobs, remember that the more intense the competition, the **less** attractive the market. Likewise for job market risk: the riskier the market, the **less** attractive. Conversely, and more intuitively, the greater the number of jobs the more attractive; likewise for growth in jobs.)

job market. Demand for jobs is sizeable and growing; competition for jobs is not as bad as for most jobs, and it doesn't seem too risky once in. Jobs A and F follow, A being a bit more risky than B, and F with less growth in jobs. D's market seems the least attractive—it's small, declining, and highly competitive.

Suppose job D is this person's most preferred job or business of all? The one with *hwyl* in spades? Shame, because even if in the next section she emerges reasonably well placed to get in and succeed in that job, it's unlikely that it would be advisable to do so. The market will be against her. She'll be pushing uphill. She won't be backable.

How Well Placed Would You Be in These Jobs?

The second stage of the screening process is to assess how well placed you would be to get in and then succeed at this job or business.

As we saw above for assessing market attractiveness, gut feel is again all that's needed at this stage. There's no point in investing hours of time in figuring out customer needs (Chapter 4), Key Kapabilities (Chapter 5), and K2 ratings (Chapter 6) for each of these dozen jobs if they're unlikely to pass through the screening process anyway. That level of detail is for the next chapter.

Let's use a shortcut instead. For each job or business, think of two criteria only:

➤ *Your relevant capabilities*—How you would rate against the capabilities required for the job or business?

➤ *Your experience*—How you would rate against the experience needed to do the job or run the business?

The first criterion relates to how well you think you would do the job, or run the business, if you got into it. How relevant are your skills, your innate talents, to the skills needed to perform the job successfully? How suitable are your qualifications? If your qualifications are currently deficient, how readily could you raise them to the required level?

The second criterion is important in those jobs or businesses where experience is a serious barrier to entry. There may be a whole range of jobs you know you could do well, but your lack of relevant experience would make you difficult to back. Not necessarily because you couldn't do the job. More because prospective employers, or indeed your customers, would be looking for someone more experienced than you to be offering and delivering such a service.

Some words of warning on the experience rating:

➤ When screening a long list, you may think that you have no experience at all of doing a particular job. Don't be dismayed. Think about what elements of your experience to date may at least be *indirectly* or tangentially relevant to that job.

➤ Remember that we're looking primarily for relative comparisons, not absolute levels. We're looking for jobs where some aspects of your past experience may be more relevant than for others.

> If you're young—under 30 (Lucky you!)—the experience criterion may be less relevant than for those of us who are not so young, especially if over 50. Youngsters applying for jobs are typically assessed less rigorously on experience than on capability. And on *potential* capability. You may choose to drop the experience criterion altogether and just use your capability rating on its own.

Let's return to the example of the person with a long list of eight jobs or businesses. Figure 16.2 shows her rough K2 rating against each of those careers.

Figure 16.2   **Rough K2 Rating Against Long-Listed Jobs: An Example**

Long-List of Jobs and Businesses	Your Relevant Capabilities	Your Relevant Experience	Your Rough K2 Rating
A	2	1	1.5
B	2	2	2.0
C	3	4	3.5
D	3	1	2.0
E	1	2	1.5
F	1	3	2.0
G	4	2	3.0
H	3	3	3.0

Key to Rating: 1 = Weak, 2 = Okay-ish, 3 = Good, favorable, 4 = Strong, 5 = Very strong

From this crude screening process, it would seem that she'd be best placed to succeed in job C, followed by jobs G and H. In job C, she believes she would have reasonable capabilities to do the job and some of her past experience would count strongly. As for her dream job D, she doesn't seem well placed to succeed there. She thinks she could do it reasonably well, but she can think of no aspect of her experience that would count for much in the interview process.

How Backable Would You Be in These Jobs?

Now we need to combine the rough assessment of market attractiveness with the similarly rough assessment of your K2 rating. This will give us an idea of how well placed you would be in job markets of varying levels of attractiveness. We need to draw up a screening chart.

All you need is a piece of paper and a pencil. The paper should be set out horizontally ("landscape"). Next you sketch out a screening chart with your likely K2 rating along the horizontal ("x") axis and your rough assessment of the job's market attractiveness along the vertical ("y") axis. Carve up the chart into a 4-by-4 matrix. Alternatively, it's all set out for you in Appendix 1, Figure A.14, and you can use or photocopy that.

Next you plot your long-listed jobs on the chart. The better your K2 rating, the further to the right you'll place your job. The more attractive the market, the higher up you'll place it.

The better the job prospect, the closer it will be placed around or even beyond the main diagonal leading from top left to bottom right.

If the job ends up in the bottom left corner, forget it. It's an unattractive market where you'll be poorly placed. It's not for you.

If the job turns up toward the top right-hand corner, that's good news. It's in an attractive market and it seems like you'll be well placed (subject to further research in the next chapter). Whether or not it's the "perfect job" will depend on how many ticks you gave it in the *hwyl* ranking of the last chapter. We'll return to this in the next section, when we introduce the *Hwyl* Star chart.

At this stage, it's better to plot your jobs using a circle, with the job name or number inside it. In the next section you'll rub it out and replace it with a more meaningful shape.

Let's again visit the example of the person with the long list of eight jobs. Figure 16.3 shows them plotted on her screening chart.

As we suspected, job D is a nonstarter. Her K2 rating is low, *and* the job is in an unattractive market. Jobs A, F, and E are not much better.

Figure 16.3 **Initial Screening of the Long List: An Example**

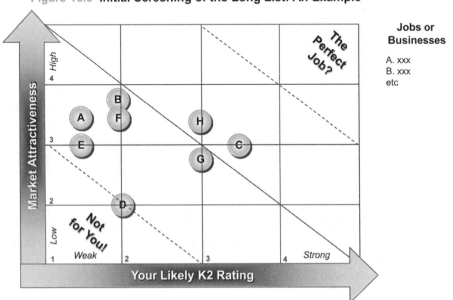

Jobs B and G offer some promise, but it is C and H that seem most promising. They lie to the right of the diagonal. For C, she is well placed in a job with reasonable market prospects. For H she is reasonably placed in a job with good market prospects.

C and H are jobs where she would be most likely to find a backer. These may well be the backable jobs that pass through her screening process and into her short list for further research.

Short Listing With the *Hwyl* Star Chart

There is, however, one final, crucial component that has been left out of the screening process until now. That is the *hwyl* factor. Jobs that proceed to the short list need to have not only good market prospects *and* be ones where you'd be reasonably placed to succeed, but they *also* need to be jobs that inspire you. If the jobs poised for short listing were ranked less favorably in the *hwyl* listings of the previous chapter, then it's possible the wrong jobs will pass through to the short list.

This is where we add the final touch to the screening chart. We replace the penciled circles with stars and make them proportional in size to the extent of *hwyl* the jobs generate. By definition, all the jobs on the long list will give you *hwyl*, but some more so than others. Give those jobs with three ticks a small star, those with four a bigger one, and those with five or more the biggest. These will be your shining stars!

Now you'll be able to see at a glance which jobs should be short listed. They will be the largest stars around and about the diagonal, preferably to its right.

The secret of success is making your vocation your vacation.—
Mark Twain

Let's return again to the example of the woman with eight jobs on her long list—see Figure 16.4.

Job H is the runaway winner for the short list. Not only would she be reasonably placed to succeed at this job, and not only is it a job with attractive market prospects, but it's one of the two jobs that give her the most *hwyl*. The other job to which she gave five ticks, by the way, is D, and that has already been ruled out as a nonstarter.

But the chart also shows that there are two other jobs that merit short listing. We've already mentioned job C, where she would be well placed in a reasonable market. But job G too is worth short listing. She would be reasonably placed for a job with reasonable market prospects *and* it's a job to which she gave four ticks in the *hwyl* listing.

In this example, then, it would be jobs H, G, and C in the long list that would pass through the screening process into the short list of jobs with *hwyl*.

Figure 16.4 **The *Hwyl* Star Chart: An Example**

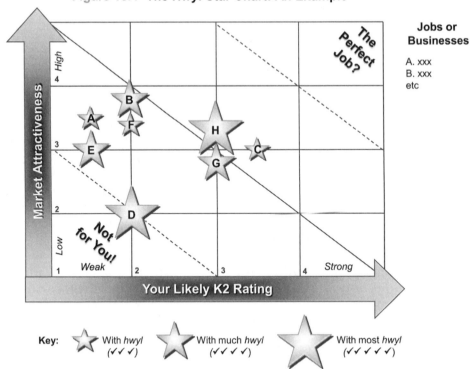

Another Iteration?

When you attempt this screening process, it may not work out quite as clearly as it did with the example chosen. This is because your long list of jobs with *hwyl* took no account whatsoever of your capability to do them. Many of those jobs at the top of your long list are just wishful thinking, and that's fine. But when you get down to the rough assessment of your K2 rating against these fanciful jobs, you may find you don't get anywhere near the diagonal. This is tough, but hardly surprising. We'd all love to be movie stars, but realistically we're not all going to make it from here!

Don't be deterred. Try another iteration. Go back to your long list and import the next dozen or so jobs. Pass them through the screening process. I bet you'll find that they get you closer to the diagonal. Still short of the two or three jobs needed for a short list? Try one more iteration and pull another dozen jobs across. Hopefully by now you'll have found two or three that are sufficiently promising to merit the short list.

Let's now take another couple of examples. First we'll return to our young, fictional friend Randy and see whether real estate, plumbing, or something completely different gets through the screening. And then we'll take a nonfictional example, me, and introduce a stiff dose of reality into my long list!

An Example: Randy's Screening

In the last chapter, we saw how Randy drew up a long list of 13 jobs with serious *hwyl*. These were jobs that Randy gave a rating of four or five ticks in terms of inspiration, joy, passion, *hwyl*. One, a pro basketball player, even rated six ticks.

Randy needed to reduce this long list to a short list of two or three. First, he did a rough and ready rating for job market attractiveness—see Figure 16.5 and found that plumbing seemed to rate the highest. Not only were there plenty of jobs around, but the demand for plumbers still seemed to be growing, competition didn't seem that tough, and it seemed much less risky a job to go into than, for example, real estate. People can often put off buying a house, but they can't hang around long when the tap springs a leak.

Car repair, air conditioning, and firefighting also seemed to have sound market prospects. However, the market attractiveness of a professional basketball player didn't seem as promising. Not many jobs (in comparison to, say, plumbing), little growth, tough competition to get into and succeed in the top teams, and relatively high risk.

Likewise, the job markets for other professional sportsmen, acting, rapping, and Wall Street trading all seemed less attractive, generally because many more people aspired to do these jobs than were opportunities available.

Next Randy had a go at rating his relevant capabilities and experience against these jobs—see Figure 16.6. He found that his rough K2 rating

Figure 16.5 Rough Market Attractiveness of Randy's Long-Listed Jobs

Long List of Jobs and Businesses	Number of Jobs	Growth in Jobs	Competition for Jobs	Job Market Risk	Market Attractiveness
Professional basketball player	2	2	2	2	2.0
Plumber, self-employed	5	4	4	4	4.3
Wall Street trader	3	3	2	3	2.8
Pipefitter	2	4	3	4	3.3
Firefighter	4	3	2	4	3.3
Air conditioning engineer	3	4	4	4	3.8
Professional footballer	2	2	2	2	2.0
Car repairer	5	4	3	4	4.0
Air Force pilot	3	3	3	3	3.0
Character actor in Hollywood	2	3	2	2	2.3
Professional baseball player	2	2	2	2	2.0
Lead actor	2	2	2	2	2.0
Rapper	2	3	3	2	2.5

Key to Rating: 1 = Unattractive, 3 = Reasonably Attractive, 5 = Highly Attractive
[For Competition for Jobs, remember that the more intense the competition, the **less** attractive the market. Likewise for Job Market Risk: the riskier the market, the **less** attractive. Conversely, and more intuitively, the greater the Number of Jobs the more attractive. Likewise for Growth in Jobs]

came out highest in plumbing and air-conditioning, due largely to the experience gained from helping out his father and uncle over the years.

Randy could think of little he had done over the years that would count as relevant experience for jobs such as Wall Street trading, flying, or acting. He felt that some of the plumbing work he'd done could be of relevance to jobs such as pipefitting and firefighting. As for his true passion, basketball, he had plenty of amateur experience, but he wasn't sure he was quite good enough to be able to rise beyond the lower echelons of the professional game. Brutal but true.

Randy then did the initial screening chart from his long list, mapping his rough K2 rating (on the X-axis) against rough job market attractiveness (on the Y-axis)—see Figure 16.7. He was delighted to see plumbing a clear leader, almost venturing into the perfect job zone. Air-conditioning, car repair, and pipe-fitting all came out well too, emerging well to the right of the main diagonal.

Firefighting, pro basketball, and even the air force weren't entirely out of the frame. Time for Randy to make the final adjustment and convert his screening chart into a *Hwyl* Star chart—see Figure 16.8.

This chart emphasizes even more why plumbing is the job for him. He figures Chuck's going to be pleased to see this chart, although he still has to face the more detailed due diligence to be undertaken in the next chapter.

The chart also shows that Randy's short list should include not just plumbing, but also pipe-fitting and firefighting. Although they seem at this rough stage less backable jobs than air-conditioning and car repair, they are jobs that fire up Randy more. And if he's going to ask Chuck to back his *hwyl,* these should be the three jobs that pass through the screen into his short list.

If further research into these three jobs results in their being shifted to the left and/or downwards in the *Hwyl* Star

Figure 16.6 Rough K2 Rating Against Randy's Long-Listed Jobs

Long List of Jobs and Businesses	His Relevant Capabilities	His Relevant Experience	His Rough K2 Rating
Professional basketball player	3.5	3	3.3
Plumber, self-employed	4	2.5	3.3
Wall Street trader	2	1	1.5
Pipefitter	4	2	3.0
Firefighter	4	1.5	2.8
Air conditioning engineer	4	2	3.0
Professional footballer	3	1	2.0
Car repairer	4	1.5	2.8
Air Force pilot	3	1	2.0
Character actor in Hollywood	3	1	2.0
Professional baseball player	3	1.5	2.3
Lead actor	1.5	1	1.3
Rapper	2	2	2.0

Key to Rating: 1 = Weak, 2 = Okay-ish, 3 = Good, favorable, 4 = Strong, 5 = Very strong

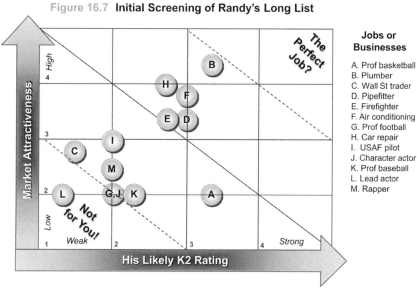

Figure 16.7 **Initial Screening of Randy's Long List**

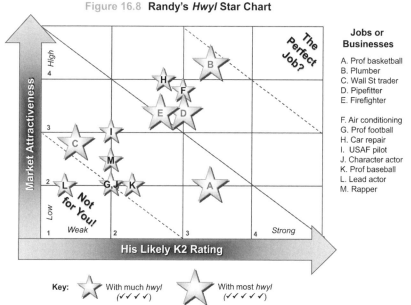

Figure 16.8 **Randy's *Hwyl* Star Chart**

chart, Randy can always return for air-conditioning and car repair and analyze them in greater depth. As for Wall Street trading and pro basketball, his other top *hwyl* jobs, the former looks hopeless while Randy figures he'll carry on with amateur basketball until a pro coach spots him and drags him off, kicking and screaming, to fame and fortune!

Another Example: Mine!

Here we go, then. Time for shattered dreams. Time to suss out just how fanciful was my long list in the last chapter. Time to see whether any of my long-list aspirations, each with four or five *hwyl* ticks, can make it through to the short list.

First, then, how attractive are the markets for these job or business? There seems to be a wide range—see Figure 16.9. Jobs such as nonfiction writing, speaking, and nonexecutive directorships have reasonable market prospects. Unlike those of a cabinet minister!

Figure 16.9 Rough Market Attractiveness of My Long-Listed Jobs

Long List of Jobs and Businesses	Number of Jobs	Growth in Jobs	Competition for Jobs	Job Market Risk	Market Attractiveness
Politics, Cabinet Minister	1	1	1	1	1.0
Politics, MP, MEP, AM	2	1.5	2.5	2	2.0
Presenter, current affairs TV	2	3	2	3	2.5
Journalist, current affairs	2	2	3	3	2.5
Screen actor	2	2	2	2	2.0
Writer, nonfiction	3	3	3.5	3.5	3.3
Speaker	2	4	3	3	3.0
Nonexecutive directorships	3	3	3	3	3.0
Charity/nonprofit, founder	3	3	2	4	3.0
Country hotel/retreat owner/mgr	2	3	3	2	2.5
Lecturer in econ/business	2	2	2	4	2.4
Newsreader on TV or radio	2	3	2	3	2.5
Writer, fiction	3	3	2	2	2.5
Stage actor	2	2	2	3	2.3

Key to Rating: 1 = Unattractive, 3 = Reasonably Attractive, 5 = Highly Attractive
(For competition for jobs, remember that the more intense the competition, the **less** attractive the market. Likewise for job market risk: the riskier the market, the **less** attractive. Conversely, and more intuitively, the greater the number of jobs the more attractive, likewise for growth in Jobs.)

Next up—and this is the bit I was dreading—is the rough K2 rating. This turns out to be not quite as bloody as I had feared, although in some fields the reality is harsh—see Figure 16.10. My rating doesn't seem wholly without hope in nonfiction writing, speaking, nonexecutive directing, and as a member of one parliament or another. Unlike my rating in writing a novel or managing a country retreat!

Then comes the initial screening chart and a few moments of truth—see Figure 16.11. The good news is that the chart suggests that nonfiction writing, speaking, and nonexecutive directing seem to offer reasonable prospects for job change. The bad news is that some aspirations have

Figure 16.10 **Rough K2 Rating Against My Long-Listed Jobs**

Long List of Jobs and Businesses	My Relevant Capabilities	My Relevant Experience	My Rough K2 Rating
Politics, Cabinet Minister	3	1	**2.0**
Politics, MP, MEP, AM	4	2	**3.0**
Presenter, current affairs TV	3	1	**2.0**
Journalist, current affairs	3	2	**2.5**
Screen actor	3	1	**2.0**
Writer, nonfiction	3.5	3	**3.3**
Speaker	3.5	3.5	**3.5**
Nonexecutive directorships	4	2	**3.0**
Charity/nonprofit, founder	2	1	**1.5**
Country hotel/retreat owner/mgr	2	1	**1.5**
Lecturer in econ/business	3	2	**2.5**
Newsreader on TV or radio	3.5	2	**2.8**
Writer, fiction	2	1	**1.5**
Stage actor	3	2	**2.3**

Key to Rating: 1 = Weak, 2 = Okay-ish, 3 = Good, favorable, 4 = Strong, 5 = Very strong

been cruelly exposed as pipe dreams. My job prospects as a movie actor are minimal, and as for becoming a cabinet minister…!

Finally, I add in the all-important *hwyl* ingredient—see Figure 16.12. It seems that speaking and nonfiction writing offer the most promise, which is just as well since I'm three-quarters of the way through writing this, my first book! Non-executive directing also makes the short list, with current affairs journalism and a return to politics not entirely out of the picture and worthy of being held in reserve.

> I don't care to belong to a club that accepts people like me as members.
> —*Groucho Marx*

As for the other most favored jobs, those with five ticks in my *hwyl* rating (A, E, and C on the chart above), it's time to say bye-bye. Barack Obama, Jack Nicholson, and Larry King on one side of the pond, and Gordon Brown, Michael Caine, and David Dimbleby on the other, can sleep easy!

You've screened your long list down to a short list of jobs that not only have *hwyl* but where you also may be backable. Time to check this out in the next chapter.

Figure 16.11 **Initial Screening of My Long-List**

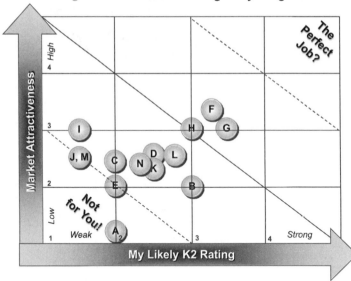

Jobs or Businesses

A. Politics, cabinet
B. Politics, MP, MEP, or AM
C. Presenter, current affairs
D. Journalist, current affairs
E. Screen actor
F. Writer, nonfiction
G. Speaker
H. Nonexec director
I. Charity/nonprofit, manager
J. Country hotel manager
K. Lecturer in econ/business
L. Newsreader on TV or radio
M. Writer, fiction
N. Stage actor

Figure 16.12 **My *Hwyl* Star Chart**

Jobs or Businesses

A. Politics, cabinet
B. Politics, MP, MEP, or AM
C. Presenter, current affairs
D. Journalist, current affairs
E. Screen actor
F. Writer, nonfiction
G. Speaker

H. Nonexec directorships
I. Charity/Nonprofit, manager
J. Country hotel manager
K. Lecturer in econ/business
L. Newsreader on TV or radio
M. Writer, fiction
N. Stage actor

Key: ⭐ With much *hwyl* (✓✓✓✓)   ⭐ With most *hwyl* (✓✓✓✓✓)

Where Best to Back?　17

▷ **How Satisfying Are These Jobs for You?**
▷ **It's Back to Part I for the Target Job, Plus a Backup**
▷ **How Attractive Are the Markets Really for These Jobs?**
▷ **How Well Placed Would You Really Be for These Jobs?**
▷ **How Do You Go About Finding Out?**
▷ **Has Your *Hwyl* Star Chart Changed Following Further Research?**
▷ **Will You Make Your Earnings Aspirations in Your Target Job?**
▷ **Will You Be Backable in Your Target Job?**
▷ **An Example: Randy's Ideal Job**
▷ **Another Example: Mine!**

In the last chapter, you short listed the most promising two or three jobs or businesses with *hwyl*. You took a long list, applied screening criteria, and emerged with a short list of potentially backable jobs with *hwyl*. In this chapter, you need to do some serious research. It should lead you to the most promising job or business with *hwyl*, the ideal job that's waiting out there for you. The target job.

This chapter will guide you through the further research needed. You'll need to read all you can about the short-listed jobs and to speak to people who do this kind of work. And to their "customers." You'll need to confirm that these jobs will inspire you with *hwyl*. You also need to confirm that they fulfill the other aspects of job satisfaction that matter to you. You'll need to dust off the tools introduced in Part I of this book and set them to work on the short-listed jobs. You'll need to *really* understand where the market is going, how tough is the competition, how well placed you would be, and how risky it would be to back U in each job.

In summary, you'll need to find out just how rosy these short-listed jobs or businesses really are. Are they really for you? You'll firm up the placement of these jobs on the *Hwyl* Star chart and conclude which job you should back yourself in—and which should be kept in reserve as a plan B.

In the next chapter, you'll see what you can do to improve your chances of getting in and succeeding in the target job or business. You may need to build on your strengths, or work on some weaknesses. You may be able to use some of the tools introduced in Part II of this book. You'll see to what extent you can improve the placement of that target job on your *Hwyl* Star chart.

But first you need to firm up on which of the short-listed jobs with *hwyl* you're really going to go for. There are three main areas where you need to do further research before you can draw firm conclusions:

➢ How satisfying are these short-listed jobs?
➢ How attractive are the markets for these jobs?
➢ How well placed would you be to do these jobs?

Let's take them one at a time.

How Satisfying Are These Jobs for You?

Let's recap. The two or three jobs or businesses that have made it into your short list are those that inspire you, fill you with *hwyl*. Hopefully they will be among those to which you gave four or five ticks in Chapter 15.

But how much do you *really* know about them? To what extent has your understanding of them been colored by what you have read in newspapers or magazines, what you have seen on the TV, what your friends or family have said about them?

Do you really understand what these jobs are like? How well paid are they? Do you have to excel to make good money? What are the working conditions like? Where will you work? Will your desk be near a window? Will you have to work long hours? Will you have to spend long periods away from your family? What sort of work will you actually do? Will you find that fulfilling? What sort of values are your colleagues likely to have? Will they be compatible with yours? What sort of status will this job have in the community? Is that important to you?

> If you do achieve what you want with your life, what about you would you like to have remembered, after you are gone from this earth?
> —Richard N. Bolles

You won't yet have answers to most of these questions. Nor should you be expected to. You're contemplating career change, after all, and it's unlikely at this stage that you'll know everything about the career you to which you are thinking about changing.

But you need to know. And now's the time to find out.

First you need to establish what constitutes satisfaction in a job or business for you personally. What would make you satisfied in your job? Loads of money? Perhaps, but at what cost? Would you accept bucketfuls of bucks every day if it meant you were expected to work in unhealthy or unsafe conditions? What if you had to compromise, even abandon your ethics? What if it meant being entirely self-centered, with no regard for others less fortunate? What if you had to bury your true self, contain your sense of humor? What if you had to be cavalier with the law?

I remember discussing with a consulting colleague a few years ago the merits of seeking a job in private equity. To do well, to get to the top in buying and selling companies, I said, you need not only to be business savvy and financially astute, but you also had to have a genuine hunger to make money, an all-embracing ambition to become rich, really rich. "I've never had that hunger," I said, "that's why I'll probably stay in consulting. What about you?" There was a pause. He looked at me with a wild-eyed determination bordering on desperation, before answering, with no trace of irony, "I'm flipping starving!" If he gets in, he'll do well. Good luck to him.

> No man or woman is an island. To exist just for yourself is meaningless. You can achieve the most satisfaction when you feel related to some greater purpose in life, something greater than yourself.
> —Denis Waitley

For most human beings, however, there are many diverse aspects of job satisfaction to take into account, not just piling up the gold. Job satisfaction criteria can be grouped under six heads:

1. *Pay*—Is this job (or business) likely to meet or exceed your desired level of wages or salary? And pension? If you expect to be rewarded in relation to performance, is this job likely to meet your expectations through a bonus scheme, profit share, or equity participation?
2. *Working conditions*—Will this job meet your expectations of type of work, hours of work, independence, work/life balance, location, frequency of overnight travel, and other working conditions?
3. *Fulfillment*—Will this type of work enable you to fulfill your manual, intellectual, and creative talents?
4. *Values*—Will the culture of the organization, the nature of the work, the character of your colleagues be compatible with your values?
5. *Status*—Would this job confer the status you require, whether to your own self-esteem or to the community?
6. *Hwyl*—Will this job inspire you, fill you with passion, fervor, spirit? Joy? Fun?

So far, you've ranked prospective jobs or businesses using only the last criterion, *hwyl*. It's the best place to start, but it's now time to see whether your short-listed jobs measure up to your other job satisfaction criteria.

The first thing you need to do is to decide which of the job satisfaction criteria matter most to you. Clearly, pay was what mattered beyond all else for my former colleague referred to above. How does it rank for you?

Try ranking the six job satisfaction criteria above in order of importance to you, from 1 to 6. Alternatively, go through each criterion and assess how important it is to you. Assign each criterion a level of importance, whether high, low, or medium, or levels in between.

Draw up a simple chart with the job satisfaction criteria in the first column, levels of importance in the second and your short-listed jobs in the next two or three columns. You can now rate each job by the extent to which it will make you satisfied against each of the criteria. You can use either words or ticks, whichever you prefer.

It may be difficult to make sensible comparative assessments at this stage. It may not be clear, for example, what the values of the organization you aspire to work for really are. To get a firmer rating may require further research. You'll get some guidance on how to do that later in this chapter in the section: *How Do You Go About Finding Out?*

Figure 17.1 shows an example, carrying on with the woman we followed in the last chapter when she screened her long list of eight jobs into a short list of three.

Figure 17.1 **Satisfaction Rating of Short-Listed Jobs: An Example**

Job Satisfaction Criteria	Importance	Job H	Job G	Job C
Pay	*Med/High*	Ok	Fine	Great
Working conditions	*High*	Great	Fine	Not so good
Fulfilment	*Med*	Great	Fine	Fine
Values	*Med/Low*	Great	Great	Okay
Status	*Med/Low*	Great	Great	Fine
Hwyl	*Med/High*	Great	Fine	Okay
Overall		**Great**	**Fine/Great**	**Okay/Fine**

Her main priority in switching careers is to gain more flexibility around working hours, to enable her to shape her working day around school drop-off and pick-up times. So she gives this job satisfaction criterion a higher importance than pay, or even *hwyl*. She finds that job H ranks highly against all her job satisfaction criteria, bar one: It doesn't pay very well. But it is one of the few jobs she has given a five-tick rating to for *hwyl* and working hours are highly flexible.

Job G pays better, and still offers some flexibility in working hours, while job C pays really well but would demand her presence on occasions irrespective of whether her children needed picking up or were unwell. She also thinks that job C would be less fulfilling, less in tune with her values (given her would-be colleagues' fixation on the bottom line), and would lend her less status in the community than either of the other two.

Overall, job H seems like a clear winner, subject to further research on all of them. Pay wouldn't be so good, but she figures she'd be able to cut her cloth accordingly and that would be a small sacrifice to enable her to do a job she'd love.

Any surprises from Figure 17.1? I'm sure you've spotted it already.

Yes, there are no numbers in it! That's not to say that populating the chart with numbers wouldn't have worked better—I think it would have. But it shows that you don't have to be a numbers nerd like me to benefit from the approach advocated in this book!

For the record, Figure 17.2 shows what the chart would have looked like if the rating had been done with numbers, instead of words or ticks.

Figure 17.2   Satisfaction Rating of Short-Listed Jobs: An Example (Rated With Numbers!)

Job Satisfaction Criteria	Weighting	Job H	Job G	Job C
Pay	20%	3	4	5
Working conditions	25%	5	4	2
Fulfilment	15%	5	4	4
Values	10%	5	5	3
Status	10%	5	5	4
Hwl	20%	5	4	3
Overall	100%	4.6	4.2	3.4

Key to Rating: 1 = Unsatisfactory, 2 = Not so satisfactory, 3 = Satisfactory, 4 = Very satisfactory, 5 = Most satisfactory

Again, the advantage of using numbers is that the final rating emerges having automatically taken into account the weighting applied to each criterion. It's difficult when using words to compare a rating of *great* against a criterion of *low/medium* importance, with an *okay* against a criterion of *high* importance. Nevertheless, the words approach still manages to yield the same answer, that is, job H looks the most promising of the three in terms of job satisfaction.

> Whoever renders service to many puts himself in line for greatness—great wealth, great return, great satisfaction, great reputation, and great joy.—*Jim Rohn*

It's Back to Part I for a Target Job, Plus a Backup

It's now time for some serious research. It's up to you whether you do this on all your short-listed jobs or businesses. Or on just the one that emerges most favorably from the job satisfaction ranking just undertaken. The target job.

Researching each target job or business will take serious time and effort. Otherwise it's not going to be convincing. It won't confirm things one way or another.

You're going to have to assess how backable you would be in this target job or business. You'll have to imagine taking your proposition to Chuck Cash. Would he back you if you were to switch to this new job or business? Would you back U?

Perhaps, but only if your job analysis is backed up by research. Chuck would ask you detailed, difficult questions. In Part I of this book when he assessed your backability in your current job, many of his questions were easy to answer. That's your job—you work in this field, you know what's going on.

But now you'll need to answer tough questions about a field you know little about. And if you can't answer them, he probably won't back you. Why should he, if you're not serious enough about this field to even research it properly?

In short, you need to repeat, more or less, Part I of this book! But not for your current job or business. For your short-listed target job or jobs with *hwyl*.

I always wanted to be somebody, but I should have been more specific.
—*Lily Tomlin*

My recommendation is that you proceed to do full Part I research on the target job, the job or business that emerged at the top of the job satisfaction rating above. And at the same time do some limited, desk-based research on a backup job, the one that came in as runner up. This should give you work enough to be getting on with as you dig up data, talk to people, draw up some charts, build the storyline.

If further research suggests that the target job may not be suitable because of too many new entrants or because it demands skills you don't have, for example, then at least you have a backup. You can upgrade research on the backup job to full Part I analysis, while starting desk-based research on the third placed job, and so on. Always keep a backup in case prospects for your target job grind to a halt.

In the example above, the woman would be well advised to undertake serious Part I research on job H, while at the same time doing some desk-based research on job G.

How Attractive Are the Markets Really for These Jobs?

The first main area of further research needed is market attractiveness. You need to firm up on the rough assessment of market attractiveness you made for Chapter 16's screening process. You know how to do it. You've already done it once in Chapters 2 and 3 for your current job or business. You just need to do it again for the target job!

To assess how attractive the markets really are for your target job, and for the backup job, you need to assess the following for each major business chunk:

$\blacktriangleright$ Market demand prospects, risks, and opportunities
$\blacktriangleright$ The nature of competition, its intensity, and how this is likely to change

You'll start by assessing market demand prospects. Just as you did in Chapter 2 of this book, you need to:
$\blacktriangleright$ Assess past growth trends. Check how market demand has grown in the past.
$\blacktriangleright$ Assess past drivers of growth. Identify what has been driving that growth in the past.
$\blacktriangleright$ Assess changes in growth drivers. Assess whether there will be any change in influence of these and other drivers in the future.
$\blacktriangleright$ Forecast future growth. Forecast market demand growth, based on the influence of future drivers.
$\blacktriangleright$ Assess market demand risks and opportunities.

I won't go into further detail on how to do the above here. It's all there in Chapter 2. Suffice to say that this will be trickier for you to research than when you did it for your current job or business. Some tips on how to go about finding the necessary information are set out later in this chapter.

Then you need to assess trends in competition in your target job or business. Again, just as you did in Chapter 3 of this book, you need to:
$\blacktriangleright$ Establish who your new competitors will be in each main business chunk.
$\blacktriangleright$ Assess whether competition is tough and/or getting tougher, using Professor Porter's Five Forces.
  o Internal rivalry
  o Threat of new entrants
  o Ease of substitution
  o Customer bargaining power
  o Supplier bargaining power

$\blacktriangleright$ Assess the market demand-supply balance and the implications for future prices or earnings.
$\blacktriangleright$ Assess competition and pricing risks and opportunities.

The above listing of a few bullets masks a lot of hard work for you in both research and analysis. But it'll be worth it, and it has to be done if you are to convince Chuck that you should switch to a career where the *hwyl* lies.

How do your researched findings compare with the rough assessment you made of the market attractiveness of this target job or business in Chapter 16? More attractive or less attractive? Why?

How Well Placed Would You Really Be for These Jobs?

Next you need to firm up how well placed you would be in this target job or business. You need to confirm the rough assessment you undertook during Chapter 16's screening process.

Again, you know how to do it. You've already done it once in Chapters 4, 5, and 6 for your current job or business. You just need to do it again for the target job.

To do this, you need to work your way carefully through the three-stage process undertaken in Part I, establishing for each main business chunk:

➢ "Customer" needs for people in your target job or business (Chapter 4).

➢ What needs to be done to succeed in that job (Chapter 5)? What are the Key Kapabilities (K2s) needed?

➢ How you would measure up against those K2s (Chapter 6)? What would your K2 rating be?

First, you need to assess what the needs of your customers are going to be in your target job. Just as you did in Chapter 4 for your current job, you'll try to establish customer needs relating to the E2-R2-P2 of your target services, namely effectiveness, efficiency, relationship, range, premises, and price.

You'll find out what level of importance customers attach to each of their needs, how this differs by business chunk, and whether this will change over time.

Undertaking this part of the research will be by no means as easy as it was when you did it for your current job or business. Then, you only had to talk to your own customers, or if you're an employee, to your colleagues and bosses. Here, you're going to need to talk to your target job's "customers," the users of the services you aspire to provide. I'll set out some tips later in the chapter on how to go about this.

Second, you need to work out what the Key Kapabilities for your target job or business are. Just as you did in Chapter 5 for your current job, you need to translate customer needs into what providers of that service need to do to meet them and succeed in that job or business. You need to apply weights reflecting the importance of each of the K2s, taking into account not just skills, qualifications, and experience, but also such factors as market share and management. And how crucial a K2 is attitude in your target job?

Now you're in a position where you can assess how well placed you'd be in your target job or business, just as you did in Chapter 6 for your current job. How would you rate against each of the K2s, in particular in relation to your peers currently performing that target job or business? How would your overall K2 rating compare with theirs?

You must be careful here. Most people doing your target job or engaged in your target business already have much more experience than you. This probably means that their overall K2 rating will be much higher than yours.

Don't be dismayed. While working out your initial K2 rating, think about what your rating could be *in three years' time*, and what you'd need to do to improve it. At the very least, the gulf in experience between you and those presently doing the job will have narrowed considerably.

And remember there's one Key Kapability where you're going to be at least on a par with those already in the field. And hopefully you may surpass many of them. That is *attitude*. The whole reason you are targeting this job is because of the *hwyl*. Some of those currently in this field may have grown jaded over the years; others may never have thought of it as their ideal job. Not so for you. From day one your enthusiasm will be radiant and your energy levels volcanic. At least on this K2, you'll be top of the tree.

These are only first cuts at your K2 rating. Where you're particularly unsure how you'd rate yourself, stick in a question mark. You'll revisit your rating once you've done your further research, in particular talking to some practitioners in the field, as well as their customers.

You've now worked out how well placed you'd be in your target job or business upon entry, and if things go according to plan, in three years' time. How does that compare with the rough assessment you made for this job during the screening process of Chapter 16? Better placed or worse? Why? What risks?

How Do You Go About Finding Out?

How can you find out about job market attractiveness and your prospective K2 rating in a field you may know little about? It's not as difficult as you may think. But it does involve picking up the telephone.

As set out in Chapter 6, there are two main sources of information available for researching job markets and your potential positioning:
1. The Internet and other sources of third-party market research
2. Structured interviewing

The Internet is a boon for doing desk-based market research—please take another look here at Chapter 2 and the section *Weave Your Web of Information.*

Then there's structured interviewing, first encountered in Chapter 6. But things were much easier then. For employees, information on customer needs and the extent to which you perform and meet those needs, in relation to your colleagues, could be readily gleaned just from talking to your bosses. For the self-employed, you could derive such information through a structured interview program with your customers.

But these were customers of your current services. They're your colleagues (if you're an employee) or your very own customers (if you're self-employed). Who then are the customers of the providers of your target job or business? And how do you get to talk to them? For that matter, who are the providers of your target job or business? It's not you any more. This is not your current job, it's a target job. How do you get to talk to these current practitioners?

You need to talk to both sets of people—providers and customers.

You need to talk to the providers to get a firmer idea of how satisfying the job would be for you. You need to accumulate further information on the nature of the work, the hours, the travel, the culture, and so forth. You need to wheedle out their views on what it takes to be successful in their field.

You need to talk to their customers to find out their needs and what providers need to have and do in order to meet them.

Again, as in Chapter 6, the answer is through structured interviewing. But this time with a couple of additional complications:

> ➤ You need to interview both customers *and* providers.
> ➤ You may well not know any customers *or* providers!

It's not as daunting as it may seem. It may help to think of Elizabeth, our market researcher of Parts I and II. Suppose her company, Consult-Co, is engaged by a private equity client to advise on whether it should invest in, say, a company providing IT outsourcing services to small- or medium-sized enterprises. Elizabeth will need to call up these customers out of the blue and charm her way through the operator and various other respondents. She'll get bounced around all over the place before she gets to the person actually responsible for engaging and monitoring the performance of an IT outsourcer. That's not easy, particularly when her storyline is questionable, but she does it regularly.

It's not so hard for you. You'll have a storyline with which *people can empathize*. You're interested in this field of work and would like to find out more about it. It's not threatening. It's highly likely you'll find people who'll be delighted to help. The biggest challenge is actually summoning the guts to pick up a phone in the first place and call a company cold.

Here in summary is how to conduct a structured interviewing program for your target job or business, which you'll see is an approach similar to that of Chapter 6:

> ➤ Select a representative range of provider and customer interviewees, preferably with some sort of a referee to break the ice.
> ➤ Prepare your storyline.
> ➤ Prepare a concise questionnaire for providers and a separate one for customers.
> ➤ Interview them, through email, telephone, or face-to-face.
> ➤ Thank them and give them some feedback.

This approach is set out in some detail in Appendix C.

Further research through structured interviewing is the key to confirming your assessment of these aspects of your target job or business:

> ➢ How satisfying is this job for you?
> ➢ How attractive is the market really for this job?
> ➢ How well placed would you be really for this job?

These are of course the three components needed for your *Hwyl* Star chart. Time to reexamine it.

Has Your *Hwyl* Star Chart Changed Following Further Research?

You've done your research. You now have a much firmer idea on how attractive the market is for your target job or business. Likewise you're clearer on how well placed you'd be in that job and on how satisfying that job would be for you.

Has your research confirmed that this is a job that would meet all, or most, of your job satisfaction criteria? That it remains a job not just with *hwyl*, but with pay, working conditions, fulfillment, values, and status that would, on balance, rank it above other short-listed jobs or businesses?

And where does your target job or business now sit on your *Hwyl* Star chart? Has it shifted significantly from your earlier drafting in Chapter 16?

Has it shifted, disappointingly, to the left, or downwards? Worse, has it headed toward the bottom left-hand corner? If so, is it looking less promising than other short-listed jobs or businesses?

Is it indeed time to draw a line under this target job? Rather than embarking on a job hunt in this field, with all that entails—job searches, application letters, chase-up calls, interviews, and all else—should you cut your losses now? And move on to researching your backup job?

Or has your research left your target job more or less where it was on the *Hwyl* Star chart? That should be encouraging. Even better, has the research improved the job's positioning, shifting it a tad upwards, or to the right, or even toward the top right-hand corner?

Has the research improved your chances of being backable in your target job or business?

Will You Make Your Earnings Aspirations in Your Target Job?

As we saw in Part I of this book, there are four pieces of the Risk Jigsaw: market demand risk, competition risk, U risk, and your plan risk. The research you've done in this chapter has helped you address the first three jigsaw pieces for your target job or business. What about the fourth? Are your earnings aspirations likely to be met?

What are your planned earnings in your target job or business in three years' time? If you're aiming to be an employee, what's your planned pay? If you're aiming to be self-employed, what are your planned revenues and profits?

Are these plans consistent with what your research suggests will happen in the market? Are they consistent with your likely lowly K2 rating when you start the job? Do they realistically reflect the likely improvement in your K2 rating over the first three years of you doing the job, or running the business?

What are the risks of you not making that plan?

Perhaps you may benefit from a quick look back at Chapter 7 of this book, where a number of examples are given that highlight the need for *consistency* in the assumptions in your plan.

Will You Be Backable in Your Target Job?

We're there! You now have all you need to be able to draw up a Suns & Clouds chart for you switching careers to your target job or business!

Have a quick skim through Chapter 8 to remind you how to do it, then give it a go! How does it look? Hopefully there will be a reasonable balance between risks and opportunities.

Don't be disheartened if the overall picture looks rather cloudy! What did you expect? You're going to be new to this job or business. It's bound to be risky! But what is this life if you take no risks?

Are you sure, however, that there are no showstopper risks? If there is one, then back out now. Don't waste any further time or effort on switching to this target job.

Are there any risks sitting uncomfortably close to the showstopper area? If so, is there anything you can do to mitigate those risks?

Would you back U in your target job or business?

Let's hope so. But before you start sending out those application letters, shouldn't you be thinking about how you can improve your chances of getting in to your target job or business? And once in, how you can improve your chances of succeeding there?

Nothing ventured, nothing gained.—*Proverb*

That's for the next chapter. Before that, let's take a look at a couple of examples of where further research may have helped confirm the backability of a target job with *hwyl*.

An Example: Randy's Ideal Job

In the last chapter, Randy's screening of his long list of jobs with *hwyl* produced a short list headed by plumbing, by quite some distance. Pipefitting and firefighting also made it through the screen, with air-conditioning and car repair in reserve.

Before embarking on some serious research on plumbing, Randy first does a check to see whether plumbing would not just be a job with *hwyl*, but also one that would fulfill other aspects of job satisfaction (see Figure 17.3).

Randy starts by assessing the relative importance of typical job satisfaction criteria to him. Pay comes first, because he feels his lifestyle demands that he has plenty of cash to throw around. The ability to start and stop working at times of his choosing is also important to him. So too is *hwyl*. He wants to be able to sing on his way to work.

He gives these three criteria the highest weighting and ranks the three short-listed jobs against them. Plumbing scores highly on all of them. Firefighting doesn't pay quite so well and falls down heavily on working hours. If there's a fire call at 4:30 P.M., you can't tell the boss that you don't want to let down your basketball buddies because you need to be at the game by 6 P.M. You've got a fire to put out.

Plumbing doesn't quite cut it in terms of status. Randy is aware that there's a public perception that plumbers rip off unsuspecting housewives with unscrupulous fault magnification ("All the valves need changing, honey") and outrageous bills. But he also knows that plumbers have recently climbed the hunk rating, thanks to the TV series *Desperate Housewives!*

Randy sees firefighting as having serious status. Being seen as cool, macho, and brave could do wonders for his already awesome social scene.

Once rated, weighted, and added up, however, firefighting is a distant third to plumbing's clear leadership in Randy's job satisfaction. He will proceed

Figure 17.3 Randy's Satisfaction Rating of Short-Listed Jobs

Job Satisfaction Criteria	Randy's Weighting	Plumbing	Pipefitting	Firefighting
Pay	30%	5	4	3.5
Working Conditions	20%	5	3	2
Fulfilment	15%	5	5	5
Values	5%	4	4	5
Status	10%	3	4	5
Hwyl	20%	5	5	5
Overall	**100%**	**4.8**	**4.2**	**4.0**

Key to Rating: 1 = Unsatisfactory, 2 = Not so satisfactory, 3 = Satisfactory,
4 = Very satisfactory, 5 = Most satisfactory

to do serious research on plumbing, and in parallel, do some desk research on pipe-fitting. Firefighting will have to take a back seat for now.

Randy's market research on plumbing could have been straight-forward. His uncle's a plumber, so all he had to do was talk to him, to two or three of his uncle's plumbing colleagues, and to half a dozen of his uncle's customers and that should do the trick.

But Randy was also interested in plumbing work for companies and institutions, where the longer jobs and greater frequency of callback appealed to the idler elements of his nature. But his uncle didn't work in that business chunk at all, and Randy suspected Chuck would want to know as much about the corporate as the household chunk.

Randy asked his uncle for contact numbers of a range of different types of plumbers. And he went and talked to them. He ended up speaking to 11 plumbers, only 5 of whom served the household chunk, including his uncle and his assistant. Two others were independents working for the corporate chunk, three worked in a plumbing firm typically engaged by larger con-struction contractors and one worked full-time in a hospital. Randy also spoke to a range of customers—three households who had recently had major plumbing jobs done, two companies, one hospital, and one school.

Randy also found good information on the Internet. Just punching in "plumbing," "Atlanta," "market growth" to Google yielded him loads of useful articles. (Try it!) He tested out some of his initial findings on the market with some of his interviewees and a consistent picture began to emerge.

He found that the plumbing market in Atlanta had been growing fast in recent years, driven by economic growth in general and social trends such as the desire for a greater number of bathrooms per house. He found that

Figure 17.4 **Market Demand Prospects for Plumbing Services in Atlanta**

Demand Drivers for Plumbing in Atlanta	Impact on Demand Growth			Comments
	Recent Past	Now	Next Few Years	
Atlanta economic growth	+	+	+	• Economic forecasts in local papers seem fine
New homes built	++	+	+	• Boom over but some developments planned
House prices	+	0	−	• House price boom had limited impact on demand for plumbing, so likewise for impending crash
Growth in offices, schools, etc., with plumbing requirement	+	+	+	• Buildings growing as fast as infrastructure
Trend toward more bathrooms per house	++	++	+	• One per bedroom already reached in many homes in upper pricing range
Trend toward more complex plumbing and heating systems	+	+	+	• More sophisticated timers, shower mechanisms, flushes etc
Trend to shoddier materials with built-in obsolescence	+	+	+	• Especially boilers, electric heaters, etc.; less so with piping
Bathrooms changing more frequently	++	++	++	• Fashion victims boosting demand
Overall Impact	++	++	++	
Market Growth Rate	*Fast*	*Fast*	*Fast*	

Key to Impact		O	None
+++	Very strong positive	−	Some negative
++	Strong positive	− −	Strong negative
+	Some positive	− − −	Very strong negative

the impending crash in house prices would have only limited impact on market demand for plumbing, just as the recent boom in house prices hadn't been a major driver in the past.

Randy dusted off his charts from Chapter 2 of this book, rubbed out all the analysis of demand for Realtor services, and applied similar thinking to demand for plumbing services—see Figure 17.4. He found that fast-growing demand for plumbing seemed set to continue. This would be good news for Chuck. He likes the wind to blow from behind.

Randy then pulled out a Five Forces competition chart from Chapter 3, slotted in his findings to the boxes, and found that the level of competitive intensity in the Atlanta plumbing market was just low to medium—see Figure 17.5. It may be set to increase a bit because of people such as him entering the market, but none he spoke to spotted any signs of an imminent invasion by an army of eager, would-be plumbers. Again, this seemed like the level of industry competition Chuck likes to back.

Next Randy sorted out the responses from his discussions with plumbing customers and slotted them into a Chapter 4 type chart on customer needs—see Figure 17.6. Household customers wanted mainly for the job to be done properly by a trustworthy, helpful, empathetic plumber. Corporate customers wanted the same to an extent, but with more emphasis on timely delivery and with a keener eye on price.

Randy then converted these customer needs into the Key Kapabilities required for a plumber to be successful, using what he had learned from Chapter 5 of this book—see Figure 17.7. Expertise is essential, including skills of manual dexterity and strength, the appropriate qualifications, and the experience of having been there, done that before. Integrity too is a K2. With a reputation for integrity, word of mouth lessens the amount of marketing needed to keep busy.

Figure 17.5 **Competition in Plumbing Services in Atlanta**

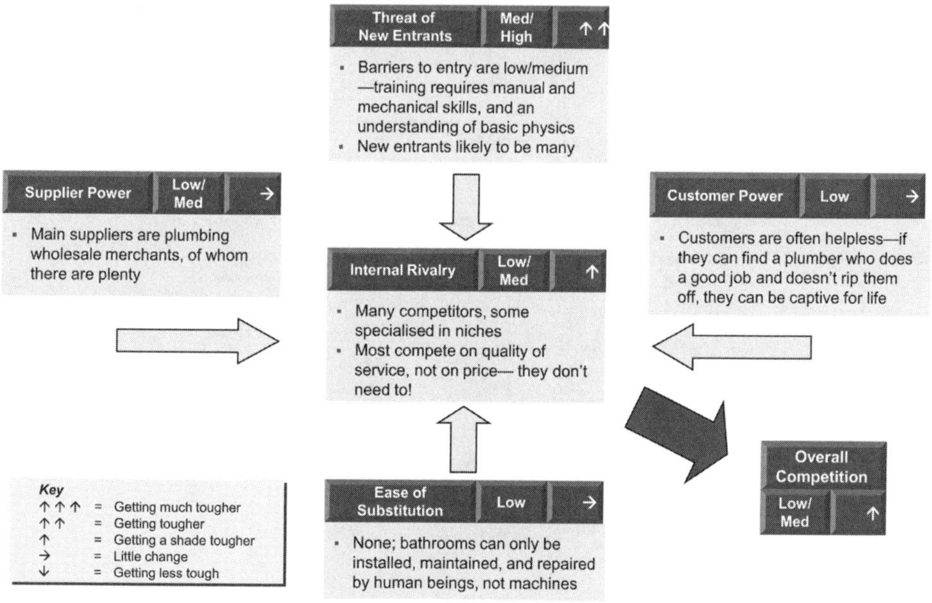

Figure 17.6 **Customer Needs From Plumbing Services in Atlanta**

Household Customer Needs		Importance	Change
Effectiveness - **Skills**	▪ In installing, repairing	High	→
- **Knowledge**	▪ Of the way plumbing systems work	Med/High	→
- **Experience**	▪ Of what can go wrong and how best it can be fixed	High	→
Efficiency	▪ Effort ▪ Timeliness	Med *Low/Med**	→ →
Relationship	▪ Trustworthiness ▪ Helpful attitude	*High** High	→ →
Range		Low	→
Premises		N/a	
Price		*Med**	↑

* Company or institutional customer needs similar to those for households,
other than in timeliness *(High)*, trustworthiness *(Med),* and price *(High)*

Figure 17.7 **Associated Key Kapabilities for Plumbing Services in Atlanta**

Household Customer Needs		Importance	Change	Associated Key Kapabilities
Effectiveness - **Skills**	▪ In installing, repairing	High	→	• **Manual dexterity, strength**
- **Knowledge**	▪ Of the way plumbing systems work	Med/High	→	• **Qualifications, diploma**
- **Experience**	▪ Of what can go wrong and how best it can be fixed	High	→	• **Direct experience**
Efficiency	▪ Effort ▪ Timeliness	Med *Low/Med**	→ →	• **Work ethic** • **Punctuality**
Relationship	▪ Trustworthiness ▪ Helpful attitude	*High** High	→ →	• **Integrity** • **Enthusiasm**
Range		Low	→	• **Range**
Premises		N/a		
Price		*Med**	↑	• **Cost competitiveness**

Randy then considered the other Key Kapabilities not derived from customer needs, namely relative market share and management factors (Chapter 5 again), and gave appropriate weightings to each of them. He thought about whether these weightings would differ between household and corporate customers and decided that improved managerial techniques, greater efficiency and a broader range of offering would be needed by companies.

He then rated how he would perform against each of these K2s, in comparison with his uncle's performance in the household business chunk—see Figure 17.8. In contrast to when he undertook this same exercise as a Realtor in Chapter 6, the results were rather dispiriting, if unsurprising. His overall rating came to just 2.5 out of 5, compared to his uncle's 4.3! His main strengths were that he would be cheap and cheerful! So how would he get work, let alone do it well when he got it?

The answer of course lies with the time-honored apprentice system. By positioning himself as his uncle's apprentice for the first 12 to 18 months, he'd have the opportunity to do plenty of work, learn how to deliver it effectively, take evening classes as he went along and eventually be able to stand on his own two feet. In three years' time, Randy figured he could have acquired similar qualifications to his uncle, though of course nothing like the same customer base or experience. He could have lifted his K2 rating to a healthy 3.4 or so.

As a check, Randy took another look at his screening work in the last chapter (Figure 16.6) to see whether his further research had had any impact on the positioning of plumbing as a

Figure 17.8 Randy's Likely K2 Rating in Plumbing Services in Atlanta

Key Kapabilities in Household Plumbing Services in Atlanta	Weighting*	Randy Today	Randy's Uncle	Randy in Three Years
Relative Market Share	15%	1	5	2
Cost Factors	15%	5	3	4
Management Factors: Marketing	5%	2	3	4
Service Factors: Effectiveness—Manual dexterity	15%	2	5	4
Effectiveness—Qualifications	10%	0	3	3
Effectiveness—Experience	20%	1.5	5	2
Efficiency—Effort, timeliness	5%	3	5	4
Relationship—Integrity, enthusiasm	15%	5	4	5
Range	0%	1	3	2
Premises (not applicable)	0%	x	x	x
K2 Rating	**100%**	**2.5**	**4.3**	**3.4**

Key to Rating: 1 = Weak, 2 = Okay-ish, 3 = Good, favorable, 4 = Strong, 5 = Very strong

* Key Kapability weighting for *companies/institutions* higher than for *households* in management factors (15%), efficiency (10%) and range (5%), and lower for relative market share (10%) and effectiveness (35% combined)

job with *hwyl*. He was rather pleased to find that not much had changed at all, meaning that his initial gut feel had been pretty much spot on. It was still a very attractive market and his initial rough K2 rating of 3.3 had turned out to be little different from the 3.4 he now feels he could achieve by year three.

It was time for Randy to put all this information together in one chart and see whether his plans would be achievable, just as he did in Chapter 7 as a Realtor—see Figure 17.9. He wanted to be earning $80,000 a year within three years. In the household chunk, he figured he could start off making $40,000 as an apprentice to his uncle. With fast market growth, low to medium competition, and a K2 rating improving from 2.5 to 3.5 in the household chunk, Randy believed he should be able to make at least $60,000 from that chunk alone in three years' time.

Randy figured he should be able to top up his earnings by year three with $20,000 from the corporate chunk. But then he tried to envision how Chuck would see it. There would be no apprenticing opportunity since his uncle didn't do corporate work, so there was nothing to build on. It's a slower growing segment of the market and

a bit more competitive. Chuck would be bound to scale back his target. If so, Randy could point out that he'd be able to spend more time on the household chunk and make up some of the $20,000 gap that way.

Finally, it was time to roll out what Randy knew to be Chuck's favorite chart, the Suns & Clouds from Chapter 8—see Figure 17.10. Just how risky would it be for Chuck to back Randy as a plumber?

Not too risky at all, Randy concluded. The only serious risk to the market as a whole was a flood of new entrants (cloud 4), and this seemed much less likely than a steady stream as in the past. The main risk to Randy's forecasts was if he made slower headway in the corporate chunk (cloud 6), but this was balanced by the alternative of Randy doing more work for households (sun 4).

Much more prominent on this chart were the suns. The market was growing fast (sun 1), Randy's uncle should help him get started (sun 2), and Randy potentially had the right skills and enthusiasm (sun 3) to succeed in this field.

Randy was done with the charts. All that remained was the storyline (Chapter 9), so Randy had a go.

Figure 17.9 How Achievable Are Randy's Revenue Plans as a Plumber in Atlanta?

Randy's Business Chunks	Randy's Revenues ($000)	Market Demand Growth (% per year)	Randy's K2 Rating (0-5)	Randy's Planned Revenues ($000)	Randy's Planned Revenue Growth (% per year)	Chuck's View: How Achievable?	More Likely Revenues ($000)
	This Year	Next Few Years	Next Few Years	In Three Years	Next Three Years		In Three Years
1	2	3	4	5	6	7	8
Household	40	Fast	2.5 to 3.4	60	22%	Likely	60+/-
Company	0	Steady	2.2 to 3.0	20	n/a	Less likely	5-10
Total	**40**			**80**	**32%**	**Possible**	**70+**

Figure 17.10 **Risks and Opportunities for Randy in Plumbing Services in Atlanta**

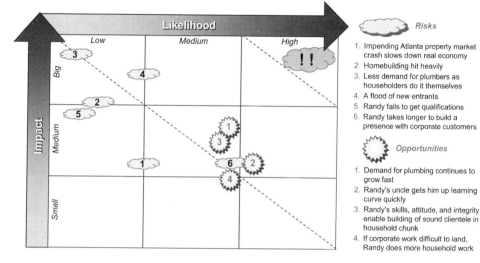

Randy has the skills, contacts, and attitude to succeed in the fast-growing and moderately competitive market of plumbing services in Atlanta:

> *Market demand prospects*—Economic growth and social trends, such as more bathrooms per house and greater frequency of renewal, should continue to drive demand for plumbing services in Atlanta.

> *Competition*—Competition among Atlanta's plumbers is moderate but may increase somewhat as people like Randy enter the market.

> *Randy's K2 rating*—Randy can gain experience with his uncle in the first couple of years and his skills, expected qualifications, and attitude should see him reasonably placed within three years.

> *Randy's plan*—Randy should come within range of his income target of $80,000 by year three.

> *Risks and opportunities*—The main risk of too many new entrants seems well outweighed by the opportunities of a growing market and Randy's contacts, skills, determination, and *hwyl*.

Would Chuck back Randy as a plumber? Surely yes, Randy thought, but just to be sure perhaps he should have a firmer strategy for how to build his plumbing business. That's for the next chapter.

Another Example: Mine!

We left off my career deliberations in Chapter 16 with professional speaking and nonfiction writing heading my short list of potential jobs with *hwyl*. Professional speaking subsequently came out best placed in my job satisfaction rating chart, and this was the field in which I decided to undertake further research.

So I joined the Professional Speakers Association (PSA), the British arm of the National Speakers Association in the United States. I went to a number of their meetings, attended the annual conference, and talked to many practitioners. I also read a number of books and articles in the field and trawled through many speakers' websites. In short, I invested in some serious research.

The research enabled me to complete the charts of Chapters 2 through 8 with some authority, subsequently leading me to these storyline conclusions (in Chapter 9 style):

My skills and experience should equip me for the professional speaking market, but I need a distinctive topic (*Backing U!?*), backed by aggressive marketing:

> ➤ *Market demand prospects*—The professional speaking market is maturing in the United States but offers stronger growth prospects in Britain and Asia.
>
> ➤ *Competition*—Competition in the United States is intense, with an array of outstanding communicators, but the earlier-stage British market has scope for differentiation.
>
> ➤ *My K2 rating*—I have reasonable speaking skills and experience of amateur speaking, but professional speaking demands a topic that *people will pay to hear* and aggressive marketing to get the speaker's name known.
>
> ➤ *My plan*—Professional speaking could enable me to meet my earnings aspirations *if* I identify a winning topic and market myself appropriately.
>
> ➤ *Risks and opportunities*—The main risk concerns whether *Backing U!* is a topic worthy of being marketed.

Finally came my Chapter 8 style Suns & Clouds for a career switch to professional speaking—see Figure 17.11.

It seemed a reasonably balanced set of risks and opportunities. The big issue was whether sun 3 happened (*Backing U!* proved a winning topic) and cloud 5, its counterpart, didn't (no winning topic). Clearly, for purposes of self-motivation, I had to put the former at a slightly higher probability than the latter (otherwise I might as well have packed up!). Overall the chart seemed more or less backable.

But imagine what the chart looked like before I started writing *Backing U!*. When I first drew up the chart and had no distinctive topic in mind, it didn't look good. That was where I was a few years ago when I joined the PSA. I let my membership lapse after a year, deciding that I needed

Figure 17.11 **Risks and Opportunities for Me in Professional Speaking**

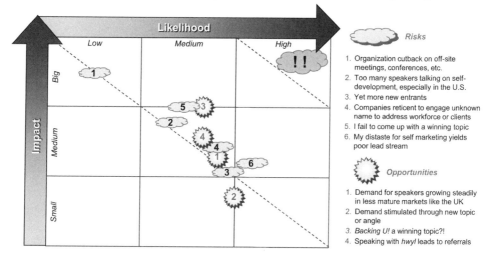

Risks

1. Organization cutback on off-site meetings, conferences, etc.
2. Too many speakers talking on self-development, especially in the U.S.
3. Yet more new entrants
4. Companies reticent to engage unknown name to address workforce or clients
5. I fail to come up with a winning topic
6. My distaste for self marketing yields poor lead stream

Opportunities

1. Demand for speakers growing steadily in less mature markets like the UK
2. Demand stimulated through new topic or angle
3. *Backing U!* a winning topic?!
4. Speaking with *hwyl* leads to referrals

to put the horse before the cart: content first, then communication. Or book first, then speaking.

So my two main short-listed careers, speaking and nonfiction writing, were interlinked. Neither seemed likely to succeed without the other. Speaking demands a topic, preferably a book. A book demands communication, preferably speaking.

But it was clear where I had to start. With the very first words of *Backing U!....*

Shortening the Odds   18

▷ **Envision the Capabilities of the Ideal Provider of Your Target Job**
▷ **Identify the K2 Gap**
▷ **Select Your Entry Strategy for Succeeding in Your Target Job**
▷ **Have You Shortened the Odds?**
▷ **An Example: Shortening Randy's Odds**
▷ **And Mine!**
▷ **A More Fascinating Example: Shortening Prince Charles' Odds!**

In the last chapter, you found a job or business where the *hwyl* lies and where you may well be backable.

Let's pause there for a moment. That's already some achievement! You've found a job or business of your dreams. Or not far off. Isn't that amazing? You're on the verge of setting off on a course that could change your life.

But before you do, there's one further step you need to consider. From all the research you conducted in the last chapter on your target job or business, did you find anything that you could or should be doing *now*, *before* you set off in pursuit of this new job or business?

Before you embark on this journey, are you are as well prepared as you could be? If you were embarking on a long hike, have you put in a good few weekends of practice carrying a heavy load on your back? Will you be carrying the right provisions and equipment? Do you have a map? Compass? Tent pegs? Stove? Waterproof clothing? Preserved foods? Water? Plasters for the inevitable blisters?

> *Don't be afraid to take a big step. You can't cross a chasm in two small jumps.*
> —David Lloyd George

What do you need to prepare and provide for yourself before you embark on this journey of career change?

This is where the tools deployed in Part II of this book may be of help. To what extent can you build on your strengths, or work on your weaknesses, before you set off or while you are pursuing your target job or business?

Which of the *Stand Out!, easyU!* or *Sharpen Act!* strategies (Chapter

12) would shorten the odds of success in your preferred field? How would they impact on positioning in the *Hwyl* Star chart? If you were to do the same or similar to prepare for other short-listed jobs or businesses, would that change their relative positioning? By the end of this chapter, you'll have planned how to go about improving your chances of success in these fields.

You'll have ensured that you're as well prepared and provisioned as you can be before you set off on the journey of the next chapter, Now Back the *Hwyl*!

Envision the Capabilities of the Ideal Provider of Your Target Job

The first thing you need to do is envision what the ideal provider of services in your target job or business will look like in three years' time. To an extent you've already done this. In the last chapter, you assessed customer needs and the Key Kapabilities needed to do your target job well.

But perhaps you could take the assessment a bit further. You could try thinking a little more "out of the box" about how things may evolve in the markets and companies you will be serving in this new job. You could try building scenarios ("What if such and such happens?") about what may happen in the future. You could then consider what would be the capabilities of the ideal provider of services under each scenario, and which of those capabilities would be common to all or most of the scenarios.

The man who does things makes many mistakes, but he never makes the biggest mistake of all—doing nothing.—*Benjamin Franklin*

If you think this approach may be useful for you, take a look at Chapter 10, where it's all set out, step by step. But there is, of course, one main difference. You'll be doing it not for your current job, but for your target job with *hwyl*.

Identify the K2 Gap

The next step is to identify the gap between your likely K2 rating in your target job and that of the ideal provider. As discussed in the last chapter, the gap will be wide at present. It should narrow over time, if only by virtue of your growing experience as time goes by, but that may not be sufficient.

To what extent does the gap differ in the various business chunks in your target job or business? You may choose to draw up a Strategic Bubble Bath for your target job, with your likely K2 rating along the x-axis and the market attractiveness of each business chunk along the y-axis—as we did in Chapter 11 for your current job.

You need to think about where you want to be in three years' time in your target job or business. Be realistic. You won't make it to the ideal provider within three years. But how close can you get? How close did you assume you'd get when you assessed your future K2 rating in the last chapter? Should you now be stretching your sights and making your plans more ambitious? Should you be "going for goal"?

In the light of your reset sights, what then is the shortfall between your expected capabilities after three years and the capabilities to which you aspire—the K2 gap?

The above drawing up of the K2 gap is set out for you in detail in Chapter 11. The difference is that now you'll be identifying the K2 gap for your target job, rather than for your current job.

Select Your Entry Strategy for Succeeding in Your Target Job

Okay, you've established the K2 gap for your target job or business. How are you going to bridge it?

You'll need to select an entry strategy on how to bridge the K2 gap. In Chapter 12, you were introduced to the three main generic strategies, which we called Stand Out!, easyU! and Sharpen Act! You were shown how to develop your strategic alternatives, investing in areas such as marketing and training for an employee, possibly self-financed. For the self-employed, further areas of investment could be in premises, equipment, staff, or partnership. You were shown how to evaluate these alternatives and how to build a realistic action plan.

Again, I won't repeat here what's already written in Chapter 12 except for this: You'll have a much better chance of getting in and succeeding in your target job if you have a sound entry strategy, if you know where you want to be in three years' time and a plan on how you're going to get there.

> I am always doing things I can't do, that's how I get to do them.—*Pablo Picasso*

And this: A Stand-Out! or easyU! strategy will typically enable you to get into your target job or business more readily than a Sharpen Act! strategy. If there is something distinctive and differentiating about you, or if you are offering a quality service at a competitive price, you'll be raising your head above the rest.

The Sharpen Act! strategy, where you work on some evident weaknesses, as opposed to building on strengths, is really more applicable to surviving, or even progressing, in your current job or business. If one of your known areas of weakness is an important Key Kapability in your target job, you may need to reconsider whether you're aiming for the right job. Having said that, if the target job is the one of your dreams, and if you think you could raise your capabilities in that area to at least parity, then why not go for it?

Having selected your generic entry strategy, what are your alternatives for realizing it? If you're to be an employee, what investment should you make in marketing or training? If you're to be self-employed, what investment is needed not just in those two areas, but also in equipment,

> The person who goes farthest is generally the one who is willing to do and dare. The sure-thing boat never gets far from shore.
> —Dale Carnegie

premises, staff, and partnering? You may want to have another look at Chapter 12 for further discussion on this.

You need to decide on the most effective strategic alternative and draw up an action plan, as set out in Chapter 12 again.

Have You Shortened the Odds?

You've envisioned the ideal provider of your target job or business, reset your sights, identified the gaps, selected a generic entry strategy, firmed up a strategic alternative, and drawn up an action plan. You'll be in better shape to embark on your job hunt.

How will that have impacted on your K2 rating chart of Chapter 17?

> You must do the thing you think you cannot do.
> —Eleanor Roosevelt

Has your forecast K2 rating in year three been raised appreciably?

Has your Suns & Clouds chart of Chapter 17 become sunnier? Has the balance of risks and opportunities shifted in your favor?

Have you been able to shorten the odds of getting in and succeeding in your target job or business with *hwyl*?

Have U become more backable?

An Example: Shortening Randy's Odds

We left off with Randy looking eminently backable in his planned job switch to plumbing. Randy figured that his Suns & Clouds chart would surely prove attractive to Chuck Cash.

But Randy wanted to go further than that. He'd read this book enthusiastically and it left him in no doubt that he'd like to Go for Goal (see Chapter 11). He'd like to get as close to being the ideal provider within three to five years as he could conceivably get.

So he kicked off with some brainstorming about what the plumbing market would look like in 5 to 10 years' time. To do this, he enlisted the help of his uncle, who, when not plumbing, is a keen fisherman. They drove out of town and spent the whole day at Bull Sluice Lake, upstream of Georgia Power's small hydroelectric dam on the Chattahoochee River. Randy's not really a fisherman, and

doesn't know a bream from a trout, so he didn't catch much other than the odd boot. But as the day progressed he found that the calm, the colors and the open air lent themselves to creative thinking.

Randy and his uncle came up with three main scenarios after their day of lakeside brainstorming:

> ➤ *PB Promo*—The settlement of the class action lawsuit in polybutylene piping should lead to greater demand for pipe replacement.

> ➤ *Go Gas, Go*—Deregulation of the marketing of natural gas in Georgia should lead to further use of natural gas as the primary energy source for home and water heating.

> ➤ *Rip-On*—Local action groups may start to use the web more as a notice board to expose local

III

trade people who have ripped customers off.

They figured that these scenarios could have the following implications for the ideal provider of plumbing services over the next few years:

> *PB Promo*—The plumber should have a name in the market for being considerate, for example, creating minimum household disruption when replacing a home's complete polybutylene piping system with copper.

> *Go Gas, Go*—The plumber should be as knowledgeable and adept at piping and controls for heating systems as for water.

> *Rip-On*—Plumbers should be more conscious of delivering not just good work but good value.

Randy was at first dismayed by the seeming chasm between his capabilities today and those of the ideal provider of tomorrow. But his uncle suggested he take it one step at a time.

First Randy drew up a Strategic Bubble Bath (as in Chapter 11). He had already assessed market attractiveness in the last chapter for his two addressed business chunks in plumbing, namely households and companies/institutions. He had also worked out his likely K2 ratings in these chunks, both today and in three years' time. He was quickly able to place the four appropriate bubbles onto his chart—see Figure 18.1. They showed clearly how he was poised to improve his strategic position in the plumbing market over time.

But that wasn't enough. Randy wanted to Go for Goal (see Chapter 11). He stuck in a arrow (shown striped in the chart), showing how he planned to

Figure 18.1 Randy's Strategic Bubble Bath and Sights Setting

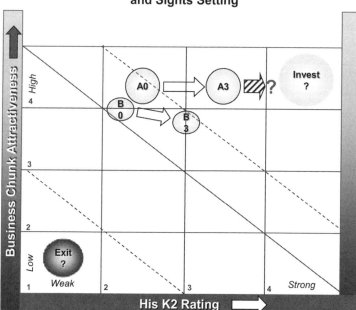

Key

Target Chunks
A. Plumbing for households, today (A0) and in three years' time (A3)
B. Plumbing for companies and institutions, today (A0) and in three years' time (A3)

Note: Diameter of bubble roughly proportional to scale of *forecast revenues in year 3*

further improve his K2 rating in the household chunk from what it would be, if he just did what he had to do, to what it could be, if he raised his sights to get closer to the ideal provider in three to five years' time.

That was the extent of Randy's K2 Gap. How was he to bridge it?

Randy was in no doubt that his should be a Stand Out! strategy to enter this market (see Chapter 12). How could it be anything else for an extrovert, athletic, socially at ease character like Randy? He and his uncle came up with this entry strategy:

Randy will set out to be the plumber of choice for householders who seek considerate and ethical solutions to all their plumbing and gas-fired heating needs, including wholesale replacement of polybutylene piping systems

Given that strategy, Randy planned a three-pronged approach to enhance his K2 rating and narrow the gap with the ideal provider, as follows:

> *Extra qualifications*—Instead of just taking twice weekly evening classes in plumbing, he'll also take an extra weekly evening class in gas-fired heating systems.

> *Targeted experience*—Specifically in polybutylene pipe replacement, with the aim of minimizing household disruption during the extensive works.

> *Targeted marketing*—Locally distributed leaflets positioning Randy as the considerate and ethical neighborhood plumber.

Randy checked to see what impact this entry strategy could have on his positioning in three years' time.

Assuming all proceeds to plan, the impact on his ratings against these K2s could be as follows:

> *Qualifications*—Rating upped from 3 to 4, higher incidentally than his uncle's!

> *Experience*—Rating upped from 2 to 2.5.

> *Marketing*—Rating upped from 4 to 4.5.

Overall, this could raise his K2 rating from 3.4 to 3.7, narrowing the gap with his uncle's 4.3. Not a bad target to go for after just three years in the job, thinks Randy.

Randy then looked at the likely impact of his entry strategy on his Suns & Clouds chart. The strategy only seemed to affect one sun, but the effect was to make the overall picture sunnier—see Figure 18.2. Chuck would like that arrow, Randy thought.

Randy was ready. He took his plans to enter the plumbing business to Chuck. Chuck was astonished. Randy had clearly learned so much from the work they had done a couple of months earlier when Chuck had been thinking of backing Randy as a Realtor. Chuck was presented with analyses of the plumbing market, on Randy's likely place within it, and on the main risks and opportunities before him. The analyses were comprehensive, coherent, and convincing.

Even more impressive, Randy had developed a stand-out entry strategy into the Atlanta plumbing market. He had thought through how to shorten his odds on success.

Chuck had little hesitation. He would back Randy as a plumber. He would back the *hwyl*.

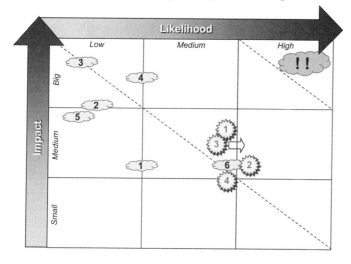

Figure 18.2 **Risks and Opportunities for Randy's Entry Strategy for Plumbing Services in Atlanta**

Risks

1. Impending Atlanta property market crash slows down real economy
2. Homebuilding hit heavily
3. Less demand for plumbers as householders do it themselves
4. A flood of new entrants
5. Randy fails to get qualifications
6. Randy takes longer to build a presence with corporate customers

Opportunities

1. Demand for plumbing continues to grow fast
2. Randy's uncle gets him up learning curve quickly
3. Randy's skills, attitude, and integrity enable building of sound clientele in household chunk
4. If corporate work difficult to land, Randy does more household work

And Mine!

I'll be brief in my tale. The most appropriate entry strategy for me in my quest to become a speaker-cum-author was, as for Randy, a Stand-Out! strategy. To prepare and provision myself, and to bridge the K2 gap, I needed to write a book with a distinctive angle and get it published. I needed to develop a series of speeches around the theme of the book and sharpen my public speaking skills. And I needed to recognize my chronic weakness in self-promotion and sign up with a marketing agent.

Here we go!

A More Fascinating Example: Shortening Prince Charles's Odds!

More fascinating may be to consider a hypothetical job switch strategy for someone whom most of us don't know in person, but we all know of. Candidates such as Bill Clinton and Tony Blair spring to mind, but perhaps even more interesting could be Charles, Prince of Wales.

Here's someone who has spent decades preparing himself for the job he's destined to do and yet can't actually start doing it until his mother either abdicates or dies. It must be a hugely frustrating position to be in, yet it's one that's shared to an extent by the offspring of many business people intent on passing on the family business to the next generation, but not until he or she is wheeled out of the office.

The big difference is that Charles's responsibilities as heir to the throne are carried out in a global goldfish bowl. Every move he makes is monitored, every word he utters noted. And he generates plenty of controversy. The tabloid newspapers write that he's too whacky to be king. He talks to flowers and believes in quack remedies. He's old-fashioned in his ways and tastes; he's reserved, even cold. It had to be his fault that his marriage with tabloid darling Princess Diana failed, ultimately leading to her singleton jet-set lifestyle and tragic, premature death. He should let the monarchy skip a generation, they say, and let his son William take the crown when the time comes.

Many others disagree. They admire Charles for being a thinker, prepared to challenge prevailing orthodoxy on a broad range of issues, such as modern architecture, urban design, and farming methods. He set up one of the most inspirational charities of his generation, the Prince's Trust, which has helped thousands of youngsters from disadvantaged circumstances get a start in life. He always takes a balanced, cerebral perspective ideal for a titular monarch with an advisory role. Not so apt perhaps for an absolute ruler in the 16th century mold, but who needs that? If the United Kingdom were a republic, many would vote for him as president.

Just suppose, however, that Charles has got fed up with waiting. Or that all the criticism he's taken over the years has finally got to him. He's now happily remarried and maintains strong bonds with his two sons. Suppose he did decide to jack it in, and rather late in life, switch to another job. He's a man with an unusually varied range of interests and passions. This may be the time for him to devote himself to one or two of them? Where should he venture?

The first thing he should do is develop a long-list inventory of jobs with *hwyl*, as in Chapter 15. He would then screen those with the most *hwyl* ticks by market attractiveness and rough K2 rating, as in Chapter 16, arriving at his *Hwyl* Star chart. Let's suppose he's done all that and Figure 18.3 is what he's come up with. Remember, this is all entirely hypothetical, and we're doing it for illustrative purposes only. I don't want to be sent to the Tower of London! (In other words, for American readers, I don't want my head chopped off!)

Of the five jobs with most *hwyl*, becoming an architect (star A), artist (star D) or homeopathist (star E) seem to be the least backable, and Charles may figure that these fields are best kept as hobbies. Becoming a full-time organic farm manager (star C), something Charles already does in a part-time capacity, offers reasonable prospects, but the outstanding job on this chart is becoming an environmental campaigner (star B). His K2 rating would be high and the market for such a job is highly attractive— with the public's growing environmental concerns driving demand, not too much competition and little risk of environmental issues becoming passé.

Another job that stands out is a portfolio of nonexecutive chairmanships and directorships (star I), in organizations ranging from business (preferably with an ethical or environmental bent) to charities such as his Prince's Trust, or in the arts or architecture. This is a job Charles gave four rather than five *hwyl* ticks to, largely because he already sits on lots of governing bodies.

Figure 18.3 **Prince Charles' Hypothetical *Hwyl* Star Chart!**

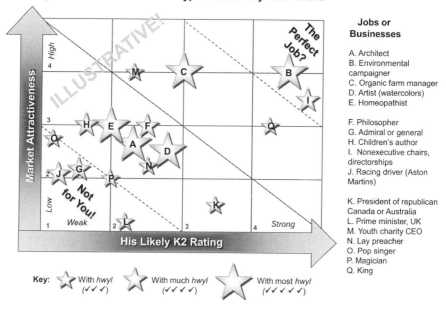

Jobs or Businesses

A. Architect
B. Environmental campaigner
C. Organic farm manager
D. Artist (watercolors)
E. Homeopathist

F. Philosopher
G. Admiral or general
H. Children's author
I. Nonexecutive chairs, directorships
J. Racing driver (Aston Martins)

K. President of republican Canada or Australia
L. Prime minister, UK
M. Youth charity CEO
N. Lay preacher
O. Pop singer
P. Magician
Q. King

The other job that stands out is king (star Q)! It has quite attractive market prospects for those in a position to be able to provide the service, and one in which many believe Charles is strongly placed to succeed. But as we hypothesized above, let's say he's fed up with waiting and feels the job no longer merits more than three *hwyl* ticks.

The clear winner is environmental campaigning. Where should he start?

To make things easier for Charles, a precedent has already been set across the pond. Al Gore reinvented himself following his dramatically narrow defeat for the U.S. presidency in 2001. He exploited global familiarity with his name to focus on a single issue, global warming, and developed a successful, part-charitable, part-commercial organization around this campaign. He has transformed his formerly rather wooden persona into a speaker capable of holding the attention of large audiences. He has developed formidable collateral in parallel with his speaking career, including a book, pamphlets—and even a movie!

Charles could do something similar. Not perhaps with global warming, since Gore has already cornered that issue. Nor perhaps with another issue dear to Charles' heart, alleviation of third world poverty, since high profile pop musicians such as Bob Geldof and Bono have arguably saturated media interest on this.

But how about organic farming? Imagine how this cause would be boosted by Charles renouncing his accession and becoming an environmental-cum-health campaigner for organic, nonintensive farming. What's more, becoming a campaigner for organic farming would combine both stars B and C in Charles' *Hwyl* Star chart. How about that for job fulfill-ment?

Before he embarks on this job switch, however, Charles needs to pre-pare and provision himself as well as possible. How can he shorten the odds of becoming a successful environmental campaigner in organic farming?

Charles studies Part II of this book. First he needs to do some brain-storming. He's fortunate to have an array of locations from which to choose, whether at his palace in London or his mansion in the Cotswolds, or even at his mother's palaces in London, Windsor, Sandringham, or Balmoral. But Charles wisely chooses his latest property, an estate in Wales, as his base for brainstorming. From there he can walk up to the bleak, often cold, wet, and windswept mountains of the Brecon Beacons to clear his head.

He's convinced that the dangers of intensive, chemically controlled farming to both the environment and to people's health are going to be-come more apparent in the future. Market demand for organic farming campaigners should grow. Charles envisages a number of grim scenarios, whereby diseases such as BSE in animals and CJD in humans multiply and spiral out of control, thereby accelerating demand for campaigning services. One such scenario sees certain genetically modified crops enter the food chain mistakenly, with grim consequences.

Charles then envisages the required capabilities of the ideal provider of these campaigning services under these scenarios. He finds that the ideal provider would be someone experienced not only in organic and alterna-tive farming methods, but one who understands and can communicate effectively the science behind modern farming methods. This will be a Key Kapability across all scenarios, but in relation to one scenario in particu-lar, the ideal provider would be someone who can debate authoritatively with the proponents of genetic modification.

Charles sets his sights and determines to become as close to the ideal provider as can be achieved. He identifies the K2 gap. He sees no great gap in experience of organic farming, he's had plenty, but the gap is much wider when it comes to its scientific underpinning. He finds gaps too in other capabilities, especially in speaking and marketing abilities.

Despite his innate diffidence, Charles recognizes that he needs a Stand-Out! strategy to succeed in this new job. He identifies three areas where he needs to prepare and provision himself for his job switch. First, he needs to raise his awareness of the underlying science from that of interested amateur to experienced, semi-professional. He realizes that he must make this a top priority, clear chunks of his diary from his plethora of other commitments and embark on an intensive tutoring program in modern agricultural science.

Second, he's aware that his clipped, rather ponderous speaking style may need to be adapted for motivational speaking. He also believes he needs to loosen up and let go as a speaker. He realizes that vocal coaches are not the answer. Regular practice in front of an empathetic audience is what can transform him, so he resolves to set up a Toastmasters Club (see Chapter 12) at St. James' Palace! He asks me for help with this…(!).

Finally, he recognizes that he's going to need a professional marketer, as opposed to his current set of royal advisers, to help him get his message across to the developed world. He resolves to meet with Al Gore's marketing agency and others to see with whom he can find the best chemistry.

Armed with these plans, Charles calls in Chuck Cash. "Backable?" he asks.

"Sure thing," replies Chuck. "How much do you need?"

Charles begins his preparations, Chuck gets the finance together and one, perhaps two, years later, Charles launches his bombshell on the kingdom. One of the most sensational job shifts in history. Watch this space!

STOP PRESS!!

I dreamed up this section on Prince Charles's future prospects in April 2007. On September 16, 2007, a feature in the *Sunday Times* suggested that Prince Charles had indeed been inspired by Al Gore and was in "advanced negotiations with Hollywood producers to make a movie in which he will tell us how to lead our lives." Initial ideas for the script, code-named "The Harmony Project," have him "praising bees for the way they work together to produce a harmonic whole."

There is no suggestion of abdication, of course, but clearly he must have been tuning in to my brainwaves, as they wafted over the river from atop my Richmond Park eyrie to his palace in Whitehall, alerting him of career development opportunities in global environmental campaigning!

Now Back the *Hwyl!* 19

- Find Your Ideal Employer
- Land the Interview
- Perform at the Interview
- Follow Up the Interview
- Or...Start Your Own Business!
- Now Back the *Hwyl!*

In Chapter 18, you developed an entry strategy for the target job or business with *hwyl* that you pinpointed in Chapter 17. Now it's time to go out and get that job. Or start that business. It's time to back the *hwyl!*

This chapter considers what you need to do to land that dream job, or start that dream business. It's not comprehensive—that's for specialist books on the process of job-hunting, for example Richard Bolles's excellent *What Color Is Your Parachute?* This chapter merely pulls out a dozen choice tips on how to back the *hwyl,* many of which have been learned by the author the hard way, along a meandering career path.

> The greatest glory in living lies not in never falling, but in rising every time we fall.
> —Nelson Mandela (from Confucius)

Here they are.

Find Your Ideal Employer

Okay. You've found your dream job. You've prepared and provisioned yourself for it. You quit your job, take a couple of weeks break, and start the job-hunting process in earnest. Smart? No!

Tip #1—It's best not to quit your job until you have the next one lined up! Employers will look more favorably on you if you have a busy work schedule than if you evidently have time on your hands. When you're working, your energy levels are higher, your time is tighter and this will come through in the interview. If you're unavoidably "in-between jobs," because you had no choice but to quit or were made

> Do, or do not. There is no try.
> —Yoda

289

redundant, you'll need to prepare carefully, to raise both knowledge and energy levels, for the interview (see later).

Okay. You start scanning through the job adverts, checking out all the online sites, as well as the traditional sites in the newspapers, magazines, journals. You write to two dozen headhunters who seem to be active in the field. You visit the local job centre. Smart? Yes and no!

Tip #2—Don't wait for the employer to come to you. Go to the employer! By the time you get to see a job advert, it may well be too late. The employer may already have someone in mind, advertising the post just to tick all the right boxes on equality of opportunity. And your response to the ad will be one of many, maybe one of hundreds. It'll be difficult to stand out from the crowd.

Likewise with introducing yourself to headhunters. They may agree to meet you, but "Don't call us, we'll call you when something comes up" is their typical response. Don't hold your breath. The odds of that headhunter receiving the mandate for the job you want are low. The odds of her then calling you, having since met scores of other hopefuls, are likewise low. Multiply those probabilities together and your chances of being asked to an interview on a specific vacancy are very low. Some get lucky, of course, but the odds aren't great.

The best strategy is to identify the companies you want to work for and approach them directly. After all, you know quite a bit about them by now. You've conducted your research on them in Chapter 17, you've even spoken to people doing the kind of work you want to do at these or similar companies.

They may not have a job vacancy available. But one may become available soon. And they could create an additional place just for you. Why? Because they'll receive an approach, whether by letter or telephone, preferably both, from you, that will be passionate. This for you is a job with *hwyl* and you'll inject that passion into all your communication with the company. They'd be fools not to take you on board. Think what they'd miss if you went to a competitor!

Land the Interview

Okay. You find a dozen companies who employ people in your target field. You get the addresses, draw up a pro forma cover letter, and insert the addresses into each cover letter, maybe with some mail merge software. Smart? No!

Tip # 3—Wherever possible, start the cover letter with a referral. Most unsolicited letters enquiring about a job opportunity end up if not in the trash can then with the standard, pro forma rejection letter. You know the one: "Very interested to receive your letter...most impressed with your qualifications and experience...however (and here it comes!)... no appropriate opportunities available at the moment...will keep you on our books...we wish you well in the future...."

Your chances of receiving one of these may well be reduced if you can sneak some sort of a referral into the opening paragraph. For example, *Dear Mr. Ford, Diana Lopez from your market research department kindly suggested that I write to you...* should be more effective than simply writing *Dear Mr. Ford, I am writing to enquire whether you have any job vacancies in your market research department...*

Even this rather tenuous referral shows that you have taken the trouble to find out about the company and to call, speak to, possibly even meet a member of staff. It's a signal of interest, enthusiasm, and initiative that could place you in a different category from other applicants.

Best of all, of course, is a genuine referral from someone you know, or someone who knows someone you know, and who actually recommends you for this job. Assuming the referee is a person of stature and known to the recipient of the letter that can be sufficient to get you through the door.

The referral is one reason why your cover letters shouldn't be standardized. But even in the absence of referral, your cover letter should be customized. The cover letter, along with the enclosed résumé, is your key to getting in the door of a company. And the more you can show in that letter that you are worth opening the door to, the better your chances.

Tip #4—Customize the cover letter for *that* job in *that* company. The cover letter is an opportunity to show that you have a sound understanding of the company and why it would be to the company's benefit to hire someone like you. The first paragraph is introductory, preferably with a referral. In the space of three further paragraphs—the cover letter should be just one page, with plenty of white space and not too much type—you need to communicate the following:

➢ Paragraph 2—Your understanding of the company, its needs, and how the company would benefit from recruiting the ideal employee for this job.

➢ Paragraph 3—Your background, leading up to why you are applying for this job.

➢ Paragraph 4—Why you are exceptionally well placed to meet the company's needs (Think of your K2 rating; highlight here your main strengths!) and why you would do so with enthusiasm, passion, *hwyl.*

This means that each letter must be special to the company to which you are writing. Much more work for you, of course, but we're talking here about switching to a job with *hwyl!* Surely that's worth a couple of extra hours on the Internet, backed up perhaps by a few calls?

Okay. You update your résumé, photocopy it a dozen times, and enclose it in each of the dozen, individually crafted cover letters. Smart? No!

Tip #5—Tailor your résumé for *that* job in *that* company. Remember, the résumé, along with the cover letter, is your key to getting in the door of a particular company. Is there any one element of your experience or qualifications that could be more relevant to that company? If so, could this be highlighted in some way in your résumé?

For example, suppose you are applying for a job in market research. You write to one company that specializes in consumer research, especially for food sector clients. So you highlight in your résumé those projects you've worked on over the years most similar to consumer research in food (or drink or consumer goods). You also write to a company that specializes in business-to-business market research, especially in IT and telecoms services. So you dig around your experience and highlight in your résumé those projects you've worked on that seem most relevant to that company (for example, some research you did a few years back on outsourcing services).

Likewise, you may want to highlight different aspects of your past job responsibilities in your résumé to make them more appropriate to the specific responsibilities likely to be demanded in the specific job for which you are applying.

The more tailored your résumé, the more customized your cover letter, the better your chances of getting through the door.

Okay. You've sent off your customized letters and tailored résumés. All you have to do is sit and wait for the mail or for a phone call. Smart? No!

Tip #6—Chase! If you hear from the company within two to three weeks, fine. If not, call them up. Chase them. Remember, this is a job with *hwyl* you're after. Maybe the delay is because they're moving your application around between departments. Fine. Maybe it's because they've made their decision, one way or another, but they've been too busy to get round to notifying you. Maybe it's because the letter got lost in the post, lost in the company, buried in one executive's in-basket. Not so fine. You need to know. Chase!

Perform at the Interview

Okay. You've landed an interview or two or more! The more the merrier, in fact, because it's good to get interview practice, even for jobs you're not hugely keen on or for jobs where it's unlikely they'll be keen on you. Practice makes perfect.

All you have to do now is roll up for the interview, be yourself, and the job's yours! Smart? No!

Tip #7—Dress to impress! Here's a rule of thumb: Be as well dressed as the best-dressed person in the room.

Companies tend to recruit in their own likeness. Period. That means looking how they look, not how you want to look. If you're a casual sort of guy and will only feel comfortable working in the kind of organization that is relaxed about dress, fine. But don't take the risk of showing up sloppy

III ▶

at the interview, thinking it's a laid-back organization. The organization may be, but what if the HR person isn't? Suppose he or she comes into the room looking drop-dead smart. No matter what the organization, sloppy dress will not come over as respectful. You may not be taken seriously.

Even if you know it to be an open-shirt type of organization, play it safe. Wear a tie.

I remember going for an interview in London in the early-1980s. I'd been working overseas for many years and went to the interview wearing a two-tone brown suit, the jacket in light herringbone pattern, which I'd bought years earlier in Carnaby Street—then at the heart of London's Swinging Sixties. It had been fashionable at the time but was dreadfully dated by the 1980s—and wholly inappropriate for an interview where the dress code turned out to be dark suits! I didn't get the job.

Okay. You put on a smart suit, walk through the door and tell the interviewer all about your past career and your hopes for the future. Smart? Yes, and no!

Tip #8—Talk about why the company needs U! Sure, you need to convey where you've been and where you hope to go. But what really impresses the interviewer is when the interviewee knows about the company and what she could do for the company. She should bubble with information on the company and with ideas on where the company is heading and how she could play her part in helping the company get there.

In today's world, it's so easy to get up to speed on most companies and their markets. So much information is sitting there on the web, begging to be read. It's just a matter of taking the time to dig around and find it.

Imagine this: The interviewer tells you that you'll be expected to spend a day or so a month going to regional team meetings, whether in the Miami, New Orleans, or Atlanta offices. And you say, "Great! I didn't know the company had more than one office in the southeast." What's the interviewer to think? That's publicly available information, accessed with just a couple of clicks on the website. "This guy didn't bother to find out much about us," she'll think. "He can't be very eager."

Whatever information there is on the company in the public space, you should know about it before you walk into the interview room. And you should let the interviewer know that you know it.

Okay. You're dressed up and clued up on the company, all you have to do now is relax and chat about yourself and how you can fit in with the company. Smart? No!

Tip #9—Sit alert. Interviews should not be relaxing. Relaxing can be dangerous. The more you relax, the less impressive you may become.

Of course, you shouldn't be tense either. If you're anxious, nervous, and jumpy, that's hardly going to impress the interviewer either.

You need to be alert, on the button. That's what does the trick. And the best place to start is how you sit. Not reclining in the chair. Not leaning on the table. But in the classic TV interview pose. Upright, but leaning slightly forward. At around 75 degrees. That posture enables you to appear at your most alert. It also enables you to perform at your best while seated.

I remember another of my laid-back interviews in the mid-1980s, where I got on so well with the guy that we talked for a half-hour about my travels round the world. He'd visited on holiday some of the countries I'd lived in and seemed genuinely interested in finding out more. We shared stories and anecdotes, enjoying each other's company. By the time we finally got round to my work experience, I was so relaxed that I'd slipped right back in my chair. I wasn't far off horizontal! I didn't get the job.

Okay. You're dressed up, clued up, and sitting up; all you need to do now is tell your story. Smart? Yes and no!

I walked in and there was a man with his feet up on the desk, reading a report. He gestured to me to sit down and continued to read, ignoring me completely. Time went by, one minute, two. What was I supposed to do? Should I pull out my newspaper? Powder my nose? Punch his? Finally, after five minutes, he raised his eyes slowly from his report and asked, "Who are you?" I kept my cool and politely told him my name. He pondered on that, for another minute or two, and then sneered: "And why should a company like ours employ someone like you?" This was a tricky one. I was tempted to counter with, "Why should someone like me join a company that employs jerks like you?" But I couldn't. The situation was so Groucho Marx. I just stood up slowly, said, "Thank you very much for telling me so much about your company" and walked out the door. I didn't get the job.— *Vaughan Evans (extract from a speech to London Corinthians Toastmasters, September 2003)*

Tip #10—Perform! It's not just what you say, it's how you say it. This one hour interview is a momentous occasion for you. This is for a job with *hwyl*. It could be for the job with the most *hwyl* of all. Imagine you're on stage. The curtain goes up, the lights come on, and yes, it's show time! Time to perform!

Your enthusiasm for this job needs to come through not just in your words and ideas, but in you. In how you communicate. In your voice—in its pitch, its pace, its volume. In your facial expressions. In your hand movements (and please, don't allow your hands to go anywhere near your face, especially your mouth—don't block your main instrument of communication!). In how you perform.

Easier said than done, you say. Dead right. But there's a simple solution.

Tip #11—Join Toastmasters! I've already given a plug for Toastmasters International in Chapter 12. But I'd be remiss in not reinforcing it here when discussing personal communication skills.

The skills you learn at Toastmasters will fully equip you for the interview process. You'll learn how to communicate better, not just speaking to a roomful of people, but one-to-one. You'll learn how to use your voice, your face, your hands, your body in improving your communicating skills. You'll learn how to work with words. You'll learn how to persuade, inspire, and entertain. You'll learn how to perform.

But Toastmasters will help with more than just communication skills. It'll provide you with group support. You're embarking on a life-enhancing career switch. This is self-development at its zenith, and that's what Toastmasters is all about. It's full of like-minded souls.

Use Toastmasters as a forum to try out your ideas. Construct a speech on why you want to change career, then deliver it and receive the feedback of your peers. And another speech on how your target job could transform your life. Try a humorous speech about your horrors of picking up the phone, or being interviewed. Get their feedback. Discuss your life-enhancing career plans in an empathetic milieu. There will be dozens like you, discussing similar themes. You are *so* not alone!

One final word on the interview. Most interviewers these days believe that the way to get the best out of interviewees is to make them feel at ease. This was not always the case in the 1980s, when some companies deployed the hostile interview. This is where the interviewee is made to feel uncomfortable to test how he will react in adverse situations. It was a ridiculous concept, now entirely discredited—but see the inset box for a memorable experience!

Follow Up the Interview

Okay. You've had the interview. It went pretty well. All you have to do is wait to hear from them. Smart? No!

Tip #12—Send a note. You enjoyed the meeting. Write and let the interviewer know. Tell her that you hope she enjoyed it too and found it useful. Remind her of your contact details. And let her know that if she needs any further information you'd be pleased to let her have it.

Your letter can be by email or snail mail—or both, whatever you feel appropriate to the way that company does business. When in doubt, write a letter.

The interviewer should receive your note preferably within a day or two of the interview. If your interview is in the morning, you should write in the evening, enabling the interviewer to receive the email the following morning. If it's a letter, she'll receive it the morning after that.

Okay. You've had the interview, written a note, now you can lean back in your chair and wait! Smart? No!

It's back to tip #6 again: Chase! Allow the company three to four weeks. If you haven't heard anything by then, send a gentle prompt. Ask them if there's been any further progress, or if they've had any further thoughts. Ask them if there's anything further they'd like to discuss with you, or anyone else they feel you should meet. Chase them—by email or post, depending on how you sent the post-interview note.

Give them a further two weeks to reply to your chaser. If there's still no reply, call them. If you can't get past the PA, leave a message on the interviewer's voicemail. If there's no reply to the message in two days, call again. And so on. Pester them. Show them you're keen. Hound them until you find out, one way or another.

Okay. That's a dozen tips. You should follow them. Smart? Yes!

Or...Start Your Own Business!

On the other hand, the target career with *hwyl* that emerged from Chapter 17 may be starting your own business. Like our fictional Randy in switching from real estate to plumbing. Like Martha Stewart in switching from stockbroking to catering/writing/presenting (Chapter 15). Like Prince Charles, perhaps, in switching from monarchy to environmental campaigning (Chapter 18)!

The problem with the French is that they don't have a word for entrepreneur.—George W. Bush

The great thing about going solo is that you won't have to do any of the above hustling for interviews and pretending you're someone you're not in the interview. Even better, you won't have to do any crawling to the boss. Ever. You're the boss.

But do think twice. It's not for everybody. It can be hard. You'll find yourself having to do "interviews" again and again, except that they'll be to customers. They're pitches for work. And although you're the boss, you're also the bookkeeper, the laptop debugger, and the gofer.

These and more pros and cons are set out in detail in Chapter 13. Have a serious read of that, and of other recommended books, and if it's for you, go for it!

This is the true joy in life, being used for a purpose recognized by yourself as a mighty one. Being a force of nature instead of a feverish, selfish little clod of ailments and grievances complaining that the world will not devote itself to making you happy…. Life is no brief candle to me. It is a sort of splendid torch which I've got hold of for the moment and I want to make it burn as brightly as possible before handing it on to future generations.—George Bernard Shaw

Remember you'll have one enormous advantage in starting this business. It's one that grew out of the *hwyl* listing of Chapter 15, and survived the screening process of Chapter 16 and the research of Chapter 17. It's a career choice that will consume you with *hwyl*.

Work will no longer seem like work. You'll want to carry through this "work" into the evenings, and at weekends, because you feel passionate about it.

You'll be a "force of nature."

Your competitors may not, or may no longer, feel the *hwyl*.

You'll have an edge.

296

Now Back the *Hwyl*!

In Part I of this book, you concluded that you weren't backable in your current job or business. In this Part III you looked at a broad range of jobs or businesses with *hwyl* (Chapter 15). You screened them (Chapter 16), researched those that came through the screen and identified the target job or business with *hwyl* where you're most backable (Chapter 17). You then embarked on an entry strategy to make you more backable (Chapter 18).

You've been reminded of a few practical tips to help you land that job or launch that business (this chapter).

You're as ready as you'll ever be. Don't procrastinate. Take the plunge. A new work life beckons. One with *hwyl*.

> Life is in the living of it.
> —*Leo Tolstoy*

You won't work to live. You won't live to work. You'll live.

It's time to back the *hwyl*. It's time to back U.

Good luck. *Pob hwyl*. You can get it if you really want.

You can get it if you really want.
You can get it if you really want.
You can get it if you really want,
But you must try, try and try, try and try,
You'll succeed at last.

Rome was not built in a day.
Opposition will come your way.
But the hotter the battle you seek,
Then the sweeter the victory.

You can get it if you really want.
You can get it if you really want.
You can get it if you really want,
But you must try, try and try, try and try,
You'll succeed at last.
—*Jimmy Cliff*

Conclusion

In the introduction to this book, we learned that roughly half of U.S. and U.K. employees were dissatisfied with their jobs. You may be, or may have been, one of them.

You may have been one of those who thought things were better elsewhere. But you found out from Part I that you're better off staying where you are. You're backable in your current job or business.

You then learned in Part II some techniques on how to make yourself more backable in your current job. And hopefully more satisfied, more fulfilled.

You must be the change you wish to see in the world.
—*Mahatma Gandhi*

On the other hand, you may have learned from Part I that you're not backable in your current job or business. This may be because of issues affecting the market as a whole, or affecting just your company. It may be because you don't have the capabilities of your peers. Or it may be because you don't enjoy your job. And this shows through in your attitude.

So you followed the techniques of Part III and found a target job or business with *hwyl*. You found a job where you'd be backable. You drew up an entry strategy to make yourself more backable. You're ready to set off, and you've picked up a few practical tips for the journey ahead.

The quality, not the longevity, of one's life is what is important.
—*Martin Luther King*

Whether you've chosen to move forward in your current job or business, or move across to one with *hwyl*, I hope you've found some of the techniques in this book useful. I hope you're now more backable.

I hope you'll carry on *Backing U!*

Postscript

Has this book helped you? If you've had a recent job shift, would it have been of help?

Please let me know.

I'm working on a follow-up to this book. It will be called *You Backed U!* and will include a series of examples of how the techniques of this book have helped people. I'd like to select a dozen or so examples of people who've benefited from Parts I and II. And a similar number who've benefited from Parts I and III.

You Backed U! aims to be inspirational. By the example of others, it hopes to inspire other people to go out and claim greater satisfaction from their current jobs, or businesses. Or switch to others where the passion lies.

Please let me know. Email me at vaughan@youbackedu.com.

I won't be able to write up all your stories, only a couple of dozen. You can appear in the book under your own name or under a pseudonym. It's up to you.

I look forward to hearing how *You Backed U!*

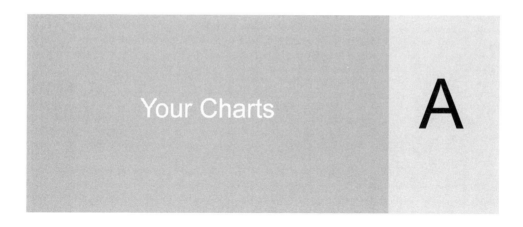

Your Charts

A

Here's a set of blank charts for you to fill out as you work your way through this book. They are grouped as follows:

> ➤ Figures A.1 to A.8 relate to Part I and should help you in deciding *Would You Back U?*
> ➤ Figures A.9 and A.10 relate to Part II and you *Becoming More Backable*
> ➤ Figures A.11 to A.15 relate to Part III; they are to help you in *Backing the* Hwyl

Each chart gives some basic instructions (in italics, with arrows indicating where to fill in what), but they are not and cannot be expected to be self-explanatory. They should be completed in conjunction with the explanations found in each appropriate chapter.

The first few charts relate to market prospects or your K2 rating in one of your main business chunks. If you are active in more than one business chunk, you may need to photocopy the relevant charts and complete one set for each of your main chunks. Alternatively, pick up a pencil, ruler and a blank piece of paper and quickly sketch a copy of the chart. None are complex, so shouldn't take more than a minute of two to sketch.

I hope you enjoy filling them in as much as I've done—whether for Leila or Oprah, Randy or Prince Charles, the Beatles or me.

Part I: WOULD YOU BACK U?

Figure A.1 **Market Demand Prospects in** ....

Enter one of your main business chunks

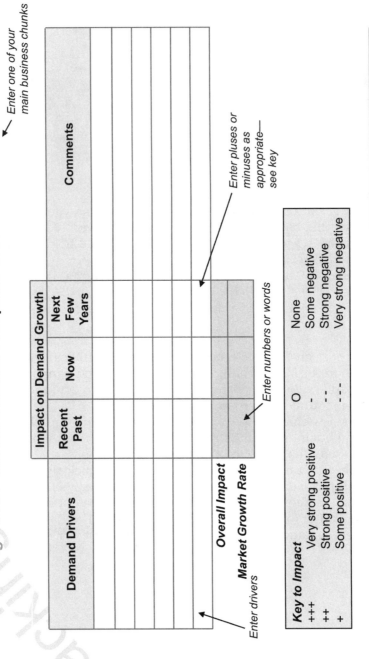

Demand Drivers	Impact on Demand Growth			Comments
	Recent Past	Now	Next Few Years	
Overall Impact				
Market Growth Rate				

Enter pluses or minuses as appropriate— see key

Enter numbers or words

Enter drivers

Key to Impact		
+++	Very strong positive	O None
++	Strong positive	- Some negative
+	Some positive	- - Strong negative
		- - - Very strong negative

For help with this chart, see Chapter 2

Source: *Backing U!*, Business & Careers Press, 2009

Figure A.2 .... Risks and Opportunities
in ....

Enter one of your
main business chunks

Enter whether these are risks and opportunities concerning Market Demand
(Chapter 2), Competition (Chapter 3), U! (Chapter 6), or Your Plan (Chapter 7)

Risks	Likeli-hood	Impact	Comments

Opportunities	Likeli-hood	Impact	Comments

Enter whether low, medium, or high

For help with this chart, see Chapters 2, 3, 6, and 7

Source: Backing U!, Business & Careers Press, 2009

Figure A.3 **Competition in** . . . .

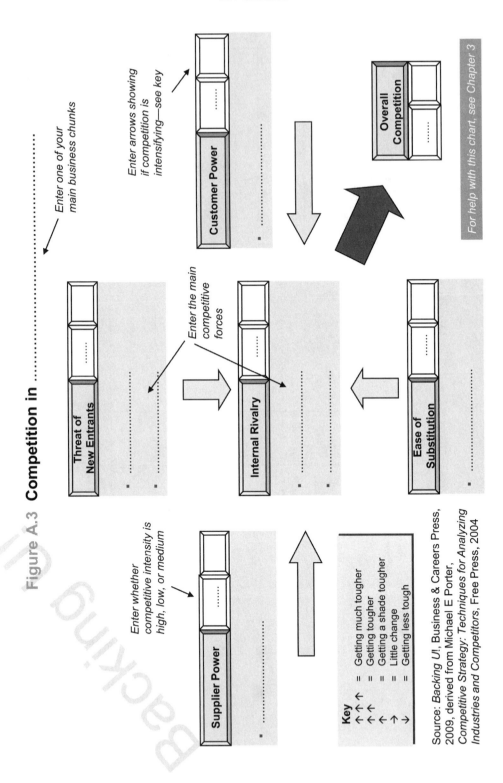

Enter one of your main business chunks

Enter arrows showing if competition is intensifying—see key

Customer Power

Overall Competition

For help with this chart, see Chapter 3

Threat of New Entrants

Enter the main competitive forces

Internal Rivalry

Ease of Substitution

Enter whether competitive intensity is high, low, or medium

Supplier Power

Key

← ← ←	=	Getting much tougher
← ←	=	Getting tougher
←	=	Getting a shade tougher
↑	=	Little change
→	=	Getting less tough

Source: *Backing UI*, Business & Careers Press, 2009, derived from Michael E Porter, *Competitive Strategy: Techniques for Analyzing Industries and Competitors*, Free Press, 2004

Figure A.4 **Customer Needs and Associated Key Kapabilities**
in ....

Enter one of your main business chunks

Customer Needs	Importance	Change	Associated Key Kapabilities
Effectiveness **- Skills** · ·············			···········
- Knowledge · ·············			···········
- Experience · ·············			···········
Efficiency · ·············			···········
Relationship · ·············			···········
Range · ·············			···········
Premises · ·············			···········
Price · ·············			···········

Enter customer needs, under E2-R2-P2 headings

Enter whether the need is of high, low, or medium importance

Enter arrows showing if the need is becoming more important over time

Enter K2 required to meet each customer need

For help with this chart, see Chapters 4 and 5

Source: *Backing UI*, Business & Careers Press, 2009

Figure A.5 Your K2 Rating in ⋯⋯⋯⋯⋯⋯⋯⋯

Enter one of your main business chunks

Enter your main competitors

Enter rating for each competitor against each K2 on a scale of 1-5 (see key below)

Key to Rating:
1 = Weak
2 = Okay-ish, not too bad
3 = Good, favorable
4 = Strong
5 = Very strong

Weighted average

For help with this chart, see Chapter 6

Key Kapabilities	Weighting (%)	U!	⋯⋯	⋯⋯	⋯⋯
Relative Market Share					
Cost Factors:					
Management Factors:					
Service Factors:					
Overall K2 Rating	**100%**				

Enter Key Kapabilities for this business chunk

Enter weighting which reflects the relative importance of each K2, taking care to ensure weightings add up to 100%

Source: *Backing U!*, Business & Careers Press, 2009

Figure A.6 How Achievable Are Your Planned Revenues or Pay?

Your Business Chunks	Your Revenues or Pay ($000)	Market Demand Growth (% / year)	Your K2 Rating (0-5)	Your Planned Revenues or Pay ($000)	Your Planned Revenue Growth (%/year)	Your Backer's View: How Achievable?	More Likely Revenues or Pay ($000)
	This Year	Next Few Years	Next Few Years	In Three Years	Next Three Years		In Three Years
1	2	3	4	5	6	7	8
	Source: Chapter 1	Source: Chapter 2	Source: Chapter 6	Source: Chapter 1	Source: Chapter 1	Source: Chapter 7	
A.							
B.							
C.							
Others							
Total							

Enter what Chuck Cash would think, not what you think, to be achievable!

For help with this chart, see Chapter 7

Source: *Backing U!*, Business & Careers Press, 2009

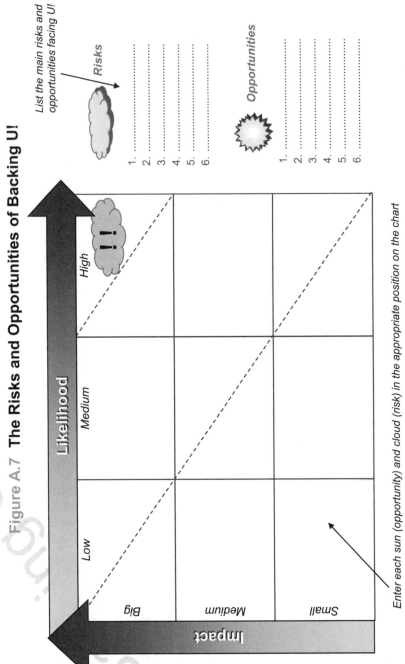

Figure A.7 **The Risks and Opportunities of Backing U!**

List the main risks and opportunities facing U!

Risks

1. ....
2. ....
3. ....
4. ....
5. ....
6. ....

Opportunities

1. ....
2. ....
3. ....
4. ....
5. ....
6. ....

For help with this chart, see Chapter 8

Likelihood

Low   Medium   High

Impact

Big   Medium   Small

Enter each sun (opportunity) and cloud (risk) in the appropriate position on the chart

Source: *Backing U!*, Business & Careers Press, 2009

Figure A.8 **Would You Back U?: The Storyline!**

Enter your overall conclusion, summarising the headlines below

Market Demand Prospects: ....

Your conclusions from Chapter 2

Competition: ....

Your conclusions from Chapter 3

Your K2 Rating: ....

Your conclusions from Chapter 6

Your Plan: ....

Your conclusions from Chapter 7

Risks and Opportunities: ....

Your conclusions from Chapter 8

For help with this chart, see Chapter 9

Source: Backing U!, Business & Careers Press, 2009

Part II: BECOMING MORE BACKABLE

Figure A.9 How Attractive Are Your Business Chunks?

Business Chunks	Market Size	Market Growth	Compet-itive Intensity	Market Risk	Enjoyment	Overall Attrac-tiveness
A.						
B.						
C.						
D.						
E (new?)						

Enter rating of attractiveness for each business chunk, using Key or, if you prefer, words or ticks

Average of ratings in previous five columns

Key to Rating: 1 = Unattractive, 3 = Reasonably Attractive, 5 = Highly Attractive
(For competitive intensity, remember that the more intense the competition, the *less* attractive the market. Likewise for market risk: the riskier the market, the **less** attractive.)

For help with this chart, see Chapter 11

Source: *Backing U!*, Business & Careers Press, 2009

Figure A.10 **How's Your Strategic Bubble Bath?**

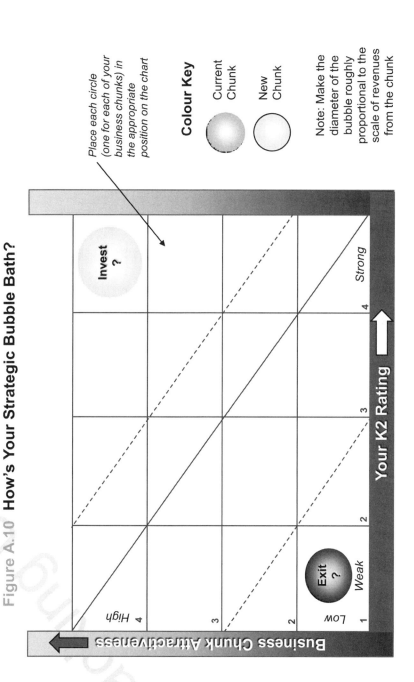

Place each circle (one for each of your business chunks) in the appropriate position on the chart

Colour Key

Current Chunk

New Chunk

Note: Make the diameter of the bubble roughly proportional to the scale of revenues from the chunk

For help with this chart, see Chapter 11

Source: *Backing UI,* Business & Careers Press, 2009

Part III: BACKING THE *HWYL*

Figure A.11 **Your Long List of Jobs with *Hwyl***

Who	Job	Hwyl
		✓✓✓✓✓
		✓✓✓✓✓
		✓✓✓✓✓
		✓✓✓✓✓
		✓✓✓✓✓
		✓✓✓✓✓
		✓✓✓✓
		✓✓✓✓
		✓✓✓✓
		✓✓✓✓
		✓✓✓
		✓✓✓

Enter those jobs from your full list with five hwyl ticks, then those with four ticks and so forth, carrying on if necessary for another page or two

For help with this chart, see Chapter 15

Source: *Backing UI*, Business & Careers Press, 2009

Figure A.12 How Attractive (Roughly)
Are the Markets of Your Long-Listed Jobs?

Long List of Jobs and Businesses	Number of Jobs	Growth in Jobs	Competition for Jobs	Job Market Risk	Overall Attractiveness
A.					
B.					
C.					
D.					
E.					
F.					
G.					
H.					

Enter rough rating of attractiveness for each job or business, using key, or if you prefer, words or ticks

Average of ratings in previous four columns

Key to Rating: 1 = Unattractive, 3 = Reasonably Attractive, 5 = Highly Attractive
(For competition for jobs, remember that the more intense the competition, the **less** attractive the market. Likewise for job market risk: the riskier the market, the **less** attractive. Conversely, and more intuitively, the greater the number of jobs the more attractive, likewise for growth in jobs.)

For help with this chart, see Chapter 16

Source: *Backing U!*, Business & Careers Press, 2009

Figure A.13 How Well Placed (Roughly) Would You Be in Your Long-Listed Jobs?

Long List of Jobs and Businesses	Your Relevant Capabilities	Your Relevant Experience	Your Rough K2 Rating
A.			
B.			
C.			
D.			
E.			
F.			
G.			
H.			

Average of ratings in previous two columns

Enter your likely ratings (very roughly at this stage) for each job or business, using key, or if you prefer, words or ticks

Key to Rating: 1 = Weak, 2 = Okay-ish, 3 = Good, favorable, 4 = Strong, 5 = Very strong

For help with this chart, see Chapter 16

Source: *Backing U!*, Business & Careers Press, 2009

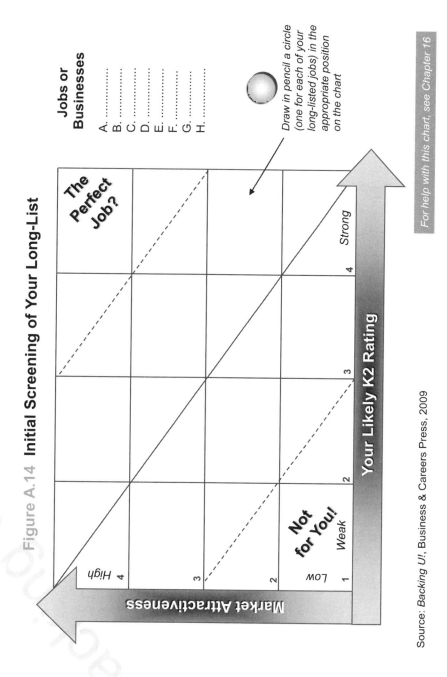

Figure A.14 Initial Screening of Your Long-List

Jobs or Businesses

A. ....
B. ....
C. ....
D. ....
E. ....
F. ....
G. ....
H. ....

Draw in pencil a circle (one for each of your long-listed jobs) in the appropriate position on the chart

The Perfect Job?

Not for You!

Market Attractiveness

High 4
3
2
Low 1

Your Likely K2 Rating

Weak 1
2
3
4 Strong

For help with this chart, see Chapter 16

Source: *Backing U!*, Business & Careers Press, 2009

315

Figure A.15 Your *Hwyl* Star Chart

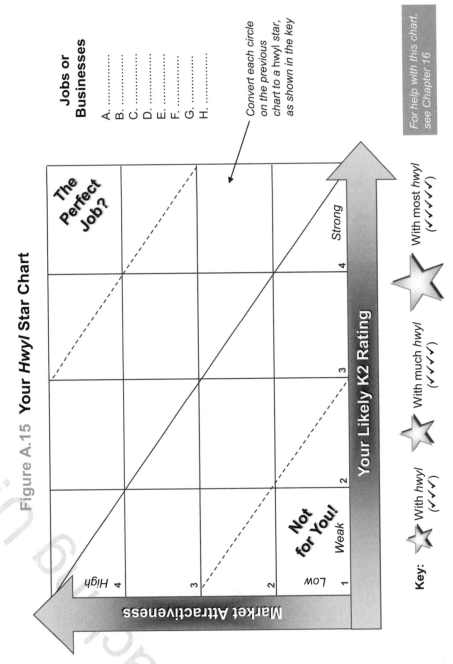

Jobs or Businesses

A. ....
B. ....
C. ....
D. ....
E. ....
F. ....
G. ....
H. ....

Convert each circle on the previous chart to a hwyl star, as shown in the key

For help with this chart, see Chapter 16

Key: With *hwyl* (✓✓✓) With much *hwyl* (✓✓✓) With most *hwyl* (✓✓✓✓)

Source: *Backing UI*, Business & Careers Press, 2009

How to Do Structured Interviewing of Your Customers

B

Chapter 6, How Do *You* Measure Up?, advised that a structured interviewing program of customers provides a methodical way for the self-employed to find out their K2 ratings.

Here's how to do it:

- ➤ Select a representative range of customer interviewees.
- ➤ Prepare your storyline.
- ➤ Prepare a concise questionnaire.
- ➤ Interview them, through email, telephone, or face-to-face.
- ➤ Thank them and give them some feedback.

The Interviewees

The interviewees should represent a broad cross-section of your business, including:

- ➤ Each of your main business chunks.
- ➤ Your top six customers in terms of revenue.
- ➤ Long-standing customers as well as recent acquisitions.
- ➤ Customers who also use, or used to use, your competitors, so they can compare you from experience rather than conjecture.
- ➤ Customers with whom you've had problems.
- ➤ Would-be customers, currently using a competitor, but on your target list.
- ➤ Former customers who switched to a competitor

That sounds like a lot, but you'll need to be selective. A dozen should suffice.

The Storyline

Here's your opportunity to put a positive light on your business. Compare these two storylines:

1. "Sorry to waste your time but can I ask for your help in figuring out how well I do my work?"

2. "As you know, my business has been rather busy over the last couple of years. But I thought I should take the time to ask some of my most important customers how their needs may be changing over time and to what extent I can serve those needs better."

Guess which line will get the better response *and* put your business in a favorable light? The first storyline conveys a negative impression and is all about you and your needs. The second leaves a positive impression and is all about your customer's needs. Stick to the second!

The Questionnaire

The questionnaire needs care. It must be taken as a guideline, not as a box-ticking exercise. It stays with you, and it doesn't get handed to the interviewee. It's a prompter to discussion, no more. It needs to be simple. And concise.

It should be in four parts:
1. The storyline
2. Customer needs—which, how important, now and in the future?
3. Performance—how you and others rate against those needs
4. The future—how you can better serve customer needs

The Storyline

The storyline should be written out at the top of the questionnaire and memorized. It must be delivered naturally and seemingly spontaneously. Stick in the odd pause, "um," or "er" to make it seem less rehearsed.

Customer Needs

These are the main questions to put on your questionnaire:
➤ What are your main needs in buying this service? What do you expect from your providers?
➤ How important are these needs? Which are more important than others? How would you rank them?
➤ Will these needs become more or less important over time?
➤ Are any other needs likely to become important in the future?

You should allow the customer to draw up her own set of needs, but it's best to prepare your own list to use as prompts, in case your customer dries up, or she misses an obvious one.

Performance

Here are some performance-related questions:
➤ How do you think I meet those needs? How do I perform?
➤ How do others perform? Do they better meet those needs?
➤ Who performs best against those most important needs?

Again you should allow the customer to select who she thinks are her alternative providers of your service, but you should include a prompt list of your main competitors—which you may or may not choose to use. No need to alert her to a troublesome competitor of whom she's not yet aware!

The Future

What should I be doing to better meet your needs and those of other customers?

The Interview

Interviews are best done face-to-face. Then you can see the nuances behind the replies—the shifting glance, the fidgeting, the emphatic hand gestures. But they are the most time consuming, unless you happen to be seeing your customer as part of your service delivery anyway.

If the interviews are done over the phone, they are best scheduled in advance. You can do this by email or with a preliminary phone call. After you've delivered the storyline, then add: "I wonder if you could spare five to ten minutes to discuss this with me. I know you're very busy, but perhaps we could set up a time later in the week for me to give you a call."

The call itself must be carefully managed. Don't launch into the questionnaire without a warmup. Ask her how she's doing, how's work, how's the family, whatever. Then gently shift to the storyline: "Well, as I was saying the other day..."

After you've finished the structured interview, don't forget the warm-down at the closing. Return to one of the topics you discussed at the outset and gently wind up the discussion, not forgetting to thank her sincerely for giving so freely of her valuable time.

The Thanks and Feedback

A few hours, a day, a couple of days, or a week later—whenever you feel it's appropriate—thank your customer again, officially. By letter is best, but that may feel overly formal for you in this electronic world. Email is probably fine, but use your judgment.

The email should be cheerful and full of sincere gratitude. If possible, it should contain a snippet of information that could be of interest or use to your customer. One or two sentences should suffice. It could pick up on one aspect of the discussion and compare what another customer had to say on the same thing. You could give her an indication of the results of your survey: "Interestingly, most customers seemed to think that experience was their most important need" or "Amazingly, most customers seemed to think my punctuality wasn't all that bad!"

That's structured interviewing. Now all you have to do is compile the results, whether on a piece of paper, on an Excel worksheet, or simply in your head, and feed them into your ratings against each K2—for you and for each of your competitors.

The intriguing thing then is to compare these customer-derived ratings with your first draft, do-it-yourself ratings. You may be in for a surprise!

How to Do Structured Cold Call Interviewing

C

Chapter 17, *Where Best to Back?,* advised that a structured interviewing program on those who currently do your target job, and their customers, provides a methodical way of finding out what you need to know about the job.

Here's how it's done, with an approach as for Appendix B, but taking a representative range of both providers and customers.

The Interviewees

If you have to go in cold in each interview, this program could be a struggle. But you may still have to do it. Preferable by far is to go into the interview warm, or even hot.

A warm interview in marketing-speak is one where someone you know has recommended that you speak to this person. A hot interview is where you actually know the interviewee.

The first step is to make a list of all those you know who are engaged in your target job or business, or who are their customers. This will be your hot list, but for many people this may only amount to one or two prospective interviewees, perhaps none.

Then you need to draw up a warm list. You need to speak to people you know who may know people in your target job or business. Speak to your family, your friends, friends of your family, family of your friends, your former classmates, your kids' friends' parents, your colleagues, past and present, friends of your colleagues, your fellow sport, society or interest group members. Speak, for example, to a friend of the family of a member of your colleague's sports club!

Defined like this, your "network" of contacts may soon run into the hundreds! Surely out of all these contacts there could be one, two, even more people who are active in your target job or business. Or at least customers. These will form your warm list.

By now, hopefully, you'll have a few names of providers or customers to whom you won't have to go in completely cold. But you'll need about a dozen interviews if you're going to satisfy Chuck. You'll probably have to do some cold-calling too.

It's easy enough to find out the names of organizations that operate in your target field. If you're planning on being self-employed, you should find plenty of people working in that field in the Yellow Pages, on the Internet, or in reference books available at your public library. Ask your librarian; she'll be delighted to help you do some research. It's much more interesting for her than just checking books in and out. She's also rather good at doing just that sort of research.

The difficulty is in finding out the actual names of people within organizations who are in your target job. In the old days, you had little choice but to call the switchboard and try to bluff your way through to the right person. But now Googling can often give up a name or two.

If you can, do try to get a name before calling an organization. If you can't, then that's too bad. You'll just have to try the old route and be prepared to duck and dive with the gatekeeper!

In summary, your interview list should be, in order of preference:
- ➤ *Hot names*, where you know the person.
- ➤ *Warm names*, where someone you know knows the person.
- ➤ *Cold names*, where you know of the person.
- ➤ *No names*, freezing cold calls, where you don't know to whom you should speak.

If all of this fills you with horror, may I suggest you seek some further guidance. John Crystal in his book *Where do I Go From Here With My Life?* suggests you should go out and talk to anybody about anything before embarking on a job-hunt-related interviewing program. Just getting out there and practicing talking should help build your confidence in talking eventually to people in your target job or business.

Daniel Porot builds on this in *The PIE Method for Career Success: A Unique Way to Find Your Ideal Job*. The I in PIE is for informational interviewing, which is similar to what I refer to here as structured interviewing. The E in PIE is for employment interviewing, where you are face-to-face with your would-be employer. But the P is for pleasure, and this is similar to what Crystal suggested. Porot suggests you take any subject you like to talk about and practice talking to like-minded people. You can talk about your likes, your interests, your hobbies, your views on hot issues—whatever gives you pleasure to talk about. It'll warm you up for the structured interviewing process to come.

The Storyline

The storyline in a structured interview program is much stronger if you can start with a reference, something like this: "Hi, Lindy. My name is Vaughan Evans, and I was recommended to talk to you by Jane Smith, who I believe you play hockey with."

When she finds out that you don't actually know Jane (!), but that she's a friend of your daughter's former classmate's mother, she may be a trifle disappointed. But you've still managed to break the ice and she may be impressed that you've gone to so much trouble to locate her. Whatever. Your chances of progressing to a five-minute discussion about her job are still higher than if you had gone in cold.

Next you proceed to tell her why you're calling. As in Appendix B, you must take care to present an upbeat message. Compare these two storylines:

1. "Look, Lindy, I'm sorry to be a bore, and I'm sure I'll be wasting your time, but could I have a chat with you for an hour or two about your job?"

2. "Anyway, Lindy, the reason for my call is that I'm trying to find out a bit more about working in PR (for example). I was wondering if you could spare just a few minutes telling me a bit about your job. Your kind of work has long struck me as being really stimulating and rewarding, certainly compared to the work I'm currently doing, and I'm seriously thinking of changing career, perhaps to PR."

What are the odds that Lindy's reply to storyline 2 will be: "What sort of work do you do at the moment?" You can then mildly disparage your current job, making Lindy feel pleased that she's in an altogether more satisfying occupation than yours. And away you go! What do you think her reply to storyline 1 would be? How about: "Look, I'm a bit busy at the moment/these days/this month. May I suggest you return to the switchboard and ask for our marketing department?"

If you have to go in cold, then storyline 2, without the reference warm-up, is all you're likely to have. It's going to have to be warm, friendly, positive, and upbeat, and leave the interviewee feeling good about herself.

The Questionnaire

For Customers

If you're interviewing a customer of your target job or business, you can use a similar questionnaire format to that suggested in Appendix B, with slight amendments and one addition:

➢ The storyline
➢ Customer needs, now and in the future
➢ How current providers rate against those needs
➢ How future providers can better serve those needs
➢ Future market demand for such services, compared to the supply of these services

The main amendment concerns the fourth bullet. You'll be asking how future providers, including possibly yourself, can better meet that customer's future needs.

The addition is the fifth bullet. You'll be taking the opportunity to get a customer's views on whether there are too many people already in this field, too few, or round about the right number. And whether market demand for such services is, in the customer's opinion, likely to grow in the future. And if so, how fast? Faster or slower than the likely number of people providing such services? Why? What are the barriers to entry? Are there likely to be too few providers, too many, round about the right number in the future?

Market information you get from customers will greatly help your assessment of the market attractiveness of your target job or business. It will supplement, and hopefully corroborate, the information you'll have found on the web.

For a further breakdown of the questions you need to ask under each of the headings in your customer survey, please take a look back at Appendix B.

For Providers

If you're interviewing a provider, that is, someone who's actually doing your target job or business, your questionnaire should be in four parts: the storyline, the nature of the job, what you need to be good at it, and how to get in.

The storyline should be typed out at the top of the page but don't read it. Learn it by heart and make sure it comes out naturally and enthusiastically.

You'll have stacks of questions relating to the nature of the job. You've already had a go at rating this job against each of your job satisfaction criteria in the first section of Chapter 17. To recap, these were grouped under pay, working conditions, fulfillment, values, status, and *hwyl*. Now's your chance to have your initial views confirmed or challenged.

Make out a list of questions under each of the job satisfaction criteria that you'd like answered. Questions under working conditions, such as hours of work, frequency of overnight travel, or holiday leave, are the easiest to ask of your interviewee. Few people really mind talking about these things. Likewise it's easy enough to ask about what sort of work they tend to do on a day-to-day basis, which will be a guide on how fulfilling this would be for you.

Questions on values are a bit more tricky, but you could try asking oblique questions on their colleagues. Do people in your line of work tend to form close friendships with their colleagues? Do they meet after work? Are they mutually supportive? Or is the workplace highly competitive, even cutthroat, and the last person you'd want to see at a Saturday night party would be a colleague?

You can touch on *hwyl* a little—do you really enjoy going to work in the morning?—but this is a highly personal criterion. What's passion-inducing to one person may be anathema to the other. Different strokes for different folks.

Toughest of all are questions relating to pay. It's inadvisable to come right out and ask, "How much do you earn?" People tend to be secretive and often sensitive about their pay. But you could try some devious comparative questions: "Is it true that most plumbers earn more than most electricians?" "Has pay in plumbing been growing reasonably over the last few years, in comparison with, say, that of electricians?"

The next set of questions concerns what you need to have or do to be good at that job or business. Have a look through your initial assessment of Key Kapabilities and their importance, as well your first cut K2 rating, in the fourth section of Chapter 17. What questions do you need to ask to get further comfort on how well placed you would be in this job?

You'll probably want to ask about qualifications and training. What's essential? What's good to have, but not absolutely necessary? What sort of skills should one preferably have? What's the minimum experience to get started? Would some of your earlier experience count as genuinely applicable for doing the job? How important is efficiency, as opposed to effectiveness? What sort of relationships does one need to form with customers?

The final set of questions relates to getting in. They may be the most important. What tips does she have on how to get in? What types of organization should you write to? To whom should you address your letters? HR or directly to your boss? Whom to talk to? What to emphasize in your resume/CV?

There are lots of questions. You won't be able to ask them all. You'll run out of time. For each of the three sets of questions, pick out the three most important. The three you really need answers to before you can realistically evaluate how well placed you would be in this job or business, and how attractive a job it is.

The Interview

The first thing to establish in an interview is how much time you have available. Once you know that, you can scope your questions accordingly.

If no time limit has been set, despite your prompting, you'll still have to prioritize. Assume that you'll only be able to get five minutes with her over the phone. Assume she'll be too busy to agree to a follow-up discussion, let alone a face-to-face meeting. Of course, you'll try for one or the other, but it's best if you assume you won't get them.

In that case, if you only have a five-minute shot, *what do you really need to know?* What must you find out from every one of the interviews to fill in your information gaps? To meet Chuck's concerns?

Under "nature of the job," which of your three most important questions do you most need to know about? If you place greatest importance on working conditions, such as the flexibility of working hours, make sure you get that question in early.

Under "what you need to be good at it," which aspect is most critical to you? Will a diploma do, or do you have to have a degree?

Remember to leave time for a final, most important question on "how to get in." For example, what type of organization has most vacancies for this kind of work?

If you manage to get these questions answered, together with the inevitable follow-up questions, in under five minutes, great. Return to the "nature of the job" and ask the second most important question to you under that heading. And so on. Ask her how much time you have left for further questions. Then ask some more from the other sections and carry on until your time has run out.

If the call ends and not all your most important questions have been answered, that can't be helped. If necessary, make them a higher priority on your list of questions for your *next* call and get them in early.

The objective must be to get at least half a dozen good responses to each of the three most important questions under each of the three headings.

With these answers under your belt, you'll be in possession of valuable information. Information that will help Chuck decide on whether to back you.

The above has been written assuming that your interview will be over the phone. Most will be. But you should try to get one or two interviews face-to-face. There is no substitute for seeing the visual response to a question, not just hearing the oral response. And it's much more awkward for an interviewee to shoo you out of the door after just five minutes!

If your interviewee is too busy to talk to you during working hours, invite him to lunch. Or for a coffee. Or to a drink after work. Or to dinner. Invest in your target job! Surely the potential returns from landing your target job are worth investing in an odd meal or three? And the information you'll draw out of him over a drink or a meal should be more abundant than what you'd have gotten out of him in a five-minute call during working hours.

The Thanks and Feedback

As advised in Appendix B, you must thank all interviewees. Both at the end of the call, and again some time later in writing—by email, by snail mail, or by both, as appropriate. And if you can throw in some element of feedback, even better—for example, "It was interesting that most respondents, like yourself, seemed to think that plumbers put in longer hours than other skilled tradesmen, like electricians, despite earning better hourly rates."

Let your life be like a snowflake: make your mark, but leave no stain.—*Anonymous, quoted by Gwyneth Evans*

Remember, this is your target job or business. The provider you talked to may be able to help you land a job. Likewise, the customer you spoke to may one day know of a provider with a job vacancy. You should aim to stay in touch with these interviewees for you never know when they may be able to help you—or you them. Write to them so they have the opportunity to remember you through your courtesy, enthusiasm, and good cheer.

D

Here are some books on career development that have been recommended in Parts I and II of this book:

Marcus Buckingham & Donald O. Clifton, *Now, Discover Your Strengths*, Free Press, 2001

Paul & Sarah Edwards and Laura Clampitt Douglas, *Getting Business to Come to You*, Tarcher Putnam, 1998

Charles Handy, *The Elephant and the Flea*, Harvard Business School Press, 2003

William Bridges, *Creating You & Co*, Perseus Books, 1997

C. J. Hayden, *Get Clients Now!*, Amacom, 1999

Roy Sheppard, *Rapid Referral Results*, Centre Publishing, 2001

Toastmasters International, *Competent Communication*, a 10-project manual (available to members), Toastmasters International, 2007

Also referred to in Parts I and II are a couple of pioneering books on business strategy and one little nugget on entrepreneurship:

Michael E. Porter, *Competitive Strategy: Techniques for Analyzing Industries and Competitors*, Free Press, 2004 (First Edition 1980)

Robert M. Grant, *Contemporary Strategy Analysis,* Blackwell, 2008 (1991)

Ken Blanchard, Don Hutson, and Ethan Willis, *The One Minute Entrepreneur,* Headline, 2008

Books recommended for further reading in Part III about career change were as follows:

Richard Nelson Bolles, *What Color Is Your Parachute? 2009: A Practical Manual for Job-Hunters and Career-Changers*, Ten Speed Press, 2008 (1970)

Po Bronson, *What Should I Do with My Life?: The True Story of People Who Answered the Ultimate Question,* Ballantine, 2005

John Crystal and Richard Nelson Bolles, *Where Do I Go from Here with My Life?,* Ten Speed Press, 1983

Vaughan Evans, *Backing U! LITE: A Quick-Read Guide to Backing Your Passion and Achieving Career Success,* Business & Careers Press, 2009

Jonathan Fields, *Career Renegade: How to Make a Great Living Doing What You Love,* Broadway Books, 2009

Howard Gardner, *Frames of Mind: The Theory of Multiple Intelligences,* Basic Books, 1993

Barrie Hopson and Mike Scally, *Build You Own Rainbow: A Workbook for Career and Life Management,* Management Books 2000, 2004

Julie Jansen, *I Don't Know What I Want, but I Know It's Not This,* Piatkus, 2003

John Lees, *How to Get a Job You'll Love, 2009/2010 Edition: A Practical Guide to Unlocking Your Talents and Finding Your Ideal Career,* McGraw-Hill Professional, 2008 (2001)

Nicholas Lore, *The Pathfinder: How to Choose or Change Your Career for a Lifetime of Satisfaction and Success,* Fireside, 1998

Carol L. McClelland, *Your Dream Career for Dummies,* For Dummies, 2005 (2001)

Daniel Porot, *The PIE Method for Career Success: A Unique Way to Find Your Ideal Job,* JIST Works, 1995

Betty Sher, *I Could Do Anything If I Only Knew What It Was: How to Discover What You Really Want and How to Get It,* Dell, 1995

Paul Tieger and Barbara Barron-Tieger, *Do What You Are: Discover the Perfect Career for You Through the Secrets of Personality Type,* Little, Brown, 2007 (1995)

Nick Williams, *The Work We Were Born to Do: Find the Work You Love, Love the Work You Do,* Element Books, 2000

And finally, just in case this book has stimulated you into writing a nonfiction book, then publishing it yourself, here are five books that have inspired and guided me:

Blythe Camenson, *How to Sell, Then Write Your Nonfiction Book,* Contemporary Books, 2002

John Kremer, *1001 Ways to Market Your Books,* Open Horizons, 2008 (1986)

Mark McCutcheon, *DAMN! Why Didn't I Write That: How Ordinary People are Raking in $100,000 or More Writing Nonfiction Books & How You Can Too!,* Quill Driver Books, 2001

Dan Poynter, *Self-Publishing Manual: How to Write, Print and Sell Your Own Book,* Para Publishing, 2007 (1979)

Tom & Marilyn Ross, *The Complete Guide to Self-Publishing: Everything You Need to Know to Write, Publish, Promote and Sell Your Own Book,* Writers Digest, 2002

Index

ARE YOU VERY BUSY?
NEED A QUICKER READ?

SLIMMED DOWN, NO CHARTS,
FOUR NEW LIVELY CASE STUDIES!

Business & Careers Press, ISBN 978-0-9561391-1-5
5"x8", 208 pages, U.S.$14.95

Give the Gift of
Backing U!
to Your Friends and Colleagues

CHECK YOUR LEADING BOOKSTORE OR ORDER HERE

Online: **www.AtlasBooks.com**

Toll-free telephone (24/7): **800-247-6553**; or fax: **419-281-0200**

Mail: **Atlas Books Distribution
30 Amberwood Parkway
Ashland, OH 44805**

☐ **YES**, I want _____ copies of *Backing U!* (ISBN 978-0-9561391-0-8) at US$24.95 each, and/or _____ copies of *Backing U! LITE* (ISBN 978-0-9561391-1-5) at US$14.95 each, plus $5.50 postage (USPS Media Mail) for one book and $1.00 for each additional book. *(Please ask about postage costs for larger, faster, or international orders. Ohio residents please add appropriate sales tax. Canadian orders must be accompanied by a postal money order in U.S. dollars.)*

Name_____

Organization_____

Address_____

City/State/Zip_____

Phone_____ E-mail_____

☐ My check or money order for $_____ is enclosed.

Or please charge my credit card:
☐ Visa ☐ MasterCard ☐ Discover ☐ American Express

Card #_____

Expiry Date_____ Signature_____

Thank you for your order!